Perspectives on
Object-Centered Learning
in Museums

Perspectives on Object-Centered Learning in Museums

Edited by

Scott G. Paris
University of Michigan

 LAWRENCE ERLBAUM ASSOCIATES, PUBLISHERS
2002   Mahwah, New Jersey   London

Lawrence Erlbaum Associates, Inc., Publishers
10 Industrial Avenue
Mahwah, NJ 07430

Cover design by Kathryn Houghtaling Lacey

Library of Congress Cataloging-in-Publication Data

Perspectives on object-centered learning in museums / edited by Scott G. Paris.
      p.   cm.
     Includes bibliographical references and indexes.
     ISBN 0-8058-3927-5 (alk. paper)
      1. Children's museums — Educational aspects. 2. Learning, Psychology of.
  3. Active learning. 4. Object-teaching. I. Paris, Scott G., 1946–
AM8 .P47 2002
069'.15 — dc21   2001040720

Printed in the United States of America
10 9 8 7 6 5 4 3 2

TO MY WIFE JAN,
a muse of whimsy and wonder,
who asks the improbable questions, paints the world
in bright colors, seeks goodness in everything,
and brings imagination to life.

Contents

Foreword

John H. Falk
Institute for Learning Innovation
Annapolis, Maryland

Understanding the interactions between objects, children, and museums is both a fascinating and daunting task. Although few topics could be more fundamental to our understanding of how museums function as educational, cultural and leisure settings, historically, little thought and even less research has been directed towards this area of inquiry. By its very existence, then, this volume makes an important contribution. However, like so many other aspects of museum visitor research, this topic too is at the earliest stages of development. Represented in this book are perspectives from a wide range of disciplines and schools of thought, many of them quite new to the museum field. Some have focused on objects, some on children, and others on the museum itself; all provide interesting ways to begin to think about how to wrap our minds around this exceedingly complex entity we call museums and the even more complex phenomenon called the museum experience.

I found particularly thought provoking the epistemological issues discussed by various authors. In fact, the theoretical framing of issues that occurs throughout the book, appropriately grounded in most cases with rich qualitative examples, is probably its most important contribution. In addition, there were some interesting methodological approaches suggested by Bain and Ellenbogen; van Kraayenoord and Paris; and Piscitelli and Weier that might prove fruitful in the future. As someone who has spent a lifetime investigating people in museums, I personally came away from reading this book with many new ideas and thoughts about not just objects and children in museums, but about how to even begin to think about the museum experience. Such is the benefit of bringing so many varied, bright people together and challenging them with an interesting topic, as was the purpose of this National Science Foundation-funded effort. However, as much as I was heartened by the new approaches and insights offered, so too was I struck by how little we still actually know.

When the search image has been appropriate, and the lens suitably selected, museums consistently emerge as extremely powerful learning institutions. In large measure, museums support successful learning experiences for the public in general, and children in particular, because they afford unprecedented opportunities to explore, observe and sense a fairly limited set of contextually relevant, highly structured, concrete experiences; all within a socially and physically novel, but safe, environment. Equally, or perhaps most importantly, museums are also one of the few places left in our society where children can exercise a high degree of personal choice and control over their behavior and learning. In a museum, children normally get to choose what and when to have an experience. They get to choose what to look at, what to touch, what to climb on, and they are permitted a high degree of discretion over whom they might choose to have experiences with. However, choice and control, as well as novelty and safety, are all relative constructs. Hence, making sense of these important constructs, and how they affect the museum experience, requires examining them within the larger context of the child's entire life, not just during the 2 hours or so they happen to be within the museum.

A similar case could be made for objects as well. Objects, although concrete, actually represent a vast continuum of abstract ideas and inter-related realities. The objects on display in a museum represent whole classes of objects, most of which do not exist only within the context of a museum. The perceived social, cultural and educational value of a steelworker's boot or an aerodynamically shaped airplane is highly dependent upon the context in which that object exists, as well as the relationship of that object to the viewer. Hence, the same boot found in a flea market stall might not arouse as much curiosity or awe as one enshrined in a museum display case with an appropriate label attached. A plane exhibited in the context of a science center exhibition on flight might evoke different experiences than one parked at the airport. And both boot and plane assume particular meanings for the visitor only because he or she has a repertoire of experiences with both footwear and transportation in general, and, ideally, boots and planes, steel workers and flight, in particular. In the absence of such repertoires of experience, the objects would take on entirely different meanings than those intended by the museum. Again, it is not possible to fully understand a museum object, or for that matter any object, by investigating it solely within the physical and temporal bounds of the museum.

It is from this perspective, then, that I would suggest an additional way to begin to think about investigations of children, objects and museums: a perspective absent from most of the papers included in this book. I am referring to the pervasive practice of conceptualizing the museum experience as something that happens uniquely within the physical and temporal envelope of the museum, rather than as an experience that happens, in part, within the museum. The context of the museum experience, including the people who visit it and the objects that reside there, is larger than the museum itself. So too should the investigations of the museum experience.

This problem I refer to, is of course not unique to this book or museums for that matter. Thinking about learning experiences, as well as efforts to investigate the phenomenon, have almost always been narrowly focused physically and temporally. On the surface this makes sense. For example, understanding museum visitors, be they children or adults, would seem most easily accomplished within the museum itself. Although not exactly a captive audience, they are at least identifiable as the audience. Similarly, any effort to understand museum objects seems to logically suggest investigation of only those specific objects displayed and interpreted within the museum; since these are the objects and interpretations in question. As reasonable and obviously convenient as this approach seems, it is arguably a limited and potentially a distorting perspective. Certainly, we need to situate our thinking and investigations of museums within an appropriate museum context. However, to limit our gaze to the spotlighted object or the ephemeral interaction between visitor and object is to risk missing the entire forest because we have focused so intently upon a single tree.

Museum professionals, and the researchers who study museums, suffer from the same myopia that has long afflicted other educationally-oriented organizations. This is the myopia of assuming that all learning and experience begins and ends with the institution — "if they don't get it here, where else?" In part, this myopia is an outgrowth of the interests and concerns of those who work within the institution. In the case of the museum professional — the curator, the museum educator, and the exhibition designer, they spend their days within the four walls of the institution. Although it is human nature to assume that one's own reality is shared by all, this view is not appropriate for individuals charged with public communication. More troubling, though, are the behaviors and beliefs of social scientists who study learning in museums; individuals who's job it is to take a broader, more "objective" view.

As a group, today's investigators of museum learning largely reject the idea that investigations conducted in schools and laboratories readily transfer to the museum context. Certainly, most of the authors in this book appropriately appreciate the highly contextual, or "situated," nature of learning; and hence the unique circumstances surrounding the museum experience. However, like the generations of learning researchers before them, many investigators working within the museum context reveal an unspoken assumption that learning, or its larger relative "experience," can somehow be readily compartmentalized and captured, as if it were something with a discrete beginning and ending. These investigators operate with the tacit assumption that learning, no matter how it is variously defined, is something that, functionally, "happens" as a direct response to some unique interaction, event or "stimulus" within the museum. In truth, learning is a continuous process, a state of becoming, rather than a unique product with distinct and totally quantifiable outcomes. I would assert that any effort to understand the visitor experience, let alone visitor learning, needs to be conceptualized within the larger context of individuals' lives. Specifically, any effort to define, observe and measure the effects of a visitor's interactions with museum objects and exhibitions, that seeks to understand how those interactions contribute to that individual's growth, change and/or development, must be conducted over a reasonably large framework of time and space. There must be a time and space framework that includes the effects of experiences both inside and outside the museum, both prior and subsequent to the museum visit. In short, it is not possible to fully understand children's museum learning and experiences with objects, or for that matter, any other group of visitors having any type of museum experience, by investigating those children and objects solely within the physical and temporal bounds of the museum. Museum experiences contribute to what children know and understand, and what meaning they make of the world, but museums are not, nor should they be assumed to be the place where "such and such" learning actually occurs. When museums succeed, which they do a remarkable percentage of the time, it is because of the contributions they make to deepening, expanding and enhancing children's understanding and appreciation of the world; but these outcomes are cumulative, long term, and not easily teased out of the fabric of children's lives.

The same perspective holds for investigations of museum objects. Museums more often than not do a wonderful job of situating objects within contexts that have personal meaning for visitors. And visitors, with or without interpretation by the museum, do a wonderful job of contextualizing objects for themselves. However, both museums and visitors contextualize objects in relation to events, experiences and realities that exist beyond the museum. Building that bridge between visitors and objects — between past and future realities, between events that occurred prior to a visitor's in-museum experience and those that will occur subsequently — is the essence of good museum design; it also needs to become a regular part of social science research on museum objects and visitors.

Accommodating this approach, or more accurately perspective, is challenging, but doable. For example, none of the theoretical frameworks or investigations described in this book are antithetical to this perspective; all could be reconfigured to accommodate this perspective. I would assert that incorporating this longer-term perspective is essential if we are to truly come to understand the museum experience; truly understand the role of museums in the lives of those who experience them. In fact, understanding how museums support lifelong learning, which is really the essence of this perspective which I an advocating, would be one way in which research on learning from museums could serve as a model for learning research in other domains, including research on learning from schools.

In conclusion, I heartily recommend this book to all who are truly interested in discovering more about how we currently understand museum experiences in general, and children and objects in particular. Not only are the chapters in this book a useful time capsule of current understanding, in most cases they represent a reasonable vision for what the near future of understanding could look like as well. Without exaggeration, it could be stated that investigations in this area are only now beginning to achieve the critical mass of time and thought necessary to propel us into a new era of understanding of the museum experience. Along with this new understanding will come the development of a whole new toolbox of valid and reliable research approaches and methodologies. This book provides encouragement that the near future will provide a better, more theoretically grounded collection of museum investigations. The hope is that these new investigations will lead to a better understanding of the meaning that children make of objects and museums and the role objects and museums can play in supporting the lifelong learning of all citizens.

Preface

The first words that you read in this book were the last ones written so I want to provide a broad perspective and a sense of anticipation for readers of this book. My intention was to write this Preface before a business trip to Washington, DC, but fortunately I missed that deadline and spent a week walking through the nation's capitol and wandering in many museums. Amidst the busloads of children and countless families in tee shirts and shorts in the summer heat, some whining and some wide-eyed, we swiveled our necks to see the sights. The majestic Washington Monument, the White House, and the Capitol dome became familiar landmarks with huge buildings of every size and shape in between. Quickly I learned to recognize the Smithsonian Institution castle, the doughnut-shaped Hirshhorn Museum, the dome of the National Museum of Natural History, and the boxy looking National Air and Space Museum. Subsequent discoveries, such as the gardens near the castle, became secret spaces of respite from the crowds. I was totally immersed in America's icons and treasures: museums, memorials, and monuments, indoors and outside, aesthetic and functional, scientific and historical, joyous and somber. The heat of the summer did not melt the exhilaration I felt each morning as much as the sheer exhaustion from investing emotional energy into the objects I saw. It is the same sense of immersion and excitement that I hope readers experience as they encounter the chapters in this book.

I do not need to convince you that a visit to Washington, DC, or a museum can be inspiring, but I would like to persuade readers that the study of such experiences is equally exciting and intellectually adventurous. For those readers who may wonder what "object-centered learning" entails, let me say that the topic represents a convergence of many approaches into a relatively new area of inquiry for psychologists and educators. There are several distinct historical precedents that deserve mention. First, museum educators and curators pioneered the study and exhibition of objects beginning in the nineteenth century. Second, anthropologists examined objects as evidence of material culture and constructed theories about objects and their meanings. Third, psychological researchers studied visitors' behavior in museums since the 1920s. Fourth, early childhood educators from Pestalozzi to Froebel to Montessori emphasized the importance of hands-on learning, play, and object study. Fifth, educational philosophers from Herbart to Dewey to Bruner have emphasized the value of educative experiences based on genuine objects. Thus, the numerous issues of pedagogy based on objects have a long and multidisciplinary history.

Let me chart the conceptual landscape that I see embodied in the chapters in this book. First, there is a broad uncharted territory of pedagogy and epistemology with authentic objects. The topography includes issues about how people of any age experience objects, that is how objects speak to them, how people read objects, and what kinds of interpretations and meanings they imbue in objects. It is a transaction between object and person that evokes and allows meaning construction. Learning about, with, and through objects involves hands-on learning and manipulation. Being in the presence of an original object can be uplifting. Talking about your own reactions to objects can be edifying. Responding to an object can deepen the experience. Authentic, unique, and first-hand experiences with objects stimulate curiosity, exploration, and emotions. These are features of an object-based epistemology that stand in contrast to the traditional methods of learning through text and discourse. Authors in this book explore many facets of object-based learning, and I hope readers consider these issues as frontiers for future exploration.

A second feature of the landscape concerns the places of learning. Informal learning environments include a wide variety of physical places and spaces and they invite analyses of their contexts. It is tempting to make contrasts between learning in schools and museums but this distinction only captures a few hills and valleys. The larger issues include the roles of context on learning and the mini-worlds created for visitors. Consider the ways that museum contexts project visitors to other places. The experiences might include: walking inside a submarine or coal mine; sitting inside a giant model of a human heart listening to the pumping sounds as an unborn child might hear them; strapping on a helmet and walking through a virtual world; or standing at a podium reading a Presidential inauguration speech while your friends see your projected image. Museums create contexts that may be authentic or imaginary but all are designed to alter the perspectives, thoughts, and feelings of visitors. Contexts may also affect visitors through the architectural design of shape, size, space, and light. Natural environments, such as gardens, ponds, and arboreta, may evoke feelings of solitude, serenity, and tranquility. The appeal of these settings is evident in their popularity as destinations for cultural tourism and family gatherings. The environments ought to be studied in order to identify how various contexts influence visitors' experiences.

A third feature of the landscape is the disciplinary orientations to objects evident in the detailed interactions of people in these environments. Museums devoted to scientific objects elicit scientific reasoning and fact-based discussions. Contexts designed to display sculptures, paintings, or art are more likely to elicit aesthetic reactions and discussions. As visitors meander through recreated historical villages or homes, they are likely to discuss historical topics, the authenticity of primary sources, and the accuracy of the curators' interpretations. Appreciation of different intellectual domains, as well as discipline-based reasoning, can be nurtured in diverse contexts and these issues, especially as they relate to children and education, are uncharted territory.

A fourth feature of the intellectual landscape mapped in this volume is the nature of object-based interactions and discourse. Objects are stimuli for conversations and explorations, a beginning point for discourses that may be scientific, historical, aesthetic, or personal. Some of these discourses may involve narratives about the object or the person that give unique meaning to their interaction. For example, touching the name of a friend on the Vietnam Memorial, touching a moon rock, or looking at an exhibit of your own cultural heritage can elicit deeply personal narratives about your own life and identity. There is a great deal to learn about how people talk about objects and how objects foster question asking and answering. Pedagogical conversations surrounding object investigations are the focus of several chapters in this volume.

Readers will find other features of the intellectual landscape of object-based learning equally provocative. If the landscape is constrained in our analyses, it is partly due to the richness of the topics that can be investigated. The chapters represent many different approaches but share underlying emphases on (a) the psychological dynamics of museum experiences and (b) the pedagogical principles of object-based learning. There are connections waiting to be made from the issues explored in this volume to research in and out of schools, to other disciplines, to museum education and exhibition design, and to theories of teaching and learning. I hope that readers share the same sense of adventure and intellectual discovery as the authors did in our discussions and writing.

— *Scott G. Paris*

Acknowledgments

The seeds of this book were planted in a Distinguished Faculty seminar at the University of Michigan, supported by the Rackham Graduate School and Department of Psychology, and taught for the first time in January through May 1999. It was a fascinating seminar, unpredictable because the ideas often tumbled forth in discussions that ranged across topics in psychology, education, anthropology, music, art, environmental education, and philosophy. Several of the authors in this book attended the seminar or gave presentations to our diverse group of faculty and students who represented many departments at Michigan. The seminar was truly transdisciplinary as well as interdisciplinary because each person worked hard to make connections from their own fields to new disciplines. I have observed similar bridge-building efforts among many groups when discussing how people experience museums and am always impressed with the inquisitive tone of these discussions. Transdisciplinary connections require an unpretentious and open attitude, and our seminar was exciting because we were all learning so much from each other. I cannot thank these colleagues enough for their inspiration and creativity: David Michener, Margaret Evans, Susanna Hapgood, Hiroyuki Hashimoto, Maurita Holland, Zilia Estrada, Melissa Mercer, Ali True, Laura Congdon, Kari Smith, Kate Theimer, Ingrid Redman, Tina Glengary, Aimee Giles, Megan Hanson, Carla Christensen, Cindy Brown, and Shannon Quesada. I am deeply indebted to Elaine Heumann Gurian, Mary Ellen Munley, John Falk, Lynn Dierking, and Kris Morissey who shared their time and ideas with our seminar and the museum community in Ann Arbor.

Special thanks go to Jennifer Jipson who provided excellent substantive and editorial suggestions to me and the authors on first drafts of chapters. I also want to extend my gratitude to Cynthia Yao, the founder of the Ann Arbor Hands-On Museum and a dedicated community leader, for her collaboration and leadership in museum education. I am also grateful to the National Science Foundation for supporting the conference in Ann Arbor during the winter of 2000.

Last only in the order of acknowledgments is the inspiration of my family. My parents George and Muriel showed me the treasures of Chicago's museums from an early age and modeled an unquenchable thirst for learning. My wife Jan teaches me to wonder about the whys and what-ifs of objects we encounter and has a knack for making museum visits adventurous. My children Jeff, Kristi, and Julie have inspired me through their curiosity, humor, and insight to try to understand the eye-opening and enduring effects of museums on each of us. I hope this book reveals some of that magic to readers.

List of Contributors

Robert Bain
School of Education
University of Michigan
Ann Arbor, MI

DeAnna Banks Beane
Association of Science-Technology
    Centers
Washington, DC

Minda Borun
The Franklin Institute Science
    Museum
Philadelphia, PA

Maureen A. Callanan
Department of Psychology
University of California, Santa Cruz
Santa Cruz, CA

Kevin Crowley
Museum Learning Collaborative
Learning Research and
    Development Center
University of Pittsburgh
Pittsburgh, PA

Lynn D. Dierking
Institute for Learning Innovation
Annapolis, MD

Sally Duensing
University of Bristol and
    The Exploratorium
San Francisco, CA

Kirsten M. Ellenbogen
School of Education
King's College London
London, England

E. Margaret Evans
Department of Psychology
University of Toledo
Toledo, OH

C. Olivia Frost
School of Information
University of Michigan
Ann Arbor, MI

Susanna E. Hapgood
School of Education
University of Michigan
Ann Arbor, MI

Jennifer L. Jipson
Department of Psychology
University of Michigan
Ann Arbor, MI

Gaea Leinhardt
Museum Learning Collaborative
Learning Research and
    Development Center
University of Pittsburgh
Pittsburgh, PA

Terence P. McClafferty
Western Australia Museum
Perth, Western Australia

David Michener
Botanical Gardens
University of Michigan
Ann Arbor, MI

Kristine A. Morrissey
Michigan State University Museum
East Lansing, MI

Melinda S. Mull
Department of Psychology
Shawnee State University
Portsmouth, OH

Annemarie Sullivan Palincsar
School of Education
University of Michigan
Ann Arbor, MI

Scott Paris
Department of Psychology
University of Michigan
Ann Arbor, MI

Barbara Piscitelli
Queensland University of
    Technology
Brisbane, Queensland, Australia

Devereaux A. Poling
Department of Psychology
University of Toledo
Toledo, OH

Myla Shanae Pope
John A. Johnson Achievement Plus
Elementary School
St. Paul, MN

Léonie J. Rennie
Science and Mathematics Education
    Centre
Curtin University of Technology
Perth, Western Australia

Shawn Rowe
Department of Education
Washington University
St. Louis, MO

Leona Schauble
Department of Educational
    Psychology
University of Wisconsin
Madison, WI

Inger J. Schultz
Nichols Arboretum
University of Michigan
Ann Arbor, MI

Monika Stampf Soennichsen
Department of Psychology
University of California, Santa Cruz
Santa Cruz, CA

Christina van Kraayenoord
Schonell Special Education
    Research Centre
The University of Queensland
Brisbane, Queensland, Australia

Katrina Weier
Queensland University of
    Technology
Brisbane, Australia

James V. Wertsch
Department of Education
Washington University
St. Louis, MO

PART I

Studying Learning
With Objects in Contexts

CHAPTER ONE

The Role of Context
in Children's Learning
from Objects and Experiences

Lynn D. Dierking
Institute for Learning Innovation

We went on a bus to the Glens of Antrim at Glenarrif (sic) forest park. Our guide was called Penny McBride. Penny took us for a walk and the first things we saw were phesants. We saw bamboo shoots. Then we went over a bridge and it was made of wood and log. Then we walked along the footpath. Then we saw the Redwood tree and it had a spongy bark. The tree came from America. [I]n America the Redwood is 300 feet tall. The redwood tree was 130 years old. Penny picked garlic leaves and let us smell them. Then we walked on the footpath and we saw a dead bird. Then we saw a squirrell (sic) going around a tree. We saw lots of beautiful waterfuls (sic). The water had foam and bubbles in it. There were platis bottle[s in] the water. We saw a wooden hut and the windows were all steamed up. We climbed up steep, steep hills and steps. Shaw dropped his money on the footpath. There were trunks there. We had our lunch at the picnic table. We tidied up the rubbish that was lying around. We went to the beach in Balleygalley. We played games like chasing Miss Armstrong a[nd] paddled in the water. We explored the rock pools. And we had a treasure hunt. At 3 o'clock we went home and we where (sic) very tired and happy. THE END.

— Sarah Jane Minford, seven-year-old Irish schoolgirl[1]

---

[1] This post-field-trip letter sent to the director of education, Glens of Antrim, Northern Ireland, appears in chapter 4 of *Learning from museums: Visitor experiences and the making of meaning* (Falk & Dierking, 2000). Sarah Jane Minford is a pseudonym.

This actual post-field-trip account of a school trip to a nature center in Northern Ireland points out both the wonder and challenge of understanding children's learning from objects and experiences. Clearly, this trip was memorable, and clearly objects and experiences played a tremendous role in making it so. Sarah's rich descriptions of walking along a footpath; seeing pheasants, bamboo shoots, a bridge made of wood and log, a redwood tree, a dead bird, a squirrel, waterfalls, and a wooden hut; smelling garlic leaves; climbing hills and steps, eating a picnic lunch, playing games and exploring rock pools, all attest to the richness of this experience.[2] At the same time, though, this rich account also demonstrates the challenges of understanding the meaning that children make of such objects and experiences, for how does one tease out the essential threads of learning from such a description? Did Sarah actually learn from this experience?

I argue that she did, but documenting this requires stepping back and thinking about learning from objects and experiences more broadly than is typically done; traditional models of learning, such as the transmission–absorption model (Hein, 1998; Hein & Alexander, 1998; Roschelle, 1995), do not account for or explain the highly interactive learning that results from such experiences and encounters with objects. An important missing ingredient is the role that context plays in facilitating learning from objects and experiences.

Traditional models of learning do not account for the richness and complexity of learning from objects and experiences, particularly not its rich contextual nature. Much of the traditional research has focused on learning in and from classrooms or laboratories, where much of the learning is decontextualized from direct experience with objects. The notion that objects and experience, with their inherent physical and sociocultural natures, might actually play an essential role in learning, and that these processes encompass much more than learning about facts and concepts but also include changes in attitudes, beliefs, aesthetic understandings, identity, etc., has been missing. Such models of learning do not work well when attempting to document the decontextualized learning in and from schools and laboratories; when these models are applied to the real object- and experience-centered world, they are seriously deficient.

This chapter describes a framework, the Contextual Model of Learning, that Falk and I have conceptualized to deal with the complexity and richness of learning and meaning-making from objects and experiences (Falk & Dierking, 2000). I then use the model to tease out and discuss some of the potential factors that might influence Sarah's learning and meaning-making from her school trip to the forest park, utilizing research done by Falk and myself and others.

---

[2]I have visited this same park and her description is quite accurate and rich!

The Contextual Model of Learning starts from the premise that all learning is situated, a dialogue between the individual and his or her environment. It is not some abstract experience that can be isolated in a test tube or laboratory, but an organic, integrated experience that happens in the real world with real objects (Ceci & Roazzi, 1994; Lewin, 1951; Mead, 1934; Shweder, 1990). In other words, learning is a contextually driven effort to find meaning in the real world. The model advocates thinking more holistically about learning as a series of related and overlapping processes that accommodate the complexity and ephemeral nature of learning and meaning-making from objects and experiences, learning that we call *free-choice learning*.[3]

THE CONTEXTUAL MODEL OF LEARNING

The Contextual Model of Learning (Falk & Dierking, 2000) grew out of a framework we developed 10 years ago that, at the time, we called the Interactive Experience Model (Falk & Dierking, 1992). In the last year we have built on and refined this model, recasting it as the Contextual Model of Learning. The Contextual Model suggests that three overlapping contexts contribute to and influence the interactions and experiences that children have with objects and the consequent learning and meaning-making — the personal context, the sociocultural context, and the physical context. Learning is the process/product of the interactions between these three contexts and is more descriptive than predictive. The power of the Contextual Model is not that it attempts to reduce complexity to one or two simple rules, but rather that it embraces and organizes complexity into a manageable and comprehensible whole.

The *personal context* refers to all that the learners bring to the learning situation, their interest and motivations, their preferences for learning modalities, their prior knowledge and experience. Four important lessons are at the heart of the personal context: (a) learning flows from appropriate motivational and emotional cues; (b) learning is facilitated by personal interest; (c) "new" knowledge is constructed from a foundation of prior experience and knowledge; and (d) learning is expressed within appropriate contexts.

The *sociocultural context* encompasses factors that recognize that learning is both an individual and a group experience. What someone learns, let

---

[3] We have begun advocating *free-choice learning* as a better term than *informal learning* for describing learning from objects and experiences, such as might happen in a museum or nature center. Rather than defining the learning by what it is not (formal) or where it occurs, as the term informal learning does, free-choice learning focuses on the characteristics of such learning — nonlinear, personally motivated, and involving considerable choice on the part of the learner as to when, where, why, and what to learn (Dierking & Falk, 1994; Falk, 1999; Falk, in press; Falk & Dierking, 1998; Johnston, 1999).

alone why and how someone learns, is inextricably bound to the cultural and historical context in which that learning occurred. At one level, learning is distributed meaning-making. Knowledge, rather than being within the domain of the individual, is a shared process, and learning and meaning-making take place within often delimited communities of learners. In other words, there exist a myriad number of communities of learners, defined by the boundaries of shared knowledge and experience. Interestingly, not only is learning a sociocultural process in the here and now, but the historical and cultural modes of communicating ideas are also sociocultural in nature. This helps to account for the fact that universally, people respond well and better remember information if it is recounted to them in a story or narrative form, an ancient sociocultural vehicle for sharing information.

The third context, the *physical context,* accounts for the fact that learning does not occur isolated from the objects and experiences of the real world. The physical context includes the architecture and "feel" of the situation — in other words, the sights, sounds, and smells, as well as the design features of the experience. Our research and that of others suggests that when people are asked to recall their experiences in free-choice settings, like Glens of Antrim Forest Park, whether a day or two later or after 20 or 30 years, the most frequently recalled and persistent aspects relate to these physical context factors — memories of what an individual saw, what they did, and how they felt about those experiences.[4]

The model also includes a fourth and very important dimension — time. Looking at free-choice learning as a snapshot in time, even a long snapshot (e.g., the time Sarah spent exploring the forest park with her classmates and teacher) is woefully inadequate. One needs to pan the camera back in time and space so that one can see the learner across a larger swath of his or her life, and can view the experience within the larger context of the community and society in which he or she lives. A convenient, though admittedly artificial, way to think about this model is to consider learning as being constructed over time as people move through their sociocultural and physical worlds; over time, meaning is built up, layer upon layer. However, even this model does not quite capture the true dynamism of the process because even the layers themselves, once laid down, are not static or necessarily even permanent. All the layers, particularly those laid down earliest, interact and directly influence the shape and form of future layers; the learners both form and are formed by their environments. For convenience, we have distinguished three separate contexts, but it is important to keep in mind that these contexts are not really separate, or even separable.

---

[4]For example, Falk, 1988; Falk & Dierking, 1990, 1992; Fivush, Hudson, & Nelson, 1984; McManus, 1993; Stevenson, 1991; Wolins et al., 1992.

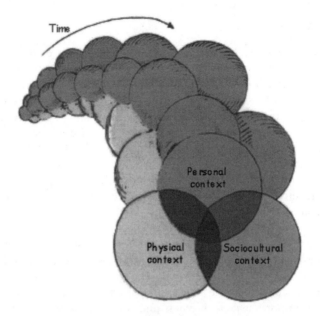

FIG. 1.1.   The Contextual Model of Learning. (Falk & Dierking, 2000).

Western science in general, and psychology in particular, are strongly tied to ideas of permanence — the brain is a constant, the environment is a given, memories are permanent. None of this appears to be, in fact, reality. None of the three contexts — personal, sociocultural, or physical — is ever stable or constant. Learning, as well as its constituent pieces, is ephemeral, always changing. Ultimately then, learning can be viewed as the never-ending integration and interaction of these three contexts over time. A valiant effort at depicting this model is shown in Fig. 1.1, appreciating that it really should be depicted in three dimensions and animated, so that both the temporal and interactive nature of learning could be captured.

The Contextual Model of Learning provides the large-scale framework within which to organize information about learning from objects and experience; the details vary depending on the specific context of the learner. After considering findings from hundreds of research studies, 10 key factors — or, more accurately, suites of factors — emerged as particularly fundamental to experiences with and from objects.[5]

---

[5]This model is a work in progress. In our recent book and at the Ann Arbor conference, only eight factors were presented. Subsequent thinking suggests that there are 10 suites of factors.

Personal Context Factors

Motivation and Expectations.   People have experiences with objects for many reasons and possess predetermined expectations for what those objects and experiences will hold. For example, children visiting a park like Glens of Antrim Forest Park expect to have a direct encounter with the outdoors, with plants and animals. These motivations and expectations directly affect what children do and what they learn from these objects and experiences. When expectations are fulfilled, learning is facilitated. When expectations are unmet, learning can suffer. Intrinsically motivated learners tend to be more successful learners than those who learn because they feel they have to. Learning situations are effective when they attract and reinforce intrinsically motivated individuals.

Interest.   Based on prior interest, learners self-select what objects and experiences with which to interact, for example, what to see and do while exploring Glens of Antrim Forest Park. The term *interest* refers to a psychological construct that includes attention, persistence in a task, and continued curiosity, all important factors when one wants to understand what might motivate someone to become fully engaged and perhaps to learn something (Hidi, 1990). In research about free-choice learning, interest emerges as an important variable that greatly influences later learning (Dierking & Pollock, 1998; Falk & Dierking, 2000), directly affecting what people do and what they learn from objects and experiences such as encountered in a place like Glens of Antrim Forest Park. For this reason, learning is always highly personal.

Prior Knowledge and Experience.   Prior knowledge and experience are fundamental factors contributing to learning (Roschelle, 1995). They play an important role in encounters that children have with objects and experiences in real world places like Glenarrif Forest Park. This prior knowledge and experience directly affects what children do and what they learn. The meaning that is made of objects and experiences is always framed within and constrained by prior knowledge and experience.

Choice and Control.   Learning is facilitated when individuals can exercise choice over what and when they learn, and feel in control of their own learning. This is certainly the case for children. Real world settings, such as the outdoors, are quintessential free-choice learning settings and afford children abundant opportunity for both. Research suggests that children are very sensitive to these issues, often preferring to encounter objects in real-world settings with their families rather than with school groups for the very reason that they feel they have more choice and control over the experience (Griffin, 1998; Griffin & Dierking, 1999; Jensen, 1994). Consequently, effective learning situations afford learners abundant opportunity for both choice and control.

Sociocultural Context

Within-Group Sociocultural Mediation. Children are inherently social creatures. They learn and make meaning as part of social groups — groups with histories, groups that separately and collectively form communities of learners, such as Sarah's class. Peers build social bonds through shared experiences and knowledge. All social groups in settings like Glens of Antrim Forest Park utilize each other as vehicles for deciphering information, for reinforcing shared beliefs, for making meaning. Such settings create unique milieus for such collaborative learning to occur. Children have experiences with objects with their peers and familiar adults, such as parents or teachers, and this collaborative learning greatly influences the meaning they make.

Facilitated Mediation by Others. Socially mediated learning does not only occur within one's own social group. Powerful socially mediated learning occurs with other people perceived to be knowledgeable such as teachers, parents, and other facilitators. Such learning has long evolutionary and cultural antecedents. Interactions with other people can either enhance or inhibit a child's object-based learning experience. When skillful, the staff of a free-choice learning setting can significantly facilitate visitor learning.

Physical Context Factors

Advance Preparation. Study after study has shown that people, particularly children, learn better when they feel secure in their surroundings and know what is expected of them, that is, when they have received advance organizers and orientation for the experience. Real-world settings, such as the outdoors, tend to be large, visually and aurally novel settings. When people feel disoriented, it directly affects their ability to focus on anything else; certainly this is the case for children. When people feel oriented, some novelty can enhance learning. Similarly, providing conceptual advance organizers significantly improves people's ability to construct meaning from experiences. When children feel oriented and are provided conceptual advance organizers, this advance preparation enhances their object-based learning.

Setting. Whatever the learning experience, learning and meaning-making are influenced by setting, that is, the ambiance, feel, and comfort of the place or situation. When children feel comfortable in a learning setting or situation, learning is enhanced. This is certainly important in real-world settings like the outdoors.

Design. Whatever the learning experience, learning and meaning-making are influenced by design, that is, the specific design elements of that experience. In real-world settings children see and experience authentic, real objects, within appropriate environments. Appropriately designed learning experiences that capitalize on the elements of the real world are compelling learning tools.

Subsequent Reinforcing Events and Experiences. Learning does not respect institutional boundaries. Children learn by accumulating understanding over time, from many sources in many different ways. Subsequent reinforcing events and experiences are as critical to learning from objects and experiences as are their immediate interactions. In a very real sense, the knowledge and experience gained from any one experience is incomplete; it requires enabling contexts to become whole. More often than not, these enabling contexts occur in other places — weeks, months, and often years later. These subsequent reinforcing events and experiences are as critical to learning from objects and experiences as are the initial encounters.

Individually and collectively, these 10 factors significantly contribute to the quality of a learning experience and influence the learning and meaning-making that results; thus, we can utilize this framework as a concrete model for understanding and facilitating children's learning from objects and experiences. We can use Sarah's experience at the forest park as a case study, to actually consider a very specific set of factors that might have influenced her learning from that experience.

SARAH'S EXPERIENCE

Clearly, personal context factors influenced her experience, evident as one reads Sarah's account, written 2 weeks after the visit. Although this was a school trip with her teacher, Miss Armstrong, her very vivid description suggests she was highly motivated and interested and paid tremendous attention to details as the trip unfolded, remembering many of those details 2 weeks later. As I said earlier, I have visited this park myself and can attest to the accuracy of her description. Clearly, she and her classmates also had expectations for what the trip would hold. For example, Shaw had brought money along, perhaps to buy a special lunch or souvenir of the trip.

Sarah's specific interests also are clear — she seemed most interested in all aspects of the natural world she was observing, in particular, the plants she encountered. She was able to describe in great detail her experience with a redwood tree, including the texture of its bark, where it came from, how tall it was, and how old. She also recalled smelling garlic leaves and seeing bamboo shoots.

Sarah's prior knowledge and experience are less evident in this account. It does not appear that she had visited the park before, although it was only about an hour from her school and is a popular place for families and schools to visit. She did describe a couple of instances of dealing with "rubbish," but it is hard to know whether she held this conservation ethic herself or whether it was encouraged by her guide and teacher. It is far easier to think about how these objects and experience will build future knowledge and experience and how they might be built on later. Her memories are so detailed and rich that one can envision these experiences being remembered and reinforced throughout her lifetime. Research documenting long-term recollections of school field trips suggests that such rich experiences are remembered and do support long-term meaning-making (Falk & Dierking, 1997).

In terms of choice and control it is not clear how free choice the day was, particularly at the park. Although the children were led on a guided tour, Sarah made no complaints about her guide, or what she did not get to see or do, suggesting that at least for Sarah, there was a feeling of freedom to look at what she was interested in looking at. Her account would suggest that she did feel that she had some choice and control in the learning situation. Certainly the time at the beach in Balleygalley, when the children played games, chased their teacher, paddled in the water, explored the rock pools, and had a treasure hunt, was free-choice in nature.

Sociocultural context factors also influenced her experience greatly. The highly social within-group nature of the school trip was very visible as Sarah describes the bus ride, Shaw's unfortunate experience losing his money, a picnic lunch, and the fun at Balleygalley Beach, playing with her classmates and teacher. In her own words, when they arrived home at 3 o'clock, they were happy, though tired. The role that such sociocultural "stamping" plays in the remembering and meaning-making process is only now coming to light, but it clearly plays an important role (Falk & Dierking, 2000; Schauble, Leinhardt, & Martin, 1998). Research suggests that in later years it will be very difficult for Sarah to think about this trip and its significance without recalling the rich sociocultural context in which it was imbedded.

Facilitation by a skillful guide also seemed to support Sarah's memory of the experience. She remembered the guide's name and all the things that they did together walking along the path, such as Penny picking garlic leaves and letting the children smell them, a very age-appropriate and effective strategy, which suggests she was a skilled guide. Our research suggests that it will not be unlikely for these memories to persist over time and for Penny McBride to be indelibly linked in a positive way to Sarah's long-term recollections of the experience (Falk & Dierking, 1997).

Probably the most obvious factors influencing her experience are the physical context factors. Seven-year-old Sarah Jane Minford, who lives in a small village approximately 30 miles north of Belfast, Ireland, was able to recall considerable details of her day-long school field trip to an outdoor environmental preserve in Northern Ireland. Although several days had elapsed between her visit and her writing about the experience, she was still able to remember quite vividly what she saw and did that day. Physical context factors obviously played a major role in the experience, none more importantly than the nature of the setting, the fact they were outside, seeing and experiencing objects in their natural environment. Sarah's detailed and vivid account of her experiences along the path attest to the power of being outside, in nature. She noticed the spongy texture of a redwood tree's bark, a bridge made of wood and log, the smell of garlic leaves, and the foam and bubbles of beautiful waterfalls. Such highly contextualized and multisensory memories are the ones that tend to persist over time (Falk & Dierking, 2000).

In terms of advance preparation, I am not sure how much the teacher prepared the class before the visit; I do know that the teacher had received a packet of advance information about the visit from the guide so that she could presumably prepare the children before the visit. I also know that on their arrival at the park, Penny McBride provided an overview to the children of what they would experience while on the visit, an advance organizer for their exploration.

However, probably most interesting, but unknown to me, is what reinforcing events and experiences Sarah has had subsequently in her life that would contribute to the long-term meaning of this school trip. I do know that the teacher had children write something about the experience, a reinforcing experience to some degree, but only 2 weeks later, so it is difficult to assess its impact. The trip occurred about 5 years ago and what would be most useful would be to be able to follow up with Sarah, to see whether she has visited this park or other parks since and what sense and meaning she now makes of the experience. Has it continued to influence her feelings and attitudes about nature, her conservation ethic, her knowledge of redwoods? Clearly, it was a powerful experience and one can hope that it did, but much depends on how the experience was used in school beyond the writing exercise and what other related experiences Sarah has had in her life. Did she continue to read about redwoods, perhaps visit the United States and see one in situ? Knowing this kind of information would make it far easier to predict just what Sarah might have taken from the experience.

Finally, we ask the question: What do we think Sarah learned from her experience in the Glens of Antrim Forest Park? At the very least, it is clear that this brief, ephemeral experience resulted in demonstrable, albeit modest, changes in her knowledge and thinking. As a direct consequence of her experience in the park, Sarah could describe facts and ideas she experienced and presumably relate them to pieces of knowledge gleaned from other sources. There was tangible evidence that the events Sarah experienced and the information she perceived during her forest park visit were not only stored in memory, but retrievable, utilized and extended subsequent to the visit. In other words, Sarah demonstrated clear evidence of having learned.

Obviously, Sarah's curiosity and interest were very much a central trait of her learning as well, as evidenced by her thorough description of the natural world she experienced. A nature center like the Glens of Antrim Forest Park is a veritable wonderland for the curious. It is also likely to anticipate the role the guide played, as well as her teacher, in influencing her learning. By taking them there in the first place, their teacher was also modeling for all of the children the role that nature centers like this park can play in their lives as places for learning and places that preserve the natural heritage of Northern Ireland. Through this experience, Sarah was learning a great deal about how to use nature centers to satisfy her many curiosities, an activity that she can enjoy throughout her life.

I believe that this case study demonstrates that, both individually and collectively, these 10 factors do significantly contribute to the quality of a child's experience with objects, contextualizing the experience, and consequently influencing the learning and meaning-making that occurs a result of these interactions. Certainly in other studies this has been demonstrated (Falk & Dierking, 2000). Thus, this framework can be utilized as a concrete model for understanding and facilitating learning from objects and experiences.

This vignette also points to the importance of documenting children's experiences with objects and framing subsequent learning and meaning-making appropriately. Instead of asking, "What did Sarah learn as a consequence of visiting Glens of Antrim Forest Park?," we should be asking "How did this experience contribute to what Sarah knows, believes, feels, or is capable of doing?" All learning is a cumulative, long-term process, a process of making meaning and finding connections among a variety of learning experiences. What we know about any particular topic is the accumulated understanding constructed from a wide variety of sources, including school, newspapers and magazines, books, conversations with friends, family and knowledgeable acquaintances, television shows, films, and interactions within real-world settings (Falk, 2001; Johnston, 1999; Miller, 2001; Miller & Pifer, 1996). It is only when we step back and look more broadly at children's experiences with objects that we can truly understand their impact in children's lives.

Clearly, the framework provided by the Contextual Model of Learning does not simplify the task of trying to understand what Sarah learned, but it does provide a road map for the inquiry. The model permits a thoughtful and reliable approach to considering the true complexity and richness of the learning process without significantly compromising either precision or generalizability. It helps us focus our attention on salient parts of the data, such as the key factors of prior knowledge and experience: interest; motivation and expectations; choice and control; within group sociocultural mediation; the role of guides as facilitators of learning; orientation and advance organizers; the importance of setting, real objects, and appropriate contexts; and finally it encourages us to frame the question of individual learning within a larger community and society-wide context. In short, the model reduces the major issues down to a manageable number, within a comprehensible framework, without losing sight of the inherently holistic and synergistic nature of learning. By no means complete, the three contexts we have proposed provided a starting point from which to both think about and describe free-choice learning outcomes. As this example demonstrates, free-choice learning environments like Glens of Antrim Forest Park emerge as particularly effective learning environments because they enable people to explore cultural, aesthetic, and scientific issues perceived as important within a socially supportive, intellectually comprehensible, and contextually appropriate environment. Utilizing the Contextual Model of Learning allows us to better document, and ultimately influence, learning in these rich environments.

FINAL THOUGHTS

So what does this all mean in terms of our efforts to meaningfully understand the nature of children's learning from objects and experiences and our efforts to research it? As we all know, children are innately curious and learning all the time, at school, at home, during structured time and free time. Although few would dispute this, interestingly, when it comes time to investigate children's learning, such broad perspectives are rarely considered and consequently almost never integrated into research designs. However, in order to design a truly meaningful research study to investigate children's learning from objects and experiences, such broad perspectives are critical. One must frame the research study broadly to include not only school, but also home and community experiences. So what would constitute the key elements of a meaningful research plan to investigate children's learning from objects and experiences?

Key Elements of a Meaningful Research Plan

- The research plan needs to investigate children engaged in authentic activities, so that their learning is studied in "real" context.
- The research design should include multiple, creative methodologies for assessing learning in a variety of ways.
- There should be opportunities for the group to be the unit of analysis, not just individual children.
- The research design should include efforts to investigate the learning that happens at home and in the community, as well as that of school,

and include efforts to demonstrate the connections between these experiences.

- There should be efforts to investigate the processes of learning as well as the products of learning.
- Research designs should be longitudinal, with opportunities to track children for several years to see how experiences are used and connected to subsequent experiences.

Investigate Authentic Activities. A high quality research study investigates learning in "real" contexts and takes into account the personal, social, and physical dimensions of learning. Although it is changing, many studies, even those designed for children, rely on paper and pencil instruments, administered to individual children, in a test-like context. Such research tools are highly decontextualized and their content validity is suspect. Authentic research designs allow children to demonstrate their skills and knowledge in rich environments filled with objects and materials that have some relationship to the learning. Authentic research designs also often provide opportunities for children to demonstrate their knowledge and skills in group situations.

Multiple Methodologies. A high quality research study for children includes a wide variety of creative methodologies such as observations, discussions, in-depth interviews, and imbedded activities such as developmentally appropriate games, drawing, and other tasks. In contrast to the paper and pencil instruments described previously, these methodologies are contextually rich and allow children to demonstrate a wide range of skills and knowledge in varied ways that are very amenable to children's personal styles.

The Group as the Unit of Analysis in Research Designs. As suggested earlier, humans are social animals and much of our learning is mediated through sociocultural interaction with others, including our parents, teachers, and peers (Falk & Dierking, 1995; Fishbein, 1976; Hansen, 1979; Ogbu, 1995; Schauble, Leinhardt, & Martin, 1998; Vygotsky, 1978; Wertsch, 1985). Despite this fact, for the most part, the unit of analysis for learning is almost always the individual. Meaningful research designs need to explore opportunities for group investigation and to experiment with the group as the unit of analysis.

Research About Learning at Home, in the Community, and at School. Children are learning all the time, at school, at home, and in the community (Epstein, 1995). Because learning is a series of overlapping and reinforcing experiences over time and place, a meaningful research design includes opportunities to investigate children using the wealth of knowledge and experience they have constructed in all parts of their life. Such research should also provide opportunities for researchers to explore the connections children have constructed among and between these experiences.

Research About the Process and Products of Learning.   Much of research currently focuses on the products of learning — what a child has figured out or created. Consequently, a meaningful research design should include methodologies for investigating how children have figured something out or created something, emphasizing the processes of learning as much as the products of learning.

Longitudinal Research.   Because learning is a series of overlapping and reinforcing experiences over time and place, to most meaningfully investigate learning, the research design needs to be comprehensive and longitudinal so the full range of understandings can be assembled across enough time that meaningful patterns and relationships can be discerned. A meaningful research design would be comprehensive, including opportunities to track children over several years to determine how experiences with objects and consequent learning are used and connected to subsequent experiences and learning. Although the specifics of some of the methodologies could differ from year to year, there would also be an effort to consistently research particular aspects of the child's learning so that meaningful patterns and relationships could be established. For example, what kind of learner is the child? How can his or her strengths be capitalized on and weaknesses strengthened? How have subsequent experiences built on and/or reinforced what and how children have learned from objects? What role have objects and experiences had in making the learning meaningful to the child?

I have suggested six elements that should be critical components of a meaningful research plan to investigate children's learning from objects and experiences. However, it is important to state that I appreciate how difficult it would be to implement such a design. It requires profound changes in some of our assumptions about learning and the best ways to document learning, and if implemented as ideally described, would be an exceedingly time-intensive endeavor for all participants. Having said that, I do believe that it is important to begin to make such changes and to take the time and effort that is really required to understand children's learning.

REFERENCES

Ceci, S. J., & Roazzi, A. (1994). The effects of context on cognition: Postcards from Brazil. In R. J. Sternberg & R. K. Wagner (Eds.), *Mind in context* (pp. 74-101). Cambridge, UK: Cambridge University Press.

Dierking, L. D., & Falk, J. H. (1994). Family behavior and learning in informal science settings: A review of the research. *Science Education, 78*(1), 57-72.

Dierking, L. D., & Pollock, W. (1998). *Questioning assumptions: An introduction to front-end studies.* Washington, DC: Association of Science–Technology Centers.

Epstein, J. E. (1995, May). School/Family/Community partnerships: Caring for the children we share. *Phi Delta Kappan,* pp. 701–711.

Falk, J. H. (1988). Museum recollections. In S. Bitgood et al. (Eds.), *Visitor studies: Theory, research, and practice* (Vol. 1, pp. 60–65). Jacksonville, AL: Center for Social Design.

Falk, J. H. (1999). Museums as institutions for personal learning. *Daedalus, 128*(3), 259–275.

Falk, J. H. (2001). Free-choice science learning: Framing the issues. In J. H. Falk (Ed.), *Free-Choice science learning: Building the informal science education infrastructure.* New York: Teachers College Press.

Falk, J. H., & Dierking, L. D. (1990). The effect of visitation frequency on long-term recollections. In S. Bitgood (Ed.), *Proceedings of the 3rd Annual Visitor Studies Conference* (pp. 94–104). Jacksonville, AL: Center for Social Design.

Falk, J. H., & Dierking, L. D. (1992). *The museum experience.* Washington, DC: Whalesback.

Falk, J. H., & Dierking, L. D. (1995). *Public Institutions for personal learning: Establishing a research agenda.* Washington, DC: American Association of Museums.

Falk, J. H., & Dierking, L. D. (1997). School field trips: Assessing their long-term impact. *Curator, 40*(3), 211–218.

Falk, J. H., & Dierking, L. D. (1998, May/June). Free-Choice learning: An alternative term to informal learning? *Informal Learning Environments Research Newsletter* (pp. 3–4). Washington, DC: American Educational Research Association.

Falk, J. H., & Dierking, L. D. (2000). *Learning from museums: Visitor experiences and the making of meaning.* Walnut Creek, CA: AltaMira.

Fishbein, H. D. (1976). *Evolution, development, and children's learning.* Pacific Palisades, CA: Goodyear.

Fivush, R., Hudson, J., & Nelson, K. (1984). Children's long-term memory for a novel event: An exploratory study. *Merrill-Palmer Quarterly 30*(3), 303–317.

Gallagher, W. (1993). *The power of place: How our surroundings shape our thoughts, emotions and actions.* New York: Poseidon.

Griffin, J. (1998). *School-museum integrated learning experiences in science: A learning journey.* Ph.D. dissertation, University of Technology, Sydney, Australia.

Griffin, J., & Dierking, L. D. (1999). *Perceptions of learning and enjoyment in informal settings.* Unpublished manuscript.

Hansen, J. F. (1979). *Sociocultural perspectives on human learning: An introduction to educational anthropology.* Englewood Cliffs, NJ: Prentice-Hall.

Hein, G. E. (1998). *Learning in the museum.* London: Routledge.

Hein, G. E., & Alexander, M. (1998). *Museums: Places of learning.* Washington, DC: American Association of Museums.

Hidi, S. (1990). Interest and its contribution as a mental resource for learning. *Review of Educational Research, 60,* 549–571.

Jensen, N. (1994). Children's perceptions of their museum experiences: A contextual perspective. *Children's Environments, 11*(4), 300–324.

Johnston, D. J. (1999). *Assessing the visiting public's perceptions of the outcomes of their visit to interactive science and technology centres.* Doctoral dissertation, Curtin University of Technology, Perth, Western Australia.

Lewin, K. (1951). *Field theory in social science.* Selected K. Lewin papers edited by D. Cartwright. New York: Harper.

McLaughlin, M. W., & Talbert, J. E. (1993). *Contexts that matter for teaching and learning.* Palo Alto, CA: Center for Research on the Context of Secondary Teaching, Stanford University.

McManus, P. (1993). Memories as indicators of the impact of museum visits. *Museum Management and Curatorship, 12,* 367–380.

Mead, G. H. (1934). *Mind, self and society.* Chicago: University of Chicago Press.

Miller, J. (2001). The acquisition and retention of scientific information by American adults. In J. H. Falk (Ed.), *Free-Choice science learning: Building the informal science education infrastructure.* New York: Teachers College Press.

Miller, J., & Pifer, L. (1996). Science and technology: The public's attitudes and the public's understanding. *Science and Engineering Indicators* (pp. 7-1-7-21). Washington, DC: National Science Board.

Ogbu, J. U. (1995). The influence of culture on learning and behavior. In J. Falk & L. Dierking (Eds.), *Public Institutions for Personal Learning* (pp. 79-95). Washington, DC: American Association of Museums.

Roschelle, J. (1995). Learning in interactive environments: Prior knowledge and new experience. In J. H. Falk & L. D. Dierking (Eds.), *Public institutions for personal learning: Establishing a research agenda* (pp. 37-51). Washington, DC: American Association of Museums.

Schauble, L., Leinhardt, G., & Martin, L. (1998). A framework for organizing a cumulative research agenda in informal learning contexts. *Journal of Museum Education, 22*(2 & 3), 3-8.

Shweder, R. A. (1990). Cultural psychology: What is it? In J. W Stigler, R. A. Shweder, & H. Herdt (Eds.), *Cultural psychology: Essays on comparative human development* (pp. 1-43). Cambridge: Cambridge University Press.

Stevenson, J. (1991). The long-term impact of interactive exhibits. *International Journal of Science Education, 13*(5), 521-531.

Vygotsky, L. S. (1978). *Mind in society: The development of higher mental processes.* (M. Cole, V. John-Steiner, S. Scribner, & E. Souberman, Eds.) Cambridge, MA: Harvard University Press.

Wertsch, J. V. (1985). *Vygotsky and the social formation of the mind.* Cambridge, MA: Harvard University Press.

Wolins, I. S., Jensen, N., & Ulzheimer, R. (1992). Children's memories of museum field trips: A qualitative study. *Journal of Museum Education, 17*(2), 17-27.

CHAPTER TWO

The Role of Objects in Active, Distributed Meaning-Making

Shawn Rowe
Washington University, Saint Louis

Although the meaning of education for museum producers and consumers has changed since the founding of America's earliest museums (Roberts, 1997), informal learning environments have taken an increasingly self-conscious place in the American educational landscape.[1] For the progressive era, this place was so important that Dewey (1900) used the museum as both the physical and metaphorical heart of the ideal school. He saw it as that place where the experiences of the child came into contact with the tools and practices "all-important in interpreting and expanding experience" (p. 85). Dewey was specifically interested in the role that objects played not only in sparking the imagination but also in the construction of knowledge.

Although one might argue that many of Dewey's visions for education have faded from the current debates concerning education, museums are now taken-for-granted elements of the educational system in the United States. The amount of funding the National Science Foundation ($46 million in 2000),[2] the National Endowment for the Arts (over $12 million in 1999),[3] and other funding sources provide for "informal" educational programs and research

---

[1]That landscape includes, as Cremin (1988) notes, any institution engaged in "the deliberate, systematic, and sustained effort to transmit, evoke, or acquire knowledge, values, attitudes, skills and sensibilities, as well as any learning that results from that effort, direct or indirect, intended or unintended" (p. x).

[2]Figures available on the NSF website at http://www.nsf.gov/bfa/bud/Fy2000/

[3]Figures available on the NEA website at http://arts.endow.gov/learn/99grants/E-A1.html

each year testifies to museums' central place in the educational landscape, especially in adult and community education.

Leaving aside temporarily the question of whether or not objects are ubiquitous to museums[4] and the question of how we should understand the term *objects,*[5] I argue that understanding the role of objects in mediating people's museum experiences requires taking a research perspective that accounts for the active, distributed, meaning-making people do in museums. Such a research perspective is grounded in a variety of what have come to be known as sociocultural approaches to mind growing out of the cultural–historical research of Vygotsky (1981), Luria (1982), and activity theory in the former Soviet Union (Leont'ev, 1981). What these approaches share is a focus on everyday cognition as it is grounded in socioculturally and historically situated, social activity. Their goal is broadly to explicate the relationships between human activity and the cultural, historical, and institutional contexts in which it takes place (Wertsch, del Río, & Alvarez, 1995, p. 3). We would expect from a sociocultural perspective that what "counts" as learning in any given museum would be quite different from what "counts" as learning in school or in any other museum. However, because most museum research and visitor studies have focused on the output of school-like knowledge (i.e., recall of discrete facts) as the most viable measure of learning, they have contributed little to understanding the unique types of learning people report anecdotally for museums or the particular cultural goals, tools, and practices of consumption museums embody and support. The result is an apparent paradox in museum education. Is the goal the transmission of accurate information about art, history or science, or is it to engage visitors in a way that validates their own knowledge, creates return visitors, or makes them critical consumers of other social texts? The role of objects in human activity can help explain this apparent paradox and is taken up near the end of this chapter.

In a broader research context, museums provide an exciting opportunity to explore group activities that we might label "learning" as they develop in more or less formal, socially mediated ways for several reasons. First, between 20% and 80% of museum visitors annually in the United States visit museums as part of a group (Bitgood, Serrell, & Thompson, 1994, p. 72). Secondly, the museum is a place where transmission of information is not necessarily the primary goal of group interaction. Rather, the primary goal of group interaction is often thought of as meaning-making. Such a view emerges from the widespread constructivist account of learning prevalent in museum learning research and among museum staff. One important implication of construc-

---

[4]Is a national battleground memorial an object? Are the html files that make up a virtual art museum objects? Are texts and photographic reproductions objects?

[5]As I argue later, it is productive to speak of the battlefield memorial, the html files, and photographs as well as very physical, three dimensional things like hammers and nails, sculptures, and the everyday objects filling history museums as all texts of one sort or another (Eco, 1981).

tivism is that the meanings people make as a result of the negotiation of different knowledges and ways of knowing cannot be judged according to authoritative standards of what is "correct" or "incorrect" as is often the case in more formal learning settings. Rather, authority for determining the correctness of an interpretation is shifted to the visitor. Without abandoning the idea that museums can and do transmit information or challenge visitors' prior knowledge, museum researchers have begun to embrace this more radical aspect of constructivism as well, seeking ways to allow visitors more room and authority to make sense. As Hein (1998) puts it, writing of the "constructivist museum,"

> Constructivist learning situations require two separate components, first a recognition that in order to learn the active participation of the learner is required. . . . Second, constructivist education requires that the conclusions reached by the learner are *not* validated by whether or not they conform to some external reality, but whether they "make sense" within the constructed reality of the learner. (p. 34)

Or as Roberts (1997) puts it, writing of the negotiation of visitor and museum meanings, "The essence of the education enterprise is thus the making of meaning" (p. 133).

These quotations from Hein and Roberts underscore the third reason museums provide a fruitful setting for exploring how group activity develops in socially mediated ways. Part of what makes the museum a unique "learning setting" is the fact that multiple ways of interacting (multiple ways of organizing social activity) around and with objects are encouraged. That is, the nature of activity and the meaning of objects in museums are up for negotiation by groups in ways that may be explicitly or implicitly prohibited in other learning settings (i.e., schools, workplaces).

To understand the roles of objects in group meaning-making in museums, it is useful to focus on the two ways in which Vygotsky (1978; 1986) saw all human activity as being distributed. First, all activity, including meaning-making, is social. It is distributed among people in groups variously described as communities of learners or communities of practice (Lave & Wenger, 1991; Rogoff, 1994) to stress their development over time in shared activities. This is not to say that individuals do not or can not learn outside of a group. Vygotsky's (1981) emphasis on the social distribution of cognitive activity stemmed from his claim that much human mental activity has its origins in social activity. From this perspective, the cognitive strategies used by individuals solving problems or interacting with objects alone retain traces of those social origins (p. 164).

To say that meaning-making is socially distributed means, first of all, that the processes of meaning-making are generally distributed among members of the group who build up a store of "knowledge" or "cultural capital."

According to Borun, Chambers, and Cleghorn (1996), family members not only help shape what each other experiences, but also together build up a fund of shared knowledge they use in later meaning-making.

As a result, the group, in effect, "knows" more than any of its individual parts. It is this kind of approach that has led to the search for what kinds of emergent properties groups have that make them distinct from individuals and more than simple amalgamations of individuals. Describing and understanding the behavior of the group is not a simple matter of describing and understanding the individual movements, statements, or knowledge of all of its members. After all, those movements and statements are always anticipatory and responsive (Bakhtin, 1981). They are in a sense strategic, responding to some other person's movements or statements and anticipating some response. Thus, understanding how a group's activity unfolds in a museum involves exploring how these actions are jointly negotiated, appropriated, and deployed.

Second, to say that meaning-making is socially distributed means that the processes of meaning-making are active coconstructions—that is, they require the active participation of and work by some or all participants using the cultural tools available to them in the setting. The meanings of what we say and do, for instance, are not necessarily obvious, waiting just to be articulated in language and transferred into brains. Rather, human meaning-making requires a great deal of assumptions and interpretive work by both speakers and addressees. Achieving understanding and making meaning are things people do actively, and that work is reflected in their conversations both in the themes of the conversations (what they say) they have during meaning-making activity and in the structures of the conversations and activities (how they say what they say).

Furthermore, Vygotsky (1978; 1986) saw human mental activity as distributed between the acting agent and the physical and cultural tools (like language) in the individual's environment. Human mental functioning is in this sense always mediated—that is, it may be distributed among multiple agents or among agents and the cultural tools available to them in a given activity. Wertsch (1998) refers to such distribution as *mediated action,* stressing that it always involves an agent working with or through cultural tools (or more likely a complex of cultural tools).

In what follows I examine two transcripts of activity at a particular exhibit in the St. Louis Science Center,[6] a large, urban, midwestern science and technology museum, to illustrate how the two types of distribution Vygotsky outlined shape the active meaning-making visitors can do with this particular

---

[6]The research from which these transcripts are drawn was funded in part by the Department of Research and Evaluation of the St. Louis Science Center, St. Louis, Missouri, through its Research and Evaluation Internship program.

object and what that means for understanding the museum as a unique learning setting and the nature of museum education. Both transcripts are from videotaped interactions at *The Great Gravity Race* exhibit, an inclined plane. The plane consists of two "tracks" down which two wheels roll. Each wheel has three weights that can be moved to any of three positions from close to the center of the wheel to close to the outer edge of the wheel. Adjusting the weights speeds up or slows down the movement of the wheels down the ramp. Specifically, if all three weights are placed closest to the center axle of the wheel, it will move fastest down the ramp, whereas if all three weights are placed closest to the outer edge of the wheel, it will move more slowly. A label near the exhibit explains that visitors should adjust the weights on the wheels, let them roll down the ramp, ask questions about their observations, and make predictions in order to think like a scientist.

Transcript 1
A man with a white beard (M). A woman in long dress (W). A teenage girl (G).
A preteen boy (B). A preteen girl (G2).

B and G approach at same time. B walks to the top of the ramp, G walks halfway up the side, brings one of the wheels half-way up, and gives it to B. B puts it at top and pushes it along. G leaves.

M approaches from end of table, watches. B rolls wheel with hand, then rolls it back up half-way, then picks it up to carry to top. M makes his way to the top of the ramp. B rolls the wheel on the left and M takes the wheel on the right.

1   B: brings left wheel to top of ramp and says **I'm gonna race ya!**
2   M: adjusts knobs.
3   W: approaches from top of table after reading label. **You can move these knobs [unintelligible]** helps boy adjust knobs. They line up the wheels with the back of the ramp.
4   M: Releases his wheel before B releases his.
5   W: **Wait [unintelligible] let me show you how to race.** Rolls both wheels back to back edge of ramp. **Hold your wheels, make sure that both your wheels are touching the back. This one.** Pointing to left wheel, pulling it back to starting point. **This one, OK.** Moves the knobs a little more. **Which one do you think will win?**
6   B: **This one.**
7   W: **OK**
8   M: Holding both wheels, releases and points with his fingers and arms outspread (i.e., don't touch)
9   W: **For heaven's sake.**
10 B: **Let's try the middle.** Takes the wheel on the right side, opposite him.
11 W: W takes the wheel from the boy to bring it back up to the top. **All right.**
12 B: **I want to try the middle.**
13 W: **What do you want to try?**
14 B: **The middle.**

15 W: **OK.**

16 B: **The middle . . . On your mark, get set, go.**

17 W: Stops them quickly. **Oh wait. We've got to start from the middle you [unintelligible].** They reposition wheels at beginning.

18 B: Releases wheels. **Oh [unintelligible].** Walks down side. Picks up wheel on the opposite side. **On the outside and middle.**

19 W: Walks to end of ramp to get wheel. **Here I'll carry mine up.** Takes wheel from B's hands.

20 B: **Let's try the outside and the middle.**

21 W: **Great, you do it. Fix em.** She lets him move both sets of knobs while she holds the wheels from rolling. Then she lets go of both of them while he finishes and steps back. Finally she moves back in to the frame only when he's about ready to start, but lets go again and points between them. **Can you do them both?**

22 B: **Yeah**

23 W: **Which one?**

24 B: Taps his wheel, then releases both of them. **This one's going sideways.** Brings them back to top and starts them over. **Cool. I know which one [unintelligible].**

25 G2: Walks up and B leaves.

I'd like to make three points using this transcript. First, as mentioned earlier, each person's actions and utterances "make sense" from an analytical perspective only in relation to the other people's actions and utterances. Their meaning comes from being situated in the group context. Each utterance is simultaneously a response to a prior one and anticipating a further response. This is most self-evident in the questions and answers (lines 5 & 6, 13 & 14, 21 & 22, for instance). But the woman's utterance in line 3, "You can move these knobs," is a response to her reading of the exhibit label — which suggests adjusting the knobs and observing the differences they make. She thus brings the information from the label (about the preferred way to use the exhibit) into the activity without directly quoting the label. The boy's statement, "Let's try the middle," in line 10 responds positively to the woman's suggested way of doing the activity (moving knobs and trying the race again) and anticipates her response to the first trial (that they should try a different configuration of weights). No utterance can be separated from this chain of responses and still make sense nor suggest alone what kinds of learning are going on in the interaction.

My second point is that B and W do an incredible amount of work to coordinate their activity, including negotiating who has authority over what parts of the activity. Without challenging B's framing of the activity as a race, W takes authority for the structure of the activity in several ways. First, she positions herself as the expert who knows not only that one "can move the knobs" (line 3) but also "how to race" (lines 5 and 17). She insists on the correct procedure, including keeping the same wheels — taking "her" wheel from the boy twice.

The boy works with her, answering the questions she asks, making predictions about what will happen, and following the rules of the game — how to race. Although she positions herself as the expert, W also works to transfer some authority for the activity to B as it progresses, going as far as stepping away from the table in line 21 to allow him control over moving the knobs on both wheels and running the race "correctly." But throughout the episode, the activity is distributed among first B, M, and W, then B and W, who must work to coordinate their activity from a shared understanding of what is going on and how to proceed.

B and W draw on at least two different "ways of knowing" to structure the interaction, both of which are supported by the museum and exhibit. The first is revealed in line 1: B interprets the activity as play, a race or competition. This is a very common response to this particular exhibit, and one which the name, *The Great Gravity Race,* suggests, although in this case B had not read the label. The second is revealed in the structure of the conversation in lines 5-7. W and B engage in a type of speech pattern very common to American classrooms: Initiation, Response, Evaluation (IRE). W initiates a question, "Which one do you think will win?" to which B responds, "This one." But W goes on to evaluate B's response, "Ok." By invoking this speech pattern common to classrooms, W shapes the activity as not "just play," but educative in some sense. Such a reading of the utterance is consistent with her early taking of authority and gradual delegation of authority to B, another common feature of educative or learning interactions between experts and novices. The race thus becomes a type of "guided participation" (Rogoff, 1990) aimed toward the boy's mastery of acceptable practices for interacting with museum objects. The situation is redefined in this sense as a teaching or learning opportunity that has (at least implicitly) the goal of reproducing social practices. The exhibit encourages both B's ways of knowing (play) and W's more formal transfer of ability to do the task correctly, but it does not limit their activity to one or the other.

Transcript 2
Two young boys (B1 & B2) approach from the end of the ramp.

1 B1: Takes the wheel on the right hand side of the ramp to the top while B2 takes the left. They carefully line the wheels up at the top
2 B 2: **Go!** They both release their wheels.
3 B1: **Whoa!**
4 B2: **Go go**
5 B1: **Oh yeah** } Both boys follow their wheels down the sides of the ramp.
6 B2: **Oh yeah**
7 B1: **Oh yeah**

Adult male (M) approaches from the end of the ramp, walks to the top, and stands to the side watching B1 and B2.

8   B2: Taking the wheel from the right side of the ramp. **This time I get that one**.

9   B1: **Yes. I want the faster one.** Picks up opposite wheel, but brings it to the right side at the top.

10   B2: Also trying to put his wheel in the right side of the ramp. **Move, move D.**

11   B1: Takes his wheel to the left side. **I get this other one**

12   B2: **Go! You pushed yours**

13   B2: reaches over and stops B1's wheel.   They both follow along beside

14   B1: **You**   the ramp

15   B2: **You pushed yours! ah yeah!**

16   B1: **You cheated**

17   B1: **You pushed yours**   Taking wheels back to top of ramp.

18   B2: **This time [unintelligible]**   B2 starts his wheel with a push then follows it down the ramp B1 starts his wheel at same time. Follows it, about $\frac{1}{3}$ of the way down, pushes it. About halfway down, he picks his wheel up and carries it to the end, arriving there be-

19   B1: **Go, yeah.**   fore B2.

20   B2: **Oh yeah. you cheated**

21   B1: Both boys carry wheels back to the top. **Let's set them up and let them go**

22   B2: **Ok.** They position wheels. **Go.**

The wheels stay in place not moving (because the weights are not evenly distributed). They each give their wheels small pushes, but only until they start to roll.

23   B2: **you had me**

24   B1: **I know**.   They both hold their hands
                                                up away from the wheels, fol-
25   B2: **oh my god. Mine's taking the lead**   lowing along the ramp.

26   B1: **They were tied!**

They bring the wheels back to the top. M steps up to the ramp and addresses B1.

27   M: **D. you're supposed to move these**, touches the weights on B1's wheel, **to see, to see if they go faster, slower, what**

28   B2: **Cool. How do you get them out of here?**

29   M: **I don't know. Let's see.** Leans over B1's wheel and manipulates the weights

30   B1: **Oh, you pull em apart**

31   B2: **Ok D. let's go**. Lets his wheel roll.

32   B1: **I can't get it.**

33   M: **Which one?** starting to move wheel and adjust weights.

34   B1: **I want this one out there.**

35   B2: **Mine goes slower**

36   B1:   Watching B2's wheel, but holding on to his. **Goes a lot slower**

37   B2:   Nods his head as he drags wheel to the top of the ramp.

38   M: **Does yours go slower or faster, D.** B1 releases his wheel.

39   B2:   **Slower**

40   B1:   **Faster**

41   B2:   **Slower.** Pulling the weights on his wheel to the outside. Accidentally jams wheel diagonally in the ramp's rails.

42   B1:   **No**

43   M: **It goes slower in the middle in the middle, duhn't it.**

44   B2:   **D.**

45   M: **If you pull em all to the outside [unintelligible]**

46   B2:   Struggling to pull his wheel out of the rails. **Dad, mine won't come out.**

47   M: Steps in to pull B2's wheel out of the rails.

48   B1:   Moves his wheel back up to the top of the ramp.

49   M: Extracts B2's wheel.

50   B1:   **Dad, I want all mine to the outside.**

51   B2:   has his wheel in place. **Here, let's go, ready?**

52   B1:   Moving his weights, **I want mine. There. All mine are in [unintelligible]**

53   M: **Here,** leans over B1's wheel and adjusts one of the weights. **This one needs to go to the outside.**

54   B1:   To B2, **Are all yours on the outside?**

55   B2:   **Mine are all on the outside. Go!**

56   B1:   **Go, go, go**

57   B2:   **Hurry**

58   B1:   Pushes his about ⅓ of the way down

59   M: **They go faster with more of them on the outside, huh?**

60   B2:   **Yeah.**

61   B1:   [unintelligible] Brings wheel back to the top of the ramp.

62   B2:   Brings his wheel back to the top, but removes it from the ramp and holds it up. **Mine looks like this.** One of the weights is closer to the inside.

63   M: Moves the weight to the outside. **Now you're all set.**

64   B2:   Putting wheel back on ramp. **Go.** They both follow along. **It looks like**

65   B1:   **That was my side.**

66   B2:   in an exaggerated way. **That was my side.**

As in the first transcript, B1 and B2 begin by racing. They do not read the label. The race itself casts the activity as a shared one. One person can do the exhibit alone. But as a shared activity, the race is different. At least in the beginning of the transcript, the boys certainly see it as a competition rather than a "learning opportunity." They urge "their" wheels on (lines 4, 5, 6, 19 — and later in 56-57). They make exclamations about "their" wheels' performance (lines 7, 19, 20, 23, 25-26), they accuse each other of cheating (lines 12-17,

20), argue over procedure (lines 8–11), and later negotiate procedure (lines 21–22). Although the exhibit label suggests using the object to "think like a scientist," the closest thing to an experiment in the early part of the activity is B2's explicit move to exchange wheels (lines 8–9), but this is framed in terms of winning the race — a potential argument over who gets the "faster one" (line 9), and who gets to use which ramp (lines 10–11).

It is only in line 27 that the man, having read the label, makes an authoritative bid for a different way of using the exhibit: "D. You're supposed to move these." The otherwise innocuous phrase "supposed to" suggests that there is a preferred, correct way to use the exhibit that the boys have not yet tried. This leads to some discussion of how to adjust the weights, and the activity changes significantly. The boys adjust the weights on their own wheels, then let them roll without setting up a "race." Arguably the group activity has changed from "race" to something more like what the label of the exhibit calls "thinking like a scientist." The boys and man ask questions about the object (lines 25, 33, 38, 43, 45, 54, 55, 59), adjust variables (lines 29, 33, 41, 52, 63), and observe the resulting action and comment on it (lines 35, 36, 39, 40, 41, 62). M particularly models the types of observations the boys "should" be making as they engage in the activity in the way they are supposed to (lines 38, 43, 45, 59). Unlike W in the first transcript, M does not invoke a particular, authoritative speech genre to shape the activity and model it. As already noted, he does invoke the authority of the museum voice — what one is "supposed to" do — but his questions have to do with seeking information, modeling the types of questions the boys should ask, and making confirmations of observations.

Having made their adjustments, the activity changes again, however, when the boys return to competition. The next two minutes of activity (not included in this transcript) are a return to the competitive race. The boys return to mostly exclamations and disagreements over procedure. But they continue to adjust the weights, evidently trying to outdo each other by trying different combinations of positions. Thus, over the course of a 6-minute interaction with this object, B1, B2, and M also draw on at least two "ways of knowing" about the exhibit. The first, I labeled "racing" to reflect its competitive, playful nature. Again, as with the group in Transcript 1, the "racing" scenario seems quite natural given the structure of the object itself: a ramp with two wheels. In fact, as mentioned earlier, the race is the preeminent way visitors use this exhibit regardless of whether or not anyone in the group reads the label or observes a previous group using the object. But M introduces a second way of knowing about and interacting with the exhibit. I labeled this one "thinking like a scientist" to reflect the fact that with it, the participants seem to engage in just the sorts of activities the museum considers the point of the exhibit (at least as the museum's voice is embodied in the content of the label).

In both transcripts, making sense out of the participants' activities requires understanding how the action is distributed among the members of the group, each of whom adjusts his or her roles, statements, and actions to those of the others involved. In both cases, how the activity is socially distributed has some bearing on the kinds of resulting activities, and from at least one point of view, this is just the point of the museum. Multiple activities can be constructed around a given object resulting in multiple meanings. However, as mentioned earlier, meaning-making is distributed in another way as well. In order to solve problems like how to remember or divide by fractions, but also how to reach shared understanding of an activity, we must rely on cultural tools (Wertsch, 1998) — things like language, word processors, calculators, algebra, even museum exhibits are tools we draw on to solve practical problems, including achieving understanding or making meaning. The question that arises, then, in such cases is, "Who is doing the acting in such situations?" The answer may be "multiple agents" — the group — as demonstrated in the discussion of the transcripts, but it may also be "both the agents and the tools they use."

Throughout his work, Vygotsky was concerned with semiotic mediation, with how semiotic means such as language, but also mathematics, music, or mnemonic devices of any kind mediated thinking. In his own work, he studied the "semiotic potentials" of a variety of cultural tools — syllogisms, the use of complexes as opposed to concepts to organize thought, the use of mnemonic devices for memory games. We may conceive of such potentials now in terms of the affordances (Gibson, 1979) and constraints objects have for particular uses. Put simply, some objects are better used for some activities than others. That is, they afford certain practices and constrain others. It has been argued, for instance, that narrative structure affords the learning of national history — or even the structuring of historical thought and argument in general. At the same time, however, that narrative structure constrains what may be included as an historical fact in that history (White, 1987) and what must be relegated to the sidebars of history books as tangential to the main story (Mink, 1978). On a more mundane level, the use of a daily calendar affords my scheduling meetings, but if I leave it at home, my memory for meetings and ability to plan for future ones is arguably constrained.

The inclined plane and wheels making up *The Great Gravity Race* afford a variety of social interactions. As Transcript 1 demonstrates, the exhibit encourages B and W to bring at least two ways of knowing to the task, both of which are "privileged" in the interactive science museum: play (the St. Louis Science Center's motto is, after all, "The Playground for Your Head") and display of knowledge for evaluation by an "expert." Transcript 2 demonstrates how the object affords playing (racing), but also the activities defined by the label as thinking like a scientist (observing, predicting, and controlling variables). But how does it constrain activity? If the point of the exhibit (as suggested by the label) is to illustrate and encourage visitors to participate in the scientific method, is it successful? Put another way, could this object in fact adequately illustrate the scientific method by leading visitors through it in a way that would lead to their understanding (if not mastery) of it? After all, isn't that precisely what the interactive science museum exhibit should do — allow the visitor to participate in an activity that illustrates and teaches some scientific concept?

We can, in fact, imagine an object that might. First, if the key to the scientific method is control of variables (and that "if" is potentially a big one here), then we could imagine a design where as many variables as possible could be manipulated; for instance, not just the position of weights, but the incline and length of the "racing" plane could be manipulated. We could imagine a design where one wheel's weights stayed put, while the other's were systematically manipulated one at a time. The point is that we could, in fact, design an object that would allow for much more sophisticated control of variables and thus afford the illustration and participation of visitors in the scientific method (or the secrets of rotary inertia, for that matter) thus defined.

But would it?

These questions, and any answers one could give to them, rely on one half of what the Soviet semiotician Lotman (1988) called the "functional dualism of texts" (p. 34), and here we return to the problematic nature of objects glossed over earlier. Objects are not simply objects. That is, the nature of an object (especially, perhaps, in a museum) is not immediately self-evident. This is because the meaning of each object relies on its place in a semiotic system: a system of signs that each of us has more or less access to. Each object is thus like a text, the meaning of which we "read" or "construct" in our interactions with it. For Lotman, each text/object has at least two functions: "to convey meanings adequately, and to generate new meanings" (p. 34).

As Lotman developed it, the first function of texts is the accurate representation and transmission of information. This presupposes a shared code among those involved in the production and consumption of a text. This also presupposes that there is, in fact, one "intended" and thus best/proper/correct way to "read" (or consume) the text. In Lotman's words, "The first function is fulfilled best when the codes of the speaker and the listener most completely coincide and, consequently, when the text has the maximum degree of univocality" (p. 34). A museum object (exhibit, label, etc.) fulfills this function when it transmits information from the curator/museum as speaker to the visitor as listener. A variety of types of information (knowledge about the object, the place of the object in a narrative, a science concept, how to look at the object, etc.) can be transmitted more or less successfully from this point of view. And success is measured by whether or not visitors in fact "get the message." If they do not, it must be due to a "breakdown in communication." Either the message was not encoded correctly, some disturbance in the channel impeded communication of the message, or the visitor failed to decode the message properly. A particular version of museum education stems from this function: Visitors can be taught to decode. In fact, the museum must produce (i.e., construct/display) objects in such a way that visitors who know the code can get the message and visitors who may be novice users of the code (i.e., the "unwashed masses," the uninitiated, the art novice, the nonnative English speaker — in U.S. museums — the school child, etc.) may learn the rudiments of the code (or at least to appreciate the code and those who can decode it).

To ask whether the object can adequately illustrate what the museum decides is the standard, authoritative, canonical, or simply "correct" interpretation of the object is to consider the object in this first function. The adult visitors in Transcripts 1 and 2 seem to share this notion of the object's function in the museum setting. In both cases, the adult shapes the activity around what one is "supposed to" do, how one should proceed in order to live out the suggestions of the museum authority as represented by its voice embodied in the label. But note, also, that if we reconsider what it means to "think like a scientist," then it is not clear that this object could illustrate it and guide the visitor into experiencing it. For example, if we imagine that the most important element of thinking like a scientist is to seek answers to questions about why seemingly trivial phenomena occur (why does the wheel go faster with one arrangement of weights as opposed to the other), then this object seems well suited to the task. However, if we imagine that thinking like a scientist involves most importantly the control and systematic manipulation of all possible variables in a controlled, experimental fashion, then this object is not suitable as there is no way to control, for example, the tilt of the plane or the friction of the surface. Nor is systematic manipulation of the available variables structured into the object. Again, this line of reasoning is based on Lotman's first function of texts, to adequately transmit information. Visitors, however, are ostensibly free in the museum to interpret and consume objets in a variety of ways — some sanctioned by the museum and others not. The objects themselves may afford certain ways of consuming. Thus, *The Great Gravity Race* certainly affords the race as one way of consuming/reading/using the object, but it does not constrain visitors to only that use, as is evidenced by the transcripts. The fact that visitors can and will consume museum objects in unexpected ways leads us directly to Lotman's second function of texts.

Besides its function of adequately transmitting information, the museum object or text is also a "thinking device," a cultural tool for generating meaning. And the driving mechanism of generating meaning is the potential for a given object/text to support multiple interpretations and activities. The object's meaning is shaped not solely by the intention of the producer, but by other texts (languages, ideas, concepts, narratives, objects, ways of interacting) the visitor brings to bear in consuming (interpreting, using) the object/text. The possibility for alternative interpretations that is, in terms of the first function, a defect, is, in terms of this second function, the most important characteristic of the text/object. Let me quote Lotman (1988) at length here because I think his explanation of the difference between the two functions is quite elegant:

> The second function of a text is to generate new meaning. In this respect a text ceases to be a passive link in conveying some constant information between input (sender) and output (receiver). Whereas in the first case a difference between the message at the input and that at the output of an information circuit can occur only as a result of a defect in the communications channel, and is to be attributed to the technical imperfections of this system, in the second case such a difference is the very essence of a text's function as a "thinking device." (p. 36)

Different interpretations are not simply imposed on the object from outside. In the language used above, the object affords and constrains possible alternative messages, but also possible uses, possible alternative ideas, concepts, languages, and practices that can be brought to bear in consuming it. The object itself thus affords and constrains the meanings that can be appropriated by visitors (because they had a hand in generating them) rather than being simply taken on authority. This is not to say that visitors freed of curatorial authority can and will generate an infinite number of possible interpretations of objects. The fact that the languages (ways of speaking about, ways of knowing, ways of demonstrating knowledge) that may interact within the "semiotic space" (p. 37) organized by the object are not equally valued or equally powerful shapes the meaning that may be generated. As Lotman (1988) said, within the text, "languages interact, interfere, and organize themselves hierarchically" (p. 37). In coming together to generate meaning, these social languages (of visitors — hierarchized by race, gender, age, nationality, etc. — and museums as well as disciplines or social authorities including politicians, funders, activists) draw on the relative social positions of their speakers, more or less reproducing the social hierarchy. This "more or less" is important as the possibility for social change appears in the current social hierarchy being a little less reproduced with each encounter.

Within this second function, museum education has a different role. The history museum becomes a space offering the visitor objects, texts, and narratives that may be organized in a number of ways including what we might call creating an available past or, alternatively, commemorating the past or reinforcing identity projects. The art museum becomes a space where visitors/museum/objects may generate personal sense, demonstrate their cultural capital (Bourdieu, 1984) for each other, escape the world, study art history, meet friends, or date. The science museum may encourage critical thinking, or the development of critical consumers of science, or elevate the scientific aspects of everyday life practices. All of these goals exist side-by-side in museums with the goals of the first function of texts, dispensing knowledge, training visitors in a code, and defining a canon. Education, in this sense, represents the possibility of providing learners space where heterogeneous, even conflicting interpretations meet on the field of visitors' experiences with objects.

This is exactly what Roberts (1997) posits as the goal of constructivist education in the museum setting. She makes explicit the connection between interanimation of visitor and museum interpretations, activities, and voices and opening access to authoritative positions from which to speak:

> First, if a message is presented in a way that acknowledges its own nature — in other words, that is explicit about being not only a version but being the museum's version — then it does not exclude the possibility of alternative versions held by visitors. Second, if a message is presented in a way that allows for argument, complexity, or multiple perspectives, then it may begin to engage visitors in the process of evaluating it against their own perspectives. The result is a relation of shared authority, as both visitors and museums engage in constructive activities that give rise to the possible meanings of things. This is the essence of education (p. 145).

However, sharing authority is not as simple as constructing new museum texts that ask visitors to share their knowledge. True, some objects and texts may afford shared authority better than others, but the voices of visitors are not automatically made equal to those of experts. Moreover, the voices of all visitors are not valued nor engaged equally. Museums have, in fact, been struggling over just how to value the voices of constituencies including African Americans, Native Americans, women, and multilingual people since at least the progressive era.

So, should museums use their objects to transmit accurate information or to transfer authority for interpretation to visitors? I am not claiming that this explication of the functional dualism of texts (embodied in museum objects) does away with the paradox of museum education thus articulated. Yes, the goal of museum education is to transmit correct information about art, science, or history by teaching visitors the code and how to decode it. In fact, entry into that code is an important part of the museum's potential social role. After all, withholding information does museum visitors no good. But is the transmission of accurate information exactly what the National Science Foundation has in mind when it charges science museums "to increase the number of youth, particularly underrepresented (e.g., minorities, girls, the physically disabled) and underserved (e.g., rural communities), who are excited about [science, math, and technology] and who pursue such activities both in and out of school" (National Science Foundation, 1999)? These goals seem to be more aligned with the second function of museum objects and the concomitant account of museum education. Yes, then, the goal of museum education is to invite visitors into the meaning-making experience, drawing on what they know and the alternative possible meanings museum objects afford and multiple ways of interacting with and around objects. The real question is just what Roberts (1997) points to: How can this invitation be done in a way that acknowledges how and why the "standard" information that objects transmit is privileged and creates spaces where alternative interpretations of objects (and ways of interacting with objects) are encouraged rather than constrained?

REFERENCES

Bakhtin, M. M. (1981). *The dialogic imagination: Four essays by M.M. Bakhtin.* (C. Emerson & M. Holquist, Trans.). M. Holquist (Ed.). Austin: University of Texas Press.

Bitgood, S., Serrell, B., & Thompson, D. (1994). The impact of informal education of visitors to museums. In V. Crane, M. Chen, S. Bitgood, B. Serrell, D. Thompson, H. Nicholson, F. Weiss, and D. Campbell (Eds.), *Informal science learning: What the research says about television, science museums, and community-based projects* (pp. 61-106). Dedham, MA: Research Communication, Ltd.

Borun, M., Chambers, M., & Cleghorn, A. (1996). Families are learning in science museums. *Curator, 39*(2), 124-138.

Bourdieu, P. (1984). *Distinction: A social critique of the judgement of taste.* Cambridge, MA: Harvard University Press.

Cremin, L. (1988). *American education, the metropolitan experience, 1876-1980.* New York: Harper & Row.

Dewey, J. (1900). *School and society.* Chicago: University of Chicago Press.

Eco, U. (1981). *Travels in hyperreality: Essays.* W. Weaver (Trans.). San Diego: Harcourt Brace Jovanovich.

Gibson, J. J. (1979). *The ecological approach to visual perception.* Boston: Houghton Mifflin.

Hein, G. (1998). *Learning in the museum.* London: Routledge.

Lave, J., & Wenger, E. (1991). *Situated learning: Legitimate peripheral participation.* Cambridge: Cambridge University Press.

Leont'ev, A. N. (1981). The problem of activity in psychology. In J. Wertsch (Ed.), *The concept of activity in soviet psychology* (pp. 40-71). Armonk, NY: M. E. Sharpe.

Lotman, Yu. M. (1988). Text within a text. *Soviet Psychology, 26*(3), 32-51.

Luria, A. R. (1982). *Language and cognition.* New York: John Wiley & Sons.

Mink, L. O. (1978). Narrative form as a cognitive instrument. In R. H. Canary and H. Kozicki (Eds.), *The writing of history: Literary form and historical understanding* (pp. 129-149). Madison: University of Wisconsin Press.

National Science Foundation (1999). *Informal science education program statement.* Washington, DC: National Science Foundation. Retrieved October 12, 1999 from the World Wide Web: http://www.ehr.nsf.gov/ehr/esie/ISE.htm

Roberts, L. (1997). *From knowledge to narrative: Educators and the changing museum.* Washington, DC: Smithsonian Institution Press.

Rogoff, B. (1990). *Apprenticeship in thinking: Cognitive development in social context.* Cambridge: Cambridge University Press.

Rogoff, B. (1994). Developing understanding of the idea of communities of learners. *Mind, culture, and activity, 1*(4), 209-229.

Vygotsky, L. S. (1978). *Mind in society: The development of higher psychological processes.* M. Cole, V. John-Steiner, S. Scribner, & E. Souberman (Eds.), Cambridge, MA: Harvard University Press.

Vygotsky, L. S. (1981). The genesis of higher mental functions. In J. V. Wertsch (Ed.), *The concept of activity in Soviet psychology* (pp. 144-188). Armonk, NY: M. E. Sharpe.

Vygotsky, L. S. (1986). *Thought and language.* (A. Kozulin, Trans.). Cambridge, MA: MIT Press.

Wertsch, J. V. (1998). *Mind as action.* New York: Oxford University Press.

Wertsch, J. V., del Río, P., & Alvarez, A. (1995). Sociocultural studies: History, action, and mediation. In J. V. Wertsch, P. del Río, & A. Alvarez (Eds.), *Sociocultural studies of mind* (pp. 1–34). Cambridge, MA: Harvard University Press.

White, H. (1987). *The content of the form: Narrative discourse and historical representation.* Baltimore: Johns Hopkins University Press.

CHAPTER THREE

Children Learning with Objects in Informal Learning Environments

Scott G. Paris
Susanna E. Hapgood
University of Michigan

Children spend an increasing amount of time in informal learning environments such as museums, but there has been little research on how those experiences contribute to their social and cognitive development. We consider several areas for future research that have potential for informing parents and educators about the dynamics of experiential learning including object-centered learning, inquiry-guided learning, aesthetics and artistic appreciation, and learning to use technology. The cumulative experiences in these novel and motivating contexts may shape children's thinking, values, aspirations, group membership, and identities throughout their lives. Studies of children in informal learning environments can complement traditional research on children in homes and schools and provide a broader variety of everyday contexts to examine motivation, socialization, and reasoning. Research on children in these diverse contexts represents an integration of contextualized theories of practices with constructivist theories of meaning-making (Paris & Ash, in press). The new field of research is pragmatic and ecological with reciprocal benefits for understanding children's development and promoting their learning.

SITUATING CHILDREN'S LEARNING EXPERIENCES

A persistent challenge for developmental psychologists is to examine and understand the ever-changing contexts in which children develop. The renewed interest in cultural and historical contexts of development, stimulated by Vygotsky's work, has shown how developing expertise is intertwined with situational opportunities and participation with others. The nondualistic and irreducible interweaving of person and context has led many theorists to proclaim that the appropriate unit of analysis is a person in a setting performing an action, a "supra-individual envelope of development" (Cole, 1995). Recent contextualist theories of development have emphasized everyday cognition (Rogoff & Lave, 1984), socially shared cognition (Resnick, Levine, & Teasley, 1991), cognitive apprenticeship and academic crafts (Brown, Collins, & Duguid, 1989), situated learning and legitimate peripheral participation, (Lave & Wenger, 1991), guided participation (Rogoff, 1993), social constructivist perspectives (Schauble, Leinhardt, & Martin, 1997), and communities of practice (Lave, 1991) as illustrations of the specialized knowledge and practices of people in specific situations. These approaches stand in sharp contrast to theories of child development that neglect or minimize the role of context, but the contrast is not simply between normative and individual descriptions of development.

Lave (1993) distinguished between two broad classes of theories that attempt to contextualize development, theories that emphasize actions and theories that emphasize meanings. The first type emphasizes the nature of engagement with a task and is often based on activity theories that focus on subject–object relationships within contexts. It has strong ties to the role of experience as espoused by Dewey (e.g., Ansbacher, 1998; Cohen, 1998; Fenstermacher & Sanger, 1998). The second type is based on meanings constructed during social interactions and is exemplified by Vygotsky and sociocultural theories (e.g., Palincsar, 1998; Wertsch, Tulviste, & Hagstrom, 1993). It is the integration of these two broad approaches that poses a significant new and potentially fruitful area of research in child development, according to Goodnow, Miller, and Kessel (1995). This leads to analyses of what children do with whom in which settings and for what purposes. How they accomplish their actions, what meanings they acquire from an experience, and why it is significant for their lives are issues of contextual interpretation.

Studies of children have always been guided by tenets of good observation and explanation, but the new thrust emphasizes analyses of the contexts as more than background variables. Instead, contexts afford and privilege some practices over others, contexts constrain and shape interactions with objects, and contexts help structure sanctioned social dynamics. Traditionally, developmental psychologists have studied children's homes and community environments as their "contexts," but new approaches are specifying in much greater detail the settings and practices that influence children's development. These are analyses of ordinary learning in everyday situations (cf. Paris & Cross, 1983), for example, selling Girl Scout cookies (Rogoff, Baker-Sennett, Lacasa, & Goldsmith, 1995) or using mathematics in and out of school (Nunes,

Schliemann, & Carraher, 1993). Such contextualized analyses may provide quite different information about children's development than studies with contrived tasks or artificial settings. The fundamental issues in this line of inquiry are to determine how the child's acquisition and expression of knowledge, beliefs, and practices of the family or community are embedded in specific contexts.

It is within the zeitgeist of theories that strive to contextualize child development that researchers are mapping a new direction for basic research, theory building, educational applications, and social policies. The new research takes place in community settings beyond home and school, such as museums, zoos, historical parks, and gardens because they provide opportunities for significant experiences in the lives of children. More than 500 million people visit American museums each year (Hein & Alexander, 1998). There are nearly 300 science museums in America and half of their visitors are under 18 years of age. Cleaver (1992) described 265 hands-on museums built on the principle of "hands-on = minds-on," a philosophy related to theorists such as John Dewey, Maria Montessori, Jean Piaget, Eleanor Duckworth, and Howard Gardner. Museums, of course, may include environments specifically designed for children, as well as buildings that house artifacts of art, science, history, and so forth. The more inclusive term is *informal learning environments* (ILE), which refers to a variety of community settings such as museums, zoos, aquaria, parks, and botanical gardens. The term ILE might also encompass community institutions such as libraries, churches, and community centers; community events such as music and cultural festivals; and groups such as Scouting and youth organizations because they all involve gatherings outside home and school to share new experiences (Forman, Minick, & Stone, 1993; Villarruel & Lerner, 1994). These contexts provide incredibly rich and diverse opportunities for learning and are ubiquitous in children's lives.

Two caveats about ILEs deserve mention. First, there is always some uneasiness with the term *learning* because acquisition of facts and knowledge is not always the purpose of the interaction in an ILE. Sometimes visitors want to play, relax, enjoy, or have a social outing in an ILE. Sometimes the impact of the experience may be implicit, subtle, and difficult to articulate or assess. At other times, learning might be intentional and structured by docents or families. Therefore, learning (in the traditional sense) may or may not occur and learning does not have to be the goal of a visit to an ILE. Second, ILEs do not have to be organized places and designated spaces. They can be defined by the social interaction. In the same way that a Muslim teacher under a tree helping young boys memorize verses from the Koran is an instance of schooling, so is a mother helping her child learn to cook or experiment in a kitchen an instance of an ILE. Thus, ILEs may reflect the nature of the social activity or learning that occurs more than a specific place. The first caveat qualifies *learning* and the second caveat qualifies *environment,* and it is clear that the intended meaning of ILE is difficult to pinpoint but more encompassing than the traditional meaning of a museum.

Moreover, as families pursue venues that provide shared opportunities for education and leisure, they increasingly seek ILEs as destinations (Borun, Cleghorn, & Garfield, 1995). Why? Some parents regard the visits as educational experiences for children to learn about history, science, and art with authentic artifacts and knowledgeable experts. Others want to strengthen family ties through shared experiences, much like vacations with educational value added. Other families regard museum visits as part of their ongoing participation in community events, a sign of active citizenship perhaps. These varied contexts extend and complement parental values and instruction; they are activities that can fuel children's aspirations as well as bolster personal, family, and cultural identity. A visit to the Museum of Science and Industry in Chicago or the Museum of Modern Art in New York may transform children's knowledge and notions of possible selves as much as a visit to the Statue of Liberty or the Holocaust Memorial may stimulate national or religious identity. However, it is important to recognize that not all families share these values and motivations for exploring ILEs. Families who are unfamiliar with local ILEs, who are less involved in children's education, or who have been disenfranchised from community participation may avoid museums (Hood, 1983). Research is needed on families who seek as well as avoid visits to ILEs. Our purpose in this chapter is to identify mutually important topics in museum education and child development because detailed studies of the social, cognitive, and developmental aspects of children and families exploring these environments can enrich theories and applications in both fields.

FEATURES OF INFORMAL LEARNING ENVIRONMENTS

Informal learning environments (ILEs) are difficult to define but are usually contrasted with formal learning opportunities in school. For example, Resnick (1987) noted that learning outside school emphasizes shared cognition, tool manipulation, contextualized reasoning, and situation-specific competencies in contrast to individual cognition, pure mentation, symbol manipulation, and generalized learning in school. However, it seems that in both schools and museums, on some occasions and in some places, learning might be more or less structured and guided, more or less formal. ILEs are also difficult to specify because learning is a broad term that encompasses many outcomes. Visiting nature parks can lead to restorative feelings (S. Kaplan, 1995) but is it learning? Participating in Girl Scouts may lead to better managerial skills and citizenship but is it learning (Edwards, 1994)? Visiting the Vietnam Memorial may move people to tears but is it learning?

Two features of ILEs are noteworthy. First, ILEs allow and promote encul-turation of visitors into social practices. The objects in museums are selected as valued objects within a culture, whether they represent art, science, or history. There are, of course, political and social overtones to the choices of objects that reflect local and national perspectives. Likewise, experiences in ILEs are intended to enculturate visitors by eliciting senses of identity and participation with specific groups and values. The cultural participation af-forded by schools and ILES may be similar. Second, ILEs are venues that foster exploration and knowledge-seeking. Self-direction and self-regulation may be allowed in schools, but students are more often directed by others as they learn, whereas museum visitors often choose their own routes, pace, level of engagement, and social group as they explore exhibits. More active and less restricted learning in ILEs may be a key feature that parents and teachers can strive to emulate.

Part of the problem of neatly circumscribing ILEs, of course, is defining learning, but part of the problem are the blurry lines between learning and development, education and entertainment, memory of facts and memory of cumulative experiences, and knowledge acquisition and affective outcomes. Despite the difficulties in classification and boundaries, ILEs are generally char-acterized as learning based on objects and experiences rather than text, per-haps the key distinction between traditional school and nonschool learning. ILEs provide authentic artifacts and allow children to determine their own goals for exploration, discovery, and learning. Falk and Dierking (1998) preferred the term *free-choice learning* to *informal learning* because visitors have choice and control in ILEs. Paris (1997) described situated motivation in museums ac-cording to some key features of intrinsic motivation. These features include the visitor's opportunities to construct personal meaning, make choices, exer-cise control, engage in collaboration and conversation, adjust task challenges, and derive consequences of performance that promote self-efficacy.

At this point, it may be noted that all these features of intrinsic motivation are evident, or at least possible, in formal schools. Many educational ap-proaches promote students' sense of control, responsibility, ownership, and collaboration as they learn. This is the key point, not the difficulty in differen-tiating formal and informal learning environments. Schools might foster chil-dren's learning more effectively if they embraced the same features that moti-vate children in ILEs. Gardner (1991) argued that schools might be more invit-ing and more effective if they resembled museums. He noted that "science museums and children's museums have become the loci for exhibitions, ac-tivities, and role models drawn precisely from those domains that do engage youngsters; their customary wares represent the kinds of vocations, skills, and aspirations that legitimately animate and motivate students" (p. 202). Schools and museums can benefit by reciprocal trade agreements and importing suc-cessful practices from each venue (Paris & Ash, in press).

Trying to understand the impact on a person of a visit to an ILE begins with a description of the situation and the experiences afforded by elements in the setting. The analogy to perceptual affordances is important because just as objects afford certain properties such as surface or support, a situation affords or promotes certain types of interactions and experiences. For example, standing on the deck of a reconstructed slave ship or descending into a replica of a coal mine can elicit strong emotional reactions. The situations are, in fact, designed to afford and evoke visitors' reactions. The authenticity of the artifacts and the affordances of the ILE foster the acquisition of knowledge because of the embeddedness of the desired knowledge and responses in the situation. This necessary embeddedness of learning and development in practical experiences is the centerpiece of theories of situated learning (Lave & Wenger, 1991) and apprenticeship (Rogoff, 1990) and illustrates the potential linkages among research in ILEs and contemporary developmental theories.

Studies of ILEs extend beyond affordances and practices; they must include examination of the motives of the person in the situation and the ways whereby meaning is created. This is the fusion of social and anthropological theories of practice with constructivist theories of meaning-making. For example, contemporary theories of children's motivation are almost entirely based on achievement strivings and failure avoidance because they emanate from research in schools (Pintrich & Schunk, 1996). Theories of mastery motivation, expectancy values, self-efficacy, or attributions were derived from academic settings and may not generalize much beyond them. Our notions of children's motivation would be enriched considerably if theories were designed to explain behavior in ILEs and nonschool contexts. Consider some of the motives for people to visit museums noted by Roberts (1997): social interaction, reminiscence, fantasies, personal involvement, and restoration. These goals for seeking and immersing oneself in ILEs need to be studied in order to understand why children choose to spend their time in certain groups, activities, and environments beyond school.

We want to promote research in community contexts of learning beyond the school and home because they have been neglected by basic psychological research and because the contexts are fertile grounds for building theories of learning, motivation, and socialization based on children's common experiences. Despite occasional studies of children and families in museums during the past 70 years (see Hein & Alexander, 1998), only recently have researchers begun systematic research and theorizing in informal environments (e.g., Matusov & Rogoff, 1995; Schauble, Banks, Coates, Martin, & Sterling, 1996). The rationale for this new area of research is predicated on the following claims: (a) children spend an increasing amount of leisure and family time in ILEs; (b) children in ILEs are exposed to unique objects and culturally informative experiences that afford construction and sharing of meanings; (c) children in ILEs encounter experts, teachers, craftspeople, artisans, artists, and role models that are often unavailable to them at home and school; (d) ILEs provide natural community venues for familial and intergenerational learning; (e) ILEs provide grounds for theory building that complement extant theories of formal learning and motivation in schools; (f) ILEs afford learning with technology through practice and social collaboration; and (g) ILEs can have cumulative and life-long effects on people's aspirations, values, and interests.

We highlight fruitful areas for research on children in ILEs that illustrate how developmental processes and outcomes can be shaped by experiences in these contexts. Parenthetically, the lack of these experiences, although not described, is presumed to detract from children's development. Each area of research is noted briefly to illustrate the kinds of issues relevant to children that could be investigated. The topics include (a) learning about objects, (b) inquiry-guided learning, (c) aesthetic development, (d) family interactions, (e) using technology, and (f) transformative personal experiences.

LEARNING WITH OBJECTS

The raison d'être of any museum is the collection of objects. The objects might reflect a discipline, person, or historical events, but the distinctive aspect of most museums is the collection and display of objects, which is the basis for a public interface (Carr, 1991). It seems strange that so little attention has been paid to the nature of children's learning about, with, and through objects. Tudge and Winterhoff (1993), in a discussion of Vygotskian notions of the culturally and socially embedded nature of cognitive development, say that "social and cultural institutions, technologies, and tools channel the nature and focus of interpersonal interactions, which in turn mediate the development of children's higher mental functions . . ." (p. 66). Developmental research usually assigns object-based learning to an elementary stage of thinking that is concrete rather than symbolic, in which learning is due to trial-and-error rather than systematic experimentation, but this ignores how children become skilled at viewing objects or inferring their uses and history. Sometimes the developing expertise about viewing objects is described as *museum literacy* or *visual literacy,* but there is much more that needs to be studied from a developmental perspective (see van Kraayenoord & Paris, chapter 12, this volume). How do children handle, discuss, and assemble objects that allow hands-on interactions? How do they learn about objects that are hands-off? How do children use prior knowledge, analogies, conversation, and question-asking to clarify their understanding of objects?

The answers to these questions are at the core of an emerging field referred to as *object-based epistemology* (Conn, 1998). Evans, Poling, and Mull (chapter 4, this volume) describe the advent of this approach in museums that began in the late 19th century and gave scientific authority to organized collections of objects. They suggest that there is both a natural history of objects in museums and a cultural history. The former is the domain of scientific exposition whereas the latter is the socially situated interpretations of objects. This dichotomy is parallel to the two classes of theories described by Lave (1993) that focus on meaning-making or contexts of objects. In one sense, the child's task is to navigate through both the natural and cultural histories of objects. This requires observations and appreciation of the objects as well as the discourse that surrounds them.

Museum educators know that objects are the starting point, not the ending, of a visitor's museum experience because objects stimulate thought and reflection. In historical museums, objects become cues for institutional memories of past events, but they are also cues for personally reconstructed memories. Viewing the objects allows visitors to recreate and embrace their personal memories, to express their ownership of the experiences, and to share the stories with others. Gurian (1999) said:

> Not meaning to denigrate the immense importance of museum objects and their care, I am postulating that they, like props in a brilliant play, are necessary but not sufficient. This paper points out something that we have always known intuitively, that the larger issues revolve around the stories museums tell and the way they tell them. Objects, one finds, have in their tangibility, provided a variety of stakeholders with an opportunity to fight over the meaning and control of their memories. It is the ownership of the story, rather than the object itself, that the fight has been all about. (p. 2)

The notion of story is crucial when considering knowledge derived from objects because museum educators know that objects on display may be inert knowledge in the same way as facts on a page. Many exhibitions of objects arrange the context to evoke a single story or permit the visitor to create his or her own story surrounding the object. Roberts (1997) described how an exhibit on Linnaeus at the Chicago Botanic Garden was designed not to tell facts about botanical classification but to weave a story about problem-solving. She built on Bruner's (1986) notion of the narrative mode of meaning-making and suggested that visitors learn by constructing their own narratives about objects." To acknowledge that meaning making lies at the heart of the museum enterprise and that narrative provides the means by which this activity is accomplished is to take the first step toward truly opening museums to multiple voices and views" (p. 152). We believe that there is a powerful role of learning about objects through narrative constructions that can be examined in ILEs. The developmental questions of how children of various ages and backgrounds construct their narratives about objects are abundant and important. They invite developmental research on children's understanding of scientific concepts, aesthetic meanings, and of one's place in history. These stories are the fabric of children's lives that integrate natural and cultural histories of objects, and they are fundamental to understanding children's cognitive and social development.

CURIOSITY, INQUIRY, AND MEANING-MAKING

Objects in museums are often rare and unusual; that is what makes them collectible and why museums have been called "cabinets of curiosity" (Weil, 1995). Most people agree that ILEs are interesting because they contain objects that elicit curiosity and exploration, evident in visitors' questions such as: What the heck is that? Is that really art? Why did the animal do that? In many ways, the questions reveal the intrinsically motivating aspects of objects and illustrate how ILEs can use visitors' inquisitiveness to guide learning. Indeed, a cornerstone of inquiry-guided learning is the discourse that surrounds children's knowledge-seeking. Sometimes children ask questions, but often their inquiry is internal or reflective. Bringing their questions into the open and encouraging conversations about objects is crucial for providing good explanations and deepening children's understanding (Callanan, Jipson, & Soennichsen, chapter 15, this volume). We believe that many of the principles currently espoused for inquiry-guided learning in schools are naturally evident in ILEs and that research in both contexts can be mutually informative.

We know that children exhibit more curiosity, initiative, and persistence when their inquiries are related to their interests (Renninger, 1992). ILEs provide opportunities for children to match their interests with the resources necessary to investigate them. A classroom teacher may find it difficult to accommodate one child's burning desire to know more about diamonds or dinosaurs, but a visit to a natural history museum may provide that opportunity. More and more museums attempt to create opportunities for first-hand investigations with exhibits in which visitors can manipulate materials to change variables. For example "exhibits" at the Exploratorium in San Francisco are usually stations that allow individuals or small groups of people to manipulate things, such as move mirrors and prisms in various configurations around a light source. This allows visitors to ask questions and to seek answers through experimentation.

Research on problem-based learning and project-based science has illuminated key factors that sustain student engagement (Blumenfeld et al., 1991; Krajcik et al., 1998). These factors, whether in schools or ILEs, are powerful shapers of learning and include: (a) a driving question that is anchored in a real-world problem to motivate the inquiry, (b) social collaboration during investigation, (c) multiple ways to demonstrate knowledge and display competence, often in the creation of artifacts or culminating projects, (d) scaffolding that models strategic thinking instead of providing definitive answers, (e) some choice and control about the topic to be studied and the methods used to conduct the investigation, (f) the availability of pertinent multimodal and multimedia information, and (g) the use of technological tools. Barron et al. (1998) emphasized the importance of honing driving questions and providing opportunities for reflection during project-based learning. Their work suggested that formative and summative self-assessment increases the chances of children doing activities for the sake of understanding rather than merely for the sake of getting them done.

We believe that ILEs provide objects and experiences that stimulate children's curiosity and support inquiry-guided learning. Research in ILEs might inform parents and educators about effective means of learning and instruction in other settings. Heath (1994) contended that successful youth organizations adhere to a philosophy that "learning counts" and they provide multiple ways to demonstrate competency. One of the virtues of ILEs is that there are diverse means of interacting with objects that can be aligned with an individual's specialized intelligences, according to Gardner (1991). Moreover, ILEs allow people to select their own environments in which they can display mastery. Thus, developmental studies of children's selection of environments and their demonstrations of expertise can both be accomplished in ILEs.

AESTHETIC DEVELOPMENT

Another fruitful area of future research is the nature of children's growing aesthetic appreciation. Whether measured in terms of academic theories or parental values, interest in academic achievement greatly overshadows children's aesthetic and artistic development. Perhaps that is why there is so little developmental research on children's performing and creative arts or their developing aesthetic appreciation. Research in ILEs seems perfectly suited to filling this gap in knowledge by studying how children understand and appreciate art, music, gardens, and features of the environment. Historically, theories of visual thinking and aesthetic experiences have changed their emphases from "assimilation and imitation" by simple exposure to "cognitive interpretation" of critical features of art (Davis & Gardner, 1992). Contemporary theories of aesthetics, for example, describe analytical, critical, and deconstructive views such as: (a) the "percipience" of the viewer as a fundamental "way of knowing" that provides a coherence of emotion, perception, and cognition that reveals insights about the self and humanity (Smith, 1992); (b) a cognitive interpretation of a symbolic system that goes beyond perception to create meaning from the context and culture of the piece of art (Parsons, 1992); and (c) a kind of reflective intelligence, as opposed to the impulsive and automatic experiential intelligence, that is a disposition to think deliberately, deeply, and boldly about the meanings of art (Perkins, 1994). The field of aesthetics was originally built on a foundation of philosophy but is now supported by cognitive, perceptual, developmental, and emotional theories of constructive meaning-making that focus on understanding the ideas and emotions engendered by art (Geahigan, 1992).

Project Zero and ARTS PROPEL, based on work by Gardner (1989), Perkins (1994), and Winner (1982), are good examples of theory-driven, child-centered approaches to arts education. Perkins (1994) described reflective intelligence, the fundamental process of learning to appreciate art, in terms of metacognition, motivational dispositions, global strategies to be thoughtful and effortful, and the high road to transfer through reflective analyses. These are the same constructs he used to explain learning in schools and may reveal similarities in children's cognitive and aesthetic development. Some scholars have devised theories of aesthetic development based on Piagetian notions (Housen, 1992), and others have analyzed visitors' interpretations as learning to read the material culture (Beck, Eversmann, Krill, Michael, & Twiss-Garrity, 1997). Kindler (1997) emphasized the value for children of direct, intense, affective experiences with art. We applaud the pioneering steps in theorizing about visual thinking and aesthetic development but see a need for research on children and adults transacting with art, with objects, and with nature. There is ample room for theories of universal and nonuniversal development in art education and aesthetics (Feldman, 1987; Gardner, 1989).

FAMILY INTERACTIONS IN ILES

Families interact less in the home and more in community settings today than ever before. The mobility of the family, the demise of the nuclear family, and the increase in ILEs fuel the expectations and desires of children and youth for adventurous learning in their communities. These factors motivate families to search for places to visit and things to do as a group, often in multiple types of family groups with assorted members. Several topics of research illustrate the reciprocal benefits for developmental psychology and museum education of studying families in ILEs.

Most of the research on families in museums is descriptive, following the tradition of visitor studies research that examines demographic characteristics of visitors (see review by Borun, Cleghorn, & Garfield, 1995). For example, Diamond (1986) recorded running narratives of families as they explored two science museums and found that families "shopped around" exhibits and stayed less than a minute at 57% of them. Family members were equally likely to observe someone else manipulating things in an exhibit as they were to operate it themselves. Families only read 9% of the graphics, and teaching was confined largely to showing and telling. Recently, researchers have tried to assess and document family learning in more detail (see Borun, chapter 14, this volume). Borun, Chambers, and Cleghorn (1996) developed measures of group learning by observing families at four different science museums. Videotapes and group discussions revealed three levels of learning — identifying, describing, and interpreting/applying — that were related to both the time spent at exhibits and the kinds of talking and reading performed while viewing.

The surprisingly meager evidence of deep and engaged family learning has led researchers to study family discourse and explanations as a key to learning. Crowley and Callanan (1998) studied how parents help children coordinate theory and evidence to nurture scientific thinking. They found that children had deeper engagement and talked more at exhibits when parents offered explanations. They also showed how some exhibits may stimulate conflicting goals between parents and children that thwart collaboration and learning, a finding observed by other researchers (Gelman, Massey, & McManus, 1991). Such findings have led researchers to define learning as *conversational elaboration* among visitors, a construct that is especially applicable to families in ILEs (Leinhardt & Crowley, 1998). Research on conversations as people view, explore, and reason together in ILEs has important implications for children's learning, language, and family dynamics.

TECHNOLOGY PRACTICES

Another area for future research on children and ILEs involves technology. Children are exposed to modern electronic technology from infancy — toys with microchips, bar code scanners at the grocery store, remote control car locks, not to mention computers and audiovisual equipment. How do children make sense of these tools? Some research with adolescents suggest that technological tools are simply taken for granted, used but unexamined and unquestioned (Breakwell & Fife-Schaw, 1987). When do children question and evaluate the technology in their lives? Where do they learn to use technology as tools for learning? ILEs provide excellent contexts for using technology, for learning about technology, and for working collaboratively with others. For example, libraries have computerized data bases and search engines. They often have computers with Internet access, as do most museums. Visitors can use touch screens, menus, search engines, word processing, and other tools to find and view information. Of course, children also use technology in theme parks, arcades, and home video games.

Krendl and Clark (1994) suggested that technology is an ideal medium for cooperation between ILEs and schools. For example, many museums have digitized images of their collections on websites that can be viewed remotely by students in schools. The images can be used for reports and projects in school or to augment field trips with pre or postvisit viewing (Valenza, 1998; Walter, 1997). In addition to seeing selected materials from another physical environment, a child on a computer can enter a virtual environment. One interesting example is MOOSE Crossing, a virtual reality environment that was designed with constructionist tenets (Papert, 1991) to allow children ages 8–13 (and some adult "rangers") the opportunity to create and share their own projects. Participation in MOOSE Crossing is voluntary and self-paced but not lonely. Children all over the country write programs to create their own pets, abodes, businesses, and personas, visit with each other, and support each other in learning how to access and use all the different subenvironments and "objects" that other children have created. The creations are both models and sources of inspiration for others situated in a social context (Bruckman, 1998). Another intriguing aspect of MOOSE Crossing is the interactions between people of different ages and different levels of expertise. New participants in the environment are as likely to receive help from children as they are from adults; both children and adults viewed themselves as teachers and learners. This is an important feature of many communities of learners, as noted by Rogoff (1994).

Technological tools can foster social interaction and coinvestigations, whether in the museum or in virtual reality. They might allow visualization of objects too tiny or too large to be seen directly. They might allow objects to be represented, animated, disassembled, reassembled, and manipulated in ways that are physically impossible with the genuine objects. They might provide illustrations that help visitors understand unobservable events such as dinosaur behavior or solar flares. Technology can also contextualize objects in either narrative frames or expository frames of reference. The potential for technology to enhance object-based epistemology in museums is huge. However, it requires more imaginative use of the tools than touch screens and audio recordings that simply mimic text.

TRANSFORMATIVE PERSONAL EXPERIENCES

The impact of ILEs on children's lives requires a developmental analysis and, often, a life-course lens because the influences of museum visits can be indirect, subtle, and latent. Elder's (1998) life-course paradigm provides an appropriate lens because it validates unique experiences and events that transform people's lives through time. A life-course perspective grounds analyses in history and ecology, a contextual view of ILEs and the roles they play in individual developmental trajectories. Ideally we want all children's experiences to work in concert to optimize their potential to become lifelong learners and contributors to society. We need to gather information about what it is that children do that is deeply meaningful to them and how such experiences shape their development. Anecdotal reports often pinpoint experiences in museums, camps, and ILEs, and often with influential teachers and admired role models, as pivotal.

The activities of children, for example, in 4-H clubs or Scouting groups are often deeply important to children. Bergin (1989) found that adolescents who pursued more out-of-school learning activities had higher intrinsic motivation for learning and better grades. Bergin also found that adolescents preferred goals of social affiliation and feelings of belonging to learning goals, but they also wanted to feel superior and successful so there was competition to be proficient in out-of-school activities whether it was sports or something else. Research is needed on the goals that children and youth maintain in out-of-school activities and how those goals are maintained over time because their pursuits can lead to group affiliation and identity development. There are many opportunities to conduct basic research on motivation, self-regulation, and identity development in ILEs.

Not all visits to ILEs are deeply engaging to all people. Some visitors stay at an exhibit less than a minute, and museum fatigue sets in for most visitors after 30 minutes (Brooks & Vernon, 1956; Falk & Dierking, 1992). However, other studies have found that even brief encounters with an exhibit can be highly memorable. Adults' recollections of museum visits have revealed enduring and salient effects of museum experiences (Falk & Dierking, 1995; McManus, 1993). Is there a particular combination of factors that, for different people at different points in their lives, bolster the impact of what might seem to be a fleeting experience? Carr (1991) wrote, "Critical cognitive experiences in cultural institutions create landmarks, reference points, watershed experiences that become permanent parts of an individual's repertoire of performing data" (pp. 19–20). These are personal experiences with long-lasting impact. They transform people by the power of the experience to strive for new goals or to emulate new people. Rarely are these powerful transformative experiences understood until viewed with reference to one's life course (Mezirow, 1991). How ILEs contribute to watershed experiences and personal development is a fascinating and unexplored issue that can and should be studied in contexts devoted to cultural, historical, national, ethnic, racial, and religious heritages (F. Kaplan, 1994).

CONCLUSIONS

The examples of research and issues that can be studied in ILEs illustrate the rich knowledge to be gained about child development when we examine contexts beyond home and school. The first-order investigations of objects that are the basis for an epistemology of objects advances the layman's notions of "hands-on activities" into a legitimate arena of research and scholarship. The second-order investigations of objects through text, discourse, and technology extend visitors' experiences and understanding and also provide fertile ground for new scholarship. Together, first- and second-order investigations allow children to discover both the natural and cultural histories of objects. ILEs provide venues for children and families to create these twin forms of knowledge and stories, stories that are both narrative and expository, told and retold over the years so they become part of each individual's personal cognitive development (Ferrari & Mahalingham, 1998).

There are many other ways that ILEs can promote children's learning and development, such as museum–school connections or family travel, and these are also possible avenues for research. One of our central points is simply the vast opportunity to extend traditional research on children's development in ILEs. The development of visual literacy can be revealed by studies of children viewing and interacting with objects. Children's intrinsic motivation and exploration can be studied in free-choice learning environments. Aesthetic development can be examined for domains as diverse as creative arts and appreciation of the environment. How families and groups learn collaboratively and how discourse groups promote engagement and understanding may be studied best in ILEs. The stories that children create, around single objects and total ILE experiences, may have lasting impact, not just on knowledge gained, but on enduring passion for art, appreciation of history, or stewardship for the environment. Life-long impact of these informal experiences are usually the stuff of anecdotes, but they deserve longitudinal research. We need to understand how children use experiences in ILEs to explore their possible future selves, emulate role models, form career aspirations, establish values for avocations, and confirm their identities. These transactive and transformative experiences are not limited to children; they should be studied in ILEs across the life span. In this manner, theories of practices in contexts and theories of individual and social meaning-making can be integrated in studies of everyday pursuits. A fuller and richer view of human development will be the result.

REFERENCES

Ansbacher, T. (1998). John Dewey's *Experience and Education:* Lessons for museums. *Curator, 41*(1), 36–49.

Barron, B. J. S., Schwartz, D. L., Vye, N. J., Moore, A., Petrosino, A., Zech, L., Bransford, J., & The Cognition and Technology Group at Vanderbilt. (1998). Doing with understanding: Lessons from research on problem- and project-based learning. *The Journal of the Learning Sciences, 7*(3&4), 271–311.

Beck, T. R., Eversmann, P. K., Krill, R. T., Michael, R., & Twiss-Garrity, B. A. (1997). Material culture as text: Review and reform of the literacy model for interpretation. In A. Smart-Martin & J. R. Garrison (Eds.), *American material culture: The shape of the field* (pp. 135–167). Winterthur, DE: Henry Francis Dupont Winterthur Museum, Inc.

Bergin, D. A. (1989). Student goals for out-of-school learning activities. *Journal of Adolescent Research, 4*(1), 92–109.

Blumenfeld, P. C., Soloway, E., Marx, R. W., Krajcik, J. S., Guzdial, M., & Palincsar, A. S. (1991). Motivating project-based learning: Sustaining the doing, supporting the learning. *Educational Psychologist, 26,* 369–398.

Borun, M., Chambers, M., & Cleghorn, A. (1996). Families are learning in science museums. *Curator, 39*(2), 262–270.

Borun, M., Cleghorn, A., & Garfield, C. (1995). Family learning in museums: A bibliographic review. *Curator, 38,* 262–270.

Breakwell, G. M., & Fife-Schaw, C. (1987). Young people's attitudes toward new technology: Source and structure. *New Directions for Child Development, 35,* 51–67.

Brooks, J. A. M., & Vernon, E. P. (1956). A study of children's interests and comprehension at a science museum. *British Journal of Psychiatry, 47,* 175–182.

Brown, J. S., Collins, A., & Duguid, P. (1989). Situated cognition and the culture of learning. *Educational Researcher, 18,* 32–42.

Bruckman, A. (1998). Community support for constructionist learning. *Computer Supported Cooperative Work, 7,* 47–86.

Bruner, J. (1986). *Actual minds, possible worlds.* Cambridge, MA: Harvard University Press.

Carr, D. (1991). Minds in museums and libraries: The cognitive management of cultural institutions. *Teachers College Record, 93*(1), 6–27.

Cleaver, J. (1992). *Doing children's museums.* Charlotte, VT: Williamson Publishing.

Cohen, D. K. (1998). Dewey's problem. *The Elementary School Journal, 98*(5), 427–446.

Cole, M. (1995). The supra-individual envelope of development: Activity and practice, situation and context. *New Directions for Child Development, 67,* 105–118.

Conn, S. (1998). *Museums and American intellectual life, 1876–1926.* Chicago, IL: The University of Chicago Press.

Crowley, K., & Callanan, M. (1998). Describing and supporting collaborative scientific thinking in parent–child interactions. *Journal of Museum Education, 23*(1), 12–17.

Davis, J., & Gardner, H. (1992). The cognitive revolution: Consequences for the understanding and education of the child as artist. In B. Reimer & R. Smith (Eds.), *The arts, education, and aesthetic knowing* (pp. 92–120). Chicago, IL: University of Chicago Press.

Diamond, J. (1986). The behavior of families in science museums. *Curator, 29,* 139–154.

Edwards, C. A. (1994) Leadership in groups of school-age girls. *Developmental Psychology, 30*(6), 920–927.

Elder, G. H. (1998). The life course as developmental theory. *Child Development, 69*(1), 1–12.

Falk, J. H., & Dierking, L. D. (1992). *The museum experience.* Washington, DC: Whalesback.

Falk, J. H., & Dierking, L. D. (1995). Recalling the museum experience. *Journal of Museum Education, 20*(2), 10–13.

Falk, J. H., & Dierking, L. D. (1998). Free-choice learning: An alternative term to informal learning. *Informal Learning Environments Research Newsletter, 2*(1), 2.

Feldman, D. H. (1987). Developmental psychology and art education: Two fields at the crossroads. *Journal of Aesthetic Education, 21*(2), 243–259.

Ferrari, M., & Mahalingam, R. (1998). Personal cognitive development and its implications for teaching and learning. *Educational Psychologist, 33*(1), 35–44.

Fenstermacher. G. D., & Sanger, M. (1998). What is the significance of John Dewey's approach to the problem of knowledge? *The Elementary School Journal, 98*(5), 467–478.

Forman, E. A., Minick, N., & Stone, C. A. (1993). *Contexts for learning: Sociocultural dynamics in children's development.* New York: Oxford University Press.

Gardner, H. (1989). Zero-based arts education: An introduction to ARTS PROPEL. *Studies in Art Education, 30,* 71–83.

Gardner, H. (1991). *The unschooled mind: How children think and how schools should teach.* New York: Basic Books.

Geahigan, G. (1992). The arts in education: A historical perspective. In B. Reimer & R. Smith (Eds.), *The arts, education, and aesthetic knowing* (pp. 1–19). Chicago, IL: University of Chicago Press.

Gelman, R., Massey, C., & McManus, M. (1991). Characterizing supporting environments for cognitive development: Lessons from children in a museum. In L. Resnick, J. Levine, & S. Teasley (Eds.), *Perspectives on socially-shared cognition* (pp. 226–256). Washington, DC: American Psychological Association.

Goodnow, J. J., Miller, P. J., & Kessel, F. (1995). Conclusion. *New Directions for Child Development, 67,* 119–120.

Gurian, E. H. (1999, March). What's the meaning of this exercise? A meandering look at the many meanings of objects in museums. Paper presented at the University of Michigan colloquium, *Reinventing museums for the 21st century,* Ann Arbor, MI.

Heath, S. B. (1994). The project of learning from the inner-city youth perspective. *New Directions for Child Development, 63,* 25–34.

Hein, G. E., & Alexander, M. (1998). *Museums: Places of learning.* Washington, DC: American Association of Museums.

Hood, M. G. (1983). Staying away: Why people choose not to visit museums. *Museum News,* 50–57.

Housen, A. (1992). Validating a measure of aesthetic development for museums and schools. *ILVS Review, 2*(2), 213–237.

Kaplan, F. E. S. (1994). *Museums and the making of "ourselves": The role of objects in national identity.* London: Leicester University Press.

Kaplan, S. (1995). The restorative benefits of nature: Toward an interactive framework. *Journal of Environmental Psychology, 15,* 169–182.

Kindler, A. M. (1997). Aesthetic development and learning in art museums: A challenge to enjoy. *Journal of Museum Education, 22*(2&3), 12–16.

Krajcik, J., Blumenfeld, P. C., Marx, R. W., Bass, K. M., Fredricks, J., & Soloway, E. (1998). Inquiry in project-based science classrooms: Initial attempts by middle school students. *The Journal of Learning Sciences, 7*(3&4), 313–350.

Krendl, K. A., & Clark, G. (1994). The impact of computers on learning research on in-school and out-of-school settings. *Journal of Computing in Higher Education, 5*(2), 85–112.

Lave, J. (1991). Situating learning in communities of practice. In L. B. Resnick, J. M. Levine, & S. D. Teasley (Eds.), *Perspectives on socially shared cognition* (pp. 63–82). Washington, DC: American Psychological Association.

Lave, J. (1993). The practice of learning. In S. Chaiklin & J. Lave (Eds.), *Understanding practice: Perspectives on activity and context* (pp. 3–32). New York: Cambridge University Press.

Lave, J., & Wenger, E. (1991). *Situated learning: Legitimate peripheral participation.* New York: Cambridge University Press.

Leinhardt, G., & Crowley, K. (1998). *The museum learning collaborative: Phase 2.* Unpublished document, University of Pittsburgh.

Matusov, E., & Rogoff, B. (1995). Evidence of development from people's participation in communities of learners. In J. Falk & L. Dierking (Eds.), *Public institutions for personal learning* (pp. 97–104). Washington, DC: American Association of Museums.

McManus, P. (1993). A study of visitors' memories of Gallery 33. In J. P. Jones (Ed.), *Gallery 33: A visitor study* (pp. 56–74). Birmingham, UK: Birmingham City Council.

Mezirow, J. (1991). *Transformative dimensions of adult learning.* San Francisco: Jossey-Bass.

Nunes, T., Schliemann, A. D., & Carraher, D. W. (1993). *Street mathematics and school mathematics.* New York: Cambridge University Press.

Palincsar, A. S. (1998). Social constructivist perspectives on teaching and learning. *Annual Review of Psychology, 49,* 345–375.

Papert, S. (1991). *Situating constructionism.* Norwood, NJ: Ablex.

Paris, S. G. (1997). Situated motivation and informal learning. *Journal of Museum Education, 22*(2/3), 22–26.

Paris, S. G., & Ash, D. (in press). Reciprocal theory building inside and outside museums. *Curator.*

Paris, S. G., & Cross, D. R. (1983). Ordinary learning: Pragmatic connections among children's beliefs, motives, and actions. In J. Bisanz, G. Bisanz, & R. Kail (Eds.), *Learning in children* (pp. 137-169). New York: Springer-Verlag.

Parsons, M. J. (1992). Cognition as interpretation in art education. In B. Reimer & R. Smith (Eds.), *The arts, education, and aesthetic knowing* (pp. 70-91). Chicago, IL: University of Chicago Press.

Perkins, D. N. (1994). *The intelligent eye: Learning to think by looking at art.* Santa Monica, CA: Getty Center for Education in the Arts.

Pintrich, P. R., & Schunk, D. H. (1996). *Motivation in education: Theory, research, and applications.* Englewood Cliffs, NJ: Prentice Hall Merrill.

Renninger, K. A. (1992). Individual interest and development: Implications for theory and practice. In K. A. Renninger, S. Hidi, & A. Krapp (Eds.), *The role of interest in learning and development* (pp. 361-395). Mahwah, NJ: Lawrence Erlbaum Associates.

Resnick, L. B. (1987). Learning in school and out. *Educational Researcher, 16,* 13-20.

Resnick, L. B., Levine, J. M., & Teasley, S. D. (1991). *Perspectives on socially shared cognition.* Washington, DC: American Psychological Association.

Roberts, L. (1997). *From knowledge to narrative.* Washington, DC: Smithsonian Institution.

Rogoff, B. (1990). *Apprenticeship in thinking: Cognitive development in social context.* New York: Oxford University Press.

Rogoff, B. (1993). Children's guided participation and participatory appropriation in sociocultural activity. In R. Wozniak & K. Fischer (Eds.), *Development in context: Acting and thinking in specific environments* (pp. 121-153). Hillsdale, NJ: Lawrence Erlbaum Associates.

Rogoff, B. (1994). Developing understanding of the idea of communities of learners. *Mind, Culture, and Activity, 1*(4), 209-229.

Rogoff, B., & Lave, J. (1984). *Everyday cognition.* Cambridge, MA: Harvard University Press.

Rogoff, B., Baker-Sennett, J., Lacasa, P., & Goldsmith, D. (1995). Development through participation in sociocultural activity. In J. J. Goodnow, P. J. Miller, & F. Kessel (Eds.), *Cultural practices as contexts for development* (pp. 45-65). San Francisco: Jossey-Bass.

Schauble, L., Banks, D., Coates, G. D., Martin, L. M. W., & Sterling, P. (1996). Outside the classroom walls: Learning in informal environments. In L. Schauble & R. Glaser (Eds.), *Innovations in learning* (pp. 5-24). Mahwah, NJ: Lawrence Erlbaum Associates.

Schauble, L., Leinhardt, G., & Martin, L. (1997). A framework for organizing a cumulative research agenda in informal learning contexts. *Journal of Museum Education, 22*(2&3), 3-8.

Smith, R. A. (1992). Toward percipience: A humanities curriculum for arts education. In B. Reimer & R. Smith (Eds.), *The arts, education, and aesthetic knowing* (pp. 51-69). Chicago, IL: University of Chicago Press.

Tudge, J. R. H., & Winterhoff, P. A. (1993). Vygotsky, Piaget, and Bandura: Perspectives on the relations between the social world and cognitive development. *Human Development, 36,* 61-81.

Valenza, J. K. (1998). Real art museums without walls. *Technology Connection, 4*(9), 10-13.

Villarruel, F. A., & Lerner, R. M. (1994). Promoting community-based programs for socialization and learning. *New Directions for Child Development, 63,* 3-10.

Walter, V. A. (1997). Virtual field trips. *Book Links, 7*(2), 10-14.

Weil, S. (1995). *A cabinet of curiosities: Inquiries into museums and their prospects.* Washington, DC: Smithsonian Institution Press.

Wertsch, J. V., Tulviste, P., & Hagstrom, F. (1993). A sociocultural approach to agency. In E. A. Forman, N. Minick, & C. A. Stone (Eds.), *Contexts for learning* (pp. 336-356). New York: Oxford University Press.

Winner, E. (1982). *Invented worlds: The psychology of the arts.* Cambridge, MA: Harvard University Press.

CHAPTER FOUR

The Authentic Object?
A Child's-Eye View

E. Margaret Evans
Melinda S. Mull
Devereaux A. Poling
University of Toledo

A core assumption in object-centered learning is that real objects "speak" in ways that representations of those objects do not. Objects evoke personal reactions as well as a shared knowledge and history. Furthermore, central to museum lore is the belief that it is the authenticity and uniqueness of the museum-based object that summons the most powerful reactions. Questions have been raised as to whether "the locus of authenticity and meaning resides not in the object but in its mark" (p. 104) or interpretation (Roberts, 1997). Also addressed is the role of the visitor. Different perspectives are likely to be held by visitors for whom the object might have been part of their cultural tradition or lived history (e.g., Gurian, 1999). Yet, the core idea that the authenticity of objects is a characteristic acknowledged by all has not been disputed.

Nevertheless, this assumption should be challenged. It has been argued that authenticity is a relatively recent concept, a 20th-century reaction to the industrial revolution's capacity to mass produce simulated objects (see Roberts, 1997). Such arguments suggest that the idea of authenticity is not intuitive. If authentic objects do speak for themselves (Conn, 1998), what do children make of these voices? Children are among the most frequent museum visitors, and their understanding of authenticity may provide a provocative new view of this issue. Do they appreciate that they are viewing the real object, not some made-to-order simulation? What do they make of the claim of original design? Do they even care?

In this chapter, we argue that the understanding of objects that children of different ages bring to the museum setting offers a unique perspective. Little direct work on this topic has been conducted in museums. However, there is a body of related work to be found in contemporary studies of children's emerging understanding of the natural and the artificial worlds that can be used to develop a framework for understanding how children might approach the world of museum objects. Recent evidence on the development of children's thinking on this subject is presented in the larger context of the historical development of object-based learning in museum settings.

CHAPTER PREVIEW

This chapter begins with an overview of the historical evidence for an object-based dialogue particularly as it evolves from an object-based epistemology (Conn, 1998) to an object-based discourse or narrative (Gurian, 1999; Roberts, 1997). The chapter then proceeds by relating children's (and adults') understanding of the reality, originality, and awe-inspiring nature of objects to specific features of this object-based dialogue. The central thesis is that the distinction between what is natural and what is artifactual lies at the heart of an object-based dialogue. Only by addressing this distinction can the implied initial question be adequately answered: What is an authentic object?

In the first section, we summarize the shift from an object-based epistemology, the language of late-19th-century museums, to an object-based discourse, the dominant voice in late-20th-century museums. This shift, we contend, represents important transformations in our understanding of the object. In an object-based epistemology, the focus was on the clear presentation of unembellished facts regarding the natural history and taxonomy of the object. In this case, the perspective of the visitor was virtually ignored. An object-based discourse, on the other hand, centers on the participation of the object in the cultural or lived history of the visitor. In the latter case, ironically, it is the natural history of the object that is downplayed; moreover, instead of bare facts, we maintain that there is an emphasis on explanation, which could be that of the expert or that of the visitor or both (but it is rarely that of the child).

In the subsequent two sections, we claim that the distinction between the natural history and the cultural history of the object maps onto important conceptual distinctions made by children and adults in their understanding of the natural and artifactual worlds. These distinctions should be clearly marked, we further argue, if children are to learn from and fully participate in an object-based dialogue. To this end, we first review recent evidence on children's conceptual development and their capacity to generate explanations for natural and artifactual phenomena. Then, we relate findings from such studies to three clearly identifiable aspects of authenticity: the reality, the originality, and the awe-inspiring nature of objects. In the final section, we return to our original theme and consider what this work reveals about the nature of the authentic object.

AN OBJECT-BASED EPISTEMOLOGY: A ONCE AND FUTURE DIALOGUE

The term *object-based epistemology* was coined by Conn (1998) to describe the orientation toward objects of the creators of many United States museums, during the late 19th and early 20th centuries (1876–1926). The serried ranks of meticulously ordered object-filled glass cases that dominated the museums of that period represented a widely held view of how objects should be presented to the public. Unlike the chaotic miscellany of objects found in museums of the antebellum era, this new approach was thought to reveal the inherent order and meaning of objects to the interested observer (Conn, 1998).

Given the influx of immigrants from Europe, curators were well aware that many visitors were unlikely to be fluent in English. Therefore, it fell to the curators to present the objects in ways in which their meaning was readily visually apparent (Conn, 1998). Although labels designating the name and origin of the object were evident, overt interpretation was kept to a minimum. However, the grouping and ordering of the objects themselves represented a covert interpretative act. The arrangement of objects suggested not only sentences in an object-based text, but stories in which the objects, rather than the text, were the sources of knowledge (p. 4). Each unique object was the perfect exemplar of a class of unseen objects; their arrangement depicted object taxonomies and levels of increasing object complexity, symbolizing, perhaps unconsciously, a worldview of inexorable progression (Conn, 1998). The value of a museum object may have derived from its claim to an authentic voice, yet it was the nature of the display that made this voice audible to the visitor (p. 22). Thus, an object-based epistemology provided the foundation on which the language of museums was constructed (p. 5).

Motivating this radical approach was the newly energized field of natural history (Conn, 1998). Even though Conn did not totally discount a Foucauldian analysis in which museum presentations are seen to be implicitly reproducing the power relationships apparent in society-at-large, he argued that a more potent source of influence in that period was the intellectual authority and scholarship of the natural historian. In their systematic description of the world of nature, the natural historians in their collective role as museum curators uncovered what was previously unknown; they were in the business of creating new knowledge. Moreover, this new knowledge was invested with religious significance insofar as it was thought to reveal the handiwork of God

(Shapin, 1996). Interestingly, the authority of the natural historian was manifest not only in natural history museums, but also in museums of anthropology, commerce, history, and even art, as a sustained attempt was made to put "all of the world's knowledge under glass" (Conn, 1998, p. 25).

The natural historian's authority came to a natural demise in the early part of the 20th century, when the center of scholarship moved from the museum to the university laboratory. Motivating this transfer was a change in the nature of the scholarship, from the description and classification of natural entities to a theory-based biological science in which explanation was paramount, especially that of evolutionary theory (Conn, 1998; Wilcove & Eisner, 2000). Conn claimed that a casualty of this shift was an object-based epistemology. Nonetheless, despite this decline, the mark of the natural historian is not so easy to erase, and an object-based epistemology survives, we contend, in many of today's museums but, perhaps, with a richer and more nuanced vocabulary. More recently, the focus of the exhibit designer has moved from the object itself to the relationship between visitor and object, with interesting consequences, we argue, for our understanding of the object.

From Object-Based Epistemology to Object-Based Discourse

Whether an object-based epistemology has evolved or has been completely eclipsed by the inclusion of the visitor's perspective in an object-based discourse is a question that is beyond the purview of this chapter, although the evolved role seems more likely. Nevertheless, in both cases, museum designers create stories in which objects play central characters, but different features of the object's character are highlighted. In the original object-based epistemology, the natural history of the object played center stage; in an object-based discourse the central role is likely to be that of the object's participation in the cultural or lived history of the visitor, with the scientific nature of the object relegated to a supporting part (e.g., Gurian, 1999; Roberts, 1997).

What inspired these changes? Previously, it was assumed that in an object-based dialogue, communication was virtually a one-way process, that is, from object to visitor. The reasoning behind an object-based epistemology appeared to be that once the language problem was solved, with labeling kept to a minimum, and the object appropriately displayed, then the visitor would see what the curator saw (e.g., Roberts, 1997). It was a visual act requiring minimal intellectual work. In fact, the visual act is an interpretive one, although this was not known with any certainty until much later in the 20th century (e.g., Rosenfield, 2000). The perspective of the lay visitor was effectively ignored in an object-based epistemology. The lifetime of knowledge the curator brought to bear on the object influenced the curator's perception of that object. For all intents and purposes, the curator and the lay visitor saw different objects. More recent scholarship recognizes that there is no single authentic voice: the object, the presentation, the visitor, even the friends and family accompanying the visitor, jointly participate in an act of meaning (Falk & Dierking, 1992, 1995; Gurian, 1999; Roberts, 1997).

However, the insertion of the visitor's perspective into an object-based dialogue introduced an element that effectively upended the original aim of an object-based epistemology. The natural historian cum curator of the late 19th century attempted to present objects as nature intended, stripped of human (if not God's) intent. Although in practice this is a difficult task as the curator introduces his or her own biases, it is the rationale underlying the scientific enterprise. In contrast, the modern museum designer often tries to put human intent back into the dialogue, making exhibits more attractive by emphasizing their relevance to the typical visitor. In the recently refocused mission of the University of Michigan's Botanical Gardens, for example, the taxonomic presentation of plants, with Latin labels, is gradually giving way to more dynamic exhibits in which people, plants, and cultures comingle. An exhibit on food plants from the African Diaspora provided enthusiastic audience members, many of them African American, with an opportunity to view living examples of plants, such as plantains, first-hand. For many visitors, this was the first time they had seen plants long associated with the lived history of their immediate ancestors. Such exhibits encourage visitors to engage in an object-based dialogue.

There is a downside, though, to such an approach: The natural history of the object could well become obscured in the process. This is not a problem for those objects, especially art objects, that derive much of their meaning from their role in human affairs, but it may well be a problem for the presentation of objects of nature. It is as if the intellectual authority of the natural historian, which previously was imposed on exhibits from museums that potentially had entirely different missions, has been finally reversed. In the late 19th century, for instance, anthropological objects were presented as objects of nature in much the same way that exotic species were presented in natural history museums, or even alongside such species (Conn, 1998). Now, as in the Botanical Gardens example, nature is often presented as an artifact of human culture rather than the other way round. Moreover, some have claimed that the study and practice of natural history has not only been marginalized, but it may well be headed for extinction (Wilcove & Eisner, 2000).

The tug-of-war over Kennewick Man (Lederman, 2000) gets to the heart of some of these issues (see also Gurian, 1999, for similar examples). These 9,300-year-old human remains, discovered by the U.S. Army Corp of Engineers in 1996, are considered part of the cultural history of five Native American tribes, who wish to rebury them as befits their ancestral status. Such an act would effectively deny access to the remains. However, scientists view the remains as an important source of evidence as to the origins of the first peoples in the Americas; moreover, they want to examine their DNA, an act considered offensive by the tribes. Clearly, this object, preserved human remains, has both a natural history and a cultural history, and it appears unlikely that both voices can be heard insofar as one voice stifles the expression of the other.

Yet, there have been additional, more subtle changes in the characteristics of an object-based dialogue that, we argue, could well have served as the catalyst motivating the shift to the visitor's perspective. Paralleling the historical change in the nature of scholarship, modern museum exhibits seem as likely to focus on explanation as on description. For example, Conn (1998) detailed how the dry fact, taxonomic approach to natural history exhibits has given way to one in which their ecology and relationship to the environment is emphasized. Leaving aside the question of whether facts can ever be value- or theory-free, this apparent shift in the quality of the revealed knowledge with the current emphasis on explanation evokes a whole new set of issues: Whose or what explanation should be marked? That of the scientist or the visitor? If the visitor, which visitor (see Gurian, 1999; Roberts, 1997)? In many cases this cacophony of voices has settled, somewhat, into a muted discourse in which museum curators, designers, and educators jostle for position as they try to represent the interests of both the object and the visitor (see Roberts, 1997, for an intriguing example). The future of museums rests on the ability to achieve an appropriate balance between these competing interests while still attracting and retaining the loyalty of the lay visitor as well as providing a haven for original scholarship.

What about the child's perspective? Not only is children's education an important function of the modern museum, but this relationship is a symbiotic one insofar as children's continued interest ensures the future of museums. Yet, children's emerging understanding of the world has not been systematically included in the visitor's perspective. Two aspects of this understanding are particularly pertinent to the object-based dialogue just described. Recent scholarship reveals that a critical aspect of children's developing understanding is their capacity to generate explanations for phenomena: their naïve theories. Children do not merely classify or describe, they explain, and ask why. Further, the distinction between what is artifactual and what is natural is central to children's naïve theories. Following a summary of some studies of children's emerging theories of the world around them, we relate selected aspects of these theories to children's appreciation (or not) of the singular nature of museum objects.

CHILDREN'S NAÏVE THEORIES

All good teachers have always realized that one must start where the student is. … The main barrier to learning is not what the student lacks, but rather what the student has, namely, alternative conceptual frameworks for understanding the phenomena covered by the theories we are trying to teach.
— Carey, 1998: Testimony before the House Committee on Science

Children are not sponges effortlessly absorbing all knowledge; instead, they filter or interpret information using their own sets of rules or frameworks. Characterizing the nature of children's alternative frameworks is a core component of recent programs of research in which children's knowledge systems are conceptualized as naive theories focused on specific domains of knowledge. Carey's studies on children's naïve biology were among some of the early contributions to this field. This program goes beyond the well-established body of work showing that prior knowledge places constraints on what the student, or, for that matter, the adult is likely to learn (summarized in Roschell, 1995). Although the naïve theory approach shares some of the same theoretical roots that succored the prior knowledge movement (see Roschell, 1995), the emphasis of this new approach is on causal explanation and a characterization of the body of knowledge that very young children are likely to have about the world, prior to any formal educational experiences. More importantly, it is a developmental approach. Young children appear to have causal intuitions or skeletal structures (Gelman, R., 2000) that enable them to "guess right" (Keil & Wilson, 2000) most of the time when they are trying to figure out how or why something happens. A goal of this new approach is the specification of the nature of those initial causal principles and how they are elaborated and, perhaps, transformed with the appropriation of new knowledge (Evans, 2001; Gelman, R., 2000; Keil & Wilson, 2000; Poling & Evans, in press).

Any particular domain of knowledge encompasses a set of interrelated causal principles, the rules governing their use, and the entities to which they can be applied (Gelman, R., 2000; Wellman & Gelman, 1998). Core domains are often characterized as carving the world at its joints, and they do so by focusing the young child's attention on particular kinds of inputs. These inputs are deemed privileged to the extent that they serve as building blocks for the elaboration of children's foundational or intuitive theories, which ground their understanding of the natural and intentional worlds (Gelman, R., 2000; Willman & Gelman, 1998). In effect, children would not be able to navigate the world of real entities if these entities did not easily map onto some system of analogous mental representations (Sperber, 1996). However, this approach acknowledges that the different environments encountered by children should lead to significant variability in the rate and nature of the knowledge acquired in any particular domain (Evans, 2000b, 2001; Gelman, R., 2000).

Which domains of knowledge are considered foundational? To date, several core domains have been identified that are thought to represent a limited but universal class of knowledge structures. These include naive theories of psychology, physics, biology, language, space, and number (Gelman, R., 2000; Wellman & Gelman, 1998). Most relevant to this chapter are the broad distinctions between the intentional and the natural but nonintentional worlds. Such distinctions, we contend, map onto the earlier dichotomy we identified, between the cultural history and the natural history of the object. Clearly, the world of artifactual objects is a consequence of intentional human activity, whereas the world of natural objects is only tangentially related to the intentional activities of humans. Do young children realize such distinctions?

Children's theory of mind, also known as their naïve or intuitive theory of psychology, has been one of the most heavily investigated areas of inquiry. Broadly, this domain covers mental states such as intentions or beliefs; less obviously, it covers the intentional activities of humans, including the creation of artifacts. From this research, we know that infants exhibit an early understanding that animate and inanimate objects have different properties (Wellman & Gelman, 1998). In particular they distinguish between the movements of animate objects, which seem self-propelled and goal-directed, and those of inanimate objects, which are moved by external forces. During the preschool years there is a major reorganization in children's representation of mental states. Four- to 5-year-olds, but not 3-year-olds, demonstrate an understanding that other "minds" may not necessarily view the world in the same way that they do, known as a *representational theory of mind* (Wellman & Gelman, 1998). This realization, arguably, goes along with the ability to recognize deception. By the end of the school-age years, children have acquired what has been called an *interpretive or constructive theory of mind* (e.g., Carpendale & Chandler, 1996). In this case, children recognize the complexity of intentional states; any object or event affords multiple meanings, and human minds actively construct meanings based on prior as well as current experiences.

For reasons of space, we have briefly summarized the emergence of a naïve psychology only, although there is also a burgeoning literature on children's understanding of physics, biology, and number, all of which are relevant to object-centered learning. However, from a child's-eye view, to make an object-based dialogue effective, we believe it is important to mark those objects that are of intentional origin in ways that clearly distinguish them from objects of natural origin. Otherwise, we argue, children's emerging ability to demarcate the authentic and the nonauthentic may be undermined.

These kinds of studies may give the false impression that children are not much more than budding psychologists, physicists, and mathematicians, figuring out the physical and mental worlds in which they find themselves. Yet, paradoxically, just as children appear to be plunging into the world of the real, they seem to be simultaneously confronted with inexplicable or impossible phenomena: the world of the unreal, the magical, and the illusory (Rosengren, Johnson, & Harris, 2000). Children, it has been claimed, are also budding metaphysicians (Harris, 2000; Johnson, 2000). The emerging ability to demarcate the metaphysical, the physical, and the artifactual places constraints, we argue, on children's capacity to perceive and respond to the voices in an object-based dialogue. Next, we consider the implications of this recent scholarship for children's understanding of, and participation in, the world of authentic museum objects.

AUTHENTICITY

> As museum professionals, most of the team members' knee-jerk reaction was to defend the "real," particularly since one of the museums' most sacred cows is their possession of original and uncommon objects. The designer in particular enjoyed reciting a popular bit of museum lore: that a fundamental, albeit intangible, difference exists between an original object, such as Linnaeus's microscope and its picture-prefect reproduction. — Roberts, 1997, p. 85

Roberts' (1997) description of the difficulties of presenting a seemingly straightforward exhibit on Linnaeus' contribution to the scientific world in a modern participatory format reveals some of the perils associated with an object-based discourse. Our interest here is not in the difficulties themselves (e.g., What happens if visitors handle original objects?) but to probe a little deeper: Do children appreciate the basis for this museum lore? Do they realize that they are viewing real, original, awe-inspiring objects? And, to the extent that children do not share the exhibit designer's understanding that an intangible difference exists between an original object and its copy, for example, what does that reveal about museum lore?

Drawing on the scholarship of MacCannell (1976) and Orvell (1989), Roberts (1997) made the case for two distinct, historically emerging concepts of reality. She then linked these 20th-century ideas to the pivotal roles of authentic objects in modern participatory exhibits, such as the one on Linnaeus. In the first example, the Victorian obsession with objects of all kinds (Conn, 1998) and replicas of important objects, in particular, paved the way for a reverence for the original authentic object, in the early part of the 20th century. Orvell (1989) detailed how the productive capacity of the Industrial Revolution led to the mass reproduction of poor quality substitutes of authentic objects. A yearning for a simpler, more authentic life was, he claimed, a reaction to this era of the fake and the illusory. Thus, real "original" objects, in this case, are contrasted with imitation, fake, or illusory objects (Roberts, 1997, p. 96).

In the second example, the new leisure class of the 20th century sought real authentic experiences, giving birth to the rise of tourism (MacCannell, 1976). Many late-20th-twentieth century museum exhibits underscore both senses of real, in that visitors are encouraged to participate in an authentic experience with real original objects, although it is the interpretation or signs mediating this experience that signal "reality" to the visitor (Roberts, 1997). Such experiences can be found, for instance, in recreated historic settlements such as Greenfield Village, where visitors sometimes literally try to place themselves in the shoes of their predecessors as they view authentic original historic objects. Interestingly, such participatory experiences merely create an illusion of reality. Adults should not be fooled by such illusions. What about children?

In the next three subsections, children's understanding of three aspects of authenticity — the reality, originality, and awe-inspiring nature of objects — is examined. The sense of the real detailed in Roberts' (1997) thesis focused on the authenticity of artifactual objects. We argue, however, that there is an important distinction to be made between the authenticity of artifacts and the authenticity of objects of nature. As Roberts pointed out, artifactual objects are authentic to the extent that they are original; they cannot be copies, fakes, or illusions. Natural objects, on the other hand, are authentic to the extent that they are natural, that is, they cannot be *artifacts,* fakes, or illusions. In other words, to be real, a natural object must be of natural, not of intentional origin, whereas, to be real, an artifactual object must be an original (and of intentional origin). It could be argued that gene-therapy, cloned sheep, and humanoid robots have eradicated such distinctions between the natural and the artifactual or intentional worlds. Yet, the reason such entities arouse such intense ethical debates is probably because they challenge our basic intuitions about what is real and natural.

First we provide evidence to show that children's understanding of both these senses of authenticity emerges slowly over the preschool to late school-age years; it cannot be imposed on them. Children construct such explanations online, we claim, and in doing so draw on experiences provided by a supportive environment, a constructive interactionism (Wozniak & Fischer, 1993). Finally, we address a puzzle. Adults' recognition of the awe-inspiring core of an authentic experience seems to be derived from their sense of the illusory. In this respect, perhaps, they appear to be as susceptible as children to the illusory and the magical.

The Real Object: Neither a Fake, nor an Illusion

Preschoolers grasp a variety of appearance–reality distinctions, such as pretense–reality, and real-natural versus artifactual appearances, in which they have to distinguish a (real) natural rock from a rock-like sponge (Flavell, Flavell, & Green, 1983). Moreover, they use the terms *real* and *really* with some sophistication, even as early as 3 years of age (Woolley & Wellman, 1990). Preschoolers also honor distinctions between the worlds of fantasy and reality, even though they may mistakenly assign the reality label to a fantasy figure (Woolley, 1997). However, this precocious understanding appears to break down when children are confronted with the illusory, which tends to be less clearly marked than the world of imagination or fantasy. In the Western world, events in which an intentional agent deceptively creates an illusion of reality are often labeled as *magical.*

An assumption is that adults are only temporarily fooled by such illusions, yet children are still sorting out this very basic understanding of reality. However, a brief excursion into the history of the illusory should rapidly convince the skeptical that adults were certainly not immune to such beliefs in the past, nor are they today (e.g., Aveni, 1996; Wyse, 1997). Even so, children are portrayed as more gullible than adults and more apt to tricked by the illusory. The emerging capacity to distinguish the natural from the artificial, the illusory, and the magical underlies the development of a scientific understanding and an appreciation of the real or the natural in an object-based dialogue.

The onset of magical explanations in the early preschool years is now thought to be an achievement (Rosengren, Johnson, & Harris, 2000) rather than a sign of confusion (Piaget, 1929). They signal children's increasing awareness that some phenomena may be illusory, even when they give the appearance of reality. But as children learn about the art of the artificer or magician, magical explanations for illusory events decrease and such events are more likely to be labeled as tricks rather than magic or magic-tricks (Phelps & Woolley, 1994; Rosengren & Hickling, 1994; Woolley, 1997). For example, we showed preschool and elementary-school children videotapes of different kinds of illusory transformations including deceptive sleight-of-hand transformations (e.g., a color-changing scarf) performed by a "scientist" in a white laboratory coat. We then asked children whether they thought the transformations were magic or a trick (Mull & Evans, 2001). From the preschool years into middle-to-late childhood magical explanations decreased and trick explanations increased (see Fig. 4.1).

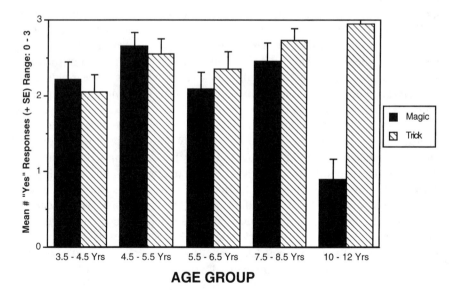

FIG. 4.1. Is it a trick? Or is it magic? Children's responses to magic and trick explanations for illusory events

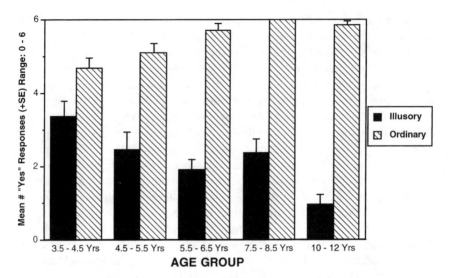

FIG. 4.2.   Can that really happen? Children's responses to questions about the reality of ordinary and illusory events

In the same study (Mull & Evans, 2001), children were asked if ordinary and illusory events could really happen (e.g., Can that person really break a pencil? Can that person really make the scarf's color change? Can dogs really talk?). Children should respond that ordinary events (breaking a pencil) could really happen, whereas illusory or fantastical events could not. A similar developmental pattern emerged. Many (but not all) young preschoolers (3- to 4-year-olds) understood that ordinary events could really happen, but they responded at chance levels for the illusory events, whereas 10-year-olds performed at an adult level, claiming that illusory events could not really happen, whereas ordinary events could (see Fig. 4.2).

We also measured children's ability to recognize false beliefs, a standard measure of a representational theory of mind. We found that both children's false belief reasoning and their recognition that illusions cannot really happen contributed, independently of each other and of age, to children's ability to mark illusory events as magical tricks. In other words, in this and related studies (Evans & Mull, 2001) we identified two of the conditions that appear to influence children's emerging realization that a deceptive agent has intentionally created an illusion of reality. One is a child's increasing ability to reason about mental states, such as false beliefs. The other is the child's level of understanding of the reality of the natural world.

To sum up, in order to identify illusory events and distinguish them from real events, children have to simultaneously integrate information from multiple sources or core domains. First, children have to recognize that certain events do not obey the laws of nature, in that they are unnatural or illusory. Second, they have to recognize that intentional agents can create illusions by manipulating natural phenomena. Clearly, children's ability to detect illusions is grounded in their emerging understanding of both the intentional and the natural worlds. This is not to say that social context does not play a part. We also assessed the parental role, independently of the effects of the previously mentioned factors. We found that children were also much less likely to label illusory events as magical when parents explained the deception underlying such events.

Given this information, it is important to consider what children might make of the reality of historical participatory exhibits, such as Greenfield Village, or even of the reality of talking dinosaurs in an amusement park. In an object-based dialogue, it would seem to be an imperative that the nonillusory or illusory nature of the objects is marked, especially in exhibits that might evoke magical responses. The uneasy relationship between conventional museums and those of Disney World rests on this distinction between what is real and what is illusory. Clearly, if the value of an object-based dialogue centers on children's experience of the real and the authentic, then the creation of an experience that gives the appearance of an illusion, as is found in many Disneyesque exhibits (Roberts, 1997), is likely to bewilder the young child, even as it entertains.

If such experiences are to contribute to a children's emerging grasp of authenticity, then more research needs to be done on exactly what happens when natural entities, such as dinosaurs or historical objects, are presented as an illusory, or, even, a virtual reality experience, versus as nature made them (e.g., in the context of a fossil hunt or an archeological dig). Natural historians, in particular, have expressed disquiet about the virtual disappearance of their topic from the curricula of elementary schools and even museum exhibits (Sicree, 2000; Wilcove & Eisner, 2000). A $250 stereo microscope can turn "a pinch of soil into a bustling world of springtails, oribatid mites, and nematodes, creatures as bizarre and engaging as anything to appear in a Star Wars movie" (Wilcove & Eisner, 2000, p. B24). Provided they understand the function of the microscope, such experiences can ground children's understanding of reality. But if the click of a plastic mouse replaces the song of birds as children navigate a virtual or a fantastical landscape rather than an authentic meadowland (p. B24), what happens to children's emerging appreciation of real authentic experiences?

The Original Object: The Very First of its Kind

If we show a child a Moore sculpture and make the claim that it is an original, what does the child make of that statement? Then we show the same child a replica of a Moore sculpture that looks just the same as "the original." The child should understand that the original object was the very first of its kind insofar as it did not previously exist, whereas the replica is a copy of a previously existing object. The authenticity of many museum artifacts rests, in most cases, on this claim of originality (Gurian, 1999). Further, to be original, not only does the idea conveyed by the object have to differ significantly from other ideas, but the object itself has to differ from other objects. The human designer has created the *very first* of a new kind of object. Although this explanation might seem obvious to any adult, we have preliminary evidence, addressed in more detail later, that this might not be as obvious to a young child.

Interestingly, if we move away from the world of artifactual objects to objects of nature, then the same kind of claim no longer makes as much sense: an original Tyrannosaurus Rex? If we replace the term *original* with *authentic,* then it becomes obvious that we mean a real fossil, not a fake. But if we carefully explain to the child that because scientists could not find all the bones, some of the bones are, in fact, fakes, how does the child (or for that matter the adult) learn to draw the line between fake and real (see Gurian, 1999)? When the term original is applied to a natural object, then it is often used in an artifactual sense. The original Tyrannosaurus Rex could be the very first of that species found by a particular fossil hunter. Less often, however, the term original might be applied to an ancestral species, such as the "original Eve," the implication being that this was the very first in a particular evolutionary line.

To complicate these issues, in order to make dinosaur exhibits more accessible, some museums have co-opted the services of a roving robot who recounts facts about the dinosaurs to any child who stops the robot and presses a button. In this case the exhibit designers may have succeeded only in confusing children. Can we be sure that the preschool or early school-age child is aware that a dinosaur and a robot have different origins, one natural, one intentional? The child may well believe that he or she is viewing a Hall of Monsters, consisting of human-created dinosaurs and robots such as the child might see on Star Wars. Returning to the theme of originality: If dinosaurs were created by humans — that is, if they were artifactual rather than natural — then it would make sense to claim that an original dinosaur is on display. Moreover, if God is substituted for human in the creation story, then biblical literalists might also find this a perfectly sensible thought. How do children sort out these issues?

We have addressed some of these questions, although we arrived at this point by a circuitous route via children's and adults understanding of origins. Earlier studies of children's understanding of the origins of species revealed that 8- or 9-year-old children endorse creationist explanations for species origins, regardless of their parents' religious or scientific beliefs: God [intentionally] created each animal kind (or species). Younger children, 5- to 7-year-olds, in contrast, endorsed a mixture of spontaneous generationist ("it came out of the ground") and creationist responses. By early adolescence there was a shift to creationist or evolutionist beliefs, which could be predicted by parental belief system as well as by children's exposure to natural history and fossil knowledge (Evans, 2000a, 2000b, 2001).

Evolutionary theory is one of those scientific ideas that radically challenges our basic preconceptions, and one predictor of its acceptance or rejection is the worldview of the individual. Young children appear to endorse an essentialist viewpoint (Gelman & Hirschfeld, 1999) in which the world is seen as stable and unchanging. From an essentialist perspective, evolutionary transformations are resisted or seen as fantastical, not as part of the natural order (Evans, 2001). Among adult Christian fundamentalist populations, such a view is not only deified but given coherent expression in sacred texts, such as the Bible.

As described earlier, one of the earliest developing and coherent of the foundational theories that young children use to explain their world appears to be children's theory of mind (Wellman & Gelman, 1998). This theory includes an understanding of mental states such as intentionality. The very power of this theory, it is claimed, leads to its overextension and use in circumstances where it is unwarranted such as in a creationist explanation for the origins of species (Evans, 2001). However, social context exerts powerful as well as more subtle effects. By early adolescence, children reared in contexts that deify these intentional explanations, such as Christian fundamentalist homes and schools, are more likely to maintain and extend their creationist ideas. Their nonfundamentalist counterparts, however, are more likely to endorse evolutionist views. The latter endorsement of evolution, however, depends crucially on two factors: exposure to the fossil evidence and a willingness to accept the (incorrect) idea that animals change in response to environmental factors (e.g., giraffes' long necks result from their habit of stretching their necks to reach into tall trees to obtain food). How do such belief systems develop? The critical process, it is argued, is the interaction between the oftentimes conflicting ideas that children construct to explain natural phenomena and an environment that either transforms or suppresses such ideas: a constructive interactionism (Evans, 2000a, 2000b, 2001).

More recent work along these lines explored the emergence of this understanding in even younger children. A particular focus was young children's ability (or not) to distinguish between the artifactual (human-made) and creationist (God-made) origins of artifactual and natural objects (Evans & Gelman, 2001; Evans, Poling, & Mull, 2001). Moreover, a further question raised by these earlier studies was investigated: Do young children realize that objects, both artifactual and natural, did not previously exist? Questions about "the very first X" would make very little sense to a child who thought that "they were always here." Young children's answers to the earlier origins questions had suggested that they believed all animals existed from the beginning of time. These findings are perfectly consistent with the young child's essentialist notions that the world is a stable and unchanging place. Nevertheless, they raise a more fundamental issue: How does a child come to contemplate questions of origins at all?

One hundred 4-to-10-year-old children viewed pictured objects, consisting of familiar and unfamiliar mammals and simple artifacts (e.g., cup). They then answered a series of questions, to which they responded "yes" or "no," about the origins ("the very first X"), the previous existence, and the death of the objects (Evans, Poling, & Mull, 2001). One crucial question, from the point of view of an object-based dialogue, is whether children distinguished between artifactual and animal (natural) objects when responding to these questions. A second question was whether they grasped the concept of original design. Not until children were 8 to 10 years old did they consistently respond "No," animals and artifacts were not "always here" (see Fig. 4.3A). Yet, at the same time even the majority of preschoolers realized that death (nonexistence) was inevitable and universal for animals, but it made no sense to claim that artifacts die (Fig. 4.3B). As for animal and artifact origins, again, it was not until children were 8 to 10 years old that they consistently agreed that God created animals, whereas humans created artifacts: a coherent creationism (Figs. 4.4A & 4.4B).

Preschool and elementary school children's responses to the death question indicated that they were sensitive to one aspect of the artifactual–natural-object distinction: animals die, whereas artifacts cannot. Yet, 4- to 7-year-old children failed to grasp more subtle aspects of this distinction. Only the 8- to

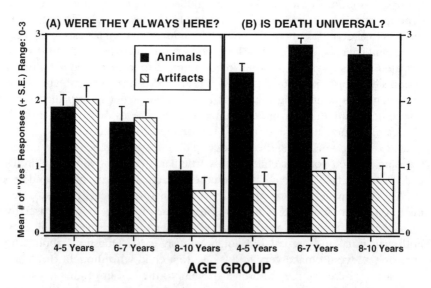

FIG. 4.3.   Children's responses to questions on (A) the permanence of objects and (B) the universality of death, for artifacts and animals

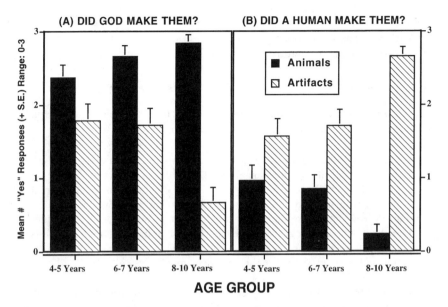

FIG. 4.4.   Children's responses to (A) creationist and (B) artificialist explanations for the origins of artifacts and animals

10-year-olds demonstrated a coherent creationism. The younger children were likely to confuse the creative capacities of God and human. Furthermore, the younger age group failed to realize that artifacts and animals did not always exist. In other words, they did not appear to have a concept of "the very first."

Further analyses demonstrated that an understanding of death, and the prior existence and origins of artifacts, predicts a coherent creationist account of origins, regardless of the effects of age. Thus, a coherent understanding of existence and nonexistence appears to be knowledge-based and to emerge by the middle to late elementary school years (8 to 10 years of age). This, we contend, is a major intellectual breakthrough for a period that is often regarded as relatively quiescent. Moreover, these results also suggest that this might be a period of radical conceptual change as children savor their new-found abilities to grasp such existential questions and assimilate them into a range of knowledge domains from evolutionary biology to philosophy to religion (Evans, Poling, & Mull, 2001). As this appears to be an age-related but not age-dependent conceptual change, its emergence could be actively promoted by a supportive environment (Wozniak & Fischer, 1993).

Studies such as these suggest that the idea of original design is not one that is normally part of the repertoire of beliefs of 4- to 7-year-olds. Preschool and early elementary school children's understanding of the very first authentic original object appears to be quite limited. In particular, they are unlikely to appreciate the special nature of original artifacts, such as art-work or historic objects, because they do not yet grasp that such objects were previously non-existent. An original Moore will not have a special status until children can value the extraordinary nature of its origins.

The Awe-Inspiring Object: Contagion Works Like Magic

In the conclusion of his book on the rise and fall of an object-based episte-mology, Conn (1998) offered a semiapologetic addendum:

> ... while these objects may no longer function epistemologically, they can still function — for me at any rate — magically. There remains something extraordi-nary, if finally inexplicable, about the experience of being in the presence of a Cézanne, a raven-mask from Alaska, or a fossil pterodactyl.... Even as prosaic a group as professional historians, most of whom do not study objects, will admit to the thrill of holding actual archival material in their hands.... Perhaps, this is why museums can still be places of education, of inspiration, or amusement, re-flection and wonder. Perhaps, in the end, there are objects. (p. 262)

What is it about authentic objects that evoke this sense of wonder? Rob-erts (1997) suggested that museums offer the visitor the potential for direct access, via the object, to "the real" — the original creative act, or a living ex-emplar of a rare natural entity. Experiencing a work of art in living color, as the artist intended, or nature in the raw, is awe-inspiring. Such an act invokes our aesthetic sensibilities, our emotions, our intellectual curiosity, and our aston-ishment at the accomplishments of others. A successful object-based dialogue kindles some sense of an authentic experience mediated, of course, by the imagination of the visitor and the interpretive aids offered by the museum. Such an experience could also be described as *magical contagion* (Nemeroff & Rozin, 2000). In reality it is an illusion and in that sense it is a false experi-ence. But in that it invokes the essence of the original, then it gives the ap-pearance of something that is very close to a true experience (Roberts, 1997; MacCannell, 1976).

Sympathetic magic, according to Nemeroff and Rozin (2000), is not a prim-itive form of reasoning. It is, instead, a singular form of thinking that can be found alongside scientific or religious thinking, in society-at-large, or in indi-viduals. Moreover, they contend that it serves important functions. We believe that such thinking lies at the heart of the awe-inspiring experiences associ-ated with authentic objects. The law of contagion, one of three principles of sympathetic magic, captures this experience: "It holds that . . . contact be-tween the source and the target results in the transfer of some effect or qual-ity (essence) from the source [authentic object] to the target [museum visi-tor]" (Nemeroff & Rozin, 2000, p. 3). This contact may be direct or mediated, and it leads to an increased feeling of connection between the target and the source, which can have a positive or negative valence.

When children play "cooties" and Western educated adults recoil from drinking out of a clean glass that may have contained poison (Nemeroff & Rozin, 2000), they are both exhibiting signs of magical contagion. Numerous studies carried out by Rozin, Nemeroff, and their colleagues indicate that negative contagion is fully appreciated by 6- to 8-year-old children, and that even preschoolers show some understanding of the principle. Its adaptive value is thought to rest on the avoidance of contact with infective agents, such as moldy foods or disease, in which the source has a negative valence (Nemeroff & Rozin, 2000). Positive contagion has not been studied in as much detail, but museum settings should provide an ideal laboratory for such investigations. When the source has a positive valence, some valued aspect of the source would be transferred to the target, who would presumably feel an enhanced sense of self (more courageous, artistic, etc.) and an increased sense of connection with the sublime. He or she feels a better person for the experience.

Museum buildings heighten this awe-inspiring experience. Reminiscent of the cathedral building of previous centuries, museums of the late 19th and early 20th centuries were built to house objects of reverence. Of course, if natural historians of this era were revealing God's handiwork (Shapin, 1996), then what better tribute to pay to the grand designer. The buildings themselves are signs signifying the appropriate veneration to be paid to the objects (Conn, 1998). Moreover, as Gurian (1999) remarked of museum professionals, "We were like priests and the museums our reliquaries" (p. 164).

In the last part of the chapter we were concerned with children's developing ability to separate the world of real objects from the illusory. Yet, in this section, on the awe-inspiring nature of objects, we expose a conundrum. We find ourselves making the claim that adults are not immune to the charms of an unreal, even a magical, participatory experience with an awe-inspiring authentic object. Moreover, museums and their staff actively promote such an experience. There is a partial solution to this puzzle. In order to truly appreciate the awe-inspiring nature of authentic objects, adults must first grasp the nature of reality and originality. Adult understanding, we claim, is qualitatively different from that of the preschool or early school-age child. Perhaps, though, some childlike illusions are never entirely abandoned. The extent to which children are sensitive to this sense of awe is unclear. Based on their understanding of original design and the contagion principle, it would seem reasonable to speculate that the awe-inspiring aspects of museum-based objects would not be appreciated fully until later in the elementary school years.

CONCLUSION: WHAT IS AN AUTHENTIC OBJECT?

Peeling back the layers of the authentic object exposes a multivoiced entity. By tracing the emergence of children's potential responsiveness to these different voices, some fundamentals that underlie an appreciation of the nature of authentic objects are uncovered. Natural objects and artifactual objects engage in subtly different aspects of an object-based dialogue. Only human-made artifacts are normally construed as both real and original. Objects of nature, on the other hand, gain their handle on reality by virtue of their contrast with the artifactual and the illusory. Any object potentially has both a natural and an artifactual voice. Which voice is heard is a function of the nature of the object, the setting in which it is placed, and the perspective of the visitor. Ideally, to engage and broaden the experience of the visitor both voices are invoked, and although one voice might be muted, it should not be stifled by the other.

In this chapter there are several examples of the ways in which an artifactual voice can be invoked when a natural object plays a central role in an object-based dialogue. For instance, if plants are displayed taxonomically, then it is their natural history that is emphasized. However, if their role in the cultural life of the visitor is also marked, then their utility as cultural artifacts is voiced (Michener & Klatt, 1999). What about the converse? Can the natural be evoked when viewing quintessentially artifactual objects such as works of art? As neurobiologist Semir Zeki pointed out, painters often have an intuitive understanding of brain function, and the way they paint reveals aspects of that organization (see Rosenfield, 2000). The act of freeing color from form, a feature of Matisse's work, for example, is made possible because these are independent brain functions (p. 61). Contrary to popular belief, it turns out that a visual experience is created by the integration of disparate functions; seeing is not a passive activity (Rosenfield, 2000). Thus, the role of visual perception in an artist's work could be exploited in an art exhibit; it might even reveal why works of art are aesthetically pleasing.

Children's developing ability to master distinctions between the worlds of the physical, the metaphysical, the artifactual, and the existential, underlies their capacity to fully engage an authentic object in an object-based dialogue. The authenticity of the object is not a given. Nevertheless, the fact that these emerging knowledge structures appear to be age-related, but not age-dependent, is a clear indication that supportive environments could promote the earlier and more nuanced emergence of such distinctions. This is the basis of a constructive interactionist approach: The child's developing conceptual structures are transformed through relevant experiences. Museums are in a unique position to capitalize on and enhance these emerging capacities. By marking these distinctions in their exhibits, the curator and museum designer both acknowledge and expand the child's-eye view.

Insofar as children are reared in an increasingly artifactual world, object-centered learning in museums has the potential of grounding (literally) their experience of reality. As described earlier, exposure to natural history knowledge, especially of fossils, undergirds children's grasp of a naturalistic theory of origins: evolution (Evans, 2001). Yet, there is a tendency to move away from displaying real objects, such as dinosaur bones, even in museums of natural history, where they are often replaced with digital objects (Sicree, 2000). We do not yet know what effects such an exposure to the artifactual might have on children's emerging grasp of reality. Nonetheless, even in advance of such knowledge, it would seem prudent to immerse children in the world of real authentic objects, before or, at least, simultaneously with, their entry into the world of virtual reality. One could argue that children have always been exposed to a world of fantastical objects and that even preschoolers grasp fantasy–reality distinctions. However, the fantastical world is clearly marked as such: It is an "imagined world" experience. It is not presented as an authentic representation of the real world. More attention needs to be paid to the broader context in which we present an authentic object because, to the extent we highlight its not-real versus its real qualities, we may only succeed in blurring the boundaries between real-world and other-world experiences for children. Robots do not really belong in a dinosaur exhibit unless their function and origins are transparent.

Paradoxically, this analysis of the authentic object reveals an enigma. Not only do the magical and illusory play a role in children's emerging grasp of the authentic, but even for adults the awe-inspiring heart of the authentic experience in an object-based dialogue is illusory, perhaps magical. We engage in a participatory act with a real object, only to grasp a semblance of a realistic, original, experience. For most of us, this is the closest we will ever come to a true encounter with the sublime.

ACKNOWLEDGMENTS

The studies reported in this chapter were supported in part by a National Academy of Education Spencer Fellowship.

REFERENCES

Aveni, A. (1996). *Behind the crystal ball: Magic, science, and the occult from antiquity through the new age.* New York: Times Books.

Carey, S. (1985). *Conceptual change in childhood.* Cambridge, MA: MIT Press.

Carey, S. (1998, July/August). Policy: Giving away research. *American Psychological Society Observer,* 6.

Carpendale, J. I., & Chandler, M. J. (1996). On the distinction between false belief understanding and subscribing to an interpretive theory of mind. *Child Development, 67,* 1263–1277.

Conn, S. (1998). *Museums and American intellectual life, 1876–1926.* Chicago: The University of Chicago Press.

Evans, E. M. (2000a). The emergence of beliefs about the origins of species in school-age children. *Merrill-Palmer Quarterly, 46*(2), 221–254.

Evans, E. M. (2000b). Beyond Scopes: Why creationism is here to stay. In K. Rosengren, C. Johnson, & P. Harris (Eds.), *Imagining the impossible: Magical scientific, and religious thinking in children* (pp. 305–331). Cambridge, UK: Cambridge University Press.

Evans, E. M. (2001). Cognitive and contextual factors in the emergence of diverse belief systems: Creation versus evolution. *Cognitive Psychology, 42,* 217–266.

Evans, E. M., & Gelman, S. A. (2001). *Revisiting the argument from design: Artificialism in young children and adults.* Manuscript in preparation.

Evans, E. M., & Mull, M. S. (2001). *Magic can happen in that world (but not this one): Constructing a naive metaphysics.* Manuscript submitted for publication.

Evans, E. M., Poling, D. A., & Mull, M. (2001, April). Confronting the existential questions: Children's understanding of death and origins. *Biennial Meeting of the Society for Research in Child Development,* Minneapolis, MN.

Falk, J. H., & Dierking, L. D. (1992). *The museum experience.* Washington, DC: Whalesback.

Falk, J. H., & Dierking, L. D. (Eds.). (1995). *Public institutions for personal learning: Establishing a research agenda.* Washington, DC: American Association of Museums.

Flavell, J. H., Flavell, E. R., & Green, F. L. (1983). Development of the appearance–reality distinction. *Cognitive Psychology, 15,* 95–120.

Gelman, R. (2000). Domain specificity and variability in cognitive development. *Child Development, 71,* 854–856.

Gelman, S. A., & Hirschfeld, L. A. (1999). How biological is essentialism? In D. L. Medin & S. Atran (Eds.), *Folkbiology* (pp. 403–447). Cambridge, MA: The MIT Press.

Gurian, E. H. (1999). What is the object of this exercise? A meandering exploration of the many meanings of objects in museums. *Daedalus, 128*(3), 163–183.

Harris, P. L. (2000). On not falling down to earth: Children's metaphysical questions. In K. Rosengren, C. Johnson, & P. Harris (Eds.), *Imagining the impossible: The development of magical, scientific, and religious thinking in children* (pp. 157–178). Cambridge, UK: Cambridge University Press.

Johnson, C. N. (2000). Putting different things together: The development of metaphysical thinking. In K. Rosengren, C. Johnson, & P. Harris (Eds.), *Imagining the impossible: The development of magical, scientific, and religious thinking in children* (pp. 179–212). Cambridge, UK: Cambridge University Press.

Keil, F. C., & Wilson, R. A. (2000). Explaining explanation. In F. C. Keil & R. A. Wilson (Eds.), *Explanation and cognition* (pp. 1–19). Cambridge, MA: MIT Press.

Lederman, D. (2000, October 6). U.S. says Indian tribes, not scientists, have rights to 9,300-year-old Kennewick Man. *The Chronicle of Higher Education,* A24.

MacCannell, D. (1976). *The tourist: A new theory of the leisure class.* New York: Stockmen.

Michener, D. C., & Klatt, B. (1999, April). Peoples, plants, and cultures at the University of Michigan Matthai Botanical Gardens. *Public Garden,* 27–30.

Mull, M. S., & Evans, E. M. (2001, April). Magic can happen in that world (but not this one): Theory of mind understanding and children's explanations for illusory events. *Biennial Meeting of the Society for Research in Child Development,* Minneapolis, MN.

Nemeroff, C., & Rozin, P. (2000). The makings of the magical mind: The nature and function of sympathetic magical thinking. In K. Rosengren, C. Johnson, & P. Harris (Eds.), *Imagining the impossible: The development of magical, scientific, and religious thinking in children* (pp. 1–34). Cambridge, UK: Cambridge University Press.

Orvell, M. (1989). *The real thing: Imitation and authenticity in American culture, 1880–1940.* Chapel Hill: University of North Carolina Press.

Phelps, K. E., & Woolley, J. D. (1994). The form and function of young children's magical beliefs. *Developmental Psychology, 30,* 385–394.

Piaget, J. (1929). *The child's conception of the world* (Joan & Andrew Tomlinson, Trans.). Totowa, NJ: Rowman & Allanhead.

Poling, D. A., & Evans, E. M. (in press). Why do birds of a feather flock together? Developmental change in the use of multiple explanations: Intention, teleology, essentialism. *British Journal of Developmental Psychology.*

Roberts, L. C. (1997). *From knowledge to narrative: Educators and the changing museum.* Washington: Simthsonian Institution Press.

Roschell, J. (1995). Learning in interactive environments: Prior knowledge and new experience. In J. H. Falk & L. D. Dierking (Eds.), *Public institutions for personal learning: Establishing a research agenda* (pp. 37-52). Washington, DC: American Association of Museums.

Rosenfield, I. (2000, September 21). A new vision of vision. *New York Review of Books, XL,* 61-64.

Rosengren, K., Johnson, C., & Harris, P. (2000). Preface. In K. Rosengren, C. Johnson, & P. Harris (Eds.), *Imagining the impossible: The development of magical, scientific, and religious thinking in children* (pp. xiii-xx). Cambridge, UK: Cambridge University Press.

Rosengren, K. S., & Hickling, A. K. (1994). Seeing is believing: Children's explanations of commonplace, magical, and extraordinary transformations. *Child Development, 65,* 1605-1626.

Shapin, S. (1996). *The Scientific Revolution.* Chicago: University of Chicago Press.

Sicree, A. (2000, October 20). Letters to the editor: Threats to natural history and to museums. *The Chronicle for Higher Education,* B21.

Sperber, D. (1996). *Explaining culture: A naturalistic approach.* Oxford, UK: Blackwell.

Wellman, H. M., & Gelman, S. A. (1998). Knowledge acquisition in foundational domains. In W. Damon (Series Ed.) & D. Kuhn & R. Siegler, (Vol. Eds.), *Handbook of child psychology: Vol. 2. Cognition, perception and language* (5th ed., pp. 523-574). New York: Wiley.

Wilcove, D. S., & Eisner, T. (2000, September 15). The impending extinction of natural history. *The Chronicle for Higher Education,* B24.

Woolley, J. D. (1997). Thinking about fantasy: Are children fundamentally different thinkers and believers from adults? *Child Development, 68,* 991-1011.

Woolley, J. D., & Wellman, H. M. (1990). Young children's understanding of realities, nonrealities and appearances. *Child Development, 61,* 946-961.

Wozniak, R. H., & Fischer, K. W. (1993). Development in context: An introduction. In R. H. Wozniak & K. W. Fischer (Eds.), *Development in context: Acting and thinking in specific environments* (pp. xi-xvi). Hillsdale, NJ: Lawrence Erlbaum Associates.

Wyse, S. A. (1997). *Believing in magic: The psychology of superstition.* Oxford, UK: Oxford University Press.

CHAPTER FIVE

When the Object is Digital: Properties of Digital Surrogate Objects and Implications for Learning

C. Olivia Frost
University of Michigan

How does the digital experience of an object differ from the physical? And how does it matter? When artistic objects are used in teaching, quite typically that object is a sculpture or a painting that instructors and students encounter in a museum. But increasingly, a digital rendering of that object may reside online, and the Internet may be used to locate and show art objects in digital form. With over 5,000 museums available for web surfers (Davis, 2000), the digital experience may become the primary exposure to the arts for many viewers, with the opportunity for instructors and learners to see more objects in virtual visits to museums than in physical museum tours. For classroom teaching, there is the potential to visit far greater numbers of digital objects than we would be able to show students in real museums. However, although digital objects are made much more accessible through online museums, experiencing the digital object is vastly different from seeing the actual object in person. These differences can extend to the visual as well as the other sensory experiences, and they affect the social experience of the museum visit as well.

When an object is digital, it offers new opportunities for learning in a way that can at once augment and limit our experience. This chapter considers features of digital objects that make the learning experience different, and the potential as well as limitations of digital representation of objects. The discussion examines ways in which digital information technologies can enhance object-centered learning, and the impact on individual and shared learning.

The focus is on general impacts as well as those with particular relevance to use of virtual objects in object-centered learning.

It is hard to even imagine that digital representations of objects will ever replace the experience encountered with an original artifact. However, both digital and real objects can contribute to object-centered learning, each in its own way. Digital technologies make it possible for learners, and users in general, to have relatively easy access to an almost limitless number of objects. These technologies also make it possible to surround the objects with rich sets of contextual information that can inform the appreciation of the object, suggest analogies from other experiences and objects, and stimulate thinking on related topics. Technologies make it possible for learners to build on objects to develop new information sources tailored to their needs and to create their own information objects. The collaborative potential of digital technologies also facilitates sharing and exchange of communication about objects. Together, both real and virtual object-centered learning can contribute to a richer educational experience.

THE DIGITAL EXPERIENCE

Online and on-site museum exhibits each offer their own unique viewing experience and provide different sensory information about the object, such as colors, textures, and spatial relationships. With these distinctive views can come differences in the way in which the object communicates an emotion as well as in the way in which it conveys information.

Although an increasing number of objects are being "born digital," including artworks created initially in digital form (Mirapaul, 2001), most digital objects have had a prior existence in a different form, and the digital version is a reproduction of some kind. A few museums exist that are entirely digital, but these are a tiny minority. In educational uses of online objects, it will be important for teachers to impart an understanding of how the digital surrogate compares with its original, and how these differences affect the experience of the object. There are many varieties of differences between the original and the digital, and many reasons why the digital version will differ. In some cases, the digital surrogate will represent a form of expression that is an entirely different medium. For example, the brief textual description accompanying a museum exhibit or digital display is clearly different from the actual object that it represents. Some visual surrogates, such as reproductions found in books or on the Internet, are black-and-white reproductions that can be easily distinguished from their original versions in color.

Research by Taylor (2000) indicated that significant differences exist between original art and digital representations, and that there is a difference in the emotional response to different formats of a representation. When the written word in print format is represented in digital form, the information value is relatively unchanged. However, when a surrogate for a three-dimensional object is created in print or digital form, there is key informational value that is lost.

There are many ways in which the surrogate object we experience can vary from its original, and each type of difference has its own impact on the quality of the experience of an object. There will be differences between the original and its reproduction, for example, between an original painting and a digital photographic copy. There are also variations among different formats of reproductions, for example, between a black-and-white copy and a color copy. In addition, however, within a particular form of reproduction there can be variations that result from the reproduction process used, the reproduction medium, or the way in which the digital data has been stored. Each type of variation may cause viewers to have different impressions of a work depending on the version that they have seen.

Arguably the most notable difference between the original object and its reproduction is that which results from translating a multidimensional object to a flat two-dimensional scale. Although virtual reality has the potential to reproduce artifacts in many dimensions, the more typical digital representation of a museum object is a two-dimensional plane. With examples from material culture, such as a doll or a piece of clothing, any two-dimensional representations of these three-dimensional objects will be diminished in some way, and the size, color, heft, and texture will not come through in the same way as with the original. Even for an object originally appearing in two dimensions, a loss of some kind may be likely; for example, if a painting is cropped and framed, or if its texture is represented only by shadings. Size matters, too. Paintings vary widely in terms of their original size, but the digital surrogate is constrained by the size of the computer screen, which is more relatively standard in its dimensions. Inasmuch as the variance of this scale is not necessarily predictable, it is not always evident to the viewer whether the tiny object on the screen is actually a wall-length painting or a miniature. Although information about the scale or the size of the original object may give an understanding of the size difference between the original and its representation, it is still an open question as to whether the impact of this difference is likely to be intellectual rather than visual (Hindle, 1978).

Even more striking is the loss that occurs when a surrogate expressed in a single two-dimensional medium stands in the place of multisensory experiences surrounding an object. If art researchers claim that there is no substitute for seeing a work in its own surroundings, then it would seem that in visiting a museum, the touch, sound, and smell associated with the experience of viewing will create a different aura in which the object is viewed (Jones, 1990). Recent initiatives suggest there will come a time when tactile sensation may be part of the digital experience of an object. At the Philadelphia

Museum of Art, two reproductions of a ceramic tea bowl and a painted scroll have been digitally recreated so that museum visitors can handle the objects. The museum curator explains that the tactile experience is particularly important in gaining an understanding of these objects because in the 17th century, the tea bowl and scroll were passed around in their original venue (Greenman, 2000). The context surrounding an original object can also include the experience the museum visitor gains by walking through the exhibit halls. Digital technology has made efforts to recreate this experience, for example in CD-ROMs in which the visitor can wander virtually through digital museum halls that simulate the corridors of a real museum. The virtual tour brings the viewer in contact with the various exhibit rooms, stops at animated displays, and even continues into the museum store (Keim, 2000). These tools may bring us a step forward in gaining a sense of place and navigation, but they still fall far short of the experience of a real museum visit. Viewing an original object in its physical milieu, walking through the halls of a gallery, is a distinctly different experience from the stationery viewing of surrogate objects on a computer screen. Taylor's research (2000) suggested that the gallery setting exerts a strong influence on how adult viewers respond to original works of art.

The display of a digital reproduction — the quality of color and crispness in the reproduction — can vary widely from the original, depending on software or system limitations. The digital rendering of an object and the quality of fidelity can also vary according to the method of digitization. Some images may be crisper and clearer because the people making the digital copy have decided to invest in a higher quality digital original. When digital information is stored, decisions made in storage may result in compression of the data, particularly with storage-intensive media such as images and video, where the storage of the original image can result in large and unmanageable files. When a visual object is rendered in digital form, some color fidelity compression loss may occur. Because of the different available methods of storage, decisions must be made that carry a trade-off: Some images may be poorer in quality due to a decision to use storage methods that create smaller files but result in a loss in image fidelity, as well as a loss in resolution. To achieve more efficient storage, some compression techniques may even result in loss of data that cannot be retrieved (Research Libraries Group, 1996). Ideally, sharp image resolution and fidelity of color representation are desired in rendering image reproductions. A decision in favor of higher resolution and richer color may result in a larger file size and thus more costly storage.

These differences can have real impacts on the experiences of the viewer. The more knowledgeable viewer may have in mind the original object and may see the digital through the lens of the original experience. At the same time, the seasoned viewer may view the digital surrogate as a poor substitute, because of this comparison. In selecting objects for pedagogical purposes, difficult choices are often at hand. Suppose we are faced with the choice be-tween a good black-and-white reproduction, or a poor quality color one. Which is the better choice, given that our young learners may respond more favorably to color, while seeing black-and-white as an anachronistic way of representing images?

In a recent study of digital surrogates, art historians and teachers in focus groups stressed that image quality was the primary criterion in deciding what kind of reproduction to use in their teaching. One art history faculty member in a focus group emphasized the priority he gave to image quality when de-ciding what types of reproductions to use in his class. "I would say that the image quality is key. Absolutely key. I would prefer actually for my students to see a black-and-white photograph than a bad color reproduction of a paint-ing, if it comes to that. As close as you can get to the original color" (Frost et al., 2000, p. 303).

In contrast, Thompson (1982) reported an experiment in which British grammar school students, when shown different formats, clearly preferred bright and comparatively crude color slides to original paintings with more subtle modulations of color. The youngsters found the copy photographs more eye-catching, stronger, and clearer. At the same time, Taylor's study (2000) focusing on nonspecialist adult viewers of art works found that these adult viewers had strong preference for representations in color, for example, color slides, but also clearly preferred the original painting to any representations.

The digital reproduction of an object takes on special significance in light of the potential for digital technologies to alter features of the original object and the implications for assessing whether what we have seen is the "real" or an altered content. Art historians are mindful that digital technologies make it possible for people to distort or alter an image deliberately. Commonly avail-able software tools for image management make it relatively easy to insert or delete portions of an image as well as change the color and shape. For this rea-son, art scholars place great emphasis on fidelity to the original, particularly in an environment where digital reproductions could easily be altered and en-hanced, and recognize that a poor quality reproduction is actually false data that would cause a scholar to come up with completely erroneous conclu-sions. One art history faculty member of a focus group said:

> I think if there were a database that people were using where images had been altered, like if it was a ceramic piece and mends had been kind of camouflaged in Photoshop, so it looked like it was a whole piece, when in fact it was a recon-structed piece, I think you'd throw out the whole database and say, "You can't touch any of it." (Frost et al., 2000, p. 303)

In other cases, methods of digitization may result in copies that are intended to be close to the original but may create distorting effects that do, in fact, mis-lead the viewer. Is it possible to make a digital representation "authoritative" in the sense that experts would be able to distinguish a faithful representation from a less effective one? Perhaps a kind of "digital literacy" that documents methods used in the reproduction would be useful in assessing digital documents, so that researchers looking for online digital versions of original works of art would be able to determine the authenticity and fidelity to the original works (Bearman & Trant, 1998).

It becomes clear that if educators are using reproductions as a surrogate for the original, it is important to stress that the scale, definition, and color of the two-dimensional image do not provide the same viewing experience as the original three-dimensional object. Learners who are inexperienced viewers may not realize the ways in which the original differs from the reproduction and that the reproduction is not a substitute for seeing the real work. As one art history teacher member of a focus group explained,

> We would regard the use of reproductions as a surrogate for the original always to help the students to understand and experience as closely as possible the nature and the quality of the original, and so we are constantly, as it were, apologizing for the problem of scale, definition, color, and the way a two-dimensional image is always misleading in relation to a three-dimensional object. (Frost et al., 2000, p. 302)

Osburne (1970) argued in addition that the reproduction, in offering only a small part of experiencing the real work, has the potential to blunt the edge of our appreciation beforehand and cheat us of surprise, so that when we visit a museum and see a painting firsthand that we have seen before, something of the picture's originality and strangeness is no longer perceptible.

As more and more material becomes available in digital form across the Internet, the digital surrogate may well become an increasingly common form of our experience of objects. To some extent, and particularly when users are more accustomed to seeing digital representations than originals in museums, users may view the images as artifacts having their own intrinsic value rather than as imperfect surrogates to be compared against an original. The challenge for teachers becomes how to convey to learners that a surrogate has different properties from the real thing?

DIGITAL COMMUNITIES AND THEIR IMPACT ON INDIVIDUAL AND SHARED LEARNING

Personal computers and access to the World Wide Web are now becoming a prevalent part of our everyday lives at school, work, and home. Costs of computing are making such access more affordable, and advances in usability of computers and programs are making it easier for ordinary citizens to use increasingly sophisticated and powerful technology. In light of these developments, and the rapid proliferation of information systems that overcome barriers of place and time, the access to information objects becomes less and less dependent on where we are, who we are, and at what point in the day we use information. At the same time, although digital technologies can broaden the reach and exchange of information and ideas, there are differences in income, education status, race and ethnicity, and/or geographic region that can have broad impacts on access (National Telecommunications Infrastructure Administration, 2000).

The use of digital information can bring with it profound changes in the way in which we interact with others in society. At the same time that digital technologies make it easier for us to have access to information on an individual, and even anonymous level, these technologies give us the power to extend our reach and join or even form new communities. With the capability of disseminating information both instantly and to an infinitely large and diverse set of recipients, users can create audiences for their communication. In Galston's view (1999), the Internet makes it possible to combine individual autonomy and social ties. The ability to exchange information and opinions with others of shared interests is a powerful force in Internet communities.

Viewing materials online can be both socially enriching and isolating. The Internet can foster community, but it can also facilitate individual, one-on-one engagement between people and the information objects found on their computers, leaving out the intermediary. This direct interaction with information makes it easier to connect to resources at our own convenience, providing we have appropriate means of access to computers and connectivity. However, there are value-added benefits that an intermediary can provide that may be lost if the learner goes directly to the resources and by-passes the assistance of the librarian or museum intermediary. The personalized help that a librarian or school media specialist can bring to an information search is usually lost to the learner in online visits to libraries. Although online versions of resources can also provide their own powerful personalized assistance, this may be lost if learners lack awareness of these tools or lack the skills to take advantage of them. In visiting a museum website, the learner may lose the benefit provided by the museum guide who serves as an intermediary to bring context, personalization, and similar assistance to help enrich the understanding of museum objects. In considering the role of mediation in determining experience with objects, Hapgood and Palinscar (chapter 10, this volume) observe that "[w]hether and how one experiences objects is a function of the interplay of the characteristics of the object, the knowledge and dispositions that one brings to the viewing, and the context in which one views the object" and argue the need for providing viewers with different lenses that they can apply to their experiences with objects.

Given the relatively anonymous context in which information creation and use occurs, those who create information resources may have little idea of who uses the information they distribute, where these users are, and under what circumstances or for what purposes the information is being used. Because people are often alone when they use their computers, the experience is individual and one-on-one with their computers, rather than a shared experience with a live group. The experience becomes in some ways more personalized, with the ability of the online tools to deliver custom-tailored information. At the same time, the experience can be devoid of the shared appreciation taking place with others at a physical museum, for example, or enriched through online interaction with others who may have viewed the same object. Rowe (chapter 2, this volume) points out that a significant percentage of museum goers visit as part of a group, with group activity and meaning-making developing in socially mediated ways.

Some museums offer online access to digital objects at the physical museum site. This offers the museum visitor the opportunity to interact with virtual and actual objects, and to benefit from a shared experience with a group as well as individually, particularly as computer use by groups is not unusual in museums (Chadwick, 1992). Falk and Dierking (1992) explored the role of social context in a museum experience and noted differences between the experience of individuals and those visiting as a group (Falk & Dierking, 1998), and a study by Chadwick (1999) looked at differences in behavior between individuals and groups visiting a museum Web site. In his online questionnaire surveying visitors to a museum website, Chadwick found that nearly 30% of respondents were visiting the museum as part of a group. The study revealed differences between groups and individuals while visiting the museum. For example, groups were likely to visit more pages during an online visit than individuals and were also more likely to be engaged in browsing behaviors, whereas individual visitors engaged in more directed searches.

For young learners working independently on their computers, the experience can be both enriching in the way it provides freedom of access to new kinds of information and limiting in its absence of guidance and context, and with the new technologies come both opportunities and challenges. Opportunities arise as online connections make resources accessible to an infinite array of audiences, and sophisticated finding tools enable novice users to locate materials by chance or by design. Because of this, there is a far greater likelihood that materials that were previously in the domain of groups privileged by education, social connection, mobility, or resources will now be accessible to much wider audiences. Accordingly, there is the potential for breaking down social and age boundaries as well as interesting possibilities for exchanges across cultures, generations, and geographic boundaries. The ability to co-locate disparate groups can enrich the audience appreciation base of an object. As a result, objects in museums, archives, and libraries are now accessible to viewers around the globe. Repositories such as archival collections, a type of material previously off-limits to all but a few scholarly users, can now in effect be in the public domain when made accessible through the Internet. Accessibility to an infinitely broad and rich set of original materials can vastly increase the availability of primary resources available to learners.

Among the challenges of online access is the fact that broad access may come with its own intellectual constraints. For example, the understanding and appreciation of objects may assume a knowledge base shared by scholarly communities and other groups with specialized expertise. Access to objects and information about them is available to both novice and expert users alike; however, the impact of the object may diminish significantly without the surrounding background necessary to understand its origins. This heightens the need for contextual resources to accompany the object. For example, sites that are enriched with material explaining the significance of a photographic exhibit can make it easier for viewers to understand more fully the importance of these materials, or engage viewers in a way that can enable them to relate what they have seen to their own experience (Frost, 1999). Increasingly, archivists have become more engaged in helping develop online primary resources for incorporation into K–12 classrooms (Gilliland-Swetland, Kafai, & Landis, 1999). Learners can have access to a rich array of archival resources available online, such as the National Archives Digital Classroom and the Learning Page of the Library of Congress' American Memory Project sites. With widely available access to these kinds of online materials, young learners can observe and participate on a much more level playing field. Broadening the access can increase the audience base for an information object and thus dramatically affect the potential of its social impact.

A major force in the dynamic of digital communities results from the ability of users to become creators as well as consumers of information objects. The self-publishing aspects of digital communication now make it possible for a wide and diverse set of users to create and distribute their works. Even relatively inexperienced computer users are able to create multimedia collages of sound, images, moving pictures, and text, and with hypertext linkages, users can place a document in a contextual setting. In using digital representations of objects, learners can go well beyond the mere viewing of an object to create their own objects or information de novo or as an extension or augmentation of an original artifact they have found. For example, learners can locate an artifact on the Internet and then provide context for it by identifying background and paths to related works and information. Another potential is to provide a new version of the artifact, for example, a drawing inspired by an original art work or a poem inspired by a piece of sculpture. The ability of new technologies to facilitate collaborative work also makes possible the opportunity for participatory creation.

Because digital information objects can be so easily altered, extended, and otherwise manipulated, a user may decide to add context to a work, reconfigure it, and use it for a different purpose. For example, a high school learner may take an image from a museum website and incorporate it into a report, combining it with music clips and video images retrieved online, as well as with text from an online encyclopedia and links to related sites. With the capability that new technologies offer to combine works of different media and to bring together images, sound, text, and software programs to create new material, such creations are increasingly common. As a result, concepts of ownership of ideas and intellectual property become increasingly complex in the creation and use of digital information. Teaching information literacy in the use of these tools will require that we go beyond the technical use of these tools. Equally important is the recognition of what it means to be an informed information citizen when it comes to concepts of intellectual property and ownership of ideas and content, as learners take existing original contents and use them as building blocks of a new creation. In new information environments, it becomes critical to understand how to use information objects in a responsible way that recognizes principles of intellectual ownership. This is especially important in view of cultural forces that have tended to make it socially acceptable to share and copy information found on the World Wide Web.

In the new digital environment, our understanding of fair use may be challenged. As educators, we, like others, are likely to make extensive use of content from other sources in our teaching. We may want to alter content to suit curricular goals and also share that content with our students, as well as with other teachers and learners. The traditions of access to information and freedom of expression are prevalent in educational institutions and the repositories, such as libraries, that serve them. For the classroom teacher and museum educator, familiar assumptions regarding appropriate use of intellectual property may no longer be valid in a digital environment. In a classroom, a teacher may assume, when he or she copies the work of others to create a lesson plan, that this is "fair use" and serves a social good. However, this may change when technologies with "anytime/anyplace" properties make it possible for us to use educational materials in locales outside the classroom, for example, if we distribute a lesson plan using a personal website, or include materials for educational use in a resource to be published for commercial profit. These considerations make it difficult to relegate certain kinds of appropriate uses to specific contexts (National Research Council, 2000). The challenge will be to identify and interpret a complex and changing environment of intellectual property in the digital environment while exploiting the capabilities of digital technologies to make information relevant and meaningful through personalization and contextualization.

NAVIGATION AND INTELLECTUAL ACCESS
TO OBJECTS

Brown (2000) asserted that:

> [t]he new information literacy, beyond text and image, is one of information navigation. The real literacy of tomorrow entails the ability to be your own personal reference librarian — to know how to navigate through confusing, complex information spaces and feel comfortable doing so. "Navigation" may well be the main form of literacy for the 21st century. (p. 14)

Navigating information space in an environment where information grows exponentially and is no longer contained in neat boundaries becomes a major obstacle in gaining intellectual access to information objects. At the same time, new information tools can facilitate information discovery and can also bring us more directly into contact with representations of images and other objects. Previously, searches in the library card catalog retrieved only surrogate descriptions of a book, image, or information object. Now, online searches can retrieve not only the descriptions about information, such as index terms and annotations, but also the information object itself. Full-text retrieval of texts and retrieval of image and sound documents are now readily accessible. Learners now have easier access to reproductions of primary resources, rather than relying on descriptions.

Intellectual access to information objects is also immensely facilitated through the power of hyperlinking. In looking up information on a given topic, a user may consult the library online card catalog to help find materials on a particular subject, or may use the catalog to locate a book or a representation of an object by its title or artist. A different, and at times more powerful means of search, is to identify a document that is close to our interests, and find what works have been linked to or from this document, a process similar to scanning a known document for its footnotes or consulting a citation index. With the Web, however, there is a far easier and more powerful means of finding items related to documents identified as being of interest. Hyperlinking in today's Internet environment takes on additional dimensions in that it allows the user to determine and create the links, thus resulting in connections that indexers and catalogers may never have dreamed of. In this way, users of the site are no longer relying solely on the links established by traditional and relatively static knowledge structures such as the Dewey Decimal Classification. Instead of or in addition to this, users are creating their own networks of connections, making hypertext links to provide their own connections to information and objects, as they identify and link related sites. At the same time, networks of links can become a maze, and it is all too easy for viewers to lose their way along the information path. In going from link to link, and from one reference point to another, it is often difficult for users to remember the starting point of the search and the points along the way. Navigating effectively among related links and information space becomes an important skill.

Another powerful capability of computer searching for objects is the facilitation of browsing. Whereas search engines require a user to submit specific terms and thus assume a certain knowledge of the subject before a search can begin, there is a wide array of browsing tools that make it easier for the novice to navigate a search through unfamiliar territory or abstract concepts. Many users may have a relatively unformed notion of what they are looking for, for example, how strength and pride are conveyed in art. Their browsing may be based on the assumption that "I'll know it when I see it." In browse mode, a user may look through a set of items and, on finding one of interest, may say to the system, "Give me more like that!" As a result, the browse mode does not require the user to initiate the query with a specific search term, but it does require the user to have some idea in mind of where to start and what collections will be browsed. One of the primary attractions of browsing is that it allows users to recognize what is interesting rather than formulating a precise information query in advance.

The power of browsing has particular implications for the discovery of image objects, inasmuch as a pictorial image is able to present itself in its own medium of expression and thus has the potential to allow users to employ their cognitive abilities to scan image content within sets of images to retrieve desired information. Browsing has an added advantage of helping users navigate without prior knowledge of subject content (Kwasnik, 1992), and has the unique advantage as "a simple and convivial form of access to information sources, particularly for occasional and inexpert users" (Bawden, 1993, p. 72.). For those lacking special expertise in a subject area, this has particular relevance.

Frost's research investigated users' preferences for retrieving image data. Focus group interviews were conducted with art history faculty and museum curators, as well as with student and faculty who were not specialists in art history. The study found that whereas specialists preferred a direct search, generalists or novice users used browsing as their preferred mode. However, both specialists and novice searchers found each mode to play a role depending on information need, and found value in a system combining both browse and direct search. For example, generalist or novice users in focus groups noted the advantages gained by browsing when the user was not able to articulate a known item search or when the priority was on ideas. One generalist in the focus group pointed out the benefits of browsing if the name of an artist or title was not known:

> If you're looking for paintings or drawings or something specific by a specific artist, you might not actually know the painting by its title, you might only know

it by how you've seen it. Like I know quite a few paintings from like older periods where I would have no idea what the name is, I only know the artist, I only know what they look like. (Frost et al., 2000, p. 307)

Respondents in the focus groups also emphasized the distinct discovery appeal afforded by online browsing, and its ability to lead to new lines of thought that might stimulate the imagination. One art history specialist noted that, "My kids sit on the computer and they just look and see what's out there, they just go from image to image, just to see what's in there" (Frost et al., 2000, p. 298).

The power of serendipity in browsing often leads people to continue to search, even when they have already found what they are looking for. One art history specialist observed, "Even if you found what you wanted, or close to what you wanted, you're not likely, if you're human, to be satisfied with that, anyway. You're gonna browse anyway, just to see if there might be something a little bit better" (Frost et al., 2000, p. 298).

Whether a user chooses to browse or search often depends on the purpose of the search. An art specialist explained how the nature of a search task determined his use of the browse or search mode:

When I would search or when I would browse would depend on what I was looking for. If I'm looking for something colorful or something flashy, then I might browse a set of images and see one that strikes my eye and hopefully they'd be nicely arranged into different thumbnails. But if I'm looking for something specific, say I was writing a paper on Monet, and I wanted to put one of Monet's pictures in, I would want to be able to get to a Monet specifically and do that. (Frost et al., 2000, p. 298)

Although navigation is important, authentication and validation of digital objects are also critical skills for effective use of digital information objects. When an object or unit of information resides in a collection, that collection serves a filtering or sanctioning role. When we visit a museum, the curators of the collection have brought to bear considerable expertise in selection and organization of the objects that are available for public view. Librarian selectors, museum curators, archival appraisers, and publishers can offer value by bringing to their collections an evaluative component that assumes that the artifacts or objects represented have been carefully selected from a broader universe of objects on the basis of their quality, fit, or other criteria. With the autonomous dimension of self-publishing on the Internet, users may not have the assurance that what they are viewing represents the best of a genre. When visiting a website, a viewer may not know whether that resource is authentic or whether it has been evaluated.

Problems of authentication can also emerge when a user employs highly powerful and sophisticated search engines to retrieve small pieces of information out of context. A search query may result in identifying an individual page, but when this individual page is retrieved outside of the context of the entire document, learners may miss out on important background information; for example, when a student retrieves a page from a website, she may not realize that the site was created by amateurs rather than museum experts. Another important feature of digital information literacy worth recognizing is that objects can be distorted or provide misleading information, losing the quality and accuracy of the original. Whereas the physical artifact remains more or less constant, there is the potential for changing its digital representation.

In a distributed information environment, computer-assisted search mechanisms such as web crawlers, while powerful, can also be manipulated by creators of web pages as well as by the designers of retrieval systems. Lynch cautioned that little technology is available that allows an indexing crawler to determine whether indexing data can be believed or whether it is simply attached to a web page in an attempt to shape the outcome of the indexing process. He stressed the need for users to understand the behavior of retrieval systems, so that users can recognize why a given result was retrieved, and observed that "[a]lmost nobody understands why they get the results that they do from a search engine; they just deal with the results that they do get" (Lynch, 2001, p. 17).

The potential for deception and misuse of information in Internet communities increases the importance of mechanisms for evaluation and judgment. When we find information in a networked environment, we may know little about its creators or the circumstances of its creation. When we ourselves create and distribute information, we have little idea of who uses the information we distribute, under what circumstances, or for what purposes. Building mechanisms that allow us to decide which information can be trusted and is authoritative is an important skill that must be learned for effective Internet use.

CONCLUSION

Digital technologies can offer a wide array of learning opportunities in the discovery, representation, dissemination, and use of information objects. Learners now have access to an immense and diverse universe of objects, and can build on these objects to create new information resources and creations. Avenues for sharing information hold the potential for exchange and interaction with other learners as well as with a broadened community. The wealth of opportunities also calls for a new digital literacy that provides skills for exploiting the potential of tools for effective information discovery, recognition of appropriate use of other's intellectual property, and appreciation of the strengths and limitations of digital representations so that they can enhance, not replace, the real world experience of an object. With access to digital collections of local museums, learners can develop background knowledge needed to understand the exhibits, and pursue their own inquiries over time. This provides an opportunity for students to develop and enhance their own understanding and appreciation of objects, to create their own objects, and to share and showcase their own creativity and understanding with a wider audience.

Objects in their original format have characteristics that make the viewing of an original artifact a quite different experience from the viewing of a representation. There is undoubtedly no replacement for the experience of viewing an object in its original form and setting. However, digital representations, while they provide an inferior viewing experience in some ways, have their own advantages unique to digital information formats. Information in digital form can reach far wider audiences, can be accessible in anywhere/anytime modalities, and can provide contextual information that can enrich and inform the viewing experience. The two formats need not compete with each other. Indeed, the power of digital technologies can be used to stimulate interest in a broad array of viewers and result in greater levels of engagement with the real objects in museums.

REFERENCES

Brown, J. S. (2000, March/April). Growing up digital: How the web changes work, education, and the ways people learn. *Change,* March/April, 11-20.

Bawden, D. (1993). Browsing: Theory and practice. *Perspectives in Information Management, 3,* 71-85.

Bearman, D., & Trant, J. (1998, June). Authenticity of digital resources: Towards a statement of requirements in the research process. *D-Lib Magazine.* Available: http://www.dlib.org/dlib/june98/06bearman.html [2001, January 28]

Chadwick, J. (1999). A survey of characteristics and patterns of behavior in visitors to a museum web site. In D. Bearman & J. Trant (Eds.), Museums and the Web1999: Selected Papers from an International Conference. Archives & Museum Informatics. Available: http://www.archimuse.com/mw99/papers/chadwick/chadwick.html [2001, Jaunary 28]

Chadwick, J. C. (1992). The development of a museum multimedia program. *Journal of Educational Multimedia and Hypermedia, 1,* 331-340.

Davis, D. (2000, September 24). The virtual museum, imperfect but promising, *The New York Times,* pp. 1, 32.

Falk, J. H., & Dierking, L. D. (1992). *The museum experience.* Washington, DC: Whalesback.

Falk, J. H., & Dierking, L. D. (1998). Understanding free-choice learning: A review of the research and its application to museum web sites. In D. Bearman & J. Trant (Eds.) *Museums and the Web 98 Proceedings* (CD-ROM). Archives and Museum Informatics. Available: http://www.archimuse.com/mw98/papers/dierking/dierking_paper.html [2001, January 28]

Frost, C. O. (1999). Cultural heritage outreach and museum/school partnerships: Initiatives at the School of Information, University of Michigan. *Museums and the Web1999: Selected Papers from an International Conference.* In D. Bearman & J. Trant (Eds.), Museums and the Web1999: Selected Papers from an International Conference. *Archives & Museum Informatics,* 223-229. Available: http://www.archimuse.com/mw99/papers/frost/frost.html [2001, January 28]

Frost, C. O., Taylor, B., Noakes, A., Markel, S., & Drabenstott, K. M. (2000). Browse and search patterns in a digital image database. *Information Retrieval, 1,* 287-313.

Galston, W. A. (1999). *(How) does the Internet affect community? Some speculations in search of evidence.* Available: www.ksg.harvard.edu/visions/galston.htm [2001, January 28]

Gilliland-Swetland, A. J., Kafai, Y. B., & Landis, W. E. (1999). Integrating primary sources into the elementary school classroom: A case study of teachers' perspectives. *Archivaria, 48,* 89-116.

Greenman, C. (2000, September 14). Museum goers get a virtual hands-on experience, *The New York Times,* p. D9.

Hindle, B. (1978). How much is a piece of the true cross worth?, In I. M. G. Quimby, (Ed.), *Material culture and the study of American life* (pp. 5-20). New York: W. W. Norton.

Jones, L. S. (1990). *Art information: Research methods and resources* (3d ed.). Dubuque, IA: Kendall/Hunt.

Keim, A. (2000, Septebmer 14). Discovering dinosaurs on 2 CD-ROM's. *The New York Times,* p. D9.

Kwasnik, B. H. (1992). The functional components of browsing. *Annual Review of OCLC Research July 1991-July 1992,* 53-56.

Library of Congress. *American Memory Project.* Available: http://lcweb2.loc.gov/ammem/ndlpedu/index.html [2001, January 28]

Lynch, C. A (2001). When documents deceive: Trust and provenance as new factors for information retrieval in a tangled web. *Journal of the American Society for Information Science and Technology 52,* 12-17.

Mirapaul, M. (2001, Jaunary 8). Museum tries mounting its latest show in cyberspace. *The New York Times,* p. B2.

National Archives Digital Classroom. Available: http://www.nara.gov/education/ [2001, January 28]

National Research Council (2000) Committee on Intellectual Property Rights and Emerging Information Infrastructure. *The digital dilemma: Intellectual property in the information age.* Available: http://books.nap.edu/html/digital_dilemma/ [2001, January 28]

National Telecommunications Infrastructure Administration. (2000). *Falling through the net: Toward digital inclusion.* Available: http://www.ntia.doc.gov/ntiahome/digitaldivide/ [2001, January 28]

Osborne, H. (Ed.). (1970). *The Oxford companion to art.* Oxford: The Clarendon Press.

Research Libraries Group (1996). *Preserving digital information. Report of the Task Force on Archiving of Digital Information.* Commissioned by the Research Libraries Group and the Commission for Preservation and Access. Available: http://www.rlg.org/ArchTF/tfadl.objects.htm [2001, January 28]

Taylor, B. L. (2000). *The effect of surrogation on viewer response to expressional qualities in works of art.* Unpublished doctoral dissertation, University of Michigan, School of Information.

Thompson, C. (1982). Why do you need to see the original painting anyway? *Visual Resources, 2,* 21-36.

CHAPTER SIX

Through the Garden Gate: Objects and Informal Education for Environmental and Cultural Awareness in Arboreta and Botanic Gardens

David C. Michener
Inger J. Schultz
University of Michigan

There was a child went forth every day,
And the first object he looked upon ... that object he became.
And that object became part of him for the day or a certain part of
The day ... or for many years or stretching cycles of years.
— Walt Whitman, 1855, cited in Bradley & Blodgett (1973)

A 6-year old boy named Matthew visited the Arboretum with his school group to learn about landscape design. Landscape design is a big topic for such a small boy, but there was no hesitation on his part to experience and learn. He studied the hills closely — running up and rolling down to get a sense of the topography. He studied planting formations by lying under the tall pines at the top of a hill and peering through them as they framed the sky. He heard and felt the river as it rushed over stones. Throughout the walk Matthew collected twigs, pebbles, and fallen leaves and then, sitting in the middle of the open valley, was asked to imagine his own landscape, and with the items he collected, some PlayDoh and markers create a landscape on a plate. Matthew created his own ideal place of hills, trees, rivers, waterfalls, and bridges on a paper plate with seed pods for boats. Matthew's landscape included a very important element that was not overtly taught in the lesson — himself. He was integral to the landscape he was just experiencing. He placed himself as an object within an object.

. . .

Arboreta and botanic gardens are among the most accessible, stimulating, and rewarding places for long-lasting affective experiences related to nature for visitors of all ages. These living museums are also among the most restorative for visitors of museum-like institutions. Counterintuitively, arboreta and gardens also present to the visitor among the most strikingly complex array of collections and objects of any museum type, making the processes of discovery and self-paced informal education appear to be fundamentally violated if viewed from a "normal" museum perspective. This chapter clarifies why arboreta and gardens have and maintain these apparently contradictory approaches to their objects and why this situation is driven by institutional missions, and highlights several novel approaches to using this full spectrum of objects in informal education for environmental and cultural awareness in the United States.

ARBORETA AND BOTANIC GARDENS HAVE NONCANONICAL OBJECTS

Arboreta and botanical gardens are distinctive among museums for presenting living collections that are among the most complex for engaging visitors. This complexity is due to the overlapping scale of landscapes, garden areas, and individual plants. The diversity and number of plants simultaneously stimulate the senses. The institution may use this diversity of scales to convey a range of conceptual issues to the visitor who may have sought only a restorative visit. But what are the "objects" on display in an arboretum or garden that engage the visitor? Is it the flower of a magnolia tree, the entire mass of flowering annuals in a seasonal Victorian floral design, or the intentionally maintained vista, be it to a focal point or even out to an infinite view of nature and sky? Perhaps "objects" in these living collections are best defined in relation to the scale of the issue being addressed rather than by a traditional catalog-based perspective of discrete physical entities.

In the canonical museum model, art displays can be extremely focused to only the few pieces needed to evoke a response or convey important concepts. Csikszentmihalyi and Robinson (1990) stated in their conclusions that:

> No matter how great the works of art displayed, they will not be able to engage the viewer as long as there are distractions competing for his or her attention. The most obvious task of museums is to provide ways for this intense concentration to occur. (p. 184)

Traditionally, arboreta and botanic gardens have sought a parallel gallery structure and treated individual plants as objects and displayed them by curatorial categories as rose garden, topiary garden, and systematic beds, similar to a traditional mineral display in a natural history museum. However, some contemporary institutional educational messages cannot be achieved with reliance on canonical objects that are placed in a narrow context. For example, if the mission includes preservation or conservation of natural habitats, then the habitat in an ecologically meaningful context is the required "object," even though it may also have rare or endangered plants within them that are also "objects." The large scale of an arboretum (which can be several thousand acres) lends itself to interpreting its collections of native herbaceous and woody plants (traditional objects) in terms of the ecosystem they are found in (a very complex object). Not only is interpretation of these natural areas (a nested object) predicated on the ecosystem, but it also dictates alternative curatorial and management techniques.

Interpreting exotic plants and habitats may require environmentally controlled conservatories (tropical house, desert house, etc.) where both the simulated habitat and individual plants must be able to be seen as objects. Ironically, gardens began to grapple with these issues for horticultural purposes over two centuries ago, as alpine plants demand conditions similar to those in nature in order to survive. The great 19th-century rock gardens are the earliest ecologically contextual display gardens where both the individual plants and the entire garden are complementary and nested objects.

A central educational issue is the type of objects that the visitors perceive and the consequent informal educational exploration and discovery. Falk and Dierking (1992) stated:

> Although frustrating for museum professionals, visitors will always try to understand an exhibit in the context of their own experiences. Museum professionals do not always present objects with this in mind because often they have already personalized their *own* (italics in original) knowledge and level of understanding of the objects. (p. 139)

This is true with living collections where the nested scale of the object(s) is an inherently important part of the display, and visitors can simultaneously observe objects of different scales. One visitor may appreciate an entire landscape or view as an object. Others may focus on different but specific plants (the canonical object). Yet another may focus entirely on one flower as the object, even to the visual suppression of the individual plant bearing the flower (some rose gardens exemplify this approach). Meanwhile, other visitors may focus on the butterflies visiting these flowers, while others notice the hawk circling high above the landscape. The visitors may derive pleasure and meaning from all such levels of object existence. From an informal educational perspective, all these levels are equally real and important to the institution's mission. The fact that the objects are nested becomes an issue of interpretation. Even within a scale of "objectness" in a garden, the situation remains noncanonical. Although the plants are stationary, numerous features and phenomena are often both ephemeral and seasonal, and the resultant living collections change by the hour, day, season, year, and decade such that visitors can never return to an identical space for an identical experience.

To continue this example, many of the obvious features could be changed 2 months later, as trees having dropped their leaves in the landscape, flowers replaced by fruits with birds gathering fruits. Yet the underlying living collection, its mission, and its educational messages have not changed. It is hard to imagine a parallel structure of seasonally changing, immobile, yet nested objects as perceived by the visitor in an art or natural history museum. It is also simplistic to define the perceived object as only the individual plants (an approach that would parallel the situation in the arts as discussed by Csikszentmihalyi & Robinson, 1990) and focus the attention of informal educational programs and assessment only at that level, as this ignores both the wider institutional mission and reinforces socially or culturally based expectations of naive audience members that only "flowers" (not even entire plants) are the sole focus of personal concern as well as institutional and societal relevance. This situation is particularly acute when arboreta and gardens reinterpret their mission to include sustainable environments and the conservation of biodiversity, environmental and cultural education, and use the living collections as tools for formal and informal education.

OBJECTS OF DIVERGENT SCALES ARE NEEDED FOR A MULTIFACETED INSTITUTIONAL MISSION

Arboreta and botanic gardens have missions that typically include one or more overlapping elements that can be grouped as (a) education and research, (b) aesthetics and personal renewal, and (c) conservation and stewardship. At any time in all gardens and arboreta, at least one element of the mission drives which objects are important and how they are displayed and explained from the scale of flowers to landscapes.

However, over time the educational mission of public gardens has expanded. A reinterpreted mission may require objects of one scale to be augmented with or sacrificed for objects of another scale. The educational program's focus may shift as well. Unlike canonical museum objects, the living plants in arboreta and botanic gardens are not easily moved or rearranged, or can only be destructively removed. Consequently, redesigning an art gallery or zoo can accomplish renovations with adequate planning, funding, and preliminary audience testing, whereas for living plant collections only time — often measured in decades — allows maturity for the trees to have flowers, vistas to be enclosed as intended, and the like. This dependence on time severely compromises quick "modernizing" of the living displays for contemporary educational mission objectives. Staff thus must not only work with existing physical layouts, but also find ways to optimize visitor engagement with minimal changes to the landscapes and panoramas. This apparent liability actually fits very nicely with many of the mission-based lessons taught about conservation of biodiversity and natural processes. It also emphasizes the need for skillful landscape design as changes made can take decades to fulfill, to develop, or to repair.

Traditionally, collections were planted (literally rooted) according to didactic or aesthetic objectives. For example, systematic collections focus on individual plants that are conceptually linked by an abstract system of classification. These collections are usually frozen in time and serve as a part of our cultural heritage. A larger scale of objects includes the well-established types of aesthetic gardens defined by horticultural and cultural themes such as rose gardens and Japanese gardens. In these cases, the object as the "garden space" and the thematically linked individual plants are subservient entities that have lesser meaning when taken out of context.

The restorative aspect of the mission is often couched in language of aesthetics, pleasure, and sanctuary. The landscape composition as well as the individual plants each contribute to the overall beauty of the collection, which itself is essential to the restorative value of the environment (see Folsom, 2000, for a discussion of the role of beauty in gardens). The submersive experience in the larger object (the landscape) is a critical element of the museum experience occurring at a botanic garden.

Kaplan (1995) defined restorative environments and experiences as those that reduce directed-attention fatigue. Fascination is an important component, but the additional elements of being away, being in a rich and coherent environment, and the presence of substantial compatibility of this environment with one's purposes and inclinations are also critical. Kaplan (1995) and Kaplan, Bardwell, and Slakter (1993) found that forests, gardens, and museums all create restorative environments for at least some of their visitors. Kaplan, Kaplan, and Ryan (1998, p. 149) listed four factors of importance for enjoyable engagement of people in new environments as would be typical of infrequent visitors (here restated as positives): understanding should be facilitated, opportunities for exploration available, restful and enjoyable experiences fostered, and participation welcome. Anecdotal evidence strongly suggests most visitors find the restorative qualities of gardens and arboreta to be primary reasons for most visits. Indeed, it may be that visitors have a clearer view of the larger objects than many of the focused staff.

It is not clear to what extent objects at different scales (a view, a small garden, a specific plant) contribute to the desired fascination and restorative qualities, although certain landscapes have been identified as being more innately appealing than others (Ryan, 1998). However, the success of informal educational experiences in gardens is likely dependent on the conditions for a concurrently restorative experience as well. As stated by Falk (in Eberbach,

1997), "people go to botanical gardens to learn. They may not state it explicitly, but they are learning environments . . . when their curiosity is piqued, when something resonates with them, they find it compelling" (p. 6).

Many modern arboreta and gardens are intentionally designed and presented in the context of an ecosystem with all the levels of complexity and change that implies. In parallel, the educational mission has expanded from education only about its own plants, location, and related cultural and natural history topics (the traditional focus of the programs) to global issues of conservation, biodiversity, and environmental stewardship. This is entering a realm that is often perceived as advocacy. Roberts (1997) stated:

> This point has been driven home recently, as museums come under growing fire for controversial exhibits, interpretations, and even collection practices. Both public and staff have become increasingly aware of the productive role museums play in crafting messages about what for years were assumed to be neutral, objective collections. This awareness has freed museum personnel to express a particular orientation or point of view in their messages. At the same time, it has opened those views to challenge, because fundamentally, differences over interpretation are differences of values and interests and cannot be resolved by appeal to traditional standards of truth. (p. 114)

However, preservation of land and conservation of natural areas is not a new concept. The founding of Nichols Arboretum in 1906 (then the University of Michigan Botanical Garden and Arboretum) came about because of the burgeoning borders of the little town of Ann Arbor. Thanks to the foresight of the founders, Nichols Arboretum lies as a green gem in now what is near the center of the city. In *Landscape Gardening* (Simonds, 1920/2000), noted landscape architect Ossian Cole Simonds decried the destruction of natural resources, of woodlands and fields, and calls for careful planning and stewardship of the land.

A current expression directly related to botanical institutions is the draft of Guidelines for Botanic Gardens in Education for Sustainability (Botanic Gardens Conservation International [BGCI], 2000):

> There has been increasing recognition, by people working in the field, that environmental education as it has been traditionally taught is not enough to stem the current environmental crisis. It needs to embrace a more holistic paradigm, one that incorporates the ecological, economic, social, cultural, and personal dimensions of sustainable development and their inter-relationships. (p. 2)

Some may question how this is incorporated in a museum setting, albeit it a living museum with formal and informal educational objectives.

The BGCI report summarized that environmental education and education for sustainability may be seen at three levels: (a) education about the environment and education about sustainability, (b) education through and in the environment and education for sustainability, and (c) education for the environment and sustainability. The first level is the most common for educational programs in the United States. Objects for informal education tend to be centered on this scale of issue. The second level has been a strength of some well-respected programs. Julyan (1998) stated, "At the Arnold Arboretum, education for children has been shaped by our strong belief that the most powerful learning happened out in the landscape..." (p. 18). This attitude is the foundation for their current Seasonal Investigator program. The third level can be the most controversial, although it is arguably the most important in terms of pending ecological crises.

Fien (1998) stated:

> Common to all our work, however, must be a vision for a more socially and environmentally sustainable future. We will all hold different perspectives on the philosophy, principles and approach to environmental education for sustainability and have different levels of opportunity and freedom to develop exciting new programmes and redevelop our old ones. We look forward to reading case studies of how botanic garden educators interpret the nature of environmental education for sustainability in a variety of different cultural settings; how the ideals of environmental education for sustainability are translated into practice; and how the tensions and issues which are encountered are overcome. (p. 17)

What objects are appropriate to convey these messages, and how do they link with any of the existing plants and larger objects already existing at gardens? At the Missouri Botanic Garden (unpublished data) a recent evaluation of visitors' reactions was conducted to understand how they engaged with the extensive educational displays that linked the tropical plants of the Climatron® with the larger ecological issues of biodiversity and ecosystems, both in the tropics and in North America. This educational exhibit was presented in a gallery separate from but adjacent to the Climatron®. An informal summary of part of the visitor study (personal communication, rephrased by the authors) is that visitors were familiar with such major issues as the existence and threats to the tropical rain forests. However, they were not markedly improved in their ability, even with the exhibits, to link to larger scientific issues such as biomes, or specific concepts that underlie ecosystem stability such as photosynthesis. The visually strong elements of destruction in the exhibit (including videos, models, and sounds of a bulldozer) were so negative that they interfered with the sense of pleasure and aesthetics that are part of the visitor's positive motivation for coming to the garden. Among the several types of exhibits, visitors enjoyed the terrarium and its plants and animals, and they wanted to know what specifically they could do to help preserve threatened environments. This bold experiment in informal education is to be lauded, learned from, and we hope, its best parts emulated as the study results are published.

EDUCATION FOR CONSERVATION
OF BIODIVERSITY THROUGH ARTS,
CULTURE AND STEWARDSHIP

The University of Michigan has been involved with several projects that address larger environmental and cultural issues using the established living collections at the university's Matthaei Botanical Gardens and Nichols Arboretum. Both units include mature collections as well as areas undergoing renovation or ecological restoration in context of the larger scale objects needed for the contemporary mission. In two of these projects, the Secret Spaces of Childhood and Out of Africa, the target audience includes both school groups and the families of these students, thus spanning the school-based and informal education perspectives.

Secret Spaces of Childhood

In November, 1998, a coalescence of ideas and energies were brought together by Dr. Elizabeth Goodenough at the Residential College of the University of Michigan. *Secret Spaces of Childhood:A Symposium on Children and Their Environments* (Goodenough, 1998) included two days of speakers discussing children's special places and places of refuge, a gallery exhibition of artists' remembered spaces, and a library exhibition of children's book illustrations. In addition, children's memories of secret spaces, an international exhibition, and an outdoor exhibition were displayed. Complementary to and based on the discussions in the academy, two child-centered events were held at the outdoor "living museum," University of Michigan's Nichols Arboretum. The Arboretum's intent was to engage children in valuing natural and designed landscapes through free exploration and serendipitous discovery of cultural presenters (Schultz, in press).

The purpose of the symposium was to highlight children's exploration of their environments around the world. It provided a forum for advocacy for children of war, preservation of natural areas, and the need for child-centered design in children's play spaces (Wood, 1999). The Arboretum's events were structured to model activities oriented to a child's perspective and immerse the child in experiencing nature through the arts.

The first Arboretum event was a presymposium visit to Nichols Arboretum by 50 children aged 4 to 13. The children gathered on an October afternoon, were coached by children's theater director, Sue Roe, to use their imagination, to explore, to look into holes and trees and find spaces to play or where other creatures might like to be. Each child was equipped with a disposable camera and a graduate student (to ensure their safe return) and set off on their adventures. Upon return, they headed off to their classrooms and homes to recreate their discoveries, memories, and impressions in crayon, paint, and pen. These became part of the library exhibition for the symposium.

The purpose of the visit was to document (by a documentary film crew for PBS and by the children themselves) children's free exploration in a safe but unknown outdoor environment. The children were asked to describe their explorations of the secret spaces in art and writing. The objects the children highlighted ranged from the very small scale (a leaf or a pebble) to the larger scale object of a hill bordered by trees that they gleefully had run down. The children also often placed themselves in the pictures they drew or story they wrote. It would be difficult to separate the enthusiasm for the object from the exhilaration of the free choice exploration. A short paragraph in *The Museum Experience* where Falk and Dierking (1992) referred to Birney's unpublished doctoral thesis explained:

> Museums have focused on trying to teach content, rather than exploring ways of maximizing the affective potential of visitors. A provocative conclusion developed by Birney was that "structured" field trips resulted in superior factual knowledge among participants, but that "unstructured" field trips yielded greater interest and enthusiasm for the subject that was presented, that is, more positive attitudes. Perhaps trying to find the balance between the structured and unstructured trip is the key. (p. 159)

In the second Arboretum event of Secret Spaces, on various hills and coves were located storytellers and theatrical scenes. The goal of Secret Spaces was to create a child-centered experience and to experience it through the eyes of a child — to allow children to be self-directed. Presenters included a Young Actor's Guild interactive production of building a Wendy House from *Peter Pan,* a scene from *A Midsummer Night's Dream* by the Emerson School, storyteller Elizabeth Elling as Beatrix Potter, Jean Gordon telling tales of a child and the moon, and David Hill with North American Indian tales and stories, each interpreting their environment through their art (Lankford, 1997).

Local schools, home schools, and day-care providers brought their charges to two entrances. Almost 1,000 children appeared in the Arboretum over a 2-hour period. Greeters at the entrances provided the caretakers with a purposefully oblique map and the instruction to allow the children to wander and explore, to "discover" the storytellers in a serendipitous way. They were encouraged to explore beyond the event and to not limit themselves to that presented to them. The children were engaged, curious, and very motivated by the instruction to explore. Groups were encouraged to be small, no more than 10 to 15 children in each. They wandered on a journey of discovery and, on sighting a storyteller, would hurry over to sit down and listen, watch, and participate. After about 5 to 10 minutes, the group would get up and continue their exploration.

Upon exiting, the children were excited, talking not so much about what the presenters did or the story they told but whether they had found all of them. They spoke about a certain tree, the river, or a rock they found (exploration and discovery of objects). The act of building the Wendy House using branches and leaves especially engaged them by participating in a familiar story. But the fascination they showed when watching *A Midsummer Night's Dream* or listening to Beatrix Potter's explanation of small things demonstrated the development of a broader perspective. "A teacher who can arouse a feeling for one single good action, for one single good poem, accomplishes more than he who fills our memory with rows on rows of natural objects classified with name & form" is an observation by Goethe (1963) as valid today as then. Through such creative interpretation of objects can arboreta and botanic gardens, large or small, engender a deeper appreciation of the environment (Harms & Lettow, 1995).

Just as arboreta are filled with nested objects, "Secret Spaces of Childhood" had layers of concepts explored. In Goodenough (2000a, 2000b), the author addresses the idealized experience for these children in the Arboretum in the broader context of advocacy for children around the world; children separated by wealth, war, violence, or poverty from the natural world. She asks, "As vicarious pursuits, virtual pets and synthetic playgrounds take over, shouldn't we worry that a world where children have minimal engagement with animals and plants might also be threatening to nature itself?" (Goodenough, 2000b, p. 11). Focusing on the child and his or her environment, Goodenough's works demonstrate the urgency for environmental education and stewardship, and investing now in our future.

Out of Africa

A novel educational and outreach program under development at the University of Michigan Matthaei Botanical Gardens is Out of Africa (see Michener & Klatt, 1999). This program was conceived by volunteers who realized that a substantial percentage of the conservatory collections are plants from Africa that are of importance to contemporary African American culture, or that played significant roles in the African American experience. Furthermore, appropriate interpretation might best be done through art, drama, music, beverages, food, and storytelling, especially if visitors became participants. Now in its third year of experimentation with staff from the African American Cultural and Historical Museum of Washtenaw County, the Ypsilanti public schools, and the University of Michigan College of Engineering, the program has included an array of activities to integrate peoples, plants, and culture. Each year the program takes place during February, Black History Month.

In all cases where a specific plant is the object, the intent is to encourage the visitor to place the plant in a larger context. Diverse parts of the larger context are already familiar to the visitor in many cases. Plants so interpreted have included yams, cotton, peanuts, papyrus, coffee, spices, and medicinal herbs. Additional plants are grown and displayed during the month-long tour period — these relate specifically to plants needed by the integrative curriculum for 3rd to 5th grade for the newly promulgated state educational standards. These plants are related to in-school activities but are interpreted on-site for all visitors. Plants include those used in natural dyes, for textiles (specifically quilts), and in traditional medicines.

The organizing theme for this year is the Underground Railroad, as this county in Michigan was historically important in that activity. A range of plants and the landscape at the Gardens can be related to enslavement, survival in escape, and the cultural heritage of southeastern Michigan and adjacent Ontario. In addition, there are thematic and historical links to local African American engineers of the late 19th and early 20th centuries, the city of Ypsilanti, the rise of the automotive industry, changes in land use, and the like. The Matthaei Botanical Gardens is within a few miles of central Ypsilanti, yet possesses never-clear-cut woodland remnants, a settlement period farm with extensive former pastures, intact glacial landforms (a rarity in metro Detroit), extensive wetlands, restored prairie fragment, and several miles of nature trails, as well as traditional display gardens and the Conservatory. These objects, at scales from landscape to peanut fruit, are core elements in environmental and cultural education related to the nature of the issue being addressed.

This year we are trying this multilayered, object-rich approach with a Jubilee Night with Ardis Renaissance Academy (an elementary school in the Ypsilanti school district). The Jubilee Night culminates a series of class-related projects coordinated through the participating teachers in all the core curricular domains. All the 3rd, 4th, and 5th grade students and their families are invited to participate, and the school district is providing the bus transportation. At the Gardens the students will present and explain their models of African American inventions and their naturally dyed quilt blocks and their symbolic meaning, stage a dramatization in the Garden's auditorium of the story of an escaped young healer who fled slavery with her medicines via Michigan, and explain a collaborative art project that is a time-line of African American history that will be on public display all along the main aisle of the tropical conservatory. The conservatory's display areas feature the plants that are key to these thematic elements for all visitors.

A significant aspect of the project's appeal to the school and its community is the activities and objects. When staged in the Garden's conservatory, these activities are in a larger context rather than just a public building. The canonical cultural objects (models, quilt blocks) are evidently perceived already as being related to larger contexts, both of Michigan's history and the diverse climates of Africa as represented in the conservatory. Not to be underestimated in the educational process is the novelty of the conservatory for most participants, and its welcome sanctuary from the depths of a Michigan winter.

The mission-driven need for this type of informal to formal educational program has already impacted the "canonical" objects in the living collections. For example, perennial cotton is grown on permanent display in the Mediterranean section of the conservatory because it was grown in ancient Egypt. This is grown in an important location, although no one would ever mistake the plant as an ornamental shrub, even though the plants bloom and boll several times a year. Rather than focus on a significant permanent interpretive device for the cotton plant itself, the interpretive perspective is placed in reverse. Which plants are needed to interpret the linkage of peoples, plants, and cultures? Then, which plants need be grown for periodic public interpretation and discussion of a related product — in this case, cotton cloth in conjunction with Out of Africa. Inasmuch as cotton was the major basis for 19th-century American slavery, the textiles in the auditorium displays and interpretive program have been African kente cloth (year 1), contemporary quilts, with personal meaning and stories, made by local African American women (year 2), and quilt blocks being created and dyed with natural dyes by the entire grade of one school participating in Out of Africa (year 3).

We find that having a cultural context as an introduction to the plants and landscapes appeals to a different audience than a plant-centered focus. We apply this perspective elsewhere in the Gardens by working in a larger ecological or cultural context to create large-scale objects as restored or ecologically appropriate habitats. These are interpreted though perspectives as Native American ethnobotany, the presence and concepts of native and exotic species, and garden areas that are being redone as physical manifestations of abstract ideas. The larger, noncanonical object in all cases is as important, if not more so, than the individual plants.

The effectiveness of Secret Spaces of Childhood and Out of Africa were not measured other than by anecdotal means. How many lives have they changed? Did children learn something about Africa, cotton, and the Underground Railroad? Did exploring the Arboretum affect the perspective of the child, his or her values? Did experiencing storytellers and theater in the Arboretum engage and intrigue, provide information — do the children recall the stories, do they know more about Shakespeare? And in the larger scope, did the Secret Spaces of Childhood Symposium effect change, give information and knowledge to participants in advocacy for children in the international arena? In our literature survey, we found very little analysis of the effectiveness of object-centered learning specifically in botanic gardens or arboreta. Our conversation with several botanic garden education officers found they were frequently too understaffed, too underfunded, and too busy creating and implementing programmatic elements to incorporate a device for measuring the effectiveness of the program. If they had an in-house assessment, they had not yet published the results. There are more general studies on environmental education that are not specific to arboreta and gardens but give legitimacy to many programs found there. Yet appropriate evaluation is critical to demonstrating which program components are effective, even in the short term, in order to focus the programs on the parts that best serve their objectives. The BGCI (2000) report stated: "Evaluation is an integral part of any education programme and critical to the success of EfS (Education for Sustainability)" (p. 15).

Evaluation can take several forms. Heininger and Walter (1998) commented on an article about designing exhibits that are compatible to the goals for the audience. They wrote:

> We feel strongly that the need to assess (not the same thing as to measure) and to understand these factors is central to museums' work. One of the negative impacts of our increasing educational ambitions is that sometimes we act as if the validity of our learning environments is solely what people learn from our site. We should know better. Much of the educational value of museums is our ability to encourage learning as a way of life, to provide experiences that help people grow their delight, satisfaction and skill in making use of the museum of the world. (p. 18)

Orr (1994) suggested that environmental education should not be simply measured for knowledge base but for earth stewardship, asking the education programs to modify behavior. Botanic gardens and arboreta should become recognized by the academy, the general public, and by the gardens themselves as not only resources of technical information but also a place for leading the community in conservation and stewardship efforts. This role is called out by Botanic Garden Conservation International, the American Association of Botanical Gardens and Arboreta, and the Center for Plant Conservation at the World Botanical Garden Congress 2000. We anticipate that more focus and support will be given to the design, implementation, and analysis of effective programming.

University botanic gardens and arboreta are uniquely positioned to effect change in both encouraging good stewardship of the land and experimenting in techniques of conservation. The technical and ecological expertise found on college campuses should and can be used to help lead community and campus efforts in educating for sustainability and stewarding the land (Varley, 1973).

VOLUNTEER STEWARDSHIP

About 15 years ago Professor Robert Grese began a prairie restoration project as part of his research. Using volunteers to help burn, remove invasive plants, inventory changes, and manage the natural area, the prairie has become an important "object" in the larger landscape of the Arboretum. It could be interpreted for plant inventory, the prairie landscape, ecosystem, cultural history, and for the stewardship process (Elling, 1993).

Integral to the program goals at Nichols Arboretum are education for sustainability and conservation of biodiversity. Volunteer stewardship has become an essential ingredient in the physical management of the Arboretum's woodlands, prairie, and much of the formal collections. The stewardship program also receives a major part of the education efforts at the Arboretum. Education in the volunteer stewardship program includes the acquisition of knowledge about the plants, ecosystem, and global issues of conservation of biodiversity, and the skills and techniques needed for ecological restoration. The objects involved are the plants, the land, and the larger ecosystem and also the tools, from the loppers to the chainsaw to the tractor. The objects in this program may be large, but the objective is even larger. The expectation is not only will the restoration project within the Arboretum be successful, but also the participants will carry the behavior through the garden gate and apply their skills and knowledge in the larger community.

Volunteer stewardship programs at Nichols Arboretum include monthly workdays, Volunteers Involved Every Week, and university classes in sustainability. These programs provide service learning opportunities and special service days for sororities, fraternities and other organizations. Monthly workdays invite the community, local businesses, and high school and university students to spend a morning removing buckthorn, honeysuckle, and other invasive species from the natural areas of the Arboretum. Volunteers Involved Every Week (VIEW), a program supported by the University of Michigan's Ginsberg Center (Pickrel & Chau, 2001), encourages regular participation in a community service activity. These were principally ecological restoration activities at the Arboretum. And finally, as part of a university class, volunteer work on an eroded path provided the opportunity to study sustainability (Hackney, Bari, Vollherbst, Schillinger, & Hansen, 2000).

The questions we have as educators are: Is learning occurring during the restoration work? If so, what? Asking the Orr question, has that modified their behavior outside of the arboretum or botanic garden stewardship program? But there is a more basic question: Why do volunteers volunteer? Because volunteers are essential to the successful ecological restoration efforts across the country, we need to understand what motivates volunteers to do physical labor when there are so many other demands on their time.

Anecdotal evidence suggests that one of the major reasons volunteers volunteer is the opportunity to learn new things. Themes were identified in restoration newsletters in a newsletter study (Schroeder, 2000) as to why people choose to volunteer. These included the "Purpose of the Volunteer's Work — preserve, protect, restore biodiversity," "The Current State of Nature," "The Social Dimensions of Restoration," and others. In the category of "Personal Reward," learning and sharing knowledge had comments such as, "We can learn from this diversity, too, and use it to educate children as we take them on tours ..." In a study on the psychological benefits of volunteering (Grese, Kaplan, Ryan, & Buxton, 2000), "learning new skills" is considered part of "exploration," as are "learning new things," "doing something fascinating," "opportunity to try something new," and "learning specific plants and animals." Among the participants surveyed, exploration was ranked second to "helping the environment" in the benefits from volunteering, above spirituality and personal and social benefits. Another work (Ryan, Kaplay, & Grese, in press) suggests including exploration and learning components in stewardship programs to be critical in predicting the continued commitment of volunteers.

For those community volunteers who identified learning as a motivation and benefit for participating in volunteer stewardship activities, learning occurs. However, in a recent study on the role of ecological restoration work in university environmental education (Bowler, Florian, & Hartig, 1999), restoration work did not influence environmental knowledge but positively affected ecological behavior. The study involved three biology classes, two of which did no restoration work. The level of environmental knowledge across the three classes was high and did not vary with the involvement in physical ecological restoration work. They did not measure the skills and techniques involved in restoration work, or perhaps the specific knowledge associated with the hands on activity. This, we argue, is an essential part of understanding ecological restoration.

Bowler, Kaiser, and Hartig (1999) did point out that "ecological restoration work affects students' intentions to behave ecologically to the point that the intentions become manifest in ecological behavior" (p. 25). Both the VIEW group and the sustainability class expressed this affect on their intentions at Nichols Arboretum. The physical connection with the objects and the responsibility to care for them (the landscape, the ecosystem), prepared the participants to carry their newly acquired knowledge and skills through the garden gates.

SUMMARY

Object-centered informal education in arboreta and botanic gardens appears to be effective when presented in a rich and varied environment. Unlike traditional museums, attention is not focused on relatively few items in any given space. The objects (landscapes to flowers) in botanic gardens seem to be most engaging to visitors when there is either a selection to choose from, or a pre-existing cultural framework to provide initial meaning. In continued differentiation from the traditional museum, the visitor in an arboretum or garden is continually immersed as a participant in the visually rich landscape, not a passer-by moving from discrete object to discrete object. An important issue of object-centered informal education at arboreta and botanic gardens is to present a range of experiences and objects at various scales and engage visitors to become involved with the larger environmental and cultural issues as they re-enter society beyond the garden gate. This is a fundamental test of the effectiveness of the contemporary educational mission.

ACKNOWLEDGMENTS

We thank Beth Covitt, Liz Elling, and Bob Grese for their suggestions of references and studies. We also thank Missouri Botanical Gardens for information on their Climatron® exhibit.

REFERENCES

Botanic Gardens Conservation International. (2000). *Guidelines for Botanic Gardens in Education for Sustainability* (Draft). UK: Kew.

Bowler, P.A., Kaiser, F.G., & Hartig, T. (1999). A role for ecological restoration work in university environmental education. *The Journal of Environmental Education, 30*(4), 19–26.

Csikszentmihalyi, M., & Robinson, R. E (1990). *The art of seeing. An interpretation of the aesthetic experience.* Los Angeles: Getty Trust Publications.

Eberbach, C. (1997). John Falk: No Empty Vessels. Learning in Museums. *Public Garden, 12*(1), 6–10.

Elling, E. (1993). *An environmental education and communication plan for Nichols Arboretum.* Unpublished thesis, University of Michigan, Ann Arbor.

Falk, J. H., & Dierking, L. D. (1992). *The museum experience.* Washington, DC: Whalesback.

Fien, J. (1998). Education for sustainability: some questions for reflection. *Roots, 17,* 20–24.

Folsom, J. P. (2000). The terms of beauty. *Public Garden, 15*(2), 3–6.

Goethe, J. W. (1963). *Elective Affinities.* (E. Mayer & L. Bogan, Trans.). Chicago: H. Regnery.

Goodenough, E. (1998). Secret spaces of childhood: A symposium on children and their environments. *Program Notes.* Residential College, University of Michigan.

Goodenough, E. (Ed.). (2000a). Secret spaces of childhood I, II. *Michigan Quarterly Review.* Special publication. Ann Arbor, MI: University of Michigan.

Goodenough, E. (2000b). Time and space for children. *Michigan Today.* Ann Arbor, MI: University of Michigan.

Grese, R. E., Kaplan, R., Ryan, R. L., & Buxton J. (2000). Psychological benefits of volunteering in stewardship programs. In P. H. Gobster & R. B. Hill (Eds.), *Restoring nature, perspectives from the social sciences and humanities* (pp. 265–280). Washington, DC: Island Press.

Hackney, B., Bair D., Vollherbst, K., Schillinger, G., & Hansen, K. (2000). *A semester in the Arb.* Unpublished document, University of Michigan, Ann Arbor.

Harms, J. M., & Lettow, L. J. (1995). Supporting environmental education through poetry. *Journal of Youth Services in Libraries, 8*(2), 167–171.

Heininger M. L., & Walter, G. (1998). Compatible goals and continuing questions: a history museum response. *Journal of Museum Education, 23*(1), 18–19.

Julyan, C. L. (1998). Nature study moves into the 21st century. *Arnoldia, 158*(3), 18–24.

Kaplan, S. (1995). The urban forest as a source of psychological well being. In G. A. Bradley (Ed.), *Urban forest landscapes: integrating multidisciplinary perspectives* (100-108). Seattle: University of Washington Press.

Kaplan, S., Bardwell, L. V., & Slakter, D. B. (1993). The museum as a restorative environment. *Environment and Behavior, 25*(6), 725-742.

Kaplan, R., Kaplan, S., & Ryan R. L. (1998). *With people in mind. Design and management of everyday nature.* Washington, DC: Island Press.

Lankford, E. L. (1997). Ecological stewardship in art education. *Art Education, 50*(6), 47-53.

Michener, D. C., & Klatt, B. (1999). Peoples, plants, and cultures at the University of Michigan Matthaei Botanical Gardens. *Public Garden, 4*(2), 27-30.

Orr, D. W. (1994). Teach kids wisdom about the earth. *Utne Reader,* 87-90.

Pickrel, A., & Chau, L. (2001). A new view of the Arb. *TreeLine, 12,* 1.

Roberts, L. C. (1997). *From knowledge to narrative. Educators and the changing museum.* Washington, DC: Smithsonian Press.

Ryan, R. L. (1998). *Attachment to urban natural areas: effects of environmental experience.* Ph.D. dissertation, University of Michigan, Ann Arbor.

Ryan, R. L., Kaplan, R., & Grese, R. E. (in press). Predicting volunteer commitment in environmental stewardship programs. *Journal of Environmental Planning and Management.*

Schroeder, H. W. (2000). The restorative experience: volunteers' motives, values, and concepts of nature. In P. H. Gobster & R. B. Hill (Eds.), *Restoring nature, perspectives from the social sciences and humanities* (pp. 247-264). Washington, DC: Island Press.

Schultz, I. (in press). Education for biodiversity through arts and culture. In B. Butler & C. Pastore (Eds.), *Reaching Out.* Kennett Square, PA: AABGA.

Simonds, O. C. (2000). *Landscape gardening.* Amherst, MA: University of Massachusetts Press. (Original work published 1920)

Varley, C. R. (1973). The business officer as campus environmentalist. *NACUBO Studies in Management, 3*(4), 1-10.

Whitman, W. (1973). There was a child went forth. In S. Bradley & H. W. Blodgett (Eds.), *Leaves of Grass. Authoritative Texts* (p. 364). New York: W. W. Norton & Co.

Wood, B. (1999). *Secret spaces of childhood* [video documentary]. Ann Arbor, MI: Wood Productions.

CHAPTER SEVEN

Epistemological Issues about Objects

James V. Wertsch
Washington University, St. Louis

One of the major problems facing museum professionals today is evaluation, especially evaluation of museums' impact on visitors. One encounters many complexities when considering this issue, but none is more unsettling than a basic quandary that underlies the whole project. On the one hand, we are called upon to assess the impact that museums have on visitors. Increasing claims that museums play an important educational role have served to up the ante on this issue dramatically. On the other hand, precisely what it is that we should be evaluating remains unclear. Should visitors be acquiring new information? Should they be developing new areas of curiosity — "opening a new file folder in their brain" (Valenta, personal communication, 1997)? Should visitors be engaging in some sort of identity project? Or is there something else they should take away from a museum visit?

Lack of clarity on this issue can do more than sow confusion. When pressed to identify demonstrable educational results, for example, evaluators sometimes use off-the-shelf technology designed to assess outcomes of formal instruction, and in all too many cases the result is that museums are found not to be as good or as efficient at producing learning as instruction in standard school settings. Such findings suggest that students would be better off spending an additional hour or two in formal instruction than an entire day at a museum.

Of course this flies in the face of all sorts of beliefs and evidence about the importance of museums in modern life, and it leaves unanswered the question

113

of how to assess the impact that museums have on their visitors. More fundamentally, it challenges us to clarify just what it is that museums are *supposed*
to do even before we try to assess whether they are successful in doing it. All
too often there is a tendency to put the cart before the horse in this regard
by letting measurement instruments define what the desired outcomes of a
museum visit are instead of vice versa.

It is precisely on these issues that the chapters in this section provide some
useful insights. The authors raise important questions about what outcomes
we should seek from museum visits and what sort of research would allow us
to understand and enhance these outcomes. The sorts of inquiry we see here
also raise basic questions about the nature and development of motivation,
learning, and identity in children. Among other things, the chapters suggest
that some of our ideas may be more limited than we might otherwise suspect
because these ideas have been based largely on research in a single sociocultural setting, namely formal schooling.

In their chapter Paris and Hapgood (chap. 3, this volume) raise this point by
arguing that what constitutes learning may not be as apparent as is assumed
when we focus on the single institutional context of formal instruction. And
when it comes to motivation, these authors suggest that the problem may
be even worse, given that "contemporary theories of children's motivation are
almost entirely based on achievement strivings and failure avoidance because
they emanate from research in schools . . . and may not generalize much beyond them." Such comments suggest that we should be very cautious about
employing off-the-shelf ideas and assessment procedures when trying to understand learning and motivation in museums and other informal learning
environments.

These points by Paris and Hapgood provide a reminder that the empirical
phenomena we examine in a particular sociocultural setting can shape — and
limit — theoretical frameworks that claim to have broader applicability. Instead of developing general theoretical claims and then applying them to one
or another empirical setting, the progression is often the reverse, and this may
be at work in the case of studies of learning in museums. In this particular
instance the point is that empirical findings from a particular sociocultural
setting, namely formal instruction, have given rise to a set of claims that may
not be relevant to other contexts.

An important key to understanding what separates the museum as a sociocultural setting from formal instruction — and hence the degree that findings
from the latter apply to the former — can be found in the analysis of the
object provided in the chapter by Evans, Mull, and Poling (chap. 4, this volume). They remind us that objects, especially "authentic" objects, lie at the
core of many museums' mission. This focus on the collection, preservation,
and display of objects often competes with education as the focus of muse-

ums' institutional agenda, and it is one of the factors that differentiates them from schools as sociocultural settings for learning.

Moreover, Evans, Mull, and Poling point out that the processes at work here do not remain unchanged over time. Instead, the authors emphasize the need to introduce a historical dimension to the discussion by reviewing the shift from an "object-based epistemology," which was dominant in late 19th-century museums, to an "object-based discourse," which predominates today.

> In an object-based epistemology the focus was on the clear presentation of unembellished facts regarding the natural history and taxonomy of the subject. In this case, the perspective of the visitor was virtually ignored. An object-based discourse, on the other hand, centers on the participation of the object in the cultural or lived history of the visitor. In the latter case . . . instead of bare facts, we maintain that there is an emphasis on explanation, which could be that of the expert, or that of the visitor, or both . . .

Drawing on Conn (1998), Evans, Mull, and Poling characterize the shift from an object-based epistemology to an object-based discourse as a move away from ignoring the perspective of the visitor toward accepting and harnessing it. Instead of assuming that objects somehow tell their own story or speak for themselves, the voice and active interpretive efforts of visitors come to play a central role. This should not, however, be taken to suggest that sole authority for interpreting an object or exhibit has switched over to the museum visitor. Instead of assuming that *either* the museum *or* the visitor has sole interpretive powers, the argument is that "there is no single authentic voice: the object, the presentation, the visitor, even the friends and family accompanying the visitor, jointly participate in an act of meaning."

This line of reasoning is consistent with what Dierking (chap. 1, this volume) argues in her chapter about "The Role of Context in Children's Learning from Objects and Experiences." Echoing other authors in this volume she argues against a "transmission-absorption model," wishing to replace it with a view that recognizes "the highly interactive learning that results from . . . experiences and encounters with objects." This is part of the "Contextual Model of Learning" that Dierking and her colleagues (Falk & Dierking, 2000) have been developing over the past several years.

Included in the research plan that Dierking envisions as growing out of this model is the need to investigate "children engaged in authentic activities, so that their learning is studied in 'real' context." The call for conducting studies of "real" contexts here reflects more than a desire to avoid the limitations of laboratory research. It also reflects a desire to recognize the unique sociocultural setting of a museum visit and to differentiate it from what characterizes formal instruction in schools.

This is a point that has been taken up by Michener and Schultz in their chapter (chap. 6, this volume). In their analysis of arboreta and botanic gardens, they stress the need to consider "environmental and cultural awareness" as well as more traditional learning outcomes. While recognizing that "over time the educational mission of public gardens has expanded," they refuse to reduce the notion of education to learning. Indeed, they note that in some cases visits to arboreta may have no measurable impact in this regard. Instead, they emphasize that the interesting and lasting outcomes of such visits should be conceptualized in terms of ecological awareness, stewardship, and future behavior.

Like Paris and Hapgood, Dierking, and others, then, Michener and Schultz suggest that we must resist the temptation to rely too heavily on ideas and assessment techniques developed for formal learning environments when discussing informal learning environments such as museums and arboreta. Furthermore, Dierking provides an analytic approach for discussing these issues in a general way by considering how sociocultural, personal, and physical contexts operate in a coordinated fashion over time.

Other chapters in this section provide further insight into the sort of thing that Dierking might have in mind when talking about "authentic activities" and "real contexts." Building on a notion of sociocultural research that overlaps with that of Dierking, for example, Rowe emphasizes that the contexts in which museum visitors operate are not static, pre-existing configurations. Rather, they are constantly changing and are actively constructed and transformed by those participating in them. Again, however, this does not mean that museum visitors are viewed as being unhindered in the interpretation they can make of an object. Instead, Rowe argues that museum exhibits act both to "afford" and "constrain" certain interpretations. The dynamics of this process mean that even though museum visitors may not use or interpret objects in the way that curators or exhibit designers had intended, their activities are nonetheless fundamentally shaped by the setting.

Rowe (chap. 2, this volume) adds an important element to this line of reasoning by noting that in many cases museum objects and exhibits are not designed solely — or perhaps even primarily — for the purpose of enhancing learning. That is, the affordances and constraints presented by exhibits may stem from forces other than the desire to optimize learning. From this perspective exhibits often reflect a host of competing demands. For example, Roberts (1997) has noted that the development of a museum exhibit typically is a product of extended negotiations among many parties, including exhibit designers, collection managers, educators, and museum sponsors. And an underlying assumption for all these parties is that a high priority for any exhibit is to attract as many visitors as possible.

This last desideratum is a core consideration when trying to understand what distinguishes museums from schools. Unlike schools, museums do not have a captive audience, and as a result, the entire nature of the sociocultural setting these institutions provide differs from that characteristic of formal instruction. This gives rise to all sorts of criticisms about the "Disneyfication" of museums, criticisms that in some cases are undoubtedly well deserved. However, criticizing museums across the board for doing what it takes to attract visitors — sometimes at the expense of learning — is to miss the fact that they *must* provide a qualitatively different sociocultural setting from that found in schools.

Key to understanding this difference is an issue that is not discussed at great length in these chapters but nonetheless underlies much of what they cover, namely the issue of *authority.* Under this topic I have in mind issues of who has the power to define what the setting is and what the participants are required to do in it. Dierking touches on this issue when she writes of "authentic activities," and Rowe addresses it when he writes of "interanimation of visitor and museum interpretations, activities, and voices [that open] access to authoritative positions from which to speak."

It is also reflected in one way or another in what most of the other authors in this section discuss. For example, in her discussion of "when an object is digital" Frost (chap. 5, this volume) notes that unlike the case of standard formal instructional settings "a major force in the dynamic of digital communities results from the ability of users to become creators as well as consumers of information objects." In particular, she notes that the digital age introduces the need for kinds of critical evaluation of information that are not encouraged when sources such as teachers and textbooks are taken to be authoritative.

> Hyperlinking in today's Internet environment takes on additional dimensions in that it allows the user to determine and create links, thus resulting in connections which indexers and catalogers may never have dreamed of. In this way, the users of the site are no longer relying solely on the links established by traditional and relatively static knowledge structures such as the Dewey Decimal Classification.

Like Rowe, then, Frost suggests that the objects in informal learning environments involve a level of active engagement and definition not found in more standard educational contexts. And this inevitably involves a shift in power and authority from the producer of objects and texts to their consumers. Of particular interest in Frost's analysis is the suggestion that in addition to new flexibility and creativity, these new settings involve taking on new forms of *responsibility.* In the case of digital objects, for instance, the users of these objects must be accountable for assessing their legitimacy, something that is not encouraged in formal instructional settings.

Taken together, the chapters in this section emphasize the need to distinguish between formal instruction and museums as sociocultural settings. This is a point that needs emphasis because the constant focus on education in today's museum mission statements makes it all too easy to slip into the assumption that they are like schools and hence can be evaluated in similar ways. Both museums and schools are characterized by multiple, competing goals, but the hierarchical organization of these goals in the two cases differs in some striking ways. In particular, because museums do not have a captive audience and because they are organized around objects, their educational objectives are often quite different from those found in schools.

In short, what these chapters suggest is that the core mission of museums may not be education, at least education as understood in the sociocultural setting of formal instruction, and this has many implications for how we go about formulating research questions. As Rowe points out, figures such as Dewey have argued for decades that museums may serve as a model for what schools *should* be like, but in my view a major problem in our current discussion has been *not* recognizing the fundamental difference between the two settings. It has been the failure to do this that has led to some of the unfortunate outcomes I noted at the beginning of my comments, and it is a failure we must address if we are going to make progress in understanding what museums do and how we can assess whether they are successful at it.

ACKNOWLEDGMENT

The writing of this chapter was assisted by a grant from the Spencer Foundation. The statements made and the views expressed are solely the responsibility of the author.

REFERENCES

Conn, S. (1998). *Museums and American intellectual life, 1876–1926.* Chicago: University of Chicago Press.

Falk, J. H., & Dierking, L. D. (2000). *Learning from museums: Visitor experiences and the making of meaning.* Walnut Creek, CA: AltiMira Press.

Roberts, L. (1997). *From knowledge to narrative: Educators and the changing museum.* Washington, DC: Smithsonian Press.

PART II

Discipline-Based Explorations of Objects

CHAPTER EIGHT

Learning With, Through, and About Art: The Role of Social Interactions

Barbara Piscitelli
Katrina Weier
Queensland University of Technology, Australia

Young children respond distinctively and enthusiastically to art objects when given appropriate opportunities. Whereas traditional museum visitors may observe, discuss, or sketch alone or with friends, young children expand the repertoire of visitor behaviors to include playing, singing, dancing, and acting. Because of their unusual responses to works of art, young children's visits to art museums have provoked interest among their teachers, parents, museum staff, and the general visitor. As part of new policy and funding initiatives focusing on audience development and lifelong learning, art museums have enacted a number of innovative interactive exhibitions and programs to attract, retain, and nurture young visitors. In Australia, and around the world, the visiting public has responded very positively to interactive exhibitions and programs with high attendance numbers and public acclaim. Both children and adults show deep engagement in interactive innovations in art such as increased capacity to understand the nature of human experience, an ability to adapt to others' ways of thinking, the willingness to solve problems, use of nonverbal communication, and the ability to communicate ideas and feelings in a variety of modes (Australia Council for the Arts, 2000; Consortium of National Arts Education Associations, 1994).

Clearly, young children find museums interesting and happy places, but why? What are the key factors? In this chapter, we identify features of high quality informal learning experiences for young children in art museums. Documentation and analysis of children's experiences at a recent interactive exhibition in Australia, "The Art of Eric Carle," led to the development of a set of standards describing conditions supporting high quality experiences for young children in museums and other informal learning settings (Weier, 2000). The conditions list includes three areas regarded as important for children's involvement and learning in art museums: the physical environment, the program, and the social milieu (see Appendix). Each of these aspects is discussed, with particular emphasis given to the social interactions that enhance young children's understanding of art objects.

LEARNING THEORIES AND MUSEUM PRACTICES

Hein and Alexander (1998) defined museums as "places of learning" with a wide range of visitors who have diverse needs, interests, and desires. Consequently, museums must consider carefully their relationships with visitors. Visitors may be conceptualized as learners, and museums thus have a role in promoting learner-centered goals and educational services. Doering (1999) suggested that the museum's primary responsibility is to be accountable to the visitor. She suggested that museums must view visitors as "clients," with needs and expectations that the institution is obligated to understand and meet. Art museums in particular have an important role in providing visitors access to authentic art objects and the stories that are reflected in these. Children's capacity to make sense of the museum and its objects may be understood in various ways through different theoretical perspectives. Broadly categorized, the main educational theories ascribed to learning in museums are sociocultural, cognitive, aesthetic, and motivational theories.

Sociocultural learning theories examine meaning-making events that occur as visitors interact with tools, signs, symbols, activities, and people in the context of the museum and its exhibits (Schauble, Leinhardt, & Martin, 1997). This orientation focuses not on the content of the visitor's knowledge, but on the processes of their learning, particularly the ways in which they interact with each other and with objects (Allen, 1997). Learning in the art museum can be viewed as a kind of "situated learning" (Lave & Wenger, 1991) in which children gain an understanding of the skills and techniques of artists. As children view authentic artworks, they make connections between their own ideas, feelings, and life experiences and those of artists who created the works. Collaboration between children and adults assists children to develop artistic and aesthetic concepts, and to move beyond intuitive responses as they make meaning from objects.

Children employ a number of cognitive processes as they develop their facility with art. Cognitive learning theories encompass the belief that knowledge is acquired through interaction with objects and people (Hein, 1995;

Jacob, 1992; Jeffery-Clay, 1998). Children's competence with artistic processes such as discovery, perception, communication, skill use, analysis, and critique is dependent on an appropriate learning environment in which carefully selected artistic resources are supplied and supportive guidance from adults provided (Wright, 1994).

Aesthetic theories focus on the affective, emotional, spiritual, creative, and pleasurable experiences and activities of learners (Housen, 1992; Kindler, 1997; Parsons, 1987). This orientation to learning in museums focuses on judgments about the noncognitive dimensions examining personal responses to art objects with emotions such as joy, disgust, shock, and delight. For young children, responses are characteristically multisensory and imaginative. Through aesthetic awareness, children perceive certain images, similes, metaphors, and other imaginative expressions, and reflect on the meaning of these.

Young visitors to museums have various difficulties connecting with art and making meaning from their experiences. Vallance (1995) questioned the traditional practice of art museums in the way they deliberately portray objects in the absence of context and advocated a need to provide connections with visitors' prior knowledge to make the overall experience meaningful and motivating. Motivational theories are used by various researchers (e.g., Csikszentmihalyi & Hermanson, 1995; Paris, 1997) to indicate that visitors use a variety of processes to give direction and personal relevance to their learning in a museum setting. Paris (1997) and Perry (1993) noted that motivators for learning in museums include opportunities for construction of personal meaning, option to make choices, willingness to accept challenges, capacity to take control of own learning, as well as opportunity to work in collaboration with others and positive consequences (benefits) for action.

Within art museums, the potential for learning with, through, and about objects has been the topic of sustained debate over the 20th century, with differing views about how the museum can best meet the priorities of both the visitor and the discipline. Traditionally, museums exhibited art by hanging or installing exhibits in galleries where visitors encountered the authentic object for observation and reflection. Conventionally, art museums hang art in a particular manner to assist interpretation in an historical sense. Thus, it is possible to enter art museums around the world and trace the story of art's history by moving through various galleries where the art of different periods and movements hang alongside one another. Museums now play a special role in educating a new generation about cultural and artistic life. A mixture of interactive, collaborative, and reflective learning opportunities provides a rich array of experiences to educate, engage, and entertain young (and old) visitors. There are diverse opinions about the relative merits of traditional static exhibitions versus contemporary interactive installations. In recent years, museums have developed innovative ways to honor tradition and invite change in exhibiting art objects. Old elitist ideas are being challenged by new museum practices, which forge successful links between young visitors and art through trans-situational and personally meaningful learning opportunities. Three important innovations are central to these practices: novel exhibition designs, child-centered programs, and responsive guides (Weier, 2000). These innovations are encompassed within broader physical environment, program, and social milieu factors that museums present to visitors.

Physical Environment

Both spatial arrangement and aesthetics are important considerations in creating a setting that is welcoming, attractive, nonthreatening, and predictable for young children, while also allowing for discovery experiences (Pearce, 1998; Piscitelli, McArdle, & Weier, 1999). Such a setting attracts desired behaviors, facilitates positive interactions, and supports active, playful involvement in learning experiences. Ideal spatial organization is characterized by clearly defined learning areas, adequate separation of active and passive activities, well-defined pathways between areas, and spaces to enable individual, small, or large group participation (Falk & Dierking, 1992; McCrea & Piscitelli, 1991; Montagu, Hansen, Gurian, Kamien, & Robinson, 1987). These factors help minimize stimulation such as noise, traffic, and crowds within a given area.

Although observation and interpretation of static exhibits are vital parts of young children's learning in art museums, particularly traditional venues, an interactive component is considered highly desirable. *Interactive* is a term used to imply first-hand experience combined with opportunities for reflection and interpretation (Rennie & McClafferty, 1996). The value of interactive exhibits is highlighted when one considers that for young children in nearly every culture, the hands-on activities of play provide the process by which they interpret and make sense of their experiences (Eisner, 1990; Judd & Kracht, 1997). A distinction is made between play and exploration, where play is associated with familiar activities and objects, and exploration with the unfamiliar or novel (Snow-Dockser & Gallagher, 1987). Too much novelty within the museum environment may be overwhelming for young children, limiting interpretation possibilities. A balance between the familiar and the unfamiliar, the static and the interactive, is recommended in museum exhibits and programs (Piscitelli, McArdle & Weier, 1999; Weier, 2000). Ideally, children's involvement in art museums should include some form of studio activity, in which art materials can be manipulated (Stokrocki, 1984). Initial exploratory experiences with open-ended materials lead to explorations of ever increasing complexity (Smith, 1993) and greater knowledge of art media, techniques, and processes.

Guided by the principles of universal design (ergonomics, accessibility, and inclusivity), exhibits provide opportunities for learning and enjoyment for all visitors, regardless of age, gender, ability, and educational background (Hein, 1998; Wylde, 2000). Gardner (in Brandt, 1993) described museums as places where individuals can become familiar with new phenomena in ways that match their own "tempo, learning style, and profile of intelligences" (p. 6). Children's engagement with art objects is heightened when exhibits are presented in open-ended, motivating ways (Falk & Dierking, 1992; Paris, 1997; Pearce, 1998). Important factors include arousal of curiosity, choice and control over experiences, challenge, provision for multisensory learning, and scope for a variety of ways of responding to allow success for all visitors.

Program

Programming plays an important role in facilitating visitor access to the collections of objects presented in art museums. Doering (1999) claimed that visitors arrive at museums with an "entrance narrative," that is, a fundamental life view, some topic knowledge, and a range of personal experiences. These prior understandings are important ingredients in a successful museum visit, as they resonate with the museum's collections and confirm and enrich visitors' existing views of the world. Opportunities to participate in orientation sessions familiarize visitors with the novel aspects of the venue and introduce them to the script of the museum. Public programs, including guided tours, gallery talks, slide lectures, and special family events encourage participation, assist viewing and interpretation, and allow future, independent use of the museum (Kropf & Wolins, 1989).

A number of practical recommendations facilitate effective implementation of museum programs with groups of young children. When guides connect museum experiences to children's interests and prior knowledge, discussions can begin comfortably for children. Learning experiences within the museum may be enhanced if children's interests are followed and opportunities are taken to capitalize on spontaneous learning incidents (Galper, 1997; Grinder & McCoy, 1989). Thus, if a particular object generates a great deal of interaction or discussion, the guide should focus on the teachable moment, restructuring the rest of the program as necessary. Guides can determine the amount of time to spend at exhibits by observing children's body language, assessing their interest levels, and monitoring their attention (Grinder & McCoy, 1989). The time spent at an exhibit will vary depending on these conditions (Griffin, 1994). Guides can then extend the children's experience, moving from the familiar to less familiar topics and concepts (McNamee, 1987). Small groups of up to eight, depending on the age of the children, are the most manageable for touring, and tour segments should be no longer than 45 minutes, but again this will be determined by the age and individual needs of the children (McNamee, 1987; Piscitelli, 1988a, 1988b). Ensuring that all children can see the exhibit and are involved in discussion can maximize children's attention (Grinder & McCoy, 1989).

Program implementation can be enhanced by the use of certain strategies and resources that support young children's responses to exhibits. Children's responses to art need not always be verbal and descriptive. Eliciting nonverbal responses through such activities as role-play, pretend play, sound-making, movement, or imitation is effective with some children (Grinder & McCoy, 1989; Piscitelli, 1988a; Worthington & Martin, 1987). These experiences should be relevant to the objectives of the program. Similarly, brief games can be used to encourage involvement and support learning goals. The best games are open-ended and noncompetitive (Grinder & McCoy, 1989), for example, games employing search and identify strategies that focus on visual understanding and artistic concepts.

Social Milieu

The potential of the learning environment and its objects largely depends on the social atmosphere generated and the support young children receive through positive, reciprocal interactions. Museum staff, volunteer guides, and other adults who accompany young children should endeavor to promote a positive social atmosphere that conveys a sense of happy involvement and fun for all children. Within such an environment, adults hold developmentally appropriate expectations of children's social behavior and accept responsibility for encouraging suitable actions (McCrea & Piscitelli, 1991; Smith, 1996). The successful learning setting functions as a community of learners, where all individuals are respected, their learning is supported, and opportunities for collaboration are provided (Bredekamp & Copple, 1997; Brown & Campione, 1994; Seefeldt, 1995).

A skilled adult is sensitive to the surrounding social cues and potential for meaningful interaction with young visitors. In a positive social milieu, the adult knows when to stand back and listen, when to offer encouragement or guidance, and when to suggest an idea or strategy in order to facilitate children's engagement and reflection in the learning environment (Moyer, 1990). A variety of interactive teaching–learning behaviors is suggested for supporting children's learning with, through, and about art (Bredekamp & Rosegrant, 1992, 1995; MacNaughton & Williams, 1998; Weier, 2000). These range from nondirective, through scaffolding, to directive behaviors (see Table 8.1). Nondirective behaviors are the least intrusive of the possible interactions. They are used to create a comfortable, secure level of interaction and to sustain children's involvement without directing their learning. Listening, commenting, praising, and encouraging are among the range of important nondirective adult behaviors. When adults scaffold children's behavior by focusing their attention and posing questions, they challenge children to a deeper level of

TABLE 8.1
Interactive Teaching–Learning Behaviors

Category	*Behaviors*
Nondirective	*Physical proximity.* Close physical proximity between the adult and child/children provides security for the children, enhances conversation, and increases viewing time.
	Listening. Careful attendance by the adult builds a climate of acceptance of the children and their ideas.
	Acknowledging. A genuine response by the adult shows children they have been heard and keeps them engaged in an activity.
	Commenting. The adult's casual comments help to create a relaxed atmosphere and comfortable level of interaction for the children.
	Encouraging and Praising. The adult's positive responses inspire children's confidence to explore or continue with a task.
	Modelling. The way the adult communicates, experiments, and approaches and solves problems, forms a powerful model for how children will behave.
Scaffolding	*Reinforcing.* A particular concept or behavior is positively emphasized by the adult.
	Facilitating. The adult provides the children with appropriate assistance or materials.
	Focusing attention. The adult draws the children's attention to a particular aspect.
	Answering. The adult provides feedback in reaction to children's enquiries.
	Describing. The adult helps the children to become aware of details or characteristics.
	Providing information. The adult expands the children's experience and knowledge.
	Explaining. The adult helps the children to construct meaning.
	Reading. The adult exposes the children to details, technical information, or new vocabulary.
	Recalling. The adult remembers facts or experiences in order to encourage the children to make associations.
	Suggesting. The adult puts forward an idea for consideration by the children.
	Initiating. The adult begins a task or line of thinking that children can follow.
	Philosophising/hypothesizing/imagining/wondering. The adult speculates in order to stimulate the children's curiosity and encourage further exploration, experimentation, and questioning.
	Prompting. The adult provides cues, which encourage the children to think divergently.
	Questioning. The adult uses open-ended questions that encourage children to explore, imagine, reason, interpret, choose, and evaluate.
	Clarifying. The adult asks the children to confirm, explain, or justify their ideas, opinions, or preferences.
	Posing problems. The adult encourages the children to explore solutions.
	Challenging. The adult increases the difficulty of a task as the children gain competence and understanding.
	Coconstructing. Adults and children collaborate to form meaning and build knowledge about the world.

(Continued)

TABLE 8.1 (*continued*)

Category	Behaviors
Directive	*Demonstrating.* The adult shows the children how something is done, in order to help them acquire that skill or behavior.
	Instructing. The adult passes information on to the children, or tells them how to perform a skill.
	Directing. The adult guides the children's behavior in a step-by-step fashion, in order to assist successful task completion.
	Task Analysis. The adult helps the children identify the key steps involved in completing a task, in order to enable successful completion of the task.

understanding that moves them beyond their current level of functioning. Finally, directive behaviors place the adult (expert) between the child (novice) and the task. Adult behaviors such as demonstrating, instructing, and analyzing may be employed to ensure children's successful completion of a task.

Interactive teaching–learning behaviors (see Table 8.1) can be applied in a range of informal contexts as young children learn with, through, and about art. Although some may be employed effectively as strategies in isolation, a balance of behaviors from each of the three categories contributes significantly to the quality of an extended adult–child interaction. Just as the elements in an artwork combine to produce a balanced composition, each category of interactive behaviors fulfils an important role within the context of a total teaching–learning exchange. However, no specific pattern of interaction is recommended. Quality interactions occur when a learner-centered approach is taken as the guiding adult responds to and supports children's individual needs, interests, and abilities.

CONNECTING WITH OBJECTS
IN PERSONALLY MEANINGFUL WAYS

Authentic objects provide a starting point for social interactions that facilitate young children's learning about art. Objects are a very important aspect of the learning process, as they are intrinsically motivating. They stimulate children's curiosity and ongoing interest, especially if they can be manipulated. They invite comment and reflection, arouse memories, and encourage sharing of personal stories. Among objects displayed in art museums, those often most accessible are narrative works that allow visitors to identify with a story. Other art objects, generally the more contemporary works, can be "exotic, difficult, or even seem hostile" (Vallance, 1995, p. 6). Museum educators can help young visitors feel empowered to relate objects, difficult or not, to their own search for meaning. Children need repeated exposure to a range of authentic works of art and opportunities to respond (Jalongo & Stamp, 1997; Veale, 1992). They need to be challenged to engage with art objects and to use the language of art in personally meaningful ways. In a broad sense, the language and traditions presented in art museums are "essential tools in enabling people to have full access to their own cultures and to those created by others long ago and far away" (Vallance, 1995, p. 6) and for enlarging their own visions of the world.

Vallance (1995, p. 7) described the capacity of individuals for receptivity to the new and challenging, for illumination, for wonder, for "AHA!" connections, and generally being able to appreciate and participate in the cultural conversation recorded in the objects and images presented in art museums. Although it is important to allow space for spontaneous wonder and illumination, it is rare for young children, like all novices to the world of art, to have awe-inspiring "AHA!" moments unaided. Most children require bridges to help them connect the unfamiliar or challenging to the familiar and comfortable. However, there is a fine balance between providing enough information to make art more accessible to young children and allowing for the emergence of children's personal responses and interpretations (Walsh-Piper, 1994). Adult-initiated interactions and guided learning experiences with art should aim to arouse curiosity, stimulate imagination, and promote development of aesthetic ability while allowing connections with objects in personally meaningful ways.

Children need continued adult guidance and instruction to support and extend their ability to respond to art. Being responsive to artworks begins with a child's highly personal, "natural, untrained powers of perception," but requires socially guided experience if these are to be put to critical use (Hurwitz & Day, 1991, p. 294). A number of cognitive processes operate when children try to understand a work of art, including use of their existing knowledge base, personalized search strategies, and dispositions toward learning. Children's development depends on the inextricable link between these three facets of cognition, and occurs when knowledge, skill, or experience gained in one context is transferred to another learning context. Such development can be viewed as a continuum. At one end is the novice, who has the least relevant knowledge base, least effective search strategies, and low motivation; at the other end is the expert, who has a highly developed and relevant knowledge base, the most effective search strategies, and high motivation. Age alone does not account for the developmental difference; experience and instruction are the important factors.

Can Aesthetics be Taught to Children?

Children's potential for understanding artworks requires "educational intervention of some kind" (Koroscik, 1997, p. 147). Burchenal (1998) described an

TABLE 8.2
VTS — Informal Approach

Three Questions

1. What's going on in this picture?
2. What do you see that makes you say that?
3. What else can you find?

Process

The adult initiates discussion using the three questions.
The children look closely at the artwork and share their observations, ideas, feelings, and interpretations.
The adult facilitates the discussion, acknowledging the importance of every idea and reiterating comments to ensure that the whole group has heard.
The adult keeps the group focused on the work of art by pointing to various aspects as the children mention them.
The adult shapes the progress of the discussion by linking points of agreement and disagreement.

Note.   Based on Burchenal, 1998.

approach to learning with authentic art objects that allows adults with little or no prior art experience to lead group discussions. The Visual Thinking Strategies (VTS) approach, originally developed by Yenawine and Housen as part of Visual Understanding in Education,[1] is an informal approach in which the adult uses a set of three questions to generate discussions about works of art (see Table 8.2). During open-ended discussions, children assume a principal role, sharing their observations, ideas, feelings, and interpretations. The adult acts as a guide, listening carefully to children's comments, acknowledging the importance of all responses, and shaping the process of discussion by linking points of agreement and disagreement.

VTS centers on art objects as items rich with layers of meaning and open to multiple interpretations. Children learn from objects as they observe closely and deeply, to uncover the many dimensions of the work. Discussing what they see, children draw on their existing knowledge and experience to understand ideas and concepts that may be unfamiliar. They learn to reason and provide evidence to support their opinions. Through the sharing process, children are encouraged to remain open to the idea that art elicits many responses and can hold different meanings for different people, some of which are not immediately apparent. As all children are given equal voice and value within the discussion, they are assisted in developing confidence in understanding works of art and forming their own interpretations. The open-ended

[1]Visual Understanding in Education (VUE) is a developmentally based educational research group, whose VTS approach was piloted in Boston with fifth-grade classroom teachers.

nature of discussing and interpreting art, evident in the VTS approach, reflects the same open-ended quality of the artist's search for meaning that is recorded in the actual object of creation (Walsh-Piper, 1994). Moreover, the skills learned through the VTS approach can be used throughout other areas of children's school and daily life, as observations and interpretations become richer and more detailed.

A number of more formal analysis frameworks have been developed for use in adult guided critical-response activities with children (see Table 8.3). These assist children to look at art objects more closely and to learn about aesthetic properties. Discussion may include art elements and principles, subject

TABLE 8.3
Formal Critical-Response Models

Authority	Critical-Response Model
Feldman (1970/1997)	*Description.* The viewer's attention is focused on naming all aspects visible in the artwork.
	Formal Analysis. The viewer enquires into the structure of the artwork by focusing on the relationships among its components. Shape, size, color, texture, space, and volume relationships are described.
	Interpretation. The viewer is encouraged to speculate about the artist's meaning, drawing upon all visual facts accumulated during previous two stages.
	Judgment. The viewer makes an informed response based on his or her understanding and appreciation of the artwork.
Chapman (1978)	*Perceiving obvious and subtle qualities.* The viewer sharpens his or her perceptual capacity by: • discriminating basic properties; • building multisensory associations; • exploring symbolism and connotations; and • becoming aware of contexts.
	Interpreting qualities as sources of feeling and meaning. The viewer organizes his or her perceptions in order to understand what they mean, through: • building a vocabulary; • empathizing and maintaining psychic distance; • speculating; and • synthesizing.
	Judging the significance of perceptual experience. The viewer states criteria and offers reasons for decisions about a particular art experience.

(Continued)

TABLE 8.3 (*continued*)

Authority	Critical-Response Model
Ott (1989)	*Thought watching.* The viewer focuses and prepares for critical enquiry. Activities may include: • games to sharpen perception; • movement experiences that increase sensory responses; • literature that heightens the possibilities for understanding particular artworks; or • music selected to develop atmosphere or mood perceptible in artworks. *Image watching.* Consists of five categories that assist the viewer to interpret an artwork: • Analyzing: What is actually seen on the surface of the artwork is elicited from the viewer. • Describing: The viewer enquires into how the artwork was executed. The elements of art often provide the starting point. • Interpreting: The viewer provides personal and emotional responses to the artwork, based on an understanding of the artwork developed in the previous two categories of describing and analyzing. • Funding: The viewer is "funded" with additional knowledge from art history or art critics who have spoken or written about the artwork. • Disclosing: The viewer reveals his or her knowledge about art through an act of artistic expression.

matter, processes, techniques, materials, and personal feelings about objects. There are various models for guiding children's criticism of art (Chapman, 1978; Feldman, 1970/1997; Ott, 1989). Basic phases of the critical-response process include perceiving and describing obvious and subtle qualities of an art object, analyzing structure and relationships, interpreting one's observations as sources of feeling and meaning, and making judgments based on understanding and appreciation of the work.

Ott (1989) emphasized the need for a preparatory phase, prior to making any formal artistic response, by suggesting a two-phase systemic process for assisting children's critical response to art objects. The first phase, Thought Watching, is a system of readiness that involves the child in experiences of focusing and preparing for critical enquiry. During Thought Watching, a range of episodes may be utilized, including games to sharpen skills in perception, movement experiences that increase sensory responses, literature that heightens the possibilities for understanding particular works, or music selected to develop atmosphere or mood perceptible in artworks. The second phase, Image Watching, utilizes the basic phases in the critical-response process (outlined earlier) to help children interpret artworks in the museum setting.

Art criticism should be the focus of children's encounters with museum exhibits, but this is not a fully satisfactory process unless the child's personal characteristics, learning styles, and touring requirements are taken into consideration. In the case study that follows, we describe an innovative exhibition where trained adult guides facilitated children's learning about art.

AN INNOVATIVE EXHIBITION: "THE ART OF ERIC CARLE"

In September of 1998, "The Art of Eric Carle" project was showcased at the Queensland Performing Arts Centre (QPAC) in Brisbane, Australia. Fifty of Eric Carle's[2] original artworks were featured in an indoor, interactive exhibition space, which included zoned play areas where children drew, solved puzzles, climbed, chanted, sang, read, watched videos, and listened to stories. Children also visited a large, outdoor art studio to experiment with Eric Carle's favored illustrative techniques, painting and collage. The total environment was designed to capture children's imagination and to enhance their appreciation and understanding of the visual arts.

The key objectives of the project were for young children and their families to have a high-quality visual arts experience in a prepared environment, and to promote learning through purposeful activities and meaningful interactions. Guiding adults facilitated children's encounters with real artworks in an authentic exhibition context and encouraged expression through art-making activities, providing the beginnings of the transition from a novice knowledge base to the larger artistic concepts available to be learned. The project focused on helping children learn with, through, and about art. By helping children understand the artist's life and work, all aspects of a robust art education were evident. Children learned in face-to-face encounters with authentic art objects, through producing their own works of art, and about art by applying art criticism, recalling art history, and encountering aesthetics.

The second author was a participant observer in this setting and documented the features of the project that facilitated high quality experiences for all visitors (Weier, 2000). She observed the encounters of 4,000 young children (toddlers to 8-year-olds), families, teachers, and caregivers. She captured visitors' responses and interactions in her field notes and on audio tape, and photographed their activities during a visit to the fully interactive exhibition

---

[2]Eric Carle (1929–) is an internationally recognized children's storybook author and illustrator, most famous for his early work, "The Very Hungry Caterpillar."

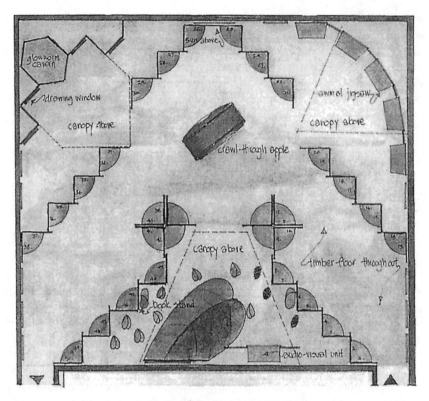

FIG. 8.1.   Exhibition installation concept.

and the art studio. Based on Weier's findings, three important facets of the project contributed to its success.

First, the environment was designed to display innovation in exhibiting art for young children. The design team from QPAC[3] devoted many months to front-end planning, refining all aspects of the interactive physical environment to be presented (see Fig. 8.1 and Fig. 8.2 for exhibition design installation concept and studio floor plan). Within the exhibition, 50 framed original artworks were hung at a level suited to children in the early childhood age group (toddlers to 8-year-olds), on screens that doubled as dividers for differentiating the various activity areas. These areas were further defined by ceiling canopies and three distinctive, low-volume soundscapes, which contributed to the ambience and theme of each activity space (e.g., insect noises in the Glow-worm Cavern where chalkboard drawing took place, and the

---

[3]The QPAC project design team included curator Beryl Davis and designer Christopher Smith.

sounds of children playing in the Storytelling Garden). A giant-sized crawl-through apple containing a large, soft caterpillar toy allowed children to engage in both large motor activity and imaginative role-play. The inclusion of soft caterpillar leaf cushions in the Storytelling Garden invited children and families to sit comfortably to enjoy stories, rhymes, and chants.

In the art studio, tables and chairs were set out for painting on one half of the tent and for collage on the other. Age-appropriate furnishings accommodated children as they worked, and adults of all ages seemed privileged to occupy the child-sized chairs as they enjoyed art making activities alongside the children (see Fig. 8.3). Positioned around these work areas were storage shelves, preparation tables, and drying racks for completed artworks. Each area was clearly and adequately separated from the others to allow assisting and accompanying adults to move comfortably about as required.

Together, the exhibition and studio environments offered a range of familiar and novel exhibits that enabled a level of interactivity consistent with the learning needs of young children. Both venues included appropriate spaces for visitors to explore and experiment alone, in pairs, and in small or large groups as they participated in a range of learning experiences. The setting was nonthreatening and aesthetically pleasing, encompassing familiar images

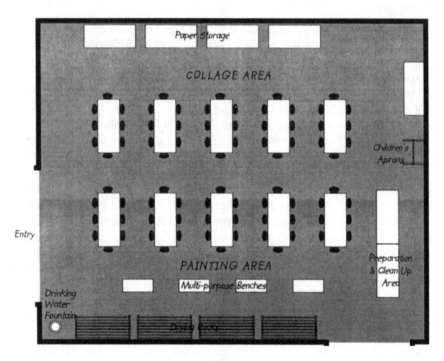

FIG. 8.2.   Studio floor plan.

FIG. 8.3.   Family involvement in the studio.

within the overall theme of art, nature, and play. The principles of universal
design were evident in the exhibition (Hein, 1998; Wylde, 2000), thus establishing an environment open to all visitors and accessible for a variety of
learner's needs.

Second, a carefully structured, child-centered program was implemented.
"The Art of Eric Carle" facilitated visitor access to original works of art by attending to the prior knowledge of the children and connecting with their
touring needs (Doering, 1999; Grinder & McCoy, 1989; McNamee, 1987;
Piscitelli, 1988a, 1988b). A carefully sequenced 2-hour program was provided
for all groups that attended the project. This included an introduction to the
experience and orientation to the venue in the form of a brief, informal discussion, followed by two sessions of equal duration spent in the interactive
exhibition and the art studio. The program capitalized on young visitors'
familiarity with Eric Carle's picture books and their interest in art-making
activities, as art appreciation activities took place in conjunction with studio
projects. Authentic objects and art media served as the "raw materials" for
children's learning about art.

Thorough planning was undertaken to prepare visitors for the project and
to provide relevant experiences during their visit.[4] As support for school and

_____

[4]An early childhood education specialist, Dr. Barbara Piscitelli, from the Queensland University of Technology, coordinated the project. Artist and teacher Raquel Redmond was the studio
coordinator.

family groups, an information sheet was distributed to teachers and parents, communicating details about what to expect in both the exhibition and studio and suggestions for previsit activities to familiarize children with Eric Carle's storybooks and illustrative techniques. In addition, a manual was prepared for use by the guides to support visitors' experiences. This extensive document listed the goals of the program, key teaching strategies, timed sequences for the exhibition and studio components of the program, and duties required in the various roles performed by guides. The manual was utilized both as a handbook during preproject training sessions for guides and as a reference tool for ongoing evaluation of the project. At regular meetings between the project coordinator and the guides during implementation, goals, touring strategies, and resources were constantly reviewed to ensure that high-quality experiences were available to visitors.

Adult guides who led small groups of visitors assumed responsibility for scheduling all aspects of the tour, ensuring that children had choice and control over the direction of their tour, thus leading to meaningful and highly personalized encounters with art (Paris, 1997; Perry, 1993). The guides allocated sufficient time for viewing of self-selected works of interest, discussion and questioning in relation to the displayed artworks, engagement in a variety of hands-on activities leading to self-expression of artistic ideas, exploration and experimentation with art materials and processes, and talking with children about their overall impressions of the project. Time was also allowed for movement of visitors between the exhibition and studio venues, satisfaction of children's physical needs, and cleaning up after studio activities. Adult–child ratios were high during group tours, consistent with recommended figures for early childhood care and education groups (National Childcare Accreditation Council, 1993). Guides, teachers, and parents worked collaboratively to support children's experiences. To enhance visitor enjoyment and involvement in the program, guides utilized a range of resources and strategies, including storytelling, search and identify or comparing games (see Fig. 8.4), simple props such as homemade cardboard viewfinders, hands-on materials to aid children's understanding of artistic concepts, and strategies like role play, sound-making, and movement to elicit nonverbal responses to artworks.

Third, trained guides provided positive social interactions for groups of visitors. A team of 40 early childhood education students from the Queensland University of Technology (QUT) became the volunteer guides for the project. This group was trained in all aspects of guiding and program implementation, under the expertise of the project and studio coordinators. A significant part of the training program focused on developing guides' interaction skills and providing them with a bank of strategies for connecting children's ideas with the exhibition's main themes and content. During implementation, the guides used positive reciprocal interactions to develop rapport with visitors and create a warm, collaborative social atmosphere, thus putting theory into action

(Csikszentmihalyi & Hermanson, 1995; Paris, 1997; see Fig. 8.5). The use of casual conversation contributed to a comfortable, effective style of interaction, while a range of more specific teaching–learning interactions assisted children to engage successfully in activities, and reflect on and interpret the exhibits. Analysis of the data gathered at the project clearly demonstrated that although the design of the physical environment and the carefully structured program made important contributions to visitors' experiences, it was the social facilitation by trained guides that most significantly affected children's experiences (Weier, 2000).

Socially Facilitated Moments at "The Art of Eric Carle"

During static and interactive experiences, guides used purposeful interaction strategies to enhance children's learning encounters with art objects. Spontaneous exchanges between visitors, including adult–child and child–child interactions, were often equally successful in achieving this goal. Established

FIG. 8.4.   Comparing picture book illustration with original artwork.

FIG. 8.5.   Developing rapport and creating a collaborative atmosphere.

relationships, shared experiences, and knowledge of children's interests and learning styles enabled parents and teachers to make young visitors' encounters with objects meaningful. For guides, who were meeting children for the first time, it was essential to acquire very quickly a sense of the group's interests and their knowledge base, in order to provide subsequent experiences that would assist interpretation of the environment, its objects, and activities. Initially, guides used casual conversation to develop rapport with young visitors and elicit personal stories. Children were eager to share information such as where they had come from, how they had travelled to the exhibition, their feelings about making art, what they knew about Eric Carle, and their favorite books or characters. A range of specific interaction strategies then came into play as guides endeavored to expand children's repertoire of experience and their knowledge, using the authentic objects and materials available to be explored and manipulated in the exhibition and studio environments. Guides combined nondirective, scaffolding, and directive teaching–learning behaviors (Weier, 2000; see Table 8.1) in isolation during episodic dialogues with visitors, or as part of longer, carefully guided learning experiences.

Responding to Children and Their Ideas.   In the exhibition, during guided viewing of displayed artworks, physical proximity was an important nondirective interaction strategy. Guides and other adults were observed bending, kneeling, and squatting to children's levels to engage in detailed observation and discussion of the works. These behaviors effectively enhanced conversation and increased viewing time. As adults supported and encouraged children's initial responses to artworks, they employed other nondirective behaviors such as careful listening, acknowledging children's ideas with genuine responses, and making casual comments to share their own ideas and observations. Similarly, adults and children interacted in intimate groups as they pored over favorite storybooks, worked on puzzles and perception games, and practiced drawing Eric Carle's eight-sided star. Each of these activities provided opportunities for heightening children's visual awareness and understanding.

Guiding Art Criticism.   Close observation and interpretation of artworks was a desired outcome of young visitors' experience in the exhibition, and required the use of a variety of interaction strategies. To allow opportunities for spontaneous responses, guides often waited for children's comments before directing the discussion. Children were then assisted to describe and analyze the works they viewed. To encourage careful looking and playful identification of colors, shapes, lines, and subject matter, guides initiated simple games:

> **Guide:** "Looking, looking, looking . . . for a zigzag line. . . . Fantastic! You've found it, right there in the fox's tail."

Guides also focused children's attention on specific aspects of works, eliciting detailed visual descriptions. Recall was used to invite associations between the artistic processes they may have used in the studio and the effects achieved in Eric Carle's works:

> **Guide:** "Remember when we were in the studio and we did our painting, do you remember how I said you can stamp on the paper to create a texture? . . . Look what Eric Carle has done here. . . . He's done exactly the same as what you did in the studio. He got something, and used it to stamp on the paint to create that texture. I wonder what he might have used here?"

Through careful questioning and modelling of artistic vocabulary, guides were able to elicit a range of informed responses to artworks from the children. The young viewers described artworks in terms of the elements of art, they analyzed works for composition, they identified techniques and processes used by the artist, and they determined what features of certain works achieved, for example, the effect of nighttime or a windy day. Where appropriate, guides described certain characteristics within artworks, to raise children's awareness, and provided information and explanations to expand children's knowledge and help them construct meaning (Hein, 1995; Schauble, Leinhardt, & Martin, 1997). In the following interaction, the guide provided general information about self-portrait as a genre, and specific information about Eric Carle's work:

> **Guide:** "This one's a picture of Eric Carle, that he painted himself. Do you know what it's called when someone paints a picture of themselves? . . . It's called a self-portrait. Can you see him drawing something there? . . . What is it? . . . Mmm. And look at his head, isn't it funny? He's got his head right open and something beautiful and big and bright and colorful is coming out the top of his head. Do you know why he's painted that? . . . He's doing this to let you know that from inside your head comes all your really bright ideas, all your big, colorful ideas."

During the same interaction, the guide consistently used technical artistic language in such a way that the meaning of each term was made clear and the children had opportunities to practice the terms in context. Analysis of the transcript reveals terms such as "transparent," "tones," "texture," "background," "signature," and "oblong shape"; and artistic concepts such as "technique" (tearing vs. cutting, drawing/painting vs. collage) and "mood" (windy feel, warm vs. cool colors; Weier, 2000).

Following carefully directed discussions about some artworks, consistent with formal critical-response models (Chapman, 1978; Feldman, 1970/1997; Ott, 1989), children were able to combine new information with existing views and preferences to make informed judgments about the artworks they viewed. It was common for children to offer information about their favorite works from the exhibition. A 5-year-old boy who had engaged in discussion with his guide about the length of time it would take the artist to complete certain works, based on the size, technique used, and amount of detail, chose as his favorite a colorful, busy zoo scene. The reason for his choice: "It has lots of artwork in it. . . . I like all the things you can see in it. There's lots and lots of things. . . . It must've taken a very long time!"

Peer Interaction. In both the exhibition and the studio, children's interactions with one another provided a scaffold as they learned from objects. Older children were often intrigued with the artist's techniques and use of materials. Two girls, for example, theorized about the specific technique used to create one of the painted works they viewed in the gallery:

> **Guide:** "How do you think Eric Carle has done this one?"
> **Rebecca:** "Well I think it's a bit of white paper and then he just, like, did a few bits of green, and a few different colors (gestures the motion of brushstrokes)."
> **Katherine:** "No. I reckon he's got all the colors and put them on that side (points to the left side of the work) and then, um, folded it, and then put it over there (points to the right side)."
> **Guide:** "Oh, folded it, like a butterfly print?"
> **Katherine:** "Yeah. But he folded it kind of, this way (gestures diagonal), and he just, like, put heaps of paint on."

Rebecca: "I don't reckon, 'cause then it'll be smudged."
Katherine: "No it wouldn't be."
Rebecca: "Yes it would be."
Guide (to Rebecca): "So you don't think it looks smudged enough to have been folded?"
Rebecca: "Mmm."
Guide: (looks and contemplates) "Can you see a fold in the paper?"
Katherine: "No."
Rebecca: "And look! Look! If he folded it, there'd be a yellow bit up here (points to yellow in bottom left, then to top right area), when there's not. There'd be — that kinda orange color up here (points to two areas again), when there's not. 'Cause there'd be a bit of green up there (points), when there's not a bit of green up there."

In the studio, children shared their expertise with one another to solve technical problems related to artistic production (see Fig. 8.6). In the following anecdote, Ethan introduced Alexander to a more effective way of applying his background paint:

Ethan: "It's better to go across. I did it like that."
Ethan takes hold of Alexander's paint brush and moves it in the direction he is advocating. Alexander initially seems surprised by Ethan's action ("Hey!"), but

FIG. 8.6.   Peer collaboration.

FIG. 8.7. Demonstrating in the studio.

accepts his advice and continues applying the background color using the techniques suggested by Ethan.

Adult Guidance. Adult initiated or guided interactions in the studio were particularly appropriate for children who experienced difficulties, lacked inspiration, or required a starting point (see Fig. 8.7). In these cases, adults took an active role to facilitate children's involvement. There was also a place for adult support in the form of nondirective behaviors such as watching, commenting, or remaining close by. A study by Kindler (1995) indicated that during art-making experiences, children employ a number of social behaviors that serve a range of functions. For instance, prior to beginning a work, children often announce the plans for their work as a means of consolidating the process of activity. Children also talk about their work in progress. They might explain details that are not communicated pictorially, or they may engage in discussion to share knowledge about the subject of their work. Sometimes, children seek recognition for their efforts or make statements to elicit help, advice, or encouraging responses from others. Appropriate responses by adults can capitilize on these kinds of behaviors to support involvement, encourage artistic expression, and extend children's knowledge of artistic concepts. Adult intervention of any kind, however, must be carefully executed to ensure that individual needs are acknowledged and the creative process is not intruded on.

When children announced plans for creations or talked about their works in progress, simple comments by guides in praise or acknowledgment of their ideas provided appropriate support for their continued enthusiastic activity:

> After pasting various pieces of paper onto his page to create a caterpillar, David comments that he has made a mistake. He proceeds to cut his page in half, cut around the caterpillar shape, and cut out a leaf shape. When asked what he intends to do, David announces:
>
> "I've got this leaf cut out and I'm going to do it like Eric Carle really does it."
> **Adult:** "Great idea! It's a good thing you know so much about the way Eric Carle makes his collages."
>
> David pastes the leaf onto the remaining half of the page, then pastes the caterpillar on top of the leaf, using the layering technique characteristic of Eric Carle's work.

The provision of advice or assistance in response to children's queries enabled them to extend their works:

> **Ashleigh** (to guide): "What else is in the sky?"
> **Guide:** "What have you got so far?" (They discuss the collage.)
> **Ashleigh:** "I know! A shooting star! . . . I can just make another star and then make a tail by drawing it on." (Ashleigh continues with her work.)
> **Ashleigh** (to guide): "What's the Milky Way again?"
> Guide explains.
> **Ashleigh:** "Oh yeah. (She sits and thinks for a while.) I think I'll make a planet."

Adult responses during the process of children's work also provided an important means of extending artistic cognition. Simple prompts encouraged divergent thinking and use of imagination, and technical vocabulary was introduced:

> **Guide:** ". . . So, what do you need in your picture to show it's a sunny day?"
> **Neah:** "A sun!"
> Neah continues her work, adding a sun. She discusses with the guide that she will also add a person sitting on a deck in the sun.
> **Guide:** "Look closely at the way the paint has made bubbles on your page, Caitlyn. That's a very interesting texture. Have you heard that word before, *texture?*"
> **Caitlyn:** "No." (tries to say it a few times)
> **Guide:** "When the paint dries, you'll be able to feel lumps where the bubbles are. That's a texture."

CONCLUSIONS

Art production and aesthetic appreciation provide tangible, visually oriented means of enlarging conceptions as learners of all ages participate in meaning-

FIG. 8.8.   Reproducing images following observation of authentic artwork.

making activities and dynamic, responsive discussions about objects. Young children's learning with, through, and about art is enhanced when children are provided with balanced opportunities to both make art and to respond to authentic works of art. Interactive exhibitions like "The Art of Eric Carle" provide children with options to build on their knowledge, interests, and preferences. These innovations have been very helpful in building secure foundations for children to develop a lifelong learning approach toward the discipline of art. As cultural institutions (such as museums) develop meaningful programs and exhibitions for young children, their families, and schools, new advances may be made in learning from artworks.

Young children's learning from art may occur in a flash as children encounter authentic objects in a gallery setting. At "The Art of Eric Carle," for example, a young boy intently observed a collage illustration of dragons and minotaurs while in the gallery. Later, in the studio, the 6-year-old child used his memory to recall salient features of the artist's work to reproduce a detailed collage of the mythical animals (see Fig. 8.8). Such potent visual thinking strategies are an important part of the learning repertoire that may be ignited and sustained through engagement with real art objects.

Social and technical supports are essential to building secure concepts and durable procedural understanding if young children are to learn about art by engaging with real objects. Social interaction is a key to enabling children to build conceptual understanding through their encounters and transactions with objects. Teachers, parents, museum educators, and peers play an influential role in helping children form ideas through dynamic discussion about art objects.

Young children, like all learners, require more than a single visit or lesson to assist them in learning about art, or any other discipline. Museums, schools, and families may together build sustainable learning communities through collaborative partnerships. Such enduring links are critically important, particularly in art. School-based education often neglects or diminishes the curricular content or time allocation for art due to perceived pressures from the academic demands of literacy and numeracy. Yet, such limited curricular content need not continue. There is a new and growing emphasis on multi-literacies that indicates that learners in contemporary societies may build expansive knowledge of their worlds — both real and virtual — through encounters with objects, experiences, and people by way of new literacies, including reading visual images and other symbol systems.

REFERENCES

Allen, S. (1997). Sociocultural theory in museums: Insights and suggestions. *Journal of Museum Education, 22*(2&3), 8-9.

Australia Council for the Arts. (2000). *Australians and the arts.* Surrey Hills, NSW: Australia Council.

Brandt, R. (1993). On teaching for understanding: A conversation with Howard Gardner. *Educational Leadership, 50*(7), 4-7.

Bredekamp, S., & Copple, C. (Eds.). (1997). *Developmentally appropriate practice in early childhood programs* (Rev. ed.). Washington, DC: National Association for the Education of Young Children.

Bredekamp, S., & Rosegrant, T. (1992). Conceptual frameworks for applying the guidelines. In S. Bredekamp & T. Rosegrant (Eds.), *Reaching potentials: Appropriate curriculum and assessment* (Vol. 1, pp. 28-42). Washington, DC: National Association for the Education of Young Children.

Bredekamp, S., & Rosegrant, T. (1995). Reaching potentials through transforming curriculum, assessment, and teaching. In S. Bredekamp & T. Rosegrant (Eds.), *Reaching potentials: Transforming early childhood curriculum and assessment* (Vol. 2, pp. 15-22). Washington, DC: National Association for the Education of Young Children.

Brown, A. L., & Campione, J. C. (1994). Guided discovery in a community of learners. In K. McGilly (Ed.), *Classroom lessons: Integrating cognitive theory and classroom practice* (pp. 229-270). Cambridge, MA: MIT Press/Bradford Books.

Burchenal, M. K. (1998). Thinking art through. *Journal of Museum Education, 23*(2), 13-15.

Chapman, L. (1978). *Approaches to art in education.* New York: Harcourt Brace Jovanovich.

Consortium of National Arts Education Associations. (1994). *National Standards for Arts Education.* Reston, VA: Music Educators National Conference.

Csikszentmihalyi, M., & Hermanson, K. (1995). Intrinsic motivation in museums: What makes visitors want to learn? *Museum News, 74*(3), 34-37, 59-61.

Doering, Z. D. (1999). Strangers, guests, or clients? Visitor experiences in museums. *Curator, 42*(2), 74-87.

Eisner, E. W. (1990). The role of art and play in children's cognitive development. In E. Klugman & S. Smilansky (Eds.), *Children's play and learning* (pp. 43–56). New York: Teachers College Press.

Falk, J. H., & Dierking, L. D. (1992). *The museum experience.* Washington, DC: Whalesback Books.

Feldman, E. (1997). *Becoming human through art.* New Jersey: Prentice-Hall. (Original work published 1970)

Galper, A. R. (1997). Opportunities for learning and development in multiple settings. In B. Hatcher & S. S. Beck (Eds.), *Learning opportunities beyond the school* (2nd ed., pp. 7–11). Washington, DC: Association for Childhood Education International.

Griffin, J. (1994, November). *Museums are educational institutions but are they always places of learning?* Paper presented at the Museums Australia Conference, Sydney, Australia.

Grinder, A. L., & McCoy, E. S. (1989). *The good guide: A sourcebook for interpreters, docents and tour guides.* Scottsdale, AZ: Ironwood Publishing.

Hein, G. E. (1995). The constructivist museum. *Journal of Education in Museums, 16,* 21–23.

Hein, G. E. (1998). *Learning in the museum.* London: Routledge.

Hein, G. E., & Alexander, M. (1998). *Museums: Places of learning.* Washington, DC: American Association of Museums.

Housen, A. (1992). Validating a measure of aesthetic development for museums and schools. *ILVS Review, 2*(2), 213–237.

Hurwitz, A., & Day, M. (1991). *Children and their art* (5th ed.). San Diego, CA: Harcourt Brace Jovanovich.

Jacob, E. (1992). Culture, contest and cognition. In M. D. LeCompte, W. L. Milroy, & J. Priessley (Eds.), *The handbook of qualitative research in education.* New York: Academic Press.

Jalongo M. R., & Stamp, L. N. (1997). *The arts in children's lives: Aesthetic education in early childhood.* Needham Heights, MA: Allyn & Bacon.

Jeffery-Clay, K. R. (1998). Constructivism in museums: How museums create meaningful learning environments. *Journal of Museum Education, 23*(1), 3–7.

Judd, M. K., & Kracht, J. B. (1997). The world at their fingertips: Children in museums. In B. Hatcher & S. S. Beck (Eds.), *Learning opportunities beyond the school* (2nd ed., pp. 21–26). Washington, DC: Association for Childhood Education International.

Kindler, A. M. (1995). Artistic learning in early childhood: A study of social interactions. *Canadian Review of Art Education, 21*(2), 91–106.

Kindler, A. M. (1997). Aesthetic development and learning in art museums: A challenge to enjoy. *Journal of Museum Education, 22*(2&3), 12–16.

Koroscik, J. S. (1997). What potential do young people have for understanding works of art? In A. M. Kindler (Ed.), *Child development in art* (pp. 143–164). Reston, VA: National Association for Education in the Arts.

Kropf, M. B., & Wolins, I. S. (1989). How families learn: Considerations for program development. *Marriage and Family Review, 13*(4), 75–86.

Lave, J., & Wenger, E. (1991). *Situated learning: Legitimate peripheral participation.* Cambridge, England: Cambridge University Press.

MacNaughton, G., & Williams, G. (1998). *Techniques for teaching young children: Choices in theory and practice.* South Melbourne, Australia: Longman.

McCrea, N., & Piscitelli, B. (Eds.). (1991). *Handbook of high quality criteria for early childhood programs* (Rev. ed.). Brisbane, Australia: Queensland University of Technology.

McNamee, A. S. (1987). Museum readiness: Preparation for the art museum (ages 3–8). *Childhood Education, 63*(3), 181–187.

Montagu, K., Hansen, S., Gurian, E. H., Kamien, J., & Robinson, J. (1987). Learning in mixed crowds: Challenges for designers of children's museum exhibitions. *Children's Environments Quarterly, 4*(1), 10–15.

Moyer, J. (1990). Whose creation is it anyway? *Childhood Education, 66*(3), 130–131.

National Childcare Accreditation Council. (1993). *Putting children first: Quality improvement and accreditation system handbook* (1st ed.). Sydney, Australia: National Childcare Association Council.

Ott, R. W. (1989). Teaching criticism in museums. In N. Berry & S. Mayer (Eds.), *Museum education: History, theory, and practice* (pp. 172–193). Reston, VA: National Art Education Association.

Paris, S. (1997). Situated motivation and informal learning. *Journal of Museum Education, 22* (2&3), 22–26.

Parsons, M. J. (1987). *How we understand art: A cognitive developmental account of aesthetic experience.* Cambridge, England: Cambridge University Press.

Pearce, J. (1998). *Centres for curiosity and imagination: When is a museum not a museum?* London: Calouste Gulbenkian Foundation.

Perry, D. L. (1993). Designing exhibits that motivate. In R. J. Hannapel (Ed.), *What research says about learning in science museums* (Vol. 2, pp. 25–29). Washington, DC: Association of Science Technology Centers.

Piscitelli, B. (1988a). Share the joy! Looking at art with preschoolers. *Links, 1,* 4–6.

Piscitelli, B. (1988b). Preschoolers and parents as artists and art appreciators. *Art Education, 41,* 48–55.

Piscitelli, B., McArdle, F., & Weier, K. (1999). *Beyond "look and learn": Investigating, implementing and evaluating interactive learning strategies for young children in museums.* Final Report, QUT–Industry Collaborative Research Project. Brisbane, Australia: Centre for Applied Studies in Early Childhood, Queensland University of Technology.

Rennie, L. J., & McClafferty, T. P. (1996). Science centres and science learning. *Studies in Science Education, 27,* 53–98.

Schauble, L., Leinhardt, G., & Martin, L. (1997). A framework for organizing a cumulative research agenda in informal learning contexts. *Journal of Museum Education, 22*(2&3), 3–7.

Seefeldt, C. (1995). Art — A serious work. *Young Children, 50*(3), 39–45.

Smith, M. K. (1996). Fostering creativity in the early childhood classroom. *Early Childhood Education Journal, 24*(2), 77–82.

Smith, N. R. (1993). *Experience and art: Teaching children to paint* (2nd ed.). New York: Teachers College Press.

Snow-Dockser, L. S., & Gallagher, J. M. (1987). Parent–child interaction in a museum for preschool children. *Children's Environments Quarterly, 4*(1), 41–45.

Stokrocki, M. (1984). The meaning of aesthetic awareness for preschoolers in a museum class. *Art Education, 37*(2), 12–16.

Vallance, E. (1995). The public curriculum of orderly images. *Educational Researcher, 24*(2), 4–13.

Veale, A. (1992). *Arts education for young children of the 21st century.* (ERIC Document Reproduction Service No. 351124). U.S. Department of Education: Educational Resources Information Center.

Walsh-Piper, K. (1994). Museum education and the aesthetic experience. In R. Moore (Ed.), *Aesthetics for young people* (pp. 105–115). Reston, VA: National Art Education Association.

Weier, K. (2000). *Lessons from an interactive exhibition: Defining conditions to support high quality experiences for young children.* Unpublished master's thesis, Queensland University of Technology.

Worthington, M., & Martin, P. (1987). The growth and development of the Los Angeles Children's Museum. *Children's Environments Quarterly, 4*(1), 41–45.

Wright, S. (1994). Artistic development and learning: An integration of processes for young children. In G. Boulton-Lewis & D. Catherwood (Eds.), *The early years* (pp. 186–221). Melbourne, Australia: The Australian Council for Educational Research Ltd.

Wylde, M. A. (2000). *It's still time for universal design.* American Society on Aging, URL: http://www.asaging.org/am/cia2/design.html (21 September 2000).

APPENDIX: CONDITIONS SUPPORTING HIGH QUALITY EXPERIENCES FOR YOUNG CHILDREN IN INFORMAL SETTINGS

1. Physical Environment

1.1 Building

    1.1.1   The entrance to the venue is visually welcoming, able to accommo-date large groups of visitors and clearly signposted to assist visitors in finding their way.

    1.1.2   The environment provides a balance between organized, pre-dictable spaces and areas of exploration and discovery.

    1.1.3   Different exhibition areas are clearly defined and adequately sepa-rated in order to minimize distractions.

    1.1.4   The space is arranged to enable individual, small, and large group participation.

    1.1.5   The space is arranged to avoid safety hazards.

    1.1.6   The environment is nonthreatening.

    1.1.7   Facilities are provided to cater for children's physical needs.

1.2 Exhibits

    1.2.1   A balance is provided between *interactive* exhibits and *static* exhibits.

    1.2.2   Exhibits cater for a variety of interests, ages, learning styles, degrees of knowledge, experiences, and skills.

    1.2.3   Exhibits promote discussion and provide opportunities for group problem solving.

    1.2.4   Exhibits provide a range of learning opportunities (psychomotor, social, affective, or cognitive goals), and consider a variety of modes of learning.

    1.2.5   Exhibits encourage repetition of activity and application of the skills or concepts presented.

    1.2.6   Exhibits stimulate visitors' natural curiosity and spark their motiva-tion to explore.

    1.2.7   Exhibits have personal utility and meaning for visitors.

    1.2.8   Visitors are given opportunities to make choices and control their experiences.

    1.2.9   The goals of exhibits are clear and manageable, allowing for self-directed behavior.

    1.2.10 Exhibits provide opportunities to receive feedback on actions per-formed.

    1.2.11 Exhibits present information in a manner that is comprehensible to both adults and children.

1.2.12 Exhibits are physically accessible to a variety of visitors.
1.2.13 The content of exhibits is sensitive to the diversity of cultural, religious, and gender groups in society.
1.2.14 Exhibits are durable.
1.2.15 Exhibits are safe and well maintained.
1.2.16 Exhibits are regularly evaluated.

2. Program

2.1 Museum Programming
   2.1.1 Public education programs and facilities are provided.
   2.1.2 Trained staff and volunteers are available to guide groups of visitors.
   2.1.3 The roles and responsibilities of the adults involved in the program are clearly defined.
2.2 Programming by School and Families
   2.2.1 In the process of preparing for a museum visit, the teacher/adult has contact with the venue.
   2.2.2 Children are prepared with previsit activities, and postvisit activities are planned as follow-up.
   2.2.3 Qualified and/or responsible adults are arranged to accompany children, at the recommended adult–child ratio.
   2.2.4 Adequate time is allowed for all aspects of the visit.
2.3 Touring Guidelines
   2.3.1 The visit begins with an introduction to the venue, as quickly as possible after entering the museum.
   2.3.2 The guide is prepared to follow the children's interests and capitalizes on teachable moments.
   2.3.3 The guide establishes a rapport with the group through quality interactions and an informal, conversational style.
   2.3.4 The tour group is kept small, appropriate to the ages of the children.
   2.3.5 Discussion of exhibits begins within children's comfort zone and moves to the less familiar.
   2.3.6 The guide ensures that all group members can see the exhibit and are included in discussion.
   2.3.7 Time spent on detailed examination of exhibits is varied over the duration of the tour.
   2.3.8 The guide uses vocabulary that can be clearly understood by the children, translating technical terms where necessary.
   2.3.9 The guide takes cues from visitors to determine the amount of time spent at individual exhibits.

2.3.10 Touring segments are no longer than 45 minutes (or less for very young children).

2.3.11 The guide is aware of time during the tour.

2.4 Touring Resources and Strategies

    2.4.1 Hands-on materials

    2.4.2 Props

    2.4.3 Strategies for evoking nonverbal responses

    2.4.4 Games

    2.4.5 Storytelling

    2.4.6 Visual thinking strategies

3. Social Milieu

3.1 Atmosphere

    3.1.1 A sense of happy involvement and fun is evident.

    3.1.2 Adults hold developmentally appropriate expectations of children's social behavior, and accept responsibility for encouraging appropriate behavior.

    3.1.3 The setting functions as a community of learners.

3.2 Interactions

    3.2.1 Nondirective behaviors

    3.2.2 Scaffolding behaviors

    3.2.3 Directive behaviors

Placing Objects Within Disciplinary Perspectives: Examples from History and Science

Robert Bain
University of Michigan

Kirsten M. Ellenbogen
King's College London

When trying to understand and improve a practice, such as learning from objects, it makes sense to look to practitioners. Historians, scientists, curators, educators, exhibit developers, and designers are all concerned with the interpretation of objects. Each belongs to a community that uses objects in its work and each community has developed a disciplinary "toolkit" filled with established modes of inquiry, evidentiary criteria, and accepted patterns of analysis to help in their object-related work. The different perspectives of these communities are reflected in the relative strengths and weaknesses of their toolkits. A disciplinary toolkit of an educator, for example, may have pedagogical strengths that contrast with the visual explanation strengths of an exhibit designer. Considering the ways practitioners situate and use objects in their work, therefore, prompts us to reconsider ways we might help learners use objects their learning.

This chapter argues that an examination of what it means to "do history" or "do science" raises fundamental questions about how children might define, observe, and interpret objects. We draw on educational, historical, scientific, philosophical, and sociological sources in order to understand what it means to use objects in doing history or doing science. Our purpose is not to make novices experts in those fields but rather to try to understand domain expertise and therefore inform our pedagogical efforts. The issues of What counts as an object? What does it mean to be an expert? and What does it mean to interpret an object? are explored as examples of the kinds of questions that

educators in and out of museums should raise in considering how our disciplinary perspectives might effect the interpretation of objects. Finally, we
conclude with a discussion of exhibitions and software that offer exemplars
of how to bring disciplinary perspectives into the interpretation of objects;
or more accurately, we discuss pedagogical attempts to place objects within
learner-centered disciplined inquiry.

OBJECTS IN HISTORY AND SCIENCE MUSEUMS

Objects in history and science museums[1] often overlap. You can go to the
Henry Ford Museum in Dearborn, Michigan or the Museum of Science and
Industry, Chicago to see planes, trains, and automobiles. Both institutions display important transportation artifacts that are interpreted regarding their
historical and technological significance. What, then, are the differences in the
objects found in history and science museums?

Objects in History Museums

The purpose of historic sites in America was initially focused on preservation
and inspiring patriotism; education was a later development (Schell, 1992).
History museums have been criticized for failing to move from a focus on objects to people, activities, and ideas (Carson, 1992). Such a move presents a
unique challenge to a history museum's use and display of objects. There is,
however, a simple power in being in the presence of objects from the past,
and therein lies the key issue for history museums. Witnessing an object first
hand is quite different from seeing it in a book or reading about it. The experience itself generates an air of authenticity and a sense that one is experiencing the past directly. After all, Charles Lindberg did fly that plane across the
Atlantic.

Yet, regardless of the object's authenticity, we cannot experience the past
directly. Museums necessarily display historical objects apart from their original context and therefore, the museum setting mediates the historical experience. Displays encourage meaning making that may add to or detract from the
types of historical conclusions learners draw from an object.

History curators are sensitive to these issues and work to display objects
within an appropriate historical context. Helping learners to see both the
object and the display setting is a unique challenge for history museums.

---

[1]Although there are important distinctions between science museums and science centers
(Durant, 1992), the boundaries between the two types of institutions are blurring. In this chapter
the two terms are used in one instance to draw an important contrast about uses of objects.
Otherwise, the term "science museum" is used broadly to encompass all types of informal science
education institutions.

Curatorial presence in the form of contextualizing display settings is thus a key component in the learner's use of objects in history museums.

Objects in Science Museums

There is very little curatorial presence on the staff of most modern science museums. The exceptions tend to be the science museums that grew out of collections gathered for World's Fairs (Danilov, 1982). Many of these World's Fair institutions still preserve and display their collections. Modern science centers founded in the wake of the Exploratorium and the Ontario Science Centre, however, have little or no artifacts of curatorial significance. These institutions tend to represent ideas rather than objects (McManus, 1992) and are more likely to have a scientist or artist on staff than a curator. The objects on display in modern science centers tend to be purpose-built exhibits that demonstrate a particular scientific phenomenon. These exhibits often carry the name of the phenomenon they demonstrate: Critical Angle, Convection Current, Bernoulli Blower, or Water Waves. The object involved is only a means to an end; it exists primarily to demonstrate a phenomenon.

Even in instances in which a science exhibit is object-based, the focus tends to be on what the object produces rather than the object itself. For example, in an exhibition about the human body, you may find a magnetic resonance imaging unit, but the focus is on the images it produces, not the machine itself. The exceptions are the cut-in-half exhibits showcasing a technological artifact, such as a computer, that has been modified to reveal its inner workings. So the plane you see at the Henry Ford Museum is mounted from the ceiling and interpreted with graphics at the floor level. At the Museum of Science and Industry, Chicago, the plane has been cut in half, attached to the balcony, and filled with interpretative graphics and interactive devices so that you can step inside and examine its inner workings. Such differences in interpretations often raise questions of an object's authenticity, another disciplinary consideration.

Authenticity

Visitors recognize and value authenticity in history (Korn, 1996) and science (Jones & Wageman, 2000) museums. Yet authenticity has different meanings in history and science. Authenticity for historians involves determining an object's legitimacy and creating its historic context. Inasmuch as all knowledge of the past is mediated by evidence, the trustworthiness of these links to the past is critical. Historical knowledge rests on historical evidence, and historians must be vigilant in investigating the reliability of any piece of evidence (Collingwood 1946; Hexter, 1971; Stanford, 1990). Determining the authentic value of a piece of evidence is no simple matter and cuts to the heart of the historian's dilemma of using "present" evidence to understand the past. To use an object, the historian must not only situate it in time and space, but also in relationship to a particular historical question.

The authenticity and importance of a museum's collection is determined in part, then, by the intellectual problems or questions the researchers bring to study that collection. Researchers' questions make an object a site for scholarly investigation. This might be clearest in history where historians' historical problems turn objects into "primary sources." "The whole perceptible world, then, is potentially and in principle evidence to the historian," according to philosopher R. G. Collingwood. "Evidence is evidence only when someone contemplates it historically. Otherwise it is merely perceived fact, historically dumb" (1946, p. 247). Our use of objects turns them into sources of meaning.

What are the implications for science museums? A computer simulation of the function and products of a scanning electron microscope is not authentic, but it is appropriate given the constraints of function, money, and location. In an institution where many of the objects on display are simulations or simply devices to demonstrate a scientific principle, what is the importance of authenticity? Authenticity in science is related to ideas and theories more than to objects.

For example, Crew and Sims (1991) explained that in addition to emphasizing the authenticity of objects themselves, it may also be useful to consider authenticity of the interpretation. In a history museum, the curators are ideally able to develop an interpretation of an object in a manner that approaches its authentic context, or provenance. Consider the Mattox House, a Depression Era sharecropper's home relocated from rural Georgia to the Henry Ford Museum & Greenfield Village in Dearborn, Michigan. This relocated southern house provides a rich context for studying the migration of millions of rural African Americans to the industrial north between 1930 and 1970. Yet an examination of archival material reveals that over 80% of the original home was replaced with new material due to termite infection. A lack of match between interpretation and provenance, however, should not preclude the use of the object. The question of authenticity should lie not in the object, but in the event. The context, interpretation, and experience of the object are of critical importance (Martin, 1996; Roberts, 1997). Although the electron microscope sitting behind glass is more authentic to a scientist visiting the science museum, it is the computer simulation of the electron microscope that is real to most visitors. The interpretation and subsequent experience of an object may be more real than the object itself.

EXPERT/NOVICE INTERPRETATION OF OBJECTS

Museums can make it hard for visitors to interpret an object by using disciplinary categories known to experts but not to the novice viewer (Alpers, 1991).

Viewing an object becomes even more difficult when the immediately visible evidence does not support the expert categories. For example, an art museum may organize its works chronologically, despite visible variations within the collection that demonstrate that the artists were not constrained by the time in which they lived. A novice sees a range of objects united only by the dates on their labels. In contrast, an expert knows the theories and histories supporting the interpretation of the objects and therefore has a richer experience. Thus a useful question is: How do expert and novice experiences differ, and how might we use our understanding of these differences to support and deepen the experiences of learners with quite varying degrees of expertise?

Expert and Novice Interpretation

Comparisons of expert–novice approaches to objects show that the primary issue is one of strategy, not volume of information (Bransford, Brown, & Cocking, 1999; Chi, Glaser, & Farr, 1991; Gobo & Chi, 1986; Wineburg, 1991). A study in the domain of dinosaurs showed that novices (children who knew little about dinosaurs) tended to focus on surface features when making category judgments. In contrast, children with extensive knowledge of dinosaurs categorized on the basis of cohesive features that were more implicit (Gobo & Chi, 1986). This cohesive knowledge structure allows experts to use information in a more structured and accessible way.

Wineburg's (1991) study of expert–novice approaches to using historical sources revealed that experts, in this case historians, used multiple strategies to "read" sources, such as corroborating and contextualizing. Novices rarely used such heuristics, seldom trying to situate a source in its context or connect it to other sources. Instead, novices attended to objects' surface features or scanned texts for facts. Wineburg concluded that these were not merely differences in age, reading strategies, or amount of factual knowledge. Rather, it was the novices' understanding of primary sources as providing direct access to the past that constrained their interpretations of objects, focusing attention on that which is most evident (see also Husbands, 1992). Wineburg's study demonstrated the dangers in assuming that access to real objects or sources is transformative. Without attending to the assumptions and presuppositions learners bring with them as they stand before an object, even the most authentic encounter with an object runs the risk of being subsumed in inauthentic, ahistoric frames.

Asking the Wrong Question?

It is tempting to ask if educators should try to turn novices into instant experts by duplicating for novices the expert's experience with an object. Such pedagogical alchemy is not what we are suggesting here, if for no other reason than the tremendous complexity involved in such transformation. Simply reconstructing the external trappings of the expert's experience is no guarantee that learners will reconstruct the "inside" of that experience. Clearly, novices can mimic expert behavior — such as reading primary sources or analyzing an object — without engaging in the thinking that characterizes the disciplinary essence of that behavior (see, for example, Wineburg, 1991). The expert–novice studies suggest ways that differences in knowledge organization, habits of mind, points of entry, and analytic styles impact experiences that on the surface appear to be similar. These studies also suggest ways educators might use the expert experience to help us enrich the learner's experience with objects.

Research on children's reasoning (Barton & Levstik, 1996; Booth, 1993; Duschl & Gitomer, 1997; Lee & Ashby, 2000; Metz, 1991, 1993; Schauble, 1990; Schauble, Glaser, Duschl, Schultze, & John, 1995) illustrates that educators have underestimated the ability of children to construct and evaluate historic interpretations and scientific explanations. Our traditional view of adult as expert and child as novice is not always appropriate. The study of experts and novices in the domain of dinosaurs described earlier (Gobo & Chi, 1986) involved children not just as novices, but also as experts. Additionally, visits to museums are often conducted in groups of mixed ages and expertise. It is perhaps this question of cross-generational problem solving that is most appropriate to an examination of object interpretation.

We know that parents are able to support their children's learning (Crowley et al., 2001; Wertsch, 1979; Wertsch, McNamee, McLane, & Budwig, 1980). Most studies, however, have been situated in domains in which the parents were able to act as experts. In other settings, such as those in which parent–child dyads were asked to solve unfamiliar problems, dyads were able to generate and interpret evidence, but parents tended to assume the most difficult conceptual tasks, delegating manual tasks to the children (Gleason & Schauble, 2000). Parents encouraged their children to physically participate, but missed opportunities to encourage children to participate in domain-specific activities, such as interpreting evidence. (See also chapter 15 by Callanan, Jipson, & Soennichsen, in this book.) This highlights the need to understand and encourage domain-specific interpretive strategies.

Considering domain-specific strategies for using and interpreting objects assists educators in helping learners expand the ways they use and interpret objects. By highlighting what is important in a discipline's approach to objects, educators can expand on their understanding of the knowledge and strategies needed for a successful museum visit. What knowledge and strategies, for example, are needed for a successful history or science museum visit? How might learners employ those strategies? An examination of the varying definitions of literacies sheds light on the discipline-specific nature of interpreting objects.

COMPARING LITERACIES

Object knowledge and *museum literacy* are terms that were introduced to highlight the belief that a command of the language and an interpretive framework for studying objects are necessary but not innate skills for museum visitors (Schlereth, 1992; Stapp, 1992; Williams, 1992). It is the museum's duty to help visitors understand the language and strategies of object interpretation. Basic museum literacy is an ability to read objects, which can be developed into full museum literacy — an ability to purposefully use a museum's resources (Stapp, 1992). Museums have a vast array of secondary sources, books, magazines, catalogs, and files about their collections. Although very important, only a fragment of these sources are fully visible in an exhibit and immediately accessible to the public. For experts, these resources provide essential support in corroborating and contextualizing studies centering around objects as primary sources. Museum resources also extend to the historical, social, and cultural context of the museum itself (Schlereth, 1992), requiring institutions to make visible their role in the history, culture, and space in which they are located.

Museum literacy carefully considers the role of visitors in the museum environment. The term, introduced in an effort to move to a visitor-centered approach, (Schlereth, 1992; Stapp, 1992; Williams, 1992) moves exhibitions away from the transmission of knowledge selected by the museum staff toward the construction of narratives determined by both the museum staff and the museum visitors (Roberts, 1997). A similar learner-centered emphasis shapes current education movements in history and science.

History Literacy

Controversy has marked almost all reform movements in history education (Nash, Crabtree, & Dunn, 1997) and many recent history museum exhibitions. Yet even during intense debates over content or direction, there has been remarkable agreement that historical knowledge is more than just the memorization of facts. The emerging criterion for literacy in history is understanding the productive use of historical facts in forming interpretations and reaching conclusions. Historical understanding is an active process. In a museum it involves approaching objects with questions in mind, employing history's toolkit to interrogate objects, and utilizing the museum's resources to expand and challenge interpretations and conclusions. Developing historical understanding requires strategically negotiating the physical, temporal, and intellectual distances between exhibited objects and the other resources that support their use.

Such negotiation is rare among learners who do not typically approach museums with questions in mind or follow exhibitors' codes to archives, libraries, or to the curators themselves. Do novice learners have the knowledge, skills, dispositions, and motivation to traverse the distances between displayed objects and their supporting resources? Are such materials arranged easily for the learner's use? There often is a gap between the ways novice learners and scholars approach objects, and this gap creates obstructions for educators seeking to help learners deepen their historical understanding.

It is tempting to hold that a first-hand experience with an authentic historical object deepens a learner's historical understanding. But does a disciplinary activity, such as working with a primary source, mechanically develop understanding? Do we automatically enhance learners' experiences by transplanting objects of interest from a community of historians to a body of novices (Bain, 2000; Seixas, 1993)? We think not, as disciplinary tasks embedded within the epistemic community draw meaning from the community's frames, scripts, and schemas. Novices learning history do not yet share the assumptions of historians and, therefore, think differently about evidence, primary sources, and historical objects (Barton & Levstik, 1996; Lee & Ashby, 2000; Seixas, 1993; Wineburg, 1991). The frames of meaning that sustain the study of material evidence within the community of historians may not exist within the classroom or the museum. Hence, learners may reject the transplanted activity. Or, the culture of the classroom or group will assimilate the authentic activity, using it to sustain pre-existing novice views. Engaging learners in legitimate disciplinary activity without restructuring the social interactions or challenging learners' presuppositions may yield only ritualistic understanding.

Making objects learner-centered involves more than providing access to the object. Educational challenges surface when trying to help learners build their understandings beyond the knowledge of facts, or of an object's surface characteristics. As we suggest later, creating domain-specific technological supports, expanding opportunities for mediated and unmediated conversations, and increasing chances for learners to perform their emerging understandings hold great promise in meeting these challenges.

Science Literacy

Current science education movements highlight a view of scientific literacy in which people need to understand science in a social context that is relevant to their lives (Bybee, 1997). Like museum literacy, the learner is central. Recent reform documents, such as the *National Science Education Standards* (National Research Council [NRC], 1996) explain that scientific literacy, or the ability to succeed in "personal decision making, participation in civic and cultural affairs, and economic productivity," rests on our understanding of scientific concepts and processes (NRC, 1996, p. 22). The focus is on the ability to do science and thereby understand and evaluate the doing of science.

In contrast to that definition, some definitions of scientific literacy are concerned primarily with factual concepts (Brennan, 1992; Hirsch, 1987; Trefil, 1993) and equate understanding with knowledge. A focus on facts is not limited to classrooms; it is implicit in many science museum exhibitions. Factual scientific literacy exemplifies the belief that learners simply need to be given a list of facts and they will be able to solve the many scientific problems that they face in their everyday lives. This belief is based on a deficit model that views the public as an empty vessel to be filled with scientific information from experts. The problem with this view is that it presumes that knowledge of facts includes an understanding of their significance and implications. More importantly, a focus on scientific facts treats science as a finished product. An emphasis on facts is what Schwab (1964) called the rhetoric of conclusions over science-in-the-making. Reading a book or an exhibit label to find facts is a practice we have all been taught, but it is a practice that ignores the making of science.

Science-in-the-making does not simply mean knowing how science works. Simply knowing how science works gives inappropriate credence to the notion that there is one scientific method. The posters typically seen in middle school classrooms perpetuate the notion of one scientific method: hypothesize, test, observe, and conclude. This does not reflect the reality of the way scientists work.

The traditional view of the individual scientist proving scientific theories to add to the accumulated body of knowledge has been replaced by a view of communities of scientists acting in concert or in tension to accept, revise, or simply abandon scientific claims (Kuhn, 1970; Latour & Woolgar, 1979; Longino, 1990). Research in the history and sociology of science shows that scientific claims are based in a community of scientists that shares values and standards about why we believe what we know. Science-in-the-making is more than an issue of method; it encompasses scientific knowledge, knowledge about how we came to know, and why we believe what we know (Duschl, 1990; Shapin, 1992). Until our presentation and interpretation of scientific objects reflect these three components of scientific knowledge, we cannot expect people to truly understand scientific objects. Introducing knowledge about how we came to know what we know, and why we believe it, into object-based learning adds another layer to museum literacy, demanding attention to and supports for these expanded interpretation strategies.

STRATEGIES FOR INTERPRETING OBJECTS

In disciplined inquiry, then, objects are sites for interpretation and sources of information rather than the information itself. A central element in taking a disciplinary perspective is making visible the thinking of the actors involved in the creation and interpretation of the object. Thus when working with museum objects, learners would benefit by also considering the thinking of curators, exhibit developers, and designers. Such interpretation of objects restores the "missing" (hidden) contexts that shape the meaning of the object (Roberts, 1997). To facilitate these experiences for learners, educators must help learners see the thinking embedded in an object by those who created and used the object in the past as well as those displaying the object in the present.

Interpreting History

Learners face challenges in making objects sites for inquiry and sources of information. In turn, educators face challenges in designing experiences to help learners (a) formulate legitimate inquiry problems or driving questions that transform objects into sources; (b) use disciplinary tools to interrogate objects; (c) connect objects/sources to relevant archival and curatorial resources; and, (d) employ museum resources in their inquiries and investigations. Again, when trying to understand and improve a practice — in this case helping learners "do" history — it makes sense to look to practitioners, in this case to consider the work of history educators.

Recent discussions of history teaching illuminate the challenges in treating history as an epistemic activity, calling for educators to merge a substantive understanding of the discipline with an equally sophisticated understanding of learning history (Bain, 2000; Husbands, 1996; Stearns, Seixas, & Wineburg, 2000). History teachers understand that teaching history is more complicated than either transmitting historical facts or engaging learners in history projects using primary sources (Bain, 2000, Husbands, 1996). The instructional challenge is to design activities that engage learners in disciplinary cognition without yielding to the tempting assumption that disciplinary tasks mechanically develop learners' higher functions. Epistemically grounded learning experiences in history must carefully utilize learners' presuppositions while simultaneously helping them work beyond their preinstructional assumptions (see Bain, 2000; Husbands, 1996; Lee & Ashby, 2000). Two design principles are very useful for history educators trying to meet that paradoxical challenge: make historical thinking visible to learners, and enable learners to employ the tools in the historian's toolkit. These principles inform the design of object-centered disciplined experiences.

A central element in doing history is making visible the thinking of historical actors. Some historians have even argued that all historical work is "rethinking past thoughts" (Collingwood, 1946). Such re-enactment is complicated when using museum objects because historians must also consider the thinking of curators and exhibitors. Therefore, educators trying to use the historical discipline to help enhance object-centered learning experiences must help learners see the thinking embedded in an object by those who created and used it as well as those displaying it now.

How can educators design experiences that help learners mine objects for veins of past and present thought before learners have the skills and dispositions for such excavation? Recent research in history teaching points to the value of creating learner-centered tools specific to historical inquiry and encouraging conversation around the inquiry (Bain, 2000; Husbands 1996; Seixas, 1993). Provided with access to learner-centered tools and opportunities to converse, learners can perform many more competencies than they could independently (Tharp & Gallimore, 1988). Embedding supports for historical thinking into objects and object-centered interactions changes learner's experiences with objects by allowing learners to participate in an assisted community of disciplined inquiry. Later, we discuss The Primary Sources Network, an example of this educational design.

Interpreting Science

Presentations of science in museums have traditionally focused on scientific facts, or what we know (Arnold, 1996). Exhibitions tend to focus on verification, that is, collecting data and making observations at one end and preset explanations at the other. There is no conversation about the middle ground of science—how data and observations are transformed into explanations. Ideally, science exhibitions should include (a) selecting data to use as evidence; (b) using evidence to generate patterns; and, (c) utilizing the patterns to propose explanations. Exhibitions must focus on all three components of science-in-the-making in order to reflect the essence of doing science.

Science museums do have a history of creating exhibitions that address the issue of science-in-the-making. In the early 1980s, *Inquiry* and later *Technology: Chance or Choice?* at the Museum of Science and Industry, Chicago examined not only scientific processes, but also the human and fallible side of science (Pridmore, 1996). Now there are numerous examples of exhibitions that highlight scientific processes, including *Investigate* at the Museum of Science in Boston. *Investigate* uses three separate sections, "The Lure of Questions," "Search for Evidence," and "The Art of Drawing Conclusions," to give learners opportunities to practice science. People use the exhibits to generate data, select data to use as evidence, utilize evidence to find patterns, and formulate explanations (Bailey, Bronnenkant, Kelley, & Hein, 1999). These examples are rich sources for exploring the processes of science; however, they lack an emphasis on the contexts and sources of knowledge, for example, how we came to know something and why we believe it.

There are fewer examples of exhibitions that incorporate the sources as well as the processes of scientific knowledge. The *Empire of Physics* at the Whipple Museum at Cambridge University addresses the sources of science by presenting two views of the same subject (Arnold, 1996). Downstairs, 19th-century physics is presented as part of the private and sometimes unintelligible activities of researchers in their laboratory. Upstairs the same science is presented as finished products in the context of an international exhibition. Another approach is the *Science is . . .* exhibition at the Birmingham Museum of Science and Industry in England (Baldock, 1995). This exhibition is designed to complement a hands-on gallery about light through historic debates about views of the universe and theories about night and day. The exhibition makes the cultural aspects of science visible, calling attention to the ways in which changes in scientific thought have led to changes in our views of ourselves.

Both *The Empire of Physics* and *Science is . . .* use history of science and are located in science museums that have historic collections. But it is possible to address the issue of sources of science within a modern science center. *A Question of Truth* at the Ontario Science Centre examines how scientific ideas are formed and challenges the notion of absolute scientific truth by presenting the validity of diverse points of view about science (Pedretti & Forbes, 1999). Single topics, such as navigation, are examined through diverse objects from different cultures, presenting multiple "correct" scientific theories. *A Question of Truth* is designed to be provocative, but at its essence it is an effort to bring to the forefront the typically unexamined relationship between scientific knowledge and science-in-the-making.

These highlighted exhibitions are exemplary, but not exhaustive in scope or medium. New technological tools are another way to facilitate disciplined inquiry centering on objects as sources. Next we examine a technology-based model for facilitating disciplined inquiry around objects in history and science.

A Technology-Supported Model for Interpreting Objects

Technology in museums of the future promises to make objects more, not less accessible (Anderson, 1999). Computer databases have the potential to enrich an object-centered experience by connecting it to other related experiences, objects, and resources. We are not suggesting that electronic experiences replace the object, but technology might extend and support learners' experiences with objects. What form, then, should the technology-supported examination of an object take?

The Primary Source Network (PSN) is a partnership between the Henry Ford Museum & Greenfield Village (HFM&GV), educators and researchers at the University of Michigan, and three Detroit area schools. The collaborative effort seeks to encourage students to use HFM&GV's resources as they work on historical and scientific questions. The PSN curriculum frames authentic historical and social scientific problems (i.e., Why did/do people migrate?) or engages students in asking legitimate driving questions in science (i.e., Can we build a safe cell phone?). The curriculum anchors historical and scientific questions in students' lives and assists them in their inquiries.

PSN technology aims to support student interrogation of objects in a number of ways. First, PSN provides digitized images to allow students to "revisit" objects electronically. Second, electronic objects sit within a frame of learner-centered supports. The frame reminds students of the central questions they are investigating, and affords them space to capture text and images. Students use an electronic notebook to record ideas and are able to access an online discussion about the object.

For each object, PSN has a series of layered prompts that support students' interrogations of the object. Each prompt helps students probe the object by encouraging them to ask questions about the object's creation, use, and context. Through these electronic tools, students are prompted to look for internal contradictions or anomalies in the object or to suggest other sources that might support, expand, or contest their understandings of the object under investigation. The prompts serve as scaffolds to help students formulate questions and to see the object more strategically. Each of the prompts is layered, and each layer offers richer support for the students by asking progressively more direct and object-specific questions. Although not meant to replace a curator or teacher, the frame tries to replicate questions a facilitator might ask to help the student focus more strategically on the object.

Asking strategic questions, though, does not enable students to answer those questions. Often the questions students raise cannot be answered on site. Indeed, observations of students' visits revealed that most student-generated questions died out in rhetorical speculation (Bain, Marx, Dershermer, & Mucher, 2000). Students could not adequately answer most of their questions on the object because most of the needed resources were housed in museum archives. Students raised questions that were best pursued through the museum's extensive collection of photographs, documents, and recordings connected to the object and by talking to the museum's staff. Time, distance, and archival skills typically make such further investigation difficult for students.

PSN technology tries to address this inquiry problem by enabling students to move immediately beyond the object through links to a wealth of sources sitting electronically "behind" the object. Thus, students can connect instantly to other resources to help reconstruct the object within its appropriate context. For example, PSN's virtual Mattox house is linked to a wealth of relevant sources, putting students a mouse click away from an oral history of a Mattox neighbor describing life in the 1930s, or the 1930s census record listing the employment records for members of the Mattox family. The technology shortens the spatial and temporal distance between the object and the archive, providing learners with immediate, learner-centered access to relevant resources.

Linking varied resources to an object enables students to consider the ways in which museum objects are themselves representations. PSN also connects curatorial and exhibitor resource notes to the object. This helps learners consider how other experts think about the object and how they decide to present the object to the public. Students have access to perspectives challenging the visual evidence, such as archival photos of the object or internal museum memos discussing the authenticity of the object. Such alternative evidence challenges students' ideas of authenticity and helps them to go beyond surface appearances, to dig even deeper into the object and its variegated contexts.

The PSN tools also support students as they construct their own representations of the problem under investigation. Grounded in their analysis of objects and documents as well as their own data gleaned from interviews and surveys, the electronic tool scaffolds students' construction of their own account of the phenomenon they study. Such student work may itself become part of the virtual database as a resource connected to the object. Therefore, students can produce material that, once archived electronically, supports others' interpretations of the object.

PSN's technology assists students in analyzing, contextualizing, and interpreting objects central to their investigations in history and science. The tool, of course, does not replace the hands-on or on-site experiences; rather, it extends and expands those experiences by paying careful attention to the needs of learners in using objects in disciplined inquiry. Although clearly aimed at museum–school partnerships, we think that PSN's principles of supporting disciplined inquiry have resonance in other learning environments, as we discuss next.

CONCLUSIONS

A disciplinary perspective reorients object-centered learning by situating the object within an investigation. Though an object may motivate and anchor a learner's investigation in history or science, it is the learner's problems and driving questions that transform the object into sources, data, and evidence. Such transformation is complicated work made easier when the learner is able to employ disciplinary tools of history or science. This strategic thinking helps the learner conduct investigations; locate and employ available resources; construct, generate, and use new data sources; analyze, evaluate, and interpret all sources including objects; and finally, use evidence to build and represent their own understandings.

Technology offers robust tools to scaffold learners' object-centered experiences. These tools supplement and assist but do not replace direct experiences. Rather, they make the material objects a key component of an inquiry, and then support learners as they extend their investigations beyond a one-time field trip or visit and beyond mere reading of museum labels. An exhibit supporting learner-centered disciplinary inquiry also enables effortless links to powerful resources that support, extend, or contest learners' interpretations. The goal is to increase the number of accessible resources while shortening the time and distance a learner travels to access them. Particularly powerful are those resources that disrupt anticipated interpretations and stimulate modest dissonance to encourage learners to puzzle about their interpretations and conclusions.

Familiarity with a range of anticipated interpretations and learning strategies is essential in enhancing learner-centered designs. Providing opportunities for learners to talk about an object and then finding ways to capture that conversation or their conclusions both enhances learning and provides a way for educators to consider the range of interpretations surrounding a particular object. Constructing a community of inquirers — even if temporary — promises rich rewards for learners and educators.

In situating objects within disciplined inquiry and supporting learners to use the disciplinary toolkit to interrogate sources, educators are not trying to teach the discipline. Rather, educators help learners employ disciplinary tools to extend and enrich the experience, making more readily available the wealth of resources and interpretations already present in the museum.

REFERENCES

Alpers, S. (1991). The museum as a way of seeing. In I. Karp & S. D. Lavine (Eds.), *Exhibiting cultures: The poetics and politics of museum display* (pp. 25–32). Washington DC: Smithsonian Institution Press.

Anderson, M. L. (1999). Museums of the future: The impact of technology on museum practices. *Daedalus, 128*(3), 129–162.

Arnold, K. (1996). Presenting science as a product or as process: Museums and the making of science. In S. M. Pearce (Ed.), *Exploring science in museums.* London: Athlone.

Bailey, E., Bronnenkant, K., Kelley, J., & Hein, G. (1999). *Visitor behavior at a constructivist exhibit: Evaluating "Investigate!" at Boston's Museum of Science.* Unpublished internal report, Boston Museum of Science.

Bain, R. B. (2000). Into the breach: Using research and theory to shape history instruction. In P. Seixas, P. Stearns, & S. Wineburg (Eds.), *Knowing, teaching & learning history: National and international perspectives* (pp. 331–353). New York: New York University Press.

Bain, R. B., Marx, R. W., Dershermer, C., & Mucher, S. (2000, April). *Children and museums as resources for learning: The Primary Sources Network.* Paper presented at the American Educational Research Association (AERA-NARST special session), New Orleans.

Baldock, J. (1995). Science is . . . at the Birmingham Museum of Science and Industry. *Public Understanding of Science, 4*(3), 285–298.

Barton, K. C., & Levstik, L. S. (1996). "Back when God was around and everything:" Elementary children's understanding of historical time. *American Educational Research Journal, 33*(2), 419–454.

Booth, M. (1993). Students' historical thinking and the national history curriculum in England. *Theory and Research in Social Education, 21*(2), 105–127.

Bransford, J., Brown, A. L., & Cocking, R. R. (Eds.). (1999). *How people learn: Brain, mind, experience, and school.* Washington, DC: National Academy Press.

Brennan, R. P. (1992). *Dictionary of scientific literacy.* Chichester, England: Wiley.

Bybee, R. W. (1997). *Achieving scientific literacy: From purposes to practices.* Portsmouth, NH: Heinemann.

Carson, B. G. (1992). Interpreting history through objects. In S. K. Nichols (Ed.), *Patterns in practice: Selections from the Journal of Museum Education* (pp. 129-133). Washington, DC: Museum Education Roundtable.

Chi, M. T. H., Glaser, R., & Farr, M. (1991). *The nature of expertise.* Hillsdale, NJ: Lawrence Erlbaum Associates.

Collingwood, R. G. (1946). *The idea of history.* Oxford: Clarendon Press.

Crew, S. R., & Sims, J. E. (1991). Locating authenticity: Fragments of a dialogue. In I. Karp & S. D. Lavine (Eds.), *Exhibiting cultures: The poetics and politics of museum display* (pp. 159-175). Washington DC: Smithsonian Institution Press.

Crowley, K., Callanan, M. A., Jipson, J., Galco, J., Topping, K., & Shrager, J. (2001). Shared scientific thinking in everyday parent–child activity. *Science Education.*

Danilov, V. J. (1982). *Science and technology centers.* Washington, DC: MIT Press.

Durant, J. (1992). Introduction. In J. Durant (Ed.), *Museums and the public understanding of science.* London: Science Museum.

Duschl, R. A. (1990). *Restructuring science education: The importance of theories and their development.* New York: Teachers College Press.

Duschl, R. A., & Gitomer, D. H. (1997). Strategies and challenges to changing the focus of assessment and instruction in science classrooms. *Educational Assessment, 4*(1), 37-73.

Gleason, M. E., & Schauble, L. (2000). Parents' assistance of their children's scientific reasoning. *Cognition and Instruction, 17*(4), 343-378.

Gobo, C., & Chi, M. T. H. (1986). How knowledge is structured and used by expert and novice children. *Cognitive Development, 1,* 221-237.

Hexter, J. H. (1971). *The history primer.* New York: Basic Books.

Hirsch, E. D. (1987). *Cultural literacy: What every American needs to know.* Boston: Houghton Mifflin.

Husbands, C. (1992). Objects, evidence and learning: Some thoughts on meaning and interpretation in museum education. *Journal of Education in Museums, 13,* 1-2.

Husbands, C. T. (1996). *What is history teaching? Language, ideas, and meaning in learning about the past.* Philadelphia: Open University Press.

Jones, J., & Wageman, S. (2000). *The promise of immersive environments.* [On-line]. Available: http://www.thetech.org/rmpo/aam-tk-paper.html.

Korn, R. (1996). *Evaluation of the "Becoming Americans" theme and "Choosing Revolution" story: Responses to visitor interviews.* Unpublished manuscript. Williamsburg, VA: Colonial Williamsburg Foundation.

Kuhn, T. S. (1970). *The structure of scientific revolutions* (2nd ed.). Chicago: University of Chicago Press.

Latour, B., & Woolgar, S. (1979). *Laboratory life: The construction of scientific facts.* Princeton, NJ: Princeton University Press.

Lee, P., & Ashby, R. (2000). Progression in historical understanding. In P. Stearns, P. Seixas, & S. S. Wineburg (Eds.), *Knowing, teaching, and learning history: National and international perspectives* (pp. 199-223). New York: New York University Press.

Longino, H. (1990). *Science as social knowledge.* Princeton, NJ: Princeton University Press.

Martin, L. (1996). Learning in context. *ASTC Newsletter, 24*(2), 2-5.

McManus, P. M. (1992). Topics in museums and science education. *Studies in Science Education, 20,* 157-182.

Metz, K. E. (1991). Development of explanation: Incremental and fundamental change in children's physics knowledge. *Journal of Research in Science Teaching, 28,* 785-798.

Metz, K. E. (1993). Preschoolers' developing knowledge of the pan balance: From new representation to transformed problem solving. *Cognition and Instruction, 11*(1) 31-93.

Nash, G. B., Crabtree, C., & Dunn, R. E. (1997). *History on trial: Culture wars and the teaching of the past.* New York: Alfred A. Knopf.

National Research Council. (1996). *National science education standards.* Washington, DC: National Academy Press.

Pedretti, E., & Forbes, J. (1999, April). *A question of truth: Critiquing the culture and practice of science through science centres and schools.* Paper presented at the annual meeting of the American Educational Research Association, Montreal, Canada.

Pridmore, J. (1996). Inventive genius: The history of the Museum of Science and Industry Chicago. Chicago: Museum of Science and Industry.

Roberts, L. C. (1997). *From knowledge to narrative: Educators and the changing museum.* Washington DC: Smithsonian Institution Press.

Schauble, L. (1990). Belief revision in children: The role of prior knowledge and strategies for generating evidence. *Journal of Experimental Child Psychology 49,* 31-57.

Schauble, L., Glaser, R., Duschl, R., Schultze, S., & John, J. (1995). Students' understanding of the objectives and procedures of experimentation in the science classroom. *The Journal of the Learning Sciences, 4*(2), 131-166.

Schell, S. B. (1992). On interpretation and historic sites. In S. K. Nichols (Ed.), *Patterns in practice: Selections from the Journal of Museum Education* (pp. 102-111). Washington, DC: Museum Education Roundtable.

Schlereth, T. J. (1992). Object knowledge: Every museum visitor an interpreter. In S. K. Nichols (Ed.), *Patterns in practice: Selections from the Journal of Museum Education* (pp. 102-111). Washington, DC: Museum Education Roundtable.

Schwab, J. J. (1964). The structure of the natural sciences. In G. W. Ford & L. Pugno (Eds.), *The structure of knowledge and the curriculum* (pp. 31-49). Chicago: Rand McNally.

Seixas, P. (1993). The community of inquiry as a basis for knowledge and learning: The case of history. *American Educational Research Journal, 302,* 305-324.

Shapin, S. (1992). Why the public ought to understand science-in-the-making. *Public Understanding of Science, 1*(1), 27-30.

Stanford, M. (1990). *The nature of historical knowledge.* Oxford: Blackwell.

Stapp, C. B. (1992). Defining museum literacy. In S. K. Nichols (Ed.), *Patterns in practice: Selections from the Journal of Museum Education* (pp. 112-117). Washington, DC: Museum Education Roundtable.

Stearns, P., Seixas, P., & Wineburg, S. S. (Eds.). (2000). *Knowing, teaching, & learning history: National and international perspectives.* New York: New York University Press.

Tharp, R. G., & Gallimore, R. (1988). *Rousing minds to life: Teaching, learning and schooling in social context.* New York: Cambridge University Press.

Trefil, J. (1993). *1001 things everyone should know about science.* London: Cassell.

Wertsch, J. V. (1979). From social interaction to higher psychological processes: A clarification and application of Vygotsky's theory. *Human Development, 22*(1), 1-22.

Wertsch, J. V., McNamee, G. D., McLane, J. B., & Budwig, N. A. (1980). The adult-child dyad as a problem-solving system. *Child Development, 51,* 1215-1221.

Williams, P. B. (1992). Object contemplation: Theory into practice. In S. K. Nichols (Ed.), *Patterns in practice: Selections from the Journal of Museum Education* (pp. 118-122). Washington, DC: Museum Education Roundtable.

Wineburg, S. S. (1991). Historical problem solving: A study of the cognitive processes used in documentary and pictorial evidence. *Journal of Educational Psychology, 83*(1), 73-87.

CHAPTER TEN

Fostering an Investigatory Stance: Using Text to Mediate Inquiry with Museum Objects

Susanna E. Hapgood
Annemarie Sullivan Palincsar
University of Michigan

"The true work of art is not the object that sits in a museum nor the perform-ance captured on film or disc. Rather, it is the experience occasioned by the production or the experience of appreciating objects and performances." These words expressed by Jackson (1998) are also captured in expressions we have used ourselves on viewing exhibits of various kinds: That piece is moving. That display left me cold. I was transported by that work.

Although experience is often considered a very personal and private affair, Dewey (1934) urged that rather than thinking of experience as something that happens exclusively within the individual, we adopt a far more inclusive conception of experience: "Instead of signifying being shut up within one's private feelings and sensations, experience signifies active and alert com-merce with the world; at its height it signifies complete interpenetration of self and the world of objects and events" (p. 25).

Clearly, not all encounters with objects yield "an experience." Whether and how one experiences objects is a function of the interplay of the characteris-tics of the object, the knowledge and dispositions that one brings to the view-ing, and the context in which one views the object. In this chapter we con-sider the role that *mediation* might play in determining the nature of one's experience with objects. Specifically, we are interested in pursuing the role of textual mediation in enhancing educative experiences in museum contexts.

Dewey (1938) suggested that an educative experience is one that "pre-pare(s) a person for later experience of a deeper and more expansive quality"

(p. 28). Like all educational institutions, museums are about ideas. Although the specific ideas privileged and the ways of representing those ideas are hotly contested, the question common to all educational institutions is how to facilitate thoughtful experiences with these ideas. Thought and reflection can occur about many aspects of a topic. Furthermore, an individual can respond to any topic from many perspectives: aesthetic, personal, historical, and analytical, to name a few. We are interested in mediation for the purpose of inviting the participant to assume an investigatory stance.

An investigatory stance can be characterized in a number of ways and across a number of domains (e.g. history, science, art). For example, integral to investigation is the role of questions guiding the encounter with a phenomenon, text or object. These questions are typically pursued through close and systematic observations, often in the form of collecting data, which are in turn linked with assertions and claims. If we accept the assumption that museums consider promoting an investigatory stance, many other questions follow: What would it look like for a visitor to be engaged in an investigation in a museum exhibit? What features of an exhibit would foster this kind of interaction with museum content? What specific role might text play in supporting an investigative stance and what features of text might work particularly well? To address these questions, we first provide illustrative examples of how participants might engage in investigation in museum contexts, framing the investigation in terms of first- and second-hand experiences (Magnusson & Palincsar, 1995). We then develop a case for the value of mediating museum experiences, drawing on empirical research as well as sociocultural theory regarding the activity of museum goers. Finally, drawing on classroom research regarding the interplay of first- and second-hand experiences in guided inquiry science instruction, we identify the role of text, in general, and specific text features in supporting inquiry.

ILLUSTRATING AN INVESTIGATIVE STANCE IN MUSEUM CONTEXTS

Visitors to museum exhibits may engage in many kinds of investigations as they explore an exhibit. Often, these investigations may be of a first-hand nature. For example, coming upon a dugout canoe, someone might ask, "How on earth did someone make this?" This hypothetical visitor might then look very closely at the canoe on display and discover blackened areas as well as axe marks and conclude that the makers of the canoe had used a combination of methods — both burning and cutting — to hollow out the canoe. This would constitute a "first-hand investigation" inasmuch as the visitor had, with a question in mind, examined the object and collected data that were then used to address the question.

Museum visitors may also engage in "second-hand investigations," in which they are learning from the investigations and interpretations of others. One sort of second-hand investigation might be about the question: Why are particular objects on display? There is usually some reason for certain parts of an exhibit to be grouped and for interpretive texts to accompany displays and interactive stations. To the extent that anyone notices that objects are grouped and to the extent that anyone questions the texts, museum visitors are engaged in second-hand investigations, that is, investigations of another person's way of making sense of something.

In the research that we describe later in this chapter, we have found that children bring the tools (e.g., ideas, language, or ways of representing information) that they have gleaned during second-hand investigations and use them during first-hand investigations. We have also found the reverse to occur — that the children take tools, such as a way of questioning or an understanding of how to justify a claim with evidence, that they have used during a first-hand investigation, and use it to support a second-hand investigation. We argue in our classroom work that there is an "interplay" between first-hand and second-hand investigations. How might this work in a museum context?

In a second-hand investigation, the text and object can also work in concert to provide another view of a field of inquiry. Imagine a natural history museum with a traditional exhibit on early hominids. Within this exhibit, imagine a display case with two skulls, one identified as Neanderthal and one as early modern European human. A visitor might initially be struck by their similarity and wonder, are Neanderthals human ancestors? The text immediately available to the visitor identified the skulls as Neanderthal and early modern European human, that they were both found in the same region of Northern Croatia, and were of approximately the same age. What is a visitor to make of these skulls now? Perhaps that *homo sapiens* and *homo neanderthalenis* coexisted at some point. But did one precede the other? Were they really different species? How do we know that?

Now imagine this same exhibit with a second-hand investigation embedded in it. A text panel could describe how a paleoanthropologist compares the two skulls. A text of this sort might include a diagram of the skulls that was labeled to show the various parts. It might also say something like:

> Paleoanthropologists, or scientists who study fossils of early hominids, examine a cluster of features to distinguish Neanderthal and early modern European skulls. Here are a few of the features to look for: Neanderthal skulls have larger "occipital buns," which are the protuberances at the back of the skull. Neanderthals also have a more pronounced browridge above the eyes, and no chin. Above the back-most molar on the lower jaw and the upper molar there is a gap, called the retromolar gap on the Neanderthal. In early modern European skulls the back-most molars meet.

This text would provide more explicit information, in addition to providing the visitor with tools with which to compare these and other skulls. However, it is possible to take the second-hand investigation a step further to put the visitor in a position of understanding *how* a paleoanthropologist had thought to look at such features and confirm that they were typical of these hominid types. It would also be possible to include a sense of how observational data are combined with other forms of evidence such as DNA evidence and additional fossils and stone tools. For example, on this topic, such a text could be written in the voice of a particular paleoanthropologist who interprets the data to suggest that Neanderthals and early modern humans coexisted in large areas of Europe for thousands of years, and, contrary to what had been previously thought, Neanderthals and early humans interbred, giving rise to the possibility that Neanderthals may have been ancestors of early humans. Of course, there are other paleoanthropologists who would dispute these interpretations. A second-hand investigation text could also convey *how* interpretations of all of these data are debated and contested, by, for example, sharing actual findings of various studies, as well as multiple paleoanthropologists' interpretations of these findings.

In summary, reflecting on the occasions for first- and second-hand investigations in museum contexts may provide a useful means for people to connect with objects as well as offer museum visitors another way of thinking about objects. The intent is not to usurp vistors' own sense-making of objects, but rather to suggest additional possible ways to approach objects. In the preceding example, we hope that we illustrated how a common natural history museum exhibit (human skulls) can be transformed from an object with a singular, unambiguous meaning, to a piece of evidence at the center of a contemporary and contentious question for debate: "Were Neanderthal and early modern European humans related?" (Wong, 2000). The viewer is invited to become a member of the community engaged in the debate, and the objects become "alive" (Holt, 1990).

AN EMPIRICALLY-BASED RATIONALE
FOR MEDIATING EXPERIENCES WITH OBJECTS

Museum educators and exhibit developers alike strive to create engaging experiences, often with educational objectives (Ansbacher, 1999). Visitors who come to museums with strong interests in particular subjects may experience "flow" states (Cszikszentmihalyi & Hermanson, 1995) during which they feel so deeply engaged with an activity that they lose all track of time. But there is empirical evidence that the experience may fall far short of this. For example, in their observational study, Paris, Troop, Henderlong, & Sulfaro (1994) documented how children in Grades 1 through 8 spent time as they visited a "Hands-on Museum." Among an interesting set of findings was the observation that children spent brief amounts of time at each exhibit. The range was 48 seconds for girls in the 10-13 year range, to 83 seconds for boys in the 6-9 year range. The limited time that children spent at each exhibit precluded deep engagement with the learning opportunities afforded by particular exhibits. Paris et al. (1994) further noted that the design features of particular exhibits did not encourage sustained time; for example, exhibits that had the potential for viewers to consider and work with complex ideas were designed in such a fashion that the children were preoccupied with the procedural aspects of the exhibit. Findings such as these have prompted researchers, working in collaboration with museum personnel, to investigate design features for the purpose of enhancing engagement and learning in museum contexts. We next review several of these studies.

Mirroring the findings of Paris et al. (1994), Gelman, Massey, and McManus (1991) observed that, when viewing an exhibit that explicitly invited comparisons of the rate at which two balls raced through tubing of different lengths and configurations, children rarely used the exhibit in the fashion intended, choosing instead to repeatedly send one ball at a time through the two arrangements, precluding the opportunity to use scientific and mathematical thinking to compare, describe, and explain why the conditions lead to different outcomes. To meet the challenge of engaging children in more thoughtful experiences with the racing balls exhibit, Gelman et al. (1991) designed a computer program that verbally prompted the viewer to race the balls down the cylinders to determine which would get to the bottom first. After a suitable amount of time, the voice inquired as to which ball reached the bottom first and why. Finally, the computer script provided an explanation of the motion of the two balls relative to the distance they each had to travel. Upon introduction of the computer-generated prompts, the procedural verbalizations decreased and the number of scientific verbalizations (which the researchers defined as predictions, descriptions of patterns in the data, and explanations) increased. Gelman et al. argued that the prompts supported the development of the conceptual structures necessary for new learning and noted that this was an especially important feature to consider in the design of museum exhibits inasmuch as, typically, museums seek to engage viewers with novel experiences, experiences for which they may have limited knowledge structures. We return to this discussion of knowledge structures in our discussion of the role that text might play in guiding viewers' interactions with objects.

In an investigation of the role that parents can play in mediating children's experiences with science exhibits, Crowley and Callanan (1998) studied the experiences of children as they interacted with an exhibit either accompanied or unaccompanied by a parent. They determined that children who were accompanied by a parent were advantaged by the fact that parents often engaged in three types of explanations: explanations focused on the mechanism at work in the exhibit, explanations linking the display to real-world phenomena, and explanations introducing formal scientific principles. Informed by these findings, they set about to redesign an exhibit that had been observed to elicit low levels of interaction and engagement. The first revision was to increase the space so that it would comfortably accommodate more than one individual. Similar to the work of Gelman et al. (1991), Crowley and Callanan also introduced a computer voice that guided the visitors through the interaction. As a result of these revisions, there was a marked increase in the intended use of the exhibit. As we discuss the role that text can play, we also focus on the role of explanation; however, we are particularly interested in how text can invite children into the process of generating and testing explanations for natural phenomena.

In contrast to the fairly modest learning goals of the design projects just reviewed, Stevens and Hall (1997) were interested in the design of an exhibit for the purpose of leading the viewer through an inquiry process: from the initial experience of puzzlement regarding a phenomenon, to the detailed examination and analysis of the phenomenon that would afford the construction of new understandings, culminating in a deeper understanding of the variables and principles at work in the phenomenon. Stevens and Hall began their research observing the activity of museum goers with a particularly attractive exhibit at the Exploratorium in San Francisco that provided the opportunity for the visitor to actually climb inside a chamber in which there was a simulated tornado. Echoing the findings reported earlier, visitors spent remarkably short periods of time in the tornado exhibit, engaged in very little manipulation, and, perhaps consequently, made few verbalizations that addressed the variables interacting to cause a tornado. Stevens and Hall (1997) designed an additional experience to complement the *Tornado Exhibit*, which they referred to as *Video Traces*. They videotaped visitors interacting with the *Tornado Exhibit*. Visitors were then invited to review the videotape with one of the researchers. Visitors spent, on average, eight times as much time watching and discussing the video records of their encounters with Tornado, as they had with the actual exhibit. Indeed, many visitors became so intrigued by the phenomenon that they went back to the exhibit and continued to explore after the discussion with the videotape. The researchers suggested that the video representation of the phenomenon enabled visitors to change the "time-scale" of the phenomenon by slowing down or freezing the motion of the tornado, thereby promoting more detailed questioning and attempts to explain the forces involved at critical moments. We suggest that the researchers' participation during the discussions was also a critical factor. The researcher, being more knowledgeable, helped direct visitors' attention to salient moments and modeled some ways to ask questions about and discuss the phenomenon.

We propose that the video-record could support an exemplary second-hand investigation. If the mediating interview were also recorded, what a new visitor would see would be the recorded visitor talking with someone about his or her initial exploration of the phenomenon. In this way the new visitor would have some ways of discussing the phenomenon modeled. This could provide this new visitor with ways of thinking about and looking at the actual exhibit that they might not have thought of alone. As we describe the role that second-hand investigations designed to support inquiry might play in museum contexts, we explore how these experiences might shape or re-shape the lenses with which one views and experiences objects. Specifically, we argue that texts can engage the viewer in experiencing the object in a mode that is reflective of the community for whom this object or phenomenon is a common object of study. This idea draws heavily from sociocultural perspectives on teaching and learning, which we review next.

SOCIOCULTURAL THEORY AND INVESTIGATORY ACTIVITY

The origin of knowledge from a sociocultural perspective is located among the interactions of members of a social group that are situated within a particular and ever dynamic historical and material context (Case, 1993). Children are thought to learn by working in collaboration with peers and more expert members of a community "in carrying out activities with purposes connected explicitly with the history and current practices of the community" (Rogoff, Matusov, & White, 1996, p. 390). A child or novice to a group begins as a "newcomer" and gradually becomes an "oldtimer" through ongoing interactions with fellow newcomers and with the guidance of oldtimers (Lave & Wenger, 1991).

Furthermore, from a sociocultural perspective, inquiry is recognized as a complex form of human thought that has developed over thousands of years. Hence, it is unlikely that, even in the context of cleverly designed and attractive exhibits, viewers will assume an investigative stance in the absence of support — a finding suggested by the empirical work reviewed earlier. From a sociocultural perspective, we are encouraged to think about ways in which exhibits could be designed to facilitate systematic exploration; making transparent the ways in which an expert might approach the artifact, attempt to make sense of the artifact, and communicate his or her observations about the artifact. (For additional discussion of similar ideas, see Rowe, chapter 2, this volume.)

As one example of how this might work in a museum context, imagine someone visiting an art museum for the first time. There are many ways to react to an art work and experienced visitors and certainly art museum curators use a range of strategies (Yenawine, 1995). Many of the strategies and tools experienced art viewers have, such as the questions they ask and the language they use to describe an artwork, can be shared with more novice participants in the "art-museum-visiting community." A question becomes how to allow for visitors to interact in ways that facilitate the sharing of such tools.

One example of what this might look like comes from an exhibit in a contemporary art museum in a large midwestern city. The museum staff had set up a "talk-back" area. Talk-back areas are common in museums and typically consist of a bulletin board onto which visitors can tack comments and questions about an exhibit. Sometimes curators or museum educators also post notes in response to visitors' comments. In this talk-back area, the focus was on just one sculpture, which was mounted to the wall. Adjacent to the sculpture was a series of questions for visitors to consider. In the corner was a booth where visitors could videotape themselves commenting on the sculpture, and in front of the booth was a monitor that played a continuous tape of visitor comments. If we consider this exhibit from a sociocultural perspective, the questions on the wall could be viewed as the more experienced art viewers' guidance to newcomers and the videotape as newcomers and oldtimers participating in structuring the experience of viewing a particular sculpture.

This example lends itself to the discussion of another construct within a sociocultural perspective, the idea of a "community of practice" with, in this case, the "art-museum-visiting" community constituting a "community of practice." The practice in this case is the activity of visiting art museums, and inherent in this practice are many shared conventions about how to behave in this setting and what to value in an art museum. In our classroom research, we have been inquiring into how a particular form of text can be used to communicate the practices specific to engaging in scientific inquiry. In addition, we look at how engaging in scientific inquiry can shape the practices of the classroom community so that it more closely reflects the practices of a scientific community. We next turn to this research.

ILLUSTRATING THE ROLE OF TEXT IN SUPPORTING SECOND-HAND INVESTIGATIONS

In our work in classrooms we have collected evidence to support the notion that first-hand experiences can interact with second-hand experiences in ways that enhance learning opportunities for children. During first-hand investigations, children pose questions and use materials to test these questions. They collect their own data sets, looking for patterns and suggesting possible ways to explain these patterns. During second-hand investigations, the children in these elementary classrooms have examined a fictional scientist's "notebooks" in which the scientist's questions, experimental set up, data, and reasoning were recorded. In this investigatory mode, children are looking closely at ideas generated by someone other than themselves, hence engaging in a second-hand experience.

In the following example, we illustrate how a second-hand investigation can serve to press those who are engaged in the investigation to think more clearly and more deeply about how to collect data with objects, how to represent those data, and how to interpret those data to address a question. The example is taken from a second-grade class that was studying the motion of balls down inclined planes (see also Hapgood, Vincent, Palinscar, & Magnusson, 2000).

During a 10-day period, Mrs. MacLean and her second graders conducted first-hand and second-hand investigations of questions about the motion of balls rolling down inclined planes. The class examined issues such as whether the mass of a ball affects its speed going down a ramp, whether changing the height of the ramp affects speed, whether faster balls will hit cans further than slower balls, and whether heavier balls will hit cans further than lighter balls. These investigations took two forms: guided reading of poster-sized "big books," which were texts designed specifically for this age group and this program of study, and whole-class and small-group hands-on investigations and demonstrations. During the text-based activity, the class investigated questions and data generated by a fictional scientist, Lesley Park. The big books were loosely based on the premise that they were copies of Lesley's scientific notebooks.

As a class, the students read a big book text to begin the program of study. In this book, Lesley noted that two sledders, one big and one little, reached the bottom of a hill at about the same time. This observation led her to ask whether the mass of something affects its speed down a hill. The first several pages of the book showed the sledding scene she witnessed and how she decided to model the situation by rolling two balls of different mass down a ramp. On page 8 of this big book, the children first encountered data from trials Lesley conducted with a 10-gram ball and a 50-gram ball recorded in tabular form (see Fig. 10.1). Prior to this program of study, Mrs. MacLean's class had not used data or data tables. The children were accustomed to looking for patterns within math tables, but they had never attempted to address a question with information from a data table. Over the course of the next two days, the class spent approximately 1 hour and 20 minutes working with this one data table, eventually coming to understand how to read and interpret it. Initially, the children had difficulty understanding what the numbers in each cell represented. This was not surprising. Making a link from quantitative data to a relationship between variables that correspond to aspects of the physical world is not a trivial matter, but it is a fundamental aspect of the physical sciences. Gott and Duggan (1996) argued that having "concepts of evidence," such as

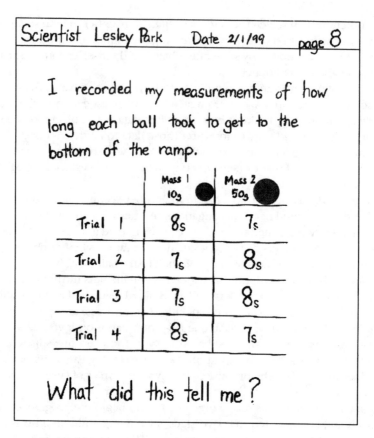

Scientist Lesley Park   Date 2/1/99   page 8

I recorded my measurements of how long each ball took to get to the bottom of the ramp.

	Mass 1 10g	Mass 2 50g
Trial 1	8s	7s
Trial 2	7s	8s
Trial 3	7s	8s
Trial 4	8s	7s

What did this tell me?

FIG. 10.1.   First data table second graders encountered in GIsML big book text for a program of study on the motion of balls rolling down inclined planes.

knowing how to use tables and graphs and thinking about variable manipulation, is at least as important as developing understandings about "substantive" scientific relationships such as the relationship between an object's mass and its speed going down a ramp

Coming to understand both what Lesley must have done to generate her data, as well as to use the data in the table to make claims about whether mass affected speed, necessitated a series of activities. Mrs. MacLean first had the class regenerate the table, cell by cell, by pantomiming what they determined must have been Lesley's actions. After all the children had begun to accept that the numbers in the table represented the time it took for the balls to go from the top to the bottom of the ramp, Mrs. MacLean asked them to consider values for just the 10g ball. Here again there was confusion; they were all sevens and eights! How could that be? What did that mean? Or, as Mrs. MacLean asked the children, "I wonder why it was not always the same number of seconds?" Spurred on by this question, the children began to consider possible sources of variation in data such as experimenter error. The class generated a list of possible reasons why the 10g ball had not always rolled down in the same number of seconds. These reasons included: aspects of the experimental set up (wind blowing) as well as procedural errors (giving the ball a slight push or not pushing the stopwatch quite right). Having determined that seven seconds and eight seconds weren't really so different, given the possibilities for error, the children were able to compare the values for the 10-gram and 50-gram balls, and one member of the class noticed that "It all adds up to 30 seconds. . . . So, it's kind of like they went down the same time so it's all 30 seconds." Because each ball had come down in 8 seconds twice and in 7 seconds twice, when this child added up the columns she got 30 seconds for both balls. This was a remarkable observation as it suggests at least one child may have been thinking quite holistically about the whole set of data for each ball and seeking to compare the two sets of data with one "average" number. This idea, once more of the children had better understood it, was quite influential. In subsequent notebook entries 5 of the 22 children referred to the observation. For example:

> I think that the 50-gram ball and 10-gram ball came down $8 + 8 + 7 + 7 = 30$. Both of the balls had tow (two) sevens on their trials and both had two eights on ther [their] trials. That is why I put $8 + 8 + 7 + 7 = 30$. If both balls got two eights and two sevens then they both got 30 seconds! The End

And

> I think that $8 + 8 + 7 + 7 = 30$ and the other trials are the same so the other trial is got to be the same as 30 so they are the same.

It seems plausible that although second graders do not yet know how to calculate an average, they are able to recognize the utility of such a concept. These notebook entries also show how the children were basing their writing on what they had learned from the data table. This was quite a leap from where they had been when they initially encountered the data table.

There are many noteworthy aspects of this example. Most pertinent to this discussion is to examine how the design of the second-hand investigation, when combined with skillful mediation on the part of the teacher, supported young children in coming to make sense of a complex representation of data, like the data table the children encountered. One could argue that having the children do the experiment and record their own data in a table would have been a more expedient way to introduce data tables and the activity of generating claims on the basis of data. However, we suggest there were advantages to having the text-based encounter precede first-hand generation of a data table. First, the number of trials and the data itself could be controlled. When the children later replicated Lesley's experiment and in their own first-hand investigations, they enthusiastically ran several dozen trials. Learning how to read a data table from such relatively huge data sets would have added even more complexity to the task. Second, the data in Lesley's notebook were quite clean.[1] In contrast, the data the children collected, though remarkably well done, were not as error free. Thus, examining their own data sets for patterns was a much more challenging task because the children needed to deal with a greater range in the results, as well as more anomalous data. At first, the children had difficulty interpreting even Lesley's relatively straightforward tables: for example, they needed a great deal of help before they would accept "7 seconds" and "8 seconds" as basically the same amount of time, given the accuracy of measurement. Once the children had practiced how to read and interpret Lesley's data, they spontaneously suggested using a data table to record data they collected themselves about the effect of ramp height on speed in a subsequent investigation. The majority of the students were then also able to write claims about the relationship between ramp height and speed on the basis of their analyses of their own data tables.

DESIGN FEATURES OF TEXTS
THAT SUPPORT INQUIRY

Via close study of teachers and students engaged in the use of the scientist notebook texts, we have identified several design features that afford students opportunities to advance both their understandings of scientific concepts and their scientific reasoning (cf. Ford, 1999; Hapgood et al., 2000; Palincsar & Magnusson, 2001; Palincsar, Magnusson, Marano, Ford, & Brown, 1998). In the design of our texts, we have been most influenced by descriptions of scientists' work and analysis of scientific activity found in writings such as Latour & Woolgar (1979) and Schwab (1962). We describe these features for the purpose of exploring how they might inform the design of text used in museum exhibits for the purpose of enhancing visitors' experiences, in particular, by engaging them in inquiry.

Explicit Reference to the Source of Questions

To model how a scientist may be motivated to explore a phenomenon, we used the first portion of each text to illustrate the circumstances that piqued

---

[1] In other notebook texts we designed, we deliberately had Lesley collect data that lacked precision. In those texts, which were for fourth graders, part of the experience of reading the text was to question Lesley's decision making about her procedures and techniques.

Lesley's curiosity and led her to ask the questions that, in turn, drove her investigations. We did this, in part, to maximize the possibility that classes would discuss how to derive a testable question from observations in the world. Similarly, in a museum context, visitors could be invited to engage in the process of identifying the questions that spring to mind upon viewing a collection of artifacts. Visitors could be invited to document their thinking, using print, audio, or video records. Excerpts of interviews with anthropologists and paleontologists, sharing the questions with which they would approach such a collection could, in turn, be shared with visitors: What do these objects suggest about the users' ways of eating, spending time, interacting with others, defending themselves? What do these objects suggest our ancestors believed, valued, honored? What new questions do these objects raise for us? How do objects such as these lead us to doubt earlier conclusions? With these questions in mind, the viewer is poised to (re)consider the exhibit in an inquiry mode.

Use of Norms and Conventions of the Scientific Community

In general, scientists adhere to certain rules as they set about conducting and reporting their research. Using consistent and well-documented procedures in an experiment, identifying the variables in a study, and then controlling as much as possible for experimental errors, are just a few of the norms and conventions of the scientific community to which Lesley draws attention in her notebook. We also provide examples in these notebooks of the scientific community questioning Lesley's conclusions, because she had not reflected the scientific norms in her research, for example, in those instances where she has failed to provide sufficiently precise data.

How might this feature be used in exhibits? Taking the visitor "behind the scenes" to learn how scientists approach their work and demonstrating how "rigor" has changed over time as new conventions arise and new technologies are introduced might be one way. For example, in the absence of microscopes, the theory of spontaneous generation, which today seems quite ludicrous, may seem entirely reasonable if properly situated in its time. Exhibits could be arranged in such a fashion that viewers were invited to share in the experience of coming to deeper and more scientifically accurate conceptions of phenomena, made possible through advances in technology.

Examples of Think-Aloud Expert Reasoning

Lesley often modeled how a scientist might reason about questions or problems. For example, in one of the big books used within the program of study on motion, Lesley tested how far a very large ball and a very small ball will hit a can that is at the bottom of a ramp. She then used this information to make a prediction about a ball that weighed less than one and more than the other balls that had been initially tested. This use of extreme cases and predicting for a case in the middle is one common way for scientists to explore a phenomenon. In this case it also allowed the entire class to join in this kind of activity.

There are many objects commonly displayed in museums that have been associated with contested ideas. Text could be used to represent the reasoning processes by which scientists have come to perhaps quite disparate ideas about the phenomenon. Visitors could be invited to evaluate the merits of opposing arguments by examining for themselves the evidence in relationship to the claims.

To illustrate, visitors could be invited to trace theory development with regard to whether dinosaurs were cold- or warm-blooded by examining the sources of evidence undergirding theory development in this domain (e.g., predator-to-prey ratios, evidence for blood vessels in bones, measures of surface area compared with total weight).

Exhibits could be arranged in such a fashion that visitors quite literally pursue the course of different theories by taking two paths through an exhibit in which two competing theories are explicated with their associated evidence. For example, one pathway could take the viewer down the path that explores the theory that our universe is expanding while another pathway takes the viewer down a path exploring the theory that the universe is contracting. Visitors could be invited to comment, at the end of their tours down each path, on their own thinking, whether and how it was influenced by their experiences on each path.

Returning to our earlier discussion of competing theories related to our human ancestors or human contemporaries, visitors could be invited to evaluate these competing theories by considering the data and commenting on the compellingness of those data.

Multiple Ways of Representing Data

In the world of science, multiple types of representations are used to communicate ideas and experimental findings. Likewise, in Lesley's notebooks we have included several types of representations, such as diagrams, graphs, and data tables.

We can imagine many ways in which visitors could be engaged in the processes of both collecting and interpreting data. The motion of an object down an inclined plane presents an interesting case in point. When Galileo was confronted with this very problem and did not have the advantage of timing devices that could record nano-seconds, he tried many approaches including the patterns created by water drips and sand emanating from the traveling object. Visitors could be invited to try their hand at suggesting ways in which data might be collected regarding a particular phenomenon and to compare their ideas with previous visitors' and scientists' ideas as well.

An important dimension related to the representation of data is the way in which the representation can influence one's thinking about the phenomenon. For example, the debate over global warming is related to the ways in which relevant data are presented; examining ocean temperatures over millennia, over centuries, or over decades influences one's thinking about whether we are looking at a mere blip or at a convincing pattern. Visitors could be invited to compare their own conclusions, presented different arrays of data regarding identical phenomena.

Use of Narrative Features: Lesley's "Voice"

Our texts have had a narrative quality to them; they were the stories of Lesley's investigations. Written in the first person, Lesley "talked" to the children via her notebooks about her thinking and, in turn, was welcomed into the children's classroom as another member of their community of "scientific thinkers." We have documented the ways in which this quality of the texts appears to have facilitated some children's questioning and criticism of the texts' content (Ford, 1999). Similarly, we can imagine ways in which presenting the " faces," as well as the "minds" behind a display could humanize the enterprise of science, revealing the role that imagination, tenacity, and passion play in the conduct of inquiry.

CHALLENGES FOR MUSEUM SETTINGS

We recognize that creating opportunities for museum visitors to engage in first- and second-hand investigations could be quite challenging for a variety of reasons. Perhaps most salient are the following two issues: the absence of someone in a "teacher" role to help mediate visitors' investigatory experiences, and the difficulty of crafting second-hand investigation texts for audiences that accommodate the age and background knowledge of diverse museum visitors. Although substantial, we do not think these challenges are insurmountable. Next we address each in turn.

In our classroom-based work, we found the teacher's role in guiding both first- and second-hand science investigations to be critical. In classrooms, teachers shoulder most of the burden for fostering a classroom culture in which inquiry can occur. Even given a supportive classroom culture, teachers must remain attentive to multiple issues such as class dynamics, individual students' needs, and curricular demands as they shape whole class discussions and interact one-on-one with students. Part of the reason for our creating the scientist's notebook texts was in an effort to lessen the burden on teachers to attend to so many factors at once. We hoped that, by introducing various forms of representation and issues such as fair-testing and control of variables, opportunities to talk about and explore the significance of these ideas would result.

Museum environments already have many characteristics found to support inquiry (cf. chapter 3 by Paris & Hapgood in this volume), and are therefore spaces ripe for investigatory activity. What may be lacking is the immediate mediation that a teacher provides a class of students. We know that most visitors to museums come in some sort of group (cf. Borun's chapter 14 and Dierking's chapter 1 in this volume), and it may be that some member(s) of a group may provide online mediation that is sensitive to the particular group's profile (interests, ages, purposes, time constraints). Or, as many programs in museums are staff or docent-led, museum educators may make use of the ideas in this chapter in these contexts most readily. The idea of guiding a first-hand or second-hand investigation could be a useful tool for encouraging docents or other museum personnel to interact with museum visitors and for school teachers preparing to visit museums with their students who would like to prime their students to visit museums. In the case of guiding a first-hand investigation, the idea would be to encourage visitors to look purposefully at an object (e.g., What can you find out about the person who wore this suit of armor? What happens if you change the slope of the ramp?) In the case of guiding a second-hand investigation, one might ask visitors to critically consider an assertion that might be in text about an object (e.g., What evidence is the paleontologist using to support the claim that dinosaurs were a kind of bird? Why do you think the curator decided to include this object in this exhibit?).

In addition to perhaps being useful for interpersonal encounters, we would like to propose that even within stand-alone exhibits, the idea of combining first-hand and second-hand investigations may be stimulating. The key would be figuring out for each context the best way to invite visitors to take up an investigatory lens. This may simply be by suggesting questions to consider while examining an object. Or, it might mean finding ways for visitors to record observations and prompting visitors to compare their observations with those made by other visitors or perhaps by "experts" in whatever discipline happens to be the focus. The idea here is never to supplant visitors' own ways of making meaning with museum objects and experiences, but rather to offer visitors ways to expand their repertoire of strategies for interacting with and questioning objects and experiences. The point is to open up realms of scholarship to visitors.

This naturally leads to the next issue, that of designing materials that invite visitors to engage in first-hand and second-hand investigations. Whether these materials consist of verbal prompts and questions, outreach lessons to schools, audio-taped tours, signage on walls, exhibit brochures, videos, CD-ROMs, entire exhibit layouts, or other forms, designing the materials is no mean feat. We know from our design of various programs of study for elementary school science instruction that have included the scientist's notebook texts that every decision we make has ramifications for how the instruction will unfold. We often talk about the "affordances and constraints" of each decision, because each decision (e.g., whether or not to include something, or about *how* to represent an idea) can foster discussions to go in particular ways. For example, in the notebook text discussed earlier in this chapter, we purposefully designed the initial question and data chart to involve only one variable. We therefore constrained discussion of the importance of the control of variables. But we used data in the data table in such a way that it afforded the opportunity to discuss possible sources of error — how else could one explain how the same ball could go down the ramp in 8 seconds sometimes and 7 seconds sometimes?

Design decisions in museum settings are perhaps even more complex because of the range of visitors that visit museums. Here we think it may be possible to offer visitors several ways of investigating exhibits. For example, some museums have begun offering visitors portable laminated sheets of information about objects. This same format might be used to suggest multiple ways of investigating a particular object or set of objects. One question might focus on the materials and craftsmanship; another prompt might suggest that visitors think about the historical context during which an object was used and compare that context to the present day. Another way to invite groups of visitors to ask questions in exhibits would be to give groups a "grab bag" of questions from which to pull a question. Of course, many museums already ask visitors to ponder certain questions, sometimes using questions as the headers for object labels. The Exploratorium often has a heading "To Do and To Notice" on its exhibits, which we know visitors find very useful indeed. But we would suggest that many exhibit labels could model ways to inquire about objects and related domains of knowledge. Perhaps adding "To Question" on some labels would encourage an investigatory stance.

CONCLUSIONS

Almost all museum exhibits are mixtures of objects and texts. We are not alone in suggesting that the ways in which texts, objects, and visitors interact can create powerful learning opportunities (Falk & Dierking, 1992, Hein, 1998). We made essentially two arguments in this chapter. One is that objects arrayed in an exhibit are, in essence, a form of text with the potential to engage the viewer in interpretation and response. (See also van Kraayenord & Paris, chapter 12 in this volume, who provide an excellent discussion on this point.) Observational research suggests that visitors do not readily approach exhibits in such a fashion. Hence, drawing on our classroom experiences using the model of a scientist's notebook, we proposed ways in which visitors can be guided to assume an inquiry stance relative to objects so that such activities as sense making, wondering, tendering claims, and drawing conclusions can be made explicit. Our thinking is that by providing the viewer with different lenses to bring to their experiences with objects, exhibits might more successfully realize their educative potential.

ACKNOWLEDGMENTS

The authors wish to acknowledge the foundational work of Dr. Shirley J. Magnusson, codirector of the Guided Inquiry supporting Multiple Literacies research group, in both conceptualizing and creating second-hand investigations for use in classroom contexts.

The classroom-based text research reported in this chapter has been supported with a grant from the McDonnell Foundation's Cognitive Studies in Educational Practice Program. In addition, partial support was provided under the Education Research and Development Centers Program PR/Award Number R305R70004, as administered by the Office of Educational Research and Improvement, U.S. Department of Education. However, the contents do not necessarily represent the positions or policies of the National Institute on Student Achievement, Curriculum, and Assessment or the National Institute on Early Childhood Development, or the U.S. Department of Education, and one should not assume endorsement by the federal government.

REFERENCES

Ansbacher, T. (1999). John Dewey's "Experience and Education": Lessons for museums. *Curator,* *41*(1), 36–49.

Case, R. (1993). Theories of learning and theories of development. *Educational Psychologist,* *28*(3), 219–233.

Crowley, K. & Callanan, M. A. (1998). Describing and supporting collaborative scientific thinking in parent–child interactions. *Journal of Museum Education, 23*(1), 12–17.

Csikszentmihalyi, M., & Hermanson, K. (1995). Intrinsic motivation in museums: What makes visitors want to learn? *Museum News, 74*(3), 34–37, 59–61.

Dewey, J. (1934). *Art as experience.* New York: Minton, Balch & Company.

Dewey, J. (1938). *The child and the curriculum.* Chicago: The University of Chicago Press.

Falk, J. H., & Dierking, L. D. (1992). *The museum experience.* Washington, DC: Whalesback.

Ford, D. J. (1999). *The role of text in supporting and extending first-hand investigations in guided inquiry science.* Unpublished doctoral dissertation, University of Michigan, Ann Arbor, Michigan.

Gelman, R., Massey, C. M., & McManus, M. (1991). Characterizing supporting environments for cognitive development: Lessons from children in a museum. In L. Resnick, J. Levine, & S. Teasley

(Eds.), *Perspectives on socially-shared cognition* (pp. 226-256). Washington, DC: American Psychological Association.

Gott, R., & Duggan, S. (1996). Practical work: Its role in the understanding of evidence in science. *International Journal of Science Education, 18*(7), 791-806.

Hapgood, S., Vincent, M. R. L., Palincsar, A. S., & Magnusson, S. J. (2000). *Inspiring inquiry: An examination of design features of a science text for young children.* Paper presented at the annual meeting of the American Educational Research Association, New Orleans, LA.

Hein, G. E. (1998). *Learning in the museum.* London: Routledge.

Holt, T. (1990). *Thinking historically: Narrative, imagination and understanding.* New York: College Entrance Examination Board.

Jackson, P. W. (1998). *John Dewey and the lessons of art.* New Haven, CT: Yale University Press.

Latour, B., & Woolgar, S. (1979). Laboratory life: The social construction of scientific facts. Beverly Hills, CA: Sage.

Lave, J., & Wenger, E. (1991). *Situated learning: Legitimate peripheral participation.* New York: Cambridge University Press.

Magnusson, S. J., & Palincsar, A. S. (1995). The learning environment as a site of science education reform. *Theory into Practice, 34,* 43-50.

Palincsar, A. S., & Magnusson, S. J. (2001). The interplay of first-hand and second-hand investigations to model and support the development of scientific knowledge and reasoning. In D. Klahr & S. Carver (Eds.), *Cognition and instruction: Twenty-five years of progress.* Mahwah, NJ: Lawrence Erlbaum Associates.

Palincsar, A. S., Magnusson, S. J., Marano, N. L., Ford, D., & Brown, N. (1998). Designing a community of practice: Principles and practices of the GIsML community. *Teaching and Teacher Education, 14*(1), 5-19.

Paris, S. G., Troop, W. P., Henderlong, J., & Sulfaro, M. M. (1994). Children's explorations in a hands-on science museum. *The Kamehameha Journal of Education, 5,* 83-92.

Rogoff, B., Matusov, E., & White, C. (1996). Models of teaching and learning: Participation in a community of learners. In D. R. Olson & N. Torrance (Eds.), *The handbook of education and human development: New models of learning, teaching and schooling* (pp. 388-414). Cambridge, MA: Blackwell.

Schwab, J. J. (1962). The teaching of science as enquiry. In J. Schwab & P. Brandwein (Eds.), *The teaching of science* (pp. 1-103). Cambridge, MA: Harvard University Press.

Stevens, R., & Hall, R. (1997). Seeing Tornado: How Video Traces mediate visitor understandings of (natural?) phenomena in a science museum. *Science Education, 81,* 735-747.

Wong, K. (2000). Who were the Neandertals? *Scientific American, 282*(4), 98-107.

Yenawine, P. (1995). Approaching art, changing styles: Victor D'Amico and Philip Yenawine at MoMA. In C. Maeda & K. Iwasaki (Eds.), *Victor D'Amico: Art as a human necessity* (pp. 29-33). Tokyo, Japan: Child Welfare Foundation of Japan, National Children's Castle.

CHAPTER ELEVEN

Objects and Learning: Understanding Young Children's Interaction with Science Exhibits

Léonie J. Rennie
Terence P. McClafferty
Curtin University of Technology
Perth, Western Australia

As adults and experienced museum goers, we have certain expectations when we visit museums and science centers. For example, at a museum we expect to see objects whose value is intrinsic, perhaps because of their uniqueness for being one of a kind, or their history of ownership, or the cultural stories they tell. In contrast, at a science center, we expect to see objects that demonstrate scientific concepts, objects that often are built specifically for that purpose. The meaning of objects depends not only on the nature, history, and purpose of the object itself, but also on the ways it is interpreted by the visitor. Gurian's (1999) analysis of objects and how people think about them conveys these ideas very clearly. For example, Gurian pointed out that a bowl, considered to be cheap tableware in its day, may assume significance if it were present in the death camps of the Holocaust. Here, it is the story that makes the object important to the museum visitor. In contrast, an object that is intentionally designed to demonstrate a concept, like an exhibit in a science center, may well be unique, but, as Gurian noted, it has no cognate in the outside world. In both examples, the visitor has a role to play in making meaning from the object, and the nature of that meaning depends, at least in part, on the prior knowledge and experience the visitor has in relation to the object.

But what meaning can be made of objects by people who have little knowledge or sense of the relevant history, culture, or science? Young children are one such group of people. What sense do they make of objects they have not seen before? How closely does the meaning they make from the object match the meaning that curators or museum staff expect (or hope) they might make of the exhibit? In this chapter we investigate how young children interact with exhibits at an interactive science and technology center, and the kinds of behavior that lead to understanding of the science and/or technology concepts embodied in those exhibits. In particular, we look at the notions of exploration and play and how they contribute opportunities to learn.

PERSPECTIVES ON YOUNG CHILDREN'S LEARNING IN MUSEUMS

The work with young children described here is part of a larger research project addressing the need for better understanding of the nature of the communicative activities of science centers (Rennie & McClafferty, 1996a). Initially, we brought together two theoretical perspectives, the first derived from visitor research in museums and similar places, and the second from research on learning with exhibits. First, Falk and Dierking (1992) provided a research-based framework that helps to describe and understand the visitor's experience. Their Interactive Experience Model represents the visitor's experience as an interaction among three contexts. The physical context is embodied in the exhibits and the physical setting in which they are displayed. The social context refers to interactions between the visitor and others at the museum. The personal context is important in terms of the visitor's age, sex, and personal characteristics. Visitors, even young children, bring widely divergent background knowledge and experience, which contribute to how they interpret the phenomena they observe. This personal context interacts with both the physical and social contexts, playing a major role in selecting what visitors notice and what they do. The Interactive Experience Model emphasizes that the visit must be considered as a contextualized experience.

Science center exhibits provide opportunities for learning, but learning is only likely to occur if the visitor chooses to interact and engage intellectually with the exhibit. The second theoretical perspective comes from the research of Feher (1990), who described learning via an exhibit as an experiential, exploratory, and explanatory process. The visitor's perceptual experience with the exhibit leads to exploration through interaction, with meaning given to that experience through the visitor's own interpretations and explanations. Each level requires further systematic investigation, and it is the visitor's decision to persist with the investigation that determines the learning outcome from each exhibit, and possibly from the science center as an environment. Thus research must investigate what it is about particular exhibits that promotes the prolonged interaction that results in understanding.

Some research on learning in museums carried out with very young children has focused on familiarity with the exhibit, that is, whether children are likely to have seen or experienced something similar before. Several such studies were carried out at the Please Touch Museum in Philadelphia, designed specifically for children aged 7 years and younger. The research by Gallagher and Dockser (1987) examined the behavior of children with adults and the amount of time they spent with exhibits that could be labeled familiar (like the grocery store) or novel (things children were unlikely to have seen before). The familiar exhibits were associated with a greater amount of "pretend play" and they concluded that "a balance between the familiar and the novel is required in designing exhibits in children's museums" (p. 44). In subsequent work at the same museum, Sykes (1993) confirmed that more pretend play occurred at familiar exhibits, and that children were more attracted to familiar exhibits than to novel ones. Sykes concurred that exhibitions should include both familiar and novel objects. She concluded that "the familiar was more attractive, held more interest, and inspired more pretend play, while the novel imparted more new information" (p. 231).

Similar findings were made recently by Siegler (1999), who compared the interactions of children aged 4 to 7 years with their parents at two exhibits at the Madison Children's Museum. One was a dairy exhibit with life-size cows and a real milking machine that Siegler described as an analogical representation with "high transparency" because it was likely to be recognized as familiar and meaningful to visitors. The other was a sewer exhibit that was not to scale and used ping pong balls to simulate water. As an analogy, this had "low transparency" and was likely to be less familiar and less immediately meaningful to visitors than the dairy exhibit. Siegler found that the dairy exhibit elicited more interest, more children's play that supported meaning, and much greater interaction between parent and child, especially in helping children to make meaningful interpretations about the exhibit. He concluded that learning is more likely to occur when hands-on activities are meaningful and children have the opportunity to engage in play.

These studies all noted the interaction between family members as a positive part of the museum visit, but did not all examine its nature. Gelman, Massey, and McManus (1991), who also conducted research at the Please Touch Museum, found that parent interaction did not always assist children to attain the outcomes from their interactions with the exhibit that its designers had in mind. They set about designing an exhibit to support learning from the interaction among family members, or by children on their own. As they pointed out, "It is one thing to provide hands-on materials designed especially for young children and quite another to be sure that these objects will be used as intended" (p. 240). These notions were confirmed in research by Crowley and Callanan (1998), who examined parent–child interactions in the children's Discovery Museum of San Jose at a prototype exhibit called Map Your Head. The initial design resulted in low success rates because children and parents had different ideas about the exhibit's purpose. Its redesign to promote complementary interaction between parents and children increased success rate dramatically.

From our own informal observations and in earlier work, we also knew that young children interact with exhibits at science centers in many ways. Sometimes, when they use the exhibit in the way we expect, we observe their exploration as they try to get the exhibit to work and we think that they are learning. Other times they use it in unexpected ways, that often are purposeful but sometimes are repetitive and apparently without purpose. Clearly, they are interacting with the exhibit in these latter cases, but how likely is it that they are learning whatever concepts the exhibit is designed to show? How can we tell whether they are learning, or "just playing"?

Playing and Learning

Once we began serious attempts to describe how children used exhibits and whether they might be learning, we found that we needed a structure to think more formally about the concept of play and its relationship with learning. Both concepts have a very large corpus of research literature, with roots in psychology, sociology, anthropology, and ethology, as well as education, but we were interested in those aspects likely to be pertinent to children interacting with hands-on exhibits in a science center or children's museum. We began by examining the meaning of play and how it might be linked with learning.

There are some commonly agreed characteristics of play. Sylva, Bruner, and Genova (1976) stressed the voluntary nature of play. They argued that in play, the process is more important than the product, thus there is a low risk of failure, less likelihood of frustration, and the freedom to explore "the possibilities inherent in things and events" (p. 244). Garvey (1991) suggested that play is pleasurable and enjoyable, intrinsically motivated, spontaneous and voluntary, and involves the player in active engagement. Further, Garvey noted that, "Play has certain systematic relations to what is not play . . . [It] has been linked with creativity, problem solving, language learning, the development of social roles, and a number of other cognitive and social phenomena" (p. 5). Similarly, Mann's (1996) analysis of play suggested that the benefits are fun, cognitive and language development, imagination and creativity, and social competence. He offered four reasons why children play: to control their world; curiosity; for the fun of it, or intrinsic motivation; and to learn. "Play is a serious activity with wonderful developmental benefits" (p. 465) he concluded, and wondered why play is underutilized as a learning strategy.

Hands-on children's museums offer great opportunities for play and learning. Diamond (1996), in her work at the Lawrence Hall of Science and the Exploratorium, found play to be a major component of family interactions with exhibits and each other. She addressed the relationship between play and learning more broadly in the museum context and concluded that play provides experiences from which learning occurs, and that museums are contexts that can encourage play and its benefits. Because our particular interest is whether children learn from their interaction with an exhibit (regardless of whether that is cognitive, affective, or social learning, or the learning of psychomotor skills), we elaborate a point made by Diamond (1996), that is, "Play is not the same as exploration" (p. 3). Diamond distinguished between the two in terms of purpose. She described play as an attempt to vary stimulation in order to remain actively involved, but exploration aimed to reduce uncertainty in a novel or complex situation.

Interestingly, having made the distinction between play and exploration early in her paper, Diamond did not develop it, but we believe the distinction is important in understanding the relationship between play and learning. Hutt studied young children's play and exploration intensively (see Hutt, 1981, for a synthesis). She distinguished between exploratory activities, which she called investigation, and play in terms of the underlying motivation: "[T]he implicit question in the child's mind during investigation seems to be 'What can this *object* do?' whereas in play it is 'What can *I* do with this object?'" (Hutt, 1970a, p. 70, original emphasis). Hutt (1981) used this distinction to produce a more precise classification of that kind of children's behavior that is usually described generically as play. Her two major divisions are epistemic and ludic behavior. She has a third division — games with rules — not described here because it is not relevant to play in museums. Hutt's taxonomy of play, which she regards as particularly suitable to the play of 3- to 5-year olds, is the basis of Fig. 11.1.

Epistemic behavior (what can this *object* do?) concerns knowledge and information. It is goal or end-product oriented and is associated with learning. During epistemic behavior, children appear to concentrate and they do not like to be interrupted. Hutt subdivided epistemic behavior into three kinds of activities: problem-solving, such as doing a jigsaw; exploration, which involves using the senses to explore objects or materials; and productive activity, such as making something using materials like sand or paper, or acquiring skills, such as throwing a hoop. The goal of productive activity is the made object or mastery of the skill acquired. Epistemic behavior is cued by external stimuli, such as a new toy or a novel situation, and is associated with new learning.

Ludic behavior (what can *I* do with this object?) concerns self-amusement. Hutt suggested two categories: symbolic or fantasy play where children engage in pretense, often ascribing personalities and roles to objects, real and imaginary; and play that has a repetitive element, that is, children repeat the same procedure or movement without introducing any new or exploratory element. Ludic behavior is fanciful, imaginative, enjoyable, and optional; it occurs only when the child is relaxed and the surroundings familiar. Hutt's research (1981) indicated that ludic behavior may include some innovative

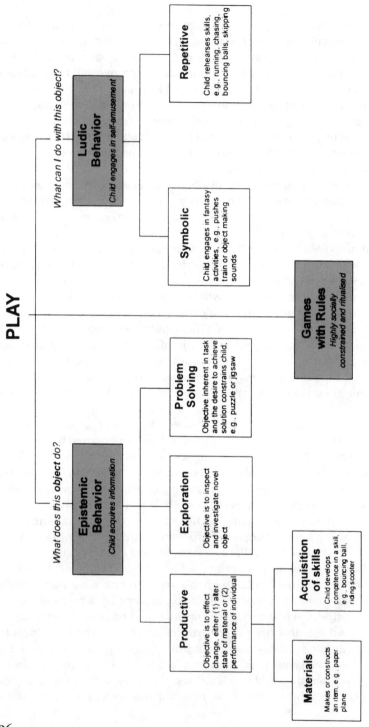

FIG. 11.1. A taxonomy of play for preschool children (after Hutt, 1981, p. 284).

elements, but mainly it consolidates skills. Further, any new learning from ludic behavior is accidental, in the sense that it is not a goal of the behavior. If something new or unexpected occurs, the child responds with further exploration in a new phase of epistemic behavior.

When presented with a novel object, children typically engage first in epistemic behavior, by looking, approaching, touching, and manipulating (Hutt, 1970b). Only when the object is sufficiently familiar and they are comfortable with it, will children engage in ludic behavior or play for self-amusement rather than investigation. Nunnally and Lemond (1973) described the sequence in a more general cycle, beginning with orienting behavior, followed by perceptual investigation, manipulating behavior, play activity, and then searching activity as the child becomes bored and seeks something else. Hutt (1970b) termed the seeking out of new activities diversive exploration, in contrast to the specific exploration in epistemic behavior. Children often alternate between exploratory behavior or investigation and play (Hodgkin, 1985; Hughes, 1983; Hutt, 1970b; Nunnally & Lemond, 1973). Thus children engaged in ludic behavior with familiar objects can be interrupted by the introduction of an unfamiliar object or the accidental discovery of a new property of the familiar object, which prompts a new cycle of epistemic, exploratory activity.

Playing and Learning With Interactive Exhibits

Using Hutt's theoretical distinction between epistemic and ludic behavior, we suggest that all playing is not learning, but that much learning is associated with play. Hutt's terminology has not become commonplace in the literature, but if we paraphrase her two questions as "What can this *exhibit* do?" and "What can *I* do with this exhibit?", we have a useful way of thinking about children's interactions with exhibits. For example, Carlisle (1985) noted in his report of a study of 5th graders' behavior at a science center that "Many children asked aloud, 'What does this do?' as they first approached an exhibit" (p. 29). Carlisle also described the frequent "roaring around" of children as they oriented themselves to the physical environment before "settling down" to more structured activity.

We suggest that a science museum or science center, which children visit infrequently, is likely to stimulate a high level of epistemic behavior because the unfamiliar environment encourages exploration. However, very new situations can be dysfunctional initially, as testified by museum researchers who described the novelty effects that interfere with learning (Falk, Martin, & Balling, 1978). Children need to orient themselves to an unfamiliar environment before they can concentrate on engaging with the exhibits. Hence, the degree of novelty of particular exhibits is important for young children. Gallagher and Dockser (1987), Siegler (1999), and Sykes (1993) all found that children were attracted to familiar settings and engaged in more "pretend play" than at the novel settings that were more likely to impart new information. These findings fit well with Hutt's description of ludic and epistemic behavior in familiar and novel situations, respectively.

Hutt's taxonomy of play also helps to illuminate the role played by interaction with others in the learning process. In particular, if interaction promotes or extends epistemic behavior, then learning is likely to occur. In research in preschools, Hutt, Tyler, Hutt, and Christopherson (1989) found that children's attention span and their concentration increased with the participation of adults, whereas the predominant activities of solitary children playing with sand or water in the familiar sand pit were stereotyped and repetitive. They concluded that being able to engage with the cognitive challenge of many activities required input from adults. This parallels the notion of scaffolding described by Vygotsky (1978) where learning occurs through interaction with others more knowledgeable. Thus, with another's help, the child is able to learn something he or she could not learn alone.

Not surprisingly, these kinds of interactions are observed in museums. Diamond's (1986) research with families and children averaging 7 years of age, provided examples of how adults' interaction could increase the likelihood of children manipulating an exhibit and influence children to spend more time with it. Similarly, from research with 4- and 5-year-olds at the Please Touch Museum, Puchner, Rapoport, and Gaskins (1997) found that (a) time-on-task was higher when adults were more highly involved in interactions, (b) learning was more likely to occur with adult interaction than without it, and (c) children's problem-solving learning was greater when given just sufficient direction by adults to help them find their own solution to problems. Puchner et al. referred to this scaffolding as "vague guidance," which seemed to work better in the child's zone of proximal development (Vygotsky, 1978) than more detailed "precise guidance," which did not allow the child freedom to explore further. Crowley and Callanan (1998) also found children interacted longer with a zoetrope when parents participated than when children were alone.

In Hutt's terms, the finding that greater learning occurs when adults are present might be explained in terms of the increased length of time spent in epistemic, problem-solving behavior, facilitated by interaction with adults, especially when they encouraged, or scaffolded, children's own exploration. It is important to note that different types of exhibits were associated with different amounts and types of involvement and also learning, so the nature of the exhibit (part of the physical context) is always a factor to be considered. A good example is the attempt by Gelman et al. (1991) to build an exhibit to support children's learning through giving them ideas about what to do with it. Early versions of their Racing Balls exhibit failed to prompt either the children to use the exhibit to race balls, as intended, or their accompanying adults to help them. Changing the exhibit by adding both images and voice from a computer eventually resulted in the desired activity. Similarly, the redesigning of the Map Your Head exhibit, reported in the Crowley and Callanan (1998) research, resulted in more effective child–adult interaction.

In summary then, our research draws from three theoretical perspectives that seem quite consistent with one another: Falk and Dierking's generic Interactive Experience Model; Feher's work with older children suggesting that learning is an experiential, exploratory and explanatory process; and Hutt's work with young children, which makes the distinction between epistemic and ludic behavior and suggests that the former is more likely to be associated with learning. Two general predictions we might make are first, that longer periods of epistemic behavior are likely to result in higher levels of learning or understanding, and second, that factors affecting the time spent in epistemic behavior include the degree of unfamiliarity of the object and interaction with others, particularly adults. Our research enabled us to test these predictions. We focused on young children who visited a cluster of exhibits designed specifically for children aged 3 to 7 years, and aimed to: (a) describe children's interactions with selected exhibits to establish typical "patterns of use" for each exhibit; (b) determine children's levels of understanding of the science and/or technology concepts that the exhibits were designed to present; and (c) interpret the relationship between patterns of use and understanding of concepts in terms of the design of the exhibit.

DESCRIBING CHILDREN'S INTERACTION WITH EXHIBITS

The venue for the project was Scitech Discovery Center in Perth, Western Australia. The work with young children was carried out in a section called *Discoverland,* which comprised 27 exhibits designed specifically for children aged 3 to 7 years. The data were collected during visits by school groups and the general public during school holidays. Most of the data were collected in the late morning when the center was busiest. Prior to their visit, school groups were informed by telephone that data collection was in progress and permission to involve the school was obtained. Signs were erected at the entrance to *Discoverland* advising that research was in progress, and researchers were identified by a name tag and label reading "evaluator." The study combined several methods of data collection and was carried out in three stages.

Establishing Patterns of Use

Using a modified version of an observational, pen and paper instrument developed in an earlier study (Rennie & McClafferty, 1996b), the nature of the interactions of over 100 children were recorded for each of four exhibits, selected on the basis of explainers' perceptions of their popularity with visitors. The observation instrument was designed to record first, the nature of the child's interaction with the exhibit, second, whether the interaction was solitary or in a group, and third, what kind of group interaction ensued. Interaction was classified at three levels: the visitor attended to (took notice of) the exhibit but did not engage with it; the visitor interacted or played with the exhibit but in a random or nonfocused way; or the visitor used the exhibit in a purposeful way. Each person was symbolized by a "g," "b," "M," "F," "E," and "T" for girl, boy, male adult, female adult, explainer, and teacher, respectively. Interaction with others was recorded by drawing links between the persons interacting. The nature of the interaction with the exhibit, or apparent pattern of use, was noted in a comment box on the instrument. To establish interrater reliability, the two researchers independently observed a total of 90 visitors interacting with three exhibits and achieved 100% agreement in coding using the instrument.

Following field testing by the researchers, the coding of subjects was refined (explainer and teacher were included at this stage, and an attempt to distinguish between parents and grandparents was abandoned because this proved too difficult) and the final version of the Visitor Observation Form was developed (see appendix). Each copy of the instrument allows coding of 30 people and data can be summarized briefly on the instrument. Even this small amount of data gives an overview of whether the exhibit is attractive to visitors and whether it is used purposefully. Incidentally, we found that design faults were quickly detected and could be listed for remedial action by exhibit staff. Volunteer staff of the science center were trained in the use of the instrument by the researchers and deployed in the collection of data from four exhibits in *Discoverland*. The exhibits were titled Magnetic Maze, Thongaphone, Periscope, and Hand Sculptures.

The first set of data recorded the behavior of at least 100 children for each of the selected exhibits. Visitors were selected at random, simply those who chose to move toward the exhibit. Observations were made on weekdays, some were made during school visits, others were made during the school holidays. An attempt was made to target children aged about 6–7 years to try to reduce the likely variance in pattern of use attributable to age and experience. Although this was easy for school groups whose characteristics were known, it was more difficult during public visits as it was not always easy to judge children's ages.

Identifying the Science and/or Technology Concepts in the Exhibits

The concepts embodied in the exhibit were determined by an expert group, comprising the education officer who oversaw the development of *Discover-*

land, the exhibit designers/builders, two science educators with research experience in other science centers, and a specialist in early childhood education. A second proforma or instrument entitled Exhibit Objectives, also initially developed for use in formative evaluation (Rennie & McClafferty, 1996b), was modified in consultation with the Education Team at Scitech Discovery Center. Its use enabled the designers' purpose of the exhibit to be described, and the cognitive, affective, and psychomotor outcomes identified. Thus, all exhibits involved in the research have a description written by the Education Team that lists the physical manipulation/operation for successful use of the exhibit by the child and the cognitive and/or affective intended message of the exhibit. Figure 11.2 gives an example of the completed Exhibit Objectives proforma for the Magnetic Maze. It lists the cognitive and affective outcomes the Education Team hoped the exhibit would promote. Of course, other outcomes, including social skills such as turn-taking, may also be developed.

Relationship between Pattern of Use and Understanding

Children's interactions with each exhibit were videotaped by leaving a video camera trained on the exhibit. The videotape record enabled a more detailed analysis of what children did in their interactions with exhibits than was possible with the Visitor Observation Form. Videotaped data were transcribed into time logs describing children's activity with the exhibit, and an example video time log for one child interacting with the Magnetic Maze is included as Fig. 11.3. In addition, and with the permission of their accompanying adult, we interviewed a sample of 15 of the children videotaped for each exhibit, who had interacted with it for at least 20 seconds. Based on the outcomes of the earlier stages of the research, interview protocols were developed for each exhibit. Interview questions related to children's level of understanding, why they had used the exhibit, and what they liked or disliked about it. Because such young children have difficulty finding the "right words," and also because they were often rather shy talking to a relative stranger about what they were doing, we encouraged them to use the exhibit to help them to talk about what they were doing and what they understood. Interviews were audiotaped with the accompanying adult's permission and later transcribed.

In sum, there are three data sets for each exhibit: first, records using the Visitor Observation Form for over 100 children; second, a videotaped record of children's interactions with the exhibit and the associated time log for about 15 children; and third, interview transcripts from this second group of children. Only some of the results are reported here by focusing on the findings for one of the exhibits, the Magnetic Maze. Although this was the exhibit's official title, it was not labeled, so visitors did not immediately realize that magnets were involved.

Exhibit Title: **Magnetic Maze**

Successful Use
What would the visitor need to do to use this exhibit successfully?

- Position the magnetic wand correctly (under the table)

- Coordinate planned movement of the dog

- Follow a path

Exhibit Message
What do we want the visitor(s) to take away from this exhibit?

Cognitive Message   *(Head — understanding the concept(s) demonstrated by exhibit)*

- Magnets can attract some objects

- Magnets can attract from a distance

- Magnetic force can pass through some materials

Affective Message   *(Heart — Attitude to the information/experience offered by exhibit)*

- Social—role play and interaction

- Relevance of the scenario

- Enjoyment in successful manipulation of wand magnet

- Mystery of how it works

Psychomotor Message   *(Hands — physical movement/manipulation needed to use exhibit)*

- Hand-eye coordination to manipulate wand out of line of sight, to move dog in a controlled manner

FIG. 11.2.   Exhibit objectives for the Magnetic Maze.

The Magnetic Maze is an exhibit set out as a diorama on a low table, the top of which simulates a park, with stylized paths and lakes marked and trees mounted on it. At each end are three houses. There are two small plastic dogs, each fixed to a base containing a magnet, and by holding a second magnet (mounted in a wand and attached to the table by a string) underneath the table and moving it in an appropriate way, the dog can be "taken for a walk" along a path around the lakes and trees. The exhibit designers expected that for successful use of the exhibit, the visitor would be able to position the wand-magnet correctly under the table and coordinate the movement of the dog along a planned path on top of the table. The cognitive, affective and psychomotor outcomes are described in the Exhibit Objectives sheet in Fig. 11.2. A simplified plan view of the table is at the top of the video time log in Fig. 11.3.

PATTERNS OF USE
FOR INTERACTIVE EXHIBITS

It was possible to determine a pattern of use for each exhibit and usually more than one. For each exhibit, there was a range of visitor interactions, varying from cursory play to prolonged purposeful activity. The length of time children spent at the exhibit was not recorded (except for those children videotaped), but observers noted that children who used the exhibit in the intended way and those who interacted with their peers or adults tended to stay longer.

Patterns of Use for the Magnetic Maze

Table 11.1 reports a breakdown of the observational data for the Magnetic Maze exhibit. It shows that of the 272 children observed to have used the Maze, about two thirds interacted with the Maze by themselves, and the others were in small groups, either adult(s) with child(ren), or children together. The possible nature of these groups is listed in the first column of Table 11.1, where the gender combination of the groups is also noted. The second column of the table shows that when children are in groups with either adults or peers, between 77% and 100% use the exhibit purposefully. In contrast, if alone, only 38% of boys and 46% of girls used the exhibit purposefully. In other words, in this sample, children in groups are about twice as likely to experience success than children alone. It did not seem to matter a great deal what the composition of this group was, and comments written by observers on the Visitor Observation Form indicate that this success was usually because one member of the group knew what to do, or because when there was more than one person, they were more likely to find the wand-magnets if they

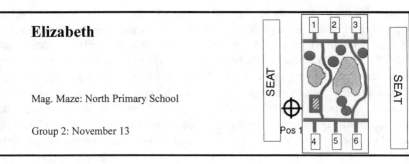

Time	Activity
13:35:53	Arrives at Pos 1
57	Picks up magnet and places above table — connects to dog.
13:36:00	Picks up dog with magnet above table
05	Looks under table at magnet/cord connection
10	Picks up dog
15	Fiddles with dog and magnet above table.
20	Snaps apart and joins dog and magnet
25	Slides dog up pathway by hand above table (no magnet):................Walk 1
30	Arrives at house 1
36	Holds dog in hand – looks under table (Returns to Pos 1)
44	Snaps dog to magnet above table
51	Accidentally flicks dog off magnet to floor
13:37:05	Plays with dog and magnet (repeatedly joining and pulling apart above the table)
12	Leaves dog at house 4
15	Looks under table
20	Picks up dog with magnet at house 6 using magnet from above (NOT under table)
23	Looks under table
26	Slides dog by hand from Exercise Ring to House 1
30	Walked around pond — moved across pond (no magnet- by hand)
	Moves dog by hand around table from Pos 1..............................Walk 2

FIG. 11.3.   Video time log for Elizabeth's interaction with the Magnetic Maze.

	45	Looks under table to get magnet and uses magnet above the table
13:38:00		Repeatedly joins and breaks apart magnet and dog at Pos 1
	05	Walks dog by hand (no magnet)
	10	Continues moving dog up and down edge of table very fast. (see figure)
	17	Repeatedly pulls apart and joins dog and magnet
13:38:34		Stops...Researcher interviews Elizabeth
13:39:00		Taylor sits on other side and uses dog and magnet purposefully. Elizabeth watches Taylor while speaking to researcher
	20	Interview ceases and researcher exits
	34	Immediately places dog near pond and takes dog to exercise ring using magnet purposefully under the table..................Walk 3
	42	Walks dog up path using magnet, negotiates dog around trees, to door of house 1
	56	Picks up dog from table and returns to Pos 1, sticking/pulling apart dog to magnet
13:40:12		Looks under table, sits on floor and feels table's metal frame under table top
	23	Replaces dog at exercise ring and exits.

FIG. 11.3 (*continued*)

TABLE 11.1
Young Children's Use of the Magnetic Maze Exhibit

	Nature of Interaction			
Nature of group	*Use Purposefully (%)*	*Interact (%)*	*Take Notice (%)*	*Total (n)*
Child–Adult groups				
boy(s) with male	86	14		7
girl(s) with male	86	14		7
boy(s) with female	83	17		24
girl(s) with female	80	10	10	10
Child groups				
boy with boy(s)	77	23		13
girl with girl(s)	93	7		15
boy with girl(s)	100			9
girl with boy(s)	100			9
Singletons				
boy	38	37	25	76
girl	46	37	17	102

had fallen under the table and were not immediately visible. There were a number of individual children who just looked at the Magnetic Maze without interacting with it. Sometimes this was because the table was crowded, and it was not always possible to tell whether these children returned later. The generalizations from these data are tentative, because the numbers of children, particularly in groups of different composition, are small, and the conclusions need to be investigated with further data. Nevertheless, the importance of social interaction in promoting opportunity to learn is clear.

There were three main patterns of use for those who interacted with the Magnetic Maze. Some children played with the dogs without noticing or using the wand-magnets, walking the dogs about the tabletop up to houses and trees by hand, often talking to them or making appropriate noises. Apart from the initial exploration of the dog and exhibit layout, which took only a few seconds, this was interpreted as "pretend play" or ludic fantasy behavior in Hutt's terms. A second pattern of use occurred when children used both dog and wand-magnet. Usually the dog and the wand-magnet stuck together and children moved them both around the tabletop. Sometimes when they apparently got bored with this, they banged the wand-magnets, or the dogs, or the wand-magnet and the dogs together in a repetitive way. This group also moved quickly from epistemic to ludic behavior, and often repetitive rather than fantasy activity. Neither of these groups of children discovered how to use the exhibit in the intended way unless they were shown how, or observed others using the wand-magnets in the way intended, and then they moved into a new exploratory phase as they tried it for themselves.

The third pattern of use was demonstrated by those children who figured out, observed, or were shown how to use the wand-magnets under the table to move the dogs. These children usually engaged in moving the wand-magnets around for a few seconds until they had the skill required to walk the dog around obstacles and the houses. Sometimes they explored other properties of the pieces, for example, using the wand-magnet to tip over and then right the dog, running it deliberately off the edge of the table, or sometimes using both wand-magnets to move the two dogs simultaneously. This kind of epistemic behavior was considered to be exploratory, followed by practicing skill. Most of these children did not stay at the exhibit long enough to engage in fantasy play, but moved off looking for new challenges when they had "mastered" the exhibit.

CHILDREN'S LEVEL OF CONCEPTUAL UNDERSTANDING

For each exhibit, the level of understanding of the relevant concepts was categorized into an hierarchical structure. This is consistent with research on exhibit evaluation, particularly the use of knowledge hierarchies described by Perry (1993). To help assess change in learning at exhibits, Perry suggested that a hierarchy could be developed from the knowledge structure inherent in each exhibit, ranging from one simple idea of the underlying concept to a full understanding of it. Perry's hierarchies were developed from examination of an exhibit, discussion with developers, and in-depth interviews with visitors who used the exhibit. We had used hierarchies with success in earlier work (McClafferty, 1995; Rennie, 1996) and found it also worked well in this study. Three or four levels were sufficient to describe children's understanding of each exhibit, and we focus here on the Magnetic Maze.

Understanding Concepts for the Magnetic Maze

We believe that children's understanding of the Magnetic Maze has to be considered in terms of what is reasonable for children of this age. Obviously, we could not expect a scientific explanation of the nature of magnetism — we are hard-pressed to provide this ourselves! The hierarchy of knowledge we developed from watching children and from our interviews with them has four levels.

At the first and simplest level, children realize that there is some attraction, or "stickiness," between the wand and the dog, but they are unable to explain more. At the second level of the hierarchy, children recognize (sometimes from being told by their companions or from their previous experience) that magnets or magnetism were involved in some way.

We propose that the third level of knowledge is recognition that the magnetism or attraction can work through the table. Perhaps not surprisingly, children were unable to explain how this might be so, although two or three suggested it might be caused by magic. (Evans, Mull, & Poling, chapter 4, this volume, discuss the likelihood of young children ascribing phenomena to "magic.") Finally, we think that the fourth and highest level of knowledge includes understanding that both the wand and the dog contain magnets. This can only be ascertained by discovering that in certain positions the dogs repel each other, and so do the wand-magnets. Although several children were observed to investigate this property, it was usually first noticed during exploratory behavior. Only one child told us there were magnets in both the dog and the wand.

RELATIONSHIP BETWEEN PATTERN OF USE
AND CONCEPTUAL UNDERSTANDING

We found clear links between patterns of use and understanding. For example, many children were observed to investigate the "stickiness" or attraction between the dogs and wand-magnets and these children were able to talk about the "stickiness." Only some of them mentioned magnets, often referring to fridge magnets as the clue to their previous experience with magnets. Further, only those children who used the Magnetic Maze to "walk," or at least manipulate, the dog by using the wand-magnet under the table reached the third level of understanding in our hierarchy, that the magnetism or attraction works through the table.

Example of Pattern of Use and Understanding the Magnetic Maze

An example of one child's pattern of use and how this reflected her understanding is documented in the videotape time log for 6-year-old Elizabeth in Fig. 11.3. Elizabeth first found the dog and wand-magnet on the table. She picked them up and explored their "stickiness." Next (at time 13:36:25), she moved the dog around the table by hand in a deliberate and orderly way. After about 10 seconds of this, she picked up a wand-magnet and began repeatedly to join it to the dog and pull them apart. She put this dog down, picked up the other one with the wand-magnet (13:37:20), and moved the second dog by hand around the table for about 25 seconds. Again Elizabeth picked up a wand-magnet from under the table and played with it and the dog, repeatedly joining and pulling them apart. Another short walk of the dog by hand (13:38:05) was followed by repetitively moving it up and down the table in a straight line. She then went back to banging a dog and a wand-magnet together (13:38:17) while looking around the room. When she seemed to have finished with the exhibit, the interviewer moved in to talk to Elizabeth next to the table. During this conversation Elizabeth continued to bang the two pieces together in an absent-minded way, but the videotape shows her also watching Taylor, who had come to the table and was correctly using the wand-magnet under the table to move the dog on the top. As soon as the interviewer finished and retired, Elizabeth began to work at the table using the dog and wand-magnet as intended. Having apparently mastered this skill to her satisfaction and explored how the magnet stuck to the metal rim under the table, she moved away (13.40.23).

Thus Elizabeth began with a brief exploration of the dog and wand-magnet, then moved into repetitive ludic behavior or play. This cycle was repeated until she saw Taylor using the exhibit in the way it was intended. She then engaged in a new cycle of exploratory, then productive, skill-mastery epistemic behavior. Each segment of epistemic behavior was associated with learning. Although Elizabeth discovered the attraction between the dog and the wand-magnet, she did not know the explicit intention of the exhibit — to "walk the dog" — using the wand-magnet under the table. She engaged in fantasy play, then repetitive play. Once "scaffolded" by watching Taylor's interaction, she moved to a new level of epistemic behavior indicative of a higher level of cognitive understanding.

In sum, we found that children whose interaction with the exhibit was epistemic invariably demonstrated higher levels of understanding of the exhibit's concepts than those whose interaction was fragmented or seemingly random. However, there were children who played with the exhibits in ways that were not intended by the designers, and these children were less likely to attain understanding of the concepts unless they also used it in the way intended. Further, children often made additional discoveries by watching or working with others, as in Elizabeth's case, by interacting with the exhibit in another round of epistemic behavior.

An Aside About the Importance of Exhibit Design

Our research drew attention to the significance of exhibit design in helping or hindering achievement of the exhibit objectives and determining what children learn. When we began observations at the Magnetic Maze, very few children, even those accompanied by adults, were able to use it successfully. The reason soon became obvious. The strings attaching the wand-magnets to the table were very short, consequently they fell under the table and visitors often did not see them. We asked the exhibit designer to lengthen the strings so the wand-magnets would stay on the table instead of falling underneath it. We discovered that the strings had been shortened deliberately because young children had been using the wand-magnets as hammers, causing damage to both the magnets and the plastic trees on the table. Again the reason was obvious. The magnets were mounted on their handles in a T-shape and looked like hammers, encouraging children to use them in this way. Shortening the strings prevented further damage to the exhibit, but also hampered its successful use. The problem was solved by reaffixing the magnets in line with their handles to look more like a wand than a hammer and lengthening the strings. We began observations again and recorded much higher levels of success with children using the exhibit as intended.

The reconfiguring of the Magnetic Maze to foster intended use is similar to the Gelman et al. (1991) series of modifications to the Racing Balls exhibit that eventually had children racing the balls as intended. In both cases, the exhibit modifications encouraged epistemic behavior that resulted in more cognitive learning. The poorly designed exhibit invited ludic behavior rather than prolonged epistemic behavior. These findings also emphasize the importance of engaging in a process of formative assessment for new exhibits.

CONCLUSIONS

This study built on the existing research base relating to young children's learning in museums, demonstrated the potential for their learning by interacting with exhibits, and tested and refined some techniques for investigating and measuring understanding about science and technology from visits to science centers. The findings make a contribution to knowledge about young children's learning and understanding of science and/or technology concepts in the informal learning environment of a science center. We used, with some success, a systematic, theoretically based approach. The Interactive Experience Model (Falk & Dierking, 1992) alerted us to plan from the beginning to consider a much broader perspective than just one child alone with an exhibit. We expected children's personal contexts to be important in how they made sense of the objects with which they interacted, but we also knew (because *Discoverland* was new) that children would find the design of the exhibits novel. We thought that young children's limited prior experience would mean that the interaction of the personal context with the physical and social contexts would assume great importance. Thus, we designed our data collection with both observation and videotapes to record social interaction with others as well as physical interaction with the exhibit. Feher's (1990) work on children's learning with exhibits also helped us to focus attention on how the design of the exhibits could prolong interaction and enhance opportunities to learn.

However, it was Hutt's (1981) distinction between epistemic and ludic behavior that enabled us to think most constructively about the nature of children's exploration of exhibits and to interpret the consequences for learning. This was especially so when we observed a child interacting alone with an exhibit, and we found it easy to decide whether behavior was epistemic and likely to be associated with learning, or ludic and associated with self-amusement. Our interviews confirmed that epistemic exploratory behavior was more likely to contribute to learning than symbolic or "pretend" play. We also found that interaction with peers and/or adults promoted learning, and our findings agree with and extend those of Crowley and Callanan (1998), Puchner et al. (1997), and Siegler (1999), who suggested that more learning occurred when there was interaction with adults.

The data collected during the study provided a great deal of feedback to Center staff about the exhibits. Although each was originally chosen because of its popularity (and therefore the likelihood of being able to collect sufficient data from it in an economical way), structured observation revealed previously unrecognized design flaws that detracted from their intended use. The hammer-like shape of the prototype wand-magnets is an example of exhibit design misleading rather than enlightening children about the appropriate use of the exhibit and hence the opportunity to learn from it. There were other examples of poor design, and some were able to be modified and data collection begun again on the improved exhibit. Thus additional outcomes of the study were to provide some guidelines for Center staff and educators to articulate the objectives for their exhibits (using the Exhibit Objectives proforma), and a means of checking whether these objectives are achieved by structured observation of visitors' interactions (using the Visitor Observation Form). We believe that effective exhibits have scope for both epistemic and ludic behavior. Both are important and should be encouraged, the former because of the greater potential for learning and the latter because it is fun.

ACKNOWLEDGMENT

The authors of this chapter thank the schools, teachers, parents, and children for their willing collaboration in the research. The research was carried out with the aid of a grant to Léonie Rennie from the Australian Research Council (ARC Large Grants Scheme). The interpretations provided in this chapter are those of the authors and should not be attributed to the granting body or other participants in the study.

REFERENCES

Carlisle, R. W. (1985). What do children do at a science center? *Curator, 28,* 27-33.

Crowley, K., & Callanan, M. A. (1998). Identifying and supporting shared scientific reasoning in parent–child interactions. *Journal of Museum Education, 23,* 12-17.

Diamond, J. (1986). The behavior of family groups in science museums. *Curator, 29*(2), 139-154.

Diamond, J. (1996). Playing and learning. *ASTC Newsletter, 24*(4), 2-6.

Falk, J. H., & Dierking, L. D. (1992). *The museum experience.* Washington, DC: Whalesback Books.

Falk, J. H., Martin, W., & Balling, J. D. (1978). The novel field trip phenomenon: Adjustment to novel settings interferes with task learning. *Journal of Research in Science Teaching, 15,* 127-134.

Feher, E. (1990). Interactive museum exhibits as tools for learning: Exploration with light. *International Journal of Science Education, 12,* 35-39.

Gallagher, J. M., & Dockser, L. S. (1987). Parent–child interaction in a museum for pre-school children. *Children's Environments Quarterly, 4*(1), 41-45.

Garvey, C. (1991). *Play* (2nd ed.). London: Fontana.

Gelman, R., Massey, C. M., & McManus, M. (1991). Characterizing supportive environments for cognitive development: Lessons from children in a museum. In L. B. Resnick, J. M. Levine, & S. D. Teasley (Eds.), *Perspectives on socially shared cognition* (pp. 226-256). Washington, DC: American Psychological Association.

Gurian, E. H. (1999). What is the object of this exercise? A meandering exploration of the many meanings of objects in museums. *Daedalus, 128*(3), 163-183.

Hodgkin, R. A. (1985). *Playing and exploring.* London: Methuen.

Hughes, M. (1983). Exploration and play. In J. Archer & L. I. A. Birke (Eds.), *Exploration in animals and humans* (pp. 230-244). Wokingham, UK: Van Nostrand Reinhold.

Hutt, C. (1970a). Curiosity and young children. *Science Journal, 6*(2), 68-71.

Hutt, C. (1970b). Specific and diversive exploration. In H. W. Reese & L. P. Lipsitt (Eds.), *Advances in child development and behavior* (Vol. 5, pp. 120-180). New York: Academic Press.

Hutt, C. (1981). Toward a taxonomy and conceptual model of play. In H. I. Day (Ed.), *Advances in intrinsic motivation and aesthetics* (pp. 251-298). New York: Plenum.

Hutt, S. J., Tyler, S., Hutt, C., & Christopherson, H. (1989). *Play, exploration and learning: A natural history of the pre-school.* London: Routledge.

Mann, D. (1996). Serious play. *Teachers College Record, 97,* 446-469.

McClafferty, T. P. (1995). Did you hear grandad? Children's and adults' use and understanding of a sound exhibit at interactive science centers. *Journal of Education in Museums, 16,* 12-16.

Nunnally, J. C., & Lemond, L. C. (1973). Exploratory behavior and human development. In H. W. Reese (Ed.), *Advances in child development and behavior* (Vol. 5, pp. 59-108). New York: Academic Press.

Perry, D. L. (1993). Measuring learning with the knowledge hierarchy. *Visitor Studies: Theory, Research and Practice, 6,* 73-77.

Puchner, L., Rapoport, R., & Gaskins, S. (1997, March). *Children and museum-based learning: A study of what and how young children learn in children's museums.* Paper presented at the annual meeting of the American Education Research Association, Chicago, IL.

Rennie, L. J. (1996). Measuring outcomes from the CSIRO Science Education Center. In M. Anderson, A. Delroy, & D. Tout-Smith (Eds.), *Identity, Icons, Artifacts: Proceedings of the Inaugural Museums Australia Conference* (pp. 259-265). Perth, Western Australia: Western Australian Museum.

Rennie, L. J., & McClafferty, T. P. (1996a). Science centers and science learning. *Studies in Science Education, 27,* 53-98.

Rennie, L. J., & McClafferty, T. P. (1996b). *Handbook for formative evaluation of interactive exhibits.* Canberra: Questacon — The National Science and Technology Center.

Siegler, J. N. (1999, April). *Analogical thinking in a children's museum context.* Paper presented at the annual meeting of the American Educational Research Association, Montreal.

Sykes, M. (1993). Evaluating exhibits for children: What is a meaningful play experience? *Visitor Studies: Theory, Research and Practice, 5,* 227-233.

Sylva, K., Bruner, J. S., & Genova, P. (1976). The role of play in the problem-solving of children 3-5 years old. In J. S. Bruner, A. Jolly, & K. Sylva (Eds.), *Play — Its role in development and evolution* (pp. 244-257). New York: Basic Books.

Vygotsky, L. S. (1978). *Mind in society: The development of higher mental processes.* Cambridge, MA: Harvard University Press.

APPENDIX

| **Visitor Observation Form** | Exhibit: _____ | Begin time: _____ |
| | Observer: _____ Date: _____ | End time: _____ |

Visitor Code:

E — Explainer
T — Teacher
M — Male Adult
F — Female Adult
b — boy
g — girl

Interaction Code:

M — g   M and g together

M ' g   M watches g

M ÷ g   M interacts with g

Takes Notice — Sub-total

| | 1 | 2 | 3 | 4 | 5 | 6 | 7 | 8 | 9 | 10 | 11 | 12 | 13 | 14 | 15 |

Interacts

| | 1 | 2 | 3 | 4 | 5 | 6 | 7 | 8 | 9 | 10 | 11 | 12 | 13 | 14 | 15 |

Uses Purposefully

| | 1 | 2 | 3 | 4 | 5 | 6 | 7 | 8 | 9 | 10 | 11 | 12 | 13 | 14 | 15 |

Sub-total · Total

Takes Notice

| | 16 | 17 | 18 | 19 | 20 | 21 | 22 | 23 | 24 | 25 | 26 | 27 | 28 | 29 | 30 |

Interacts

| | 16 | 17 | 18 | 19 | 20 | 21 | 22 | 23 | 24 | 25 | 26 | 27 | 28 | 29 | 30 |

Uses Purposefully

| | 16 | 17 | 18 | 19 | 20 | 21 | 22 | 23 | 24 | 25 | 26 | 27 | 28 | 29 | 30 |

Comments on visitor behaviour:

_____

_____

_____

Summary Recommendations:

_____

_____

_____

CHAPTER TWELVE

Reading Objects

Christina E. van Kraayenoord
The University of Queensland, Australia

Scott G. Paris
University of Michigan

"My name is Aruna and I have three daughters. Their names I will tell you, apa. They are called Diamond, Pearl and Adieu," she said proudly and everyone laughed at the old joke I was about to hear.

— Deen, 1998, p. 106

Name: EUCALYPTUS ptychocarpa; Common name: Swamp Bloodwood; Category: Tree–evergreen; Size: 15 m high, 7 m wide; Description: . . . Preferred Conditions: . . . Uses: . . . Origin: Native to Northern Territory and Western Australia.   — Miller & Ratcliffe, 1990, p. 55

Left: Multiple hand-made vase from the island of Melos in the Cyclades. Early to middle Cycladic period, c. 2000BC.   — Anderson, 1997, p. 42

IF
If I had wheels instead of feet
And roses 'sted of eyes
Then I could drive to the flower shop
And maybe win a prize.
           — Silverstein, 1981, p. 158

The Amish are not a fossilized culture from a bygone era. On first glance they do look old-fashioned. Folks who spurn high school, shun cars and read by lantern light are surely not modern. But in many ways the Amish are quite up-to-date.   — Kraybill, 1990, p. 36

As you read these texts, you may experience several reactions about your own reading. First, you may be aware that you are able to read most of the words — that is, you can attend to and identify the graphic symbols (letters) in the words and say them out loud or read them silently. However, you may be uncertain whether you have made the correct print-to-sound associations and correct pronounciations — EUCALYPTUS ptychocarpa, for example. Second, you may have become aware that you knew the meaning or understood the "gist" of the texts. On one or two occasions, however, you may have been able to decode the words but may not have been sure of their meanings — "apa," for example. You may have read a whole phrase or sentence, but had only a vague idea about the meaning or importance of the words — for example, "Early to middle Cycladic period, c. 2000BC."

These potential responses to texts illustrate how readers process text at many levels and how decoding and understanding words interact during reading. We examine the similarities between reading text and understanding objects by considering the analogous processes of constructing meaning. In the first part of this chapter, we examine different theoretical views of reading processes and the reader–text interaction by considering how the opening texts may have been read. In the second part of the chapter, we discuss a sociocritical perspective of literacy (that is, not only reading) known as the Four Resources Model (FRM; Freebody & Luke, 1990; Luke & Freebody, 1997, 1999). This perspective characterizes literacy as a broad repertoire of textual practices (known as *resources*) that suggest that learners construct meanings from texts in order to use and critically analyze them. In the third part of the chapter, we integrate the conceptualizations of reading with the FRM to demonstrate how the perceptual, cognitive, and social features of reading can be organized in an expanded framework. In the fourth section, we describe analogous processes between the reading of texts and the reading of objects. We suggest that there are a number of similarities between the reading of texts and objects, and we argue that viewers of objects use cognitive, social, personal, and contextual knowledge to construct meanings, as they do when they read text. Our view of the similarities is based on more than the visual analysis of words and objects because we emphasize how texts and objects position readers/viewers, provide stances to examine texts or objects, and promote specific kinds of transactions. Finally, we suggest a number of ways in which people employed in museums, galleries, arboreta, parks, and informal learning venues can foster multiple, complex, and deep readings of objects.

FUNDAMENTAL PROCESSES OF READING AND READERS

Different theories of reading have emphasized distinctive processes involved in apprehending meaning from printed words. During the past 75 years, some theories have been more popular than others, with the vicissitudes of positions reflecting prominent theories in education, psychology, and sociology. One of the early theories about reading emphasized the visual perceptual processes of reading. Reread the first opening text and think about your eyes and what they are doing when you read. What do you notice? You may have become aware that your eyes fixed on the text and scanned the print. Indeed, one of the earliest theories about reading emphasized the visual processing of text (Orton, 1925). According to this view, reading was concerned with the perception of graphic symbols and the identification of their orientation and properties. The reader learns to perceive the features of the print (in particular, perceiving the differences between the letters) before attaching sounds to it, which, in turn, precedes interpreting the meaning of the message. This position has regained popularity in "bottom-up" views of reading that emphasize perceptual discrimination and analyses that may be prerequisite to understanding (Adams, 1990; Bradley & Bryant, 1983; Vellutino & Denckla, 1991).

A second prominent theoretical view of reading has emphasized decoding. The decoding view refers to the translation of the graphic symbols that make up the text into phonetic sounds of the reader's language that allow interpretation. Decoding emphases are derived from the belief that reading is largely a matter of assigning sounds to symbols and then interpreting the sounds according to usual language processes (Gough, 1993; Nicholson, 1982). Reading is considered to occur at the letter, word, and sentence level. In this view, knowledge of the phonological (sound) system of language is used to assist with decoding the orthographic symbols. Phonemic awareness (an aspect of phonological knowledge that includes the blending, segmentation, and sequencing of sounds) is used to decode unknown words. Many words become recognized automatically through practice. Fluent reading involves both automatic recognition of words and rapid application of decoding skills based on phonemic awareness and sound–symbol relationships to interpret words. These skills are regarded as central processes of reading and as prerequisites to extracting meaning from text (Adams, 1990; Juel, Griffith, & Gough, 1986; Snow, Burns, & Griffin, 1998). Reading therefore involves connecting the sounds and letters in words, identifying words automatically, and decoding words.

A third view of reading emphasizes comprehension, partly as a reaction to other views that seem to neglect the making of meaning (Clay, 1991; Goodman, 1967). Some of these views are "top-down" because they assert that meaning, particularly the reader's expectations and hypotheses, guide the interpretation of individual words. In these approaches, understanding is not simply a derivative of decoding the graphic symbols on the page; it is an active part of the reader's knowledge, experience, and strategies that guides reading. According to this view, the purpose of reading is to determine the meaning of texts intended by authors by predicting and confirming the reader's predictions. The reader can create meaning simultaneously at literal and inferential levels because readers contribute more than a decoding of the words; they actively add their experiences, expectations, and knowledge to meaning-making while reading. Different reading comprehension theories emphasize the language experience approach (van Allen, 1965), the whole language approach (Goodman, 1989; Smith, 1973), and the strategic reading approach (Englert, Raphael, & Mariage, 1994; Paris, Lipson, & Wixson, 1983), but they all focus on understanding as the primary goal of reading. This contrasts with views that emphasize decoding first and meaning-making later.

These three views of reading isolate component processes that are all involved in reading, but top-down and bottom-up processes interact in contemporary theories (e.g., Stanovich, 2000). Each of these views of reading has merits for understanding how people interpret printed words. Each of these views, as we explain, also has value for understanding how people interpret objects in museums. For now, though, we want you to concentrate on the rich knowledge you bring to the task of reading. Read again the pieces of text found at the beginning of the chapter. This time, what other features do you notice?

On this occasion, during your reading of the texts, you may have linked your own knowledge or personal experiences to the ideas presented. For example, you may have thought to yourself, "I know people who have called their children by names like Diamond," or you may have chuckled when you recalled Silverstein's poetry. Such reflections mean that a reader is making sense of the words by bringing information to the text. Personal knowledge gained from one's life and one's direct and indirect experiences in the world are used to understand the ideas in text (Afflerbach, 1990; Anderson, Hiebert, Scott, & Wilkinson, 1985; Anderson & Pearson, 1984). In this view, reading comprehension involves knowledge that readers bring to the text as well as the interpretations they construct about the words that go beyond the explicit information. Consequently, reading may be variable, idiosyncratic, and contradictory among people exposed to the same text.

You may also have noticed that there is a range of types of text (genres) with a variety of structures and formats that are read in different ways. You may have tracked the print differently, and your intonation and expression probably were altered for each piece of text. Knowledge of the genre provides one with expectations about how the text will be structured, that is, how the sentences, paragraphs, and whole text are put together. Such awareness also provides information about how the text should be read. Skilled readers add voice and intonation congruent with the tone, style, and genre of the text.

As you read the poem by Shel Silverstein, you may have been reminded of other books, poems, and songs by him, or occasions when you read Silverstein's work with someone else. Making connections among different texts is known as *intertextuality*. Experiences with one text may help the reader make connections to other texts and so a rich intertextual series of meanings is created that transcends the interpretation of the individual text. You may also have reacted to the texts emotionally. Perhaps you enjoyed one, disliked another, or laughed at another. Perhaps you enjoyed the snippet that you read of "Broken Bangles" and thought that you would like to read more. You may also have been conscious of how your personal interests in a topic influenced your reading. For example, you may have been dismissive about the extract about tropical trees because you have little interest in these trees. Perhaps you decided that Kraybill's use of the adjective "fossilized" when referring to a culture (in the phrase "fossilized culture") was inappropriate and patronizing.

Each of the examples illustrates how readers actively respond to text and create meanings that transcend the printed words. Reading researchers have identified many factors that influence reading, such as prior experience and knowledge, awareness of genre, intertextuality, reader response, interest, and evaluation and judgment (Palincsar, 1998). When we add these features to visual perception, decoding, and meaning-making, we see that reading text is more complex than figuring out what the letters on the page say. Reading involves the decoding from print to sound and the application of cultural, social, and personal knowledge to the text as meanings are created. Readers may use various strategies to connect these sources of knowledge and information. For example, readers may pose questions as they read, disagree with the author, write notes in the margin, or underline sentences emphatically as a personal reaction to the text. Readers might reread puzzling sections or summarize a bit of information to recall later. Skilled readers monitor their understanding while reading and can take corrective actions to improve their comprehension if they choose.

These views of reading represent the kinds of psychological theories that emphasized *solo cognition,* that is, how individuals think about text. They were not concerned with reading that occurs among people or reading that is facilitated by social support and discussion. They were not concerned with the goals or purposes of reading nor the social situations in which reading occurred. Thus, other theories were proposed that emphasized the social nature of reading, the social discourse around reading, and the social uses of reading (Bloome, 1983; Palincsar, 1998; Street, 1995). Sociolinguistic theories of reading gained popularity along with sociocultural views of learning in the 1990s because they emphasized the situations, practices, and social supports of the activities that were inherently both cognitive and social (Lave, 1993; Rogoff, 1993; Wertsch, 1991). In the following section, we discuss one sociocritical model of literacy that was proposed by Australian researchers because it seems particularly heuristic for thinking about how one reads objects as well as texts.

THE FOUR RESOURCES MODEL OF LITERACY

The Four Resources Model (FRM; Freebody & Luke, 1990; Luke & Freebody, 1997, 1999) views literacy as a social practice. It is embedded in a paradigm broadly derived from work in the sociology, ethnography, and interactional sociolinguistics of literacy.

> It begins from the assumption that literacy is first and foremost a social and cultural practice — constructed, negotiated and achieved in relation to identifiable social, cultural, and economic contexts. Knowledge, cognition, and linguistic performance, therefore, are interactional achievements that constitute relations of power within the social fields of institutions like schools, workplaces, civic sites, and mass media. (A. Luke, personal communication, August 5, 2000)

The FRM, therefore, emphasizes that literacy is not an attribute that one "has"; rather it is an array of practices that develop in relation to and are shaped by events, contexts, and materials with which one engages.

The FRM applies to all aspects of literacy, including reading, writing, speaking, listening, and viewing, but in this chapter we confine our discussion of the FRM to reading. The FRM asserts that both understanding the purpose of a text and critical reading are necessary to understand the full meaning of text, and therefore the FRM goes beyond traditional emphases on decoding and meaning-making. In terms of the authors' purposes, authors use text as a tool for achieving particular goals that are extrinsic to the text itself (Lankshear, 1998). Readers attempt to establish the author's purpose and suggest other possible purposes. Critical reading means examining the contents and statements of the text and considering the underlying and implicit assumptions in the text. It involves examining how the reader is being positioned by the author and the degree to which the reader accepts or challenges this position. It also entails the reader's developing discourses and critical metalanguages that can be used to participate in other discourses. Morgan (1997) described the social aspects of critical literacy by noting that, "Readers focus on the cultural and ideological assumptions that underwrite texts, they investigate the politics of representations, and they interrogate the inequitable, cultural positioning of speakers and readers within discourses" (p. 42).

In many situations the critical stance taken by a reader leads to social action (Gee, 1999; The New London Group, 1996; van Kraayenoord, 2000). Such emphases on authors' purposes and critical analysis take into account the social nature of reading. The acts and the events of reading are context- and content-specific, and are used, acted on, or transformed by the reader. Thus, it is clear that the FRM adds a social and political dimension to analyses of text. Theorists in critical reading make the same point.

> Critical reading aims to enable students to question and refute the given order
> of things and it especially encourages them to dispute normalizing practices
> that define their identities and implicitly allot them a position on the grid of
> power relations within particular sites and ultimately within their society. (Mc-
> Gregor, 2000, p. 222)

What is said explicitly, as well as what is omitted from text, must be interpreted according to the social stances of both author and readers. In this view,
understanding text is not free of values or consequences; it is a contextualized
event that is a springboard for action.

Freebody and Luke (1990) proposed a family or repertoire of practices,
grouped in four areas that are used in order to read text. They are code-breaking, participating in text, using text, and analyzing text. The first two practices
are similar to processes emphasized in traditional reading theories, whereas
the latter two practices focus on the sociopolitical aspects of reading text.

Code-breaking involves perceptual and decoding processes necessary to
translate graphic symbols into meaningful words. This means that the reader
knows the patterns and conventions of the print, is able to unlock the letter
patterns of words, and can apply the sounds to the symbols on the way to ob-
taining meaning from the text. *Participating in text* means that the reader is
concerned with establishing the meanings of the text. The reader develops
an awareness of the author's intended meaning but also interrogates the text
to establish other possible meanings. The reader is involved in examining
the genre of the text and its structure and how this structure facilitates the
construction of meaning. Readers are also concerned about ways in which
their background knowledge, interests, and experiences of the world and of
text can be utilized to establish possible meanings. Code-breaking and participating in text subsume the traditional processes of reading described earlier.
The social–critical extensions of the FRM are evident in the following two
processes.

At one level, *using text* refers to developing an understanding of the intended use or uses of the text as proposed by the author. Specifically, the
reader is concerned with understanding how the audience and purpose of
the text shape its construction. How the author's choices and craft are related
to the genre, language, and format are also considered. At a second level, and
simultaneously, readers consider the potential uses of the text. That is, the
reader considers the uses or actions that can be taken as a consequence of
engaging in the text. What are the thoughts and actions of readers that can
be stimulated by the text, and what can be done with these thoughts and
actions? Thus, the purposes of the text as object, as well as the purposes of
the author as agent and reader as actor, are examined and responded to by
the reader. These instrumental uses of text and social goals of the author
and actor/reader may be open to debate or misrepresentation because they

extend beyond the literal message. However, they constitute consideration of text use in terms of authentic social situations to achieve social ends.

Analyzing text involves the application of criteria, beliefs, or standards to text in order to derive a critical stance or point of view. In this role, the reader attempts to problematize the text by questioning the authority of the author, by examining how the reader is positioned by the author, by examining whose interests are being served or whose "voice" is being heard and whose is being silenced. In other words, the reader searches for and analyzes implicit messages and assumptions that lie beneath the text. Opinion, bias, stereo-typing, and point of view are all exposed and examined. The view of reader as critic and analyst means that each reader brings personal values and per-spectives to text. Therefore, people may derive vastly different analyses of the same text. Ultimately, the reader who takes on the practices of the text an-alyst recognizes that texts are culturally crafted objects, created through the author's deliberate selection of textual features (eg., words, genre) that con-tribute to the text's ideological meanings. A reader who is a critical analyst comes to identify the text's ideological meanings and appreciate that such meanings can be endorsed or challenged (Harris, Turbill, Fitzsimmons, & McKenzie, 2001).

It is important to note that Freebody and Luke (1990) did not view these four practices as organized hierarchically by age or ability. They did not sug-gest that young, beginning readers are only able to decode text and that only more mature or sophisticated readers are able to undertake critical or analyti-cal reading. Rather they argued that all four practices are necessary and are typically employed in an overlapping and coordinated way. They are also used in flexible ways with a range of expertise according to the nature of the text and the task. The practices within the four areas are used simultaneously. Over time and with practice and developing expertise, readers apply them in skill-ful ways. The practices emphasized in the FRM have direct applications in classroom literacy instruction. For example, van Kraayenoord and Moni (2000) and Ludwig (2000) applied the FRM in the design of activities for classroom teachers in the primary grades.

INTEGRATING THE CONCEPTUALIZATIONS

Various theoretical and historical views of reading have emphasized the in-terplay of perception, decoding, automatic word recognition, making mean-ing, using previous knowledge and experiences, identifying genre, making connections across texts, responding personally, using one's interests, and making evaluations and judgments. We described how the FRM includes such processes but adds social stances and critical evaluations of the uses and pur-poses of text to provide a broader view of reading practices in social contexts. The FRM provides a framework for understanding how readers engage analytically with text in order to develop an understanding of the text, the self, and others in relation to the world and, if necessary or desired, to respond to what one learns. The practices one uses to achieve these ends, according to Freebody and Luke (1990), include the integrated use of decoding print to sound, applying cultural, social, and personal knowledge in developing an understanding of the meaning of the text, taking account of the author's position, and evaluating the ideas in terms of experiences relative to self and others (Hood, Solomon, & Burns, 1996; Ludwig, 2000).

The FRM includes a range of practices that readers apply in specific contexts that result in jointly constructed and negotiated meanings of texts. The unlocking of the code, the identification of the words, and the construction of the many meanings of the text occur in situations where readers share their ideas and respond to those of others. Reading is influenced by interactions with others to create possible meanings and, simultaneously, the meanings are shaped by the contexts in which the reading takes place. In constructing multiple understandings of the text, the reader engages in a dynamic interplay of various practices. These practices involve cognitive and linguistic skills as well as a social–critical analysis of the uses of texts, and points of view of authors and other readers of the same texts. Reading involves thinking and reasoning by predicting, problem-solving, analyzing, and critiquing the explicit and the implicit meanings, as well as the discourses used. We believe that this conceptualization of reading of texts can be applied to other domains, for example, to examine how people "read" objects.

READING OBJECTS

It is not novel for us to consider objects as texts. Anthropologists, psychologists, curators, and museum educators have noted how collected objects are like and unlike libraries of collected texts (Carr, 1991). If museums are like libraries, then objects are like books that visitors may browse. The object is like a text because it may be a representation of a class of similar objects, available for viewing, discussion, and analysis. Or it may be a unique object that might be sacred, frightening, valuable, or bizarre. Visitors look at and examine objects to determine their qualities. The individual object, like a book, may be easily read or may be difficult to interpret. Readability may depend on familiarity and complexity in texts and objects. What is apprehended from the encounter with text or object depends on the processes applied by the person.

Central to this apprehension is the knowledge that the construction of meanings is not neutral. First, objects are made by someone or selected by someone. Therefore, they are associated with a creator's or selector's history, status, language, and socialization. Second, objects are embodiments of the organization of the society in which the object's creator or selector and the object itself sit (Freebody, 1997). Third, the object's creator or selector has a relationship with the viewer (often an unequal relationship), and that relationship draws on a particular version of the individual as viewer (Ludwig, 2000). Specifically, the relationship is tied up with the creator's or selector's and the viewer's age, gender, race, ethnicity, and class. The meanings of an object are constructed as a consequence of these factors and therefore many meanings may emerge from viewing the object. These meanings are products of who the creator or selector of the object and the viewer are — within given historical, social, and economic contexts. These multiple meanings can be articulated through interactions (discourses) with others and through the acquisition and development of a metalanguage around the object. These discourses provide opportunities for the meanings to be accepted through the alignment of the viewer's meaning with the creator's position or the position can be resisted through the viewer taking a counterposition. Either acceptance or resistance of the position can lead to action. That is, the viewer can reflect on and act on the interactions about the meaning(s). Specifically, there can be personal and social consequences.

What is perhaps new in this conceptualization of viewing objects is the awareness that the viewing of objects is not neutral and that this awareness is made explicit. In addition in this conceptualization of viewing, awareness is used/exploited to permit the construction of multiple meanings. These meanings can be contested and can, and often do, have real-life effects. Such a conceptualization is different from the various accounts of object-centered learning that focus on how people respond to objects and with which we may be familiar. Some accounts describe how manipulation and physical exploration provide insight to objects through sensory impressions. Some accounts point out how objects evoke discussions among people that may involve teaching or reminiscence. Other accounts note the qualities of the object, the perceptual, spiritual, or personal features that hold a person's attention and invite deeper inspection. "Reading objects" occurs in a metaphorical sense in each of these accounts, and we think it is heuristic to explore the processes of reading objects that are suggested by the approaches of reading text, including more recent conceptualizations. We consider five aspects of this analogy.

Decoding Objects

The most direct correspondence between reading text and reading objects is at the interpretive level. Decoding objects is similar to analyses of printed words in that objects and words have both physical and symbolic representations. The perceptual analyses of words and objects allows the apprehension of distinctive features. For example, as a visitor gazes at a painting, he or she might study the color, the texture, the three-dimensional depth, and the lighting contrasts in various parts of the painting. With experience and skill, the visitor may acquire automatic recognition of these perceptual features, much like sight recognition of words. Decoding attaches sounds (familiar auditory and linguistic features) to interpreted symbols in reading and, when applied to objects, decoding attaches varied perceptual features to objects. For example, while looking at a steam locomotive, a museum visitor might consider the heat of the engine, the touch of the steel, the weight of the locomotive, or the noise of the steam escaping. These features, both apparent and imagined, can be apprehended by decoding the physical dimensions of the object.

Perkins (1994) suggested that the processes used when reading objects are similar to processes used in academic learning situations. Reading text and objects might include linear processing. Just as prior knowledge facilitates reading text, previous experience with objects facilitates understanding ramifications of objects. Perkins suggested that strategies for understanding text are like visual strategies for understanding objects. Monitoring the meaning, rereading, asking questions, and summarizing key points may be appropriate strategies in both situations. In the FRM, there is a direct analogy between code-breaking and participating in text that is like decoding objects and participating in the construction of meaning. However, this analogy is limited to the processes of the reader with the object. It neglects the larger social context and purposes of the act of reading or the experience of the larger activity signified by the text or object.

Making Sense of Objects

Understanding an object often means gathering information about it — what it is, what it is used for, and why it is important. This is especially true in science and history museums where cultural artifacts are often confusing and their purposes are opaque. Reading the nature of these objects is like reading expository text. Indeed, reading the labels may be more informative than gazing at the objects, and it is not unusual for visitors to become preoccupied with reading the labels for information rather than analyzing the objects for meaning. Sense-making is understanding the significance of the object according to someone else's criteria or context. It works well as a disciplinary-based approach to meaning both in text and objects. Seeing a ball suspended in air underneath a blower attracts attention and may cause consternation among visitors. Reading the label about the Bernouilli principle or listening to someone explain airflow and lift may provide a sensible interpretation of the phenomenon. In this case, "reading" the physical event may be more confusing or unfamiliar than reading the text label.

Reading objects in museums poses many problems for visitors who do not understand the curator's reasons for displaying some objects with others or do not understand concepts and principles that link objects (Hein &

Alexander, 1998). This is analogous to readers who do not understand the author's purpose or the connections among related texts. When objects are read
in isolation, like sentences that are not integrated in their meaning, the result
is piecemeal or superficial comprehension of insular bits of information. One
of the goals for visitors in museums is to see the connections among objects
and to make sense of the concepts they illustrate. A learning goal for people
in museums or schools is to think according to the disciplines, such as learning the rules of inquiry in science, history, art, and so forth. Reading objects
then becomes structured by disciplinary strategies and discourses much like
reading text is guided by genre and authors' purposes. But many museum objects do not fall neatly into a single disciplinary category (e.g., an old train engine exhibit may have relevance for physics, history, etc). There is an analogy
between "cultural mysteries" of objects and texts because the meaning in
both must be constructed across exemplars, within disciplines, and among
people. The sense-making involved in reading these cultural artifacts is expository or paradigmatic (Bruner, 1986) as opposed to narrative, which is considered in the following section.

Reading the Stories of Objects

Objects afford connections to concepts and disciplines but they also afford
personalized connections to individuals. For example, whereas one museum
visitor might remark that a particular old icebox on display cooled food by
evaporation, another might be reminded of an old icebox he had seen at his
grandmother's house when he was a child. The principle is sensible and the
memory is meaningful. Objects elicit stories, according to Gurian (1999), and
it is the richness, power, and emotion of the stories that ties objects to viewers
and makes the reading enjoyable. Reading objects entails making meaning
as well as sense. By making meaning, we refer to personal and idiosyncratic
responses to objects in which autobiographical references and history are
intertwined with the specific object or the class of objects represented by the
artifact (Paris & Mercer, in press). That is partly why Gurian (1999) suggested
that the specific object on display may not matter; it is the elicited story "read"
by the viewer in response to the object that matters. Certainly, there are coun-
terarguments about the importance of viewing special qualities of genuine
objects, one-of-a-kind specimens, sacred objects, and unique artifacts, but this
does not diminish the importance of visitors recalling or retelling their stories
about the objects. However, another perspective might be that objects are
also useful as starting points for personal stories (Roberts, 1997). Visitors who
are fascinated by a demonstration of the Bernouilli principle, for example,
may later make sense of other phenomena using their memory of seeing that
exhibit at the museum. It is important to consider objects as both something
to connect to prior experience as well as something that will be "past experi-

ence" for future interactions. It is the same with text. Some accounts of learning in museums ascribe these narrative stories to "personal context" variables (e.g., Falk & Dierking, 1992), whereas other accounts might emphasize autobiographical memories and reminiscence (Rosenzweig & Thelen, 1998). In either framework, we can envision visitors looking at objects and reading their own personal history in the significance of the objects.

Shared Reading of Objects

Each of the three views just described can be embedded in social situations and discourses about objects. Analyzing, perceiving, and decoding features of objects are often the most vocal and visible aspect of visitor behavior. "Look at that one! Did you see the size of that …? What the heck is that for? Have you ever seen anything so purple?" Such comments invite others to help decode the object whether it is a painting, machine, or animal. Reading text and reading objects can both be the stimulus for social interactions, perhaps on the first encounter or on re-experiencing something highly familiar. Shared readings can include instructional episodes such as scaffolded learning and questioning that are frequently observed between parents and children (Borun, Chambers, & Cleghorn, 1996). Shared reading can also be analytical, argumentative, or passionate. Like texts, objects elicit a range of personal emotions that are expressed and shared. The FRM and other models of social practices in reading emphasize the social functions of reading and the instrumental functions of text. In like manner, viewing objects with others may promote social conversations and relationships. Reading objects together as shared experiences creates a co-constructed narrative among the participants and the objects that becomes part of their shared autobiographical stories.

Never-Ending Stories Provoked
by Problematized Objects

Objects can evoke novel questions and stories that unfold among participants. For example, while viewing a piece of art, someone may ask, "What was she thinking when she made that? Why did she choose that material? Do you think it is supposed to represent a …?" Analyses do not always reach conclusions and stories do not always have definitive structures. Visitors who read objects may notice some features, ask questions, and create their own interpretations with others who may in turn challenge them or confirm the stories or create new twists on the story about the object. Just as texts can be problematized, so can objects be positioned as problems or questions. Research has shown that students become more engaged with texts and objects when driving questions and big problems are posed about them: "So, what would the world be like without insects? Why did the artist juxtapose those two objects? How did the combustion engine change the United States and who benefited from its introduction? Such questions challenge the viewer to read objects more deeply, to import previous knowledge, and to make inferences about objects that were unlikely until required. (See Ludwig 2000; Luke, O'Brien, & Comber, 1994; and O'Brien, 1994 for examples of how the roles suggested in FRM are adopted in activities around community texts — toy catalogs, Mother's Day and Father's Day catalogs, and grocery packages, etc. — in classrooms.) By asking such questions, viewers make connections among experiences and objects as they consider the range of possible stories suggested by the objects.

The viewer may form judgments and reach conclusions about the object based on a process of evaluation and decision-making. The viewer may also undertake a critical reading of the object. This would involve analyzing the object by making it problematic. For example, the object's creation, use, influence, or value may be questioned, challenged, or resisted. In this way the object and associated meanings are critiqued and new meanings are tested. This means that it could be viewed from other people's perspectives, from other time periods, and from other social situations or circumstances. Reflections on aspects such as the influence of race, gender, or economic circumstances may play a role. An understanding could be developed by the viewer that a particular stance or position has been taken by the creator and that a counterstance or alternative view is possible.

By asking questions about objects such as "What do I do with this object or what do I do with the information about this object?" (participant), we emphasize the purposes of the object, and by asking "What does this object do to me?" (analyst), we emphasize that objects are not neutral. Rather, what emerges is an understanding that there are both pragmatic and ideological codes at work (Freebody, 1992) when we view objects. The most vivid examples of this counterpositioning are evident in controversial exhibits of objects. For example, photographs of suggestive homosexuality or art that depicts desecration of religious icons may provoke community indignation. Historical reminders of racism, oppression, or genocide can elicit a wide range of reactions depending on the backgrounds and beliefs of the observers. These occasions illustrate how "reading" objects can be emotionally charged by the stances of the object, the participant, and the analyst.

HELPING VIEWERS TO READ OBJECTS

To this point we have suggested that there are many similarities between reading texts and reading objects because many of the same practices are used in reading and viewing. In this final section we suggest a number of ways in which people creating and maintaining object-centered learning environments can encourage viewers to develop more complex and deeper readings of objects.

Creating an Interactive, Responsive Environment

Based on the premise that reading objects is a social and cultural practice, it is important that situations are created in which other people are available with whom viewers can interact either during or after their engagements with the objects. A supportive individual is likely to keep the participant focussed and active as new ideas are explored and learned. Viewers can be assisted by peers, docents, and parents who model making observations, gathering details, making inferences, creating hypotheses, suggesting applications, and being analytical in their thinking. However, the "guides" do not always have to be physically present. Other opportunities to record the processes of thinking and summarize new knowledge also promote learning. Opportunities for written, drawn, or performed and shared responses can be effective. The use of written scaffolds (grids, matrices, retrieval tables) in hard copy or online, that provide a format for individuals to record data, to make predictions, relate objects to the their own experiences, and to share interpretations with others, can be created for use when a social "guide" is not present. Environments can provide viewers with feedback on their reactions and interpretations, and encourage them to stretch their thinking by using a range of strategies to read objects, create meanings, and learn how objects influence others. Feedback could include verbal, written, and symbolic support and affirmation.

Explicating the Hidden

As suggested earlier, viewers draw on a variety of sources of information to make meaning and to read objects critically. In many situations these sources of information may be implied or assumed. However, it is suggested instead that these sources should be made explicit and explained. For example, where an object has been juxtaposed with another because it can be connected historically or politically, it may be necessary to make such connections obvious and transparent. Charts and models that indicate the relations between objects or events can provide structure and support to the viewer (that is, scaffold the viewer) in developing understandings about what is implied or assumed. Viewers may also wish to add to the charts and models by noting other assumptions that are hidden. For example, the viewer may challenge the asserted historical or political link by informing other viewers of other assumptions that, from their perspective, remain hidden. Thus, the viewer might add a rejoinder or take issue with the explication.

Another way of explicating the hidden is to point out that the juxtaposition has been made for a reason, with its possible purpose being hypothesized by the viewer. Here the viewer can be creative in providing multiple explana-tions and rationalizations for the juxtaposition. At the same time, the viewer will be engaged in asking questions such as: Where did the idea for the jux-taposition come from? What did the display's creator do to create the rela-tionship? Is this juxtaposition supported/constrained by a particular piece of legislation or policy, a set of values or beliefs? Such questions do not have to be ad hoc; they are guided by the background, knowledge, and disciplinary perspectives of viewers. Bain and Ellenbogen (Chapter 9, this volume) de-scribe how scientific and historical "literacies" provide disciplinary lenses for viewing objects and asking questions. Discipline-based perspectives include rules of inquiry and evidence that distinguish novice from expert viewers and museum visitors.

Assisting Viewers to Develop Their Own Reflections and Applications

The power to develop viewers who know about themselves as learners is most important. First, visitors need to know that their personal knowledge and contributions are valued. Participants can be helped in this by being encouraged to use what they know and to draw on their personal identities. Acknowledgment of the social and cultural backgrounds of participants and acceptance of all responses and reactions to the objects will enhance en-gagement.

Second, ensuring that the environments allow the exploration of objects of importance and relevance to the viewer will also assist in the development of meaningful and applied learning. Our concern here is not to rule out or cen-sor objects that may not appeal or be relevant to the viewer, but rather to cap-italize on any connections that a viewer may be able to make to an object. Often attitudes toward (that is, liking or curiosity) an object is a trigger to an evolving interest and engagement with an object.

A third area in which viewers can be assisted is by letting them become aware that the effort that they put into their reading of objects influences their understandings. When the visitor attempts to make effortful connec-tions between what he or she knows and the object being viewed, then richer understandings are created. For example, a learner who uses observations to compare and contrast skeletons and then completes a table of similarities and differences among dinosaurs will move beyond an exotic interest in dino-saurs to the development of scientific knowledge of dinosaurs.

Finally, helping the viewer to engage in multiple readings to re-view — that is, to re-examine what he or she sees and understands — is vital. By helping the viewer to work with and against the objects, he or she will develop a deeper awareness of his or her own beliefs, assumptions, and stereotypes, and realize that there are many meanings that are both possible and legitimate.

Indeed, it is in this context that we might discuss objects considered "less than ideal in terms of content" (Gilbert, 1989). Gilbert suggested that texts that are less than ideal in terms of content "may serve the function of helping children to read critically. Perhaps in this way, teachers can take advantage of the way in which inequities are made tangible and therefore accessible, when translated into print" (p. 21). Similarly, we suggest that it is important for people involved in creating museum displays to be aware of the meanings each object affords and how meaning is constructed, so that the positioning of the viewer by the object and its creator can be understood. In this way, objects that might be regarded as controversial can also serve to develop skills of analysis and critique, hallmarks of active citizenship and democracy.

Encouraging Transformations

Object transformation refers to creating novel objects by crafting new materials, purposes, functions, or values surrounding a familiar object. During object transformation, the viewer takes his or her newly synthesized knowledge and critical awareness and makes something original — a new object or some "thing" with or of the object (either figuratively or literally). In this way the object gains a new and deeper reading. For example, following the viewing of a display of body ornaments (e.g., tattoos, body piercings, shoes, makeup), viewers may be invited to create their own body ornaments or add their comments to a computer discussion list that debates the use of such adornments. In doing so, the viewer both analyzes the purposes of such ornaments and offers reinterpretations of their function or provides a critical commentary. In such a way the viewer, like the reader, transforms the new understandings, gained from decoding, meaning-making, examining its pragmatic value, and being analytical and critical, into a new object. Such transformations are creative and allow individuals to expand their thinking and challenge traditional ways of knowing.

CONCLUSIONS

We began this chapter with various examples of texts and challenged you as a reader of these texts to examine the ways in which you might understand and engage them. We have suggested that reading text involves many more processes than perception, decoding, and comprehension. As proposed by the FRM, a reader engages in a range of practices that include these cognitive processes but that also requires an understanding of the pragmatic purposes of the text, the stances of the author, and the need for critique of the explicit and the implicit meanings. In this chapter we argued that the reading of objects involves similar social, pragmatic, and cognitive practices. Multiple readings are developed based on what is brought to the object and the ways in which the viewer engages with it. We suggest that a viewer must decode objects, make sense of objects, read the stories of objects, engage in the shared reading of objects, and be involved in reflective, never-ending stories. We encourage museum educators to assist viewers by creating interactive, responsive environments, explicating the hidden meanings, and encouraging transformations of objects through participation.

REFERENCES

Adams, M. (1990). *Beginning to read: Thinking and learning about print.* Cambridge, MA: MIT Press.

Afflerbach, P. P. (1990). The influence of prior knowledge and text genre on readers' prediction strategies. *Journal of Reading Behavior, 22,* 131-148.

Anderson, R. G. W. (Compiler). (1997). *The British Museum.* London: British Museum Press.

Anderson, R. C., Hiebert, E. H., Scott, J. A., & Wilkinson, I. A. G. (1985). *Becoming a nation of readers: The Report of the Commission on Reading.* Washington, DC: The National Institute of Education.

Anderson, R. C., & Pearson, P. D. (1984). A schema-thematic view of basic processes in reading comprehension. In P. D. Pearson, R. Barr, & M. L. Kamil (Eds.), *Handbook of reading research* (Vol. 1, pp. 255-291). New York: Longman.

Bloome, D. (1983). Reading as a social process. In B. Hutson (Ed.), *Advances in reading/language research* (Vol. 2, pp. 165-195). Greenwich, CT: JAI Press.

Borun, M., Chambers, M., & Cleghorn, A. (1996). Families are learning in science museums. *Curator, 39*(2), 262-270.

Bradley, L., & Bryant, P. E. (1983). Categorizing sounds and learning to read: A causal connection. *Nature, 301,* 419-421.

Bruner, J. S. (1986). *Actual minds, possible worlds.* Cambridge, MA: Harvard University Press.

Carr, D. (1991). Minds in museums and libraries: The cognitive management of cultural institutions. *Teachers College Record, 93*(1), 6-27.

Clay, M. M. (1991). *Becoming literate: The construction of inner control.* Portsmouth, NH: Heinemann.

Deen, H. (1998). *Broken bangles.* Sydney: Anchor Books.

Englert, C. S., Raphael, T., & Mariage, T. V. (1994). Developing a school-based discourse for literacy learning: A principled search for understanding. *Learning Disability Quarterly, 17*(1), 2-32.

Falk, J. H., & Dierking, L. D. (1992). *The museum experience.* Washington, DC: Whalesback Books.

Freebody, P. (1992). A socio-cultural approach: Resourcing four roles as a literacy learner. In A. Watson & A. Badenhop (Eds.), *Prevention of reading failure* (pp. 48-80). Lindfield, NSW: Scholastic Australia.

Freebody, P. (1997). *Critical literacy: What and why?* Paper presented at the Metropolitan East Literacy Forum, Brisbane, Australia.

Freebody, P., & Luke, A. (1990). Literacies' programs: Debates and demands in cultural context. *Prospect: A Journal of Australian TESOL, 11,* 7-16.

Gee, J. P. (1999). The new literacy studies: From "socially situated" to the work of the social. In D. Barton, M. Hamilton, & R. Ivanic (Eds.), *Situated literacies: Reading and writing in context* (pp. 180-196). London: Routledge.

Gilbert, P. (1989). *Gender, literacy and the classroom.* Melbourne: Australian Reading Association.

Goodman, K. (1967). Reading: A psycholinguistic guessing game. *Journal of the Reading Specialist, 6,* 126-135.

Goodman, K. A. (1989). Whole-language research: Foundations and development. *Elementary School Journal, 90,* 207-221.

Gough, P. B. (1993). The beginning of decoding. *Reading and Writing, 5,* 181-192.

Gurian, E. H. (1999). What is the object of this exercise? A meandering exploration of the many meanings of objects in museums. *Daedulus, 128*(3), 163-183.

Harris, P., Turbill, J., Fitzsimmons, P., & McKenzie, B. (2001). *Reading in the primary school years.* Katooma, NSW: Social Science Press.

Hein, G. E., & Alexander, M. (1998). *Museums: Places of learning.* Washington, DC: American Association of Museums.

Hood, S., Solomon, N., & Burns, A. (1996). *Focus on reading.* Sydney: National Centre for English Language Teaching and Research, Macquarie University.

Juel, C., Griffith, P. L., & Gough, P. B. (1986). Acquisition of literacy: A longitudinal study of 54 children from first through fourth grades. *Journal of Educational Psychology, 80,* 437-447.

Kraybill, D. B. (1990). *The puzzles of Amish life.* Intercourse, PA: Good Books.

Lankshear, C. (1998). Frameworks and workframes: Literacy, policies and new orders. *Unicorn, 24*(2), 43-58.

Lave, J. (1993). The practice of learning. In S. Chaiklin & J. Lave (Eds.), *Understanding practice: Perspectives on activity and context* (pp. 3-32). New York: Cambridge University Press.

Ludwig, C. (2000). *Why wait: A way to teach critical literacies in the early years.* Brisbane: The State of Queensland (Department of Education).

Luke, A., & Freebody, P. (1997). Shaping the social practices of reading. In S. Muspratt, A. Luke, & P. Freebody (Eds.), *Constructing critical literacies: Teaching and learning textual practice* (pp. 185-225). St. Leonards, NSW: Allen & Unwin.

Luke, A., & Freebody, P. (1999). A map of possible practices: Further notes on the Four Resources Model. *Practically Primary, 4*(2), 5-8.

Luke, A., O'Brien, J., & Comber, B. (1994). Making community texts objects of study. *Australian Journal of Language and Literacy, 17*(2), 139-149.

McGregor, G. (2000). Kids who "talk back" — critically literate or disruptive youth? *Journal of Adolescent and Adult Literacy, 44*(3), 221-228.

Miller, H., & Ratcliffe, R. (1990). *Top plants for tropical gardens.* Canberra, Australia: Australian Government Publishing Service.

Morgan, W. (1997). *Critical literacy in the classroom: The art of the possible.* New York: Routledge.

Nicholson, T. (1982). *An anatomy of reading.* Sydney: Martin Educational.

O'Brien, J. (1994). Critical literacy in an early childhood classroom: A progress report. *Australian Journal of Language and Literacy, 17*(1), 36-44.

Orton, S. T. (1925). Word blindness in school children. *Archives of Neurology and Psychiatry, 14,* 582-615.

Palincsar, A. S. (1998). Social constructivist perspectives on teaching and learning. *Annual Review of Psychology, 49,* 345-375.

Paris, S. G., Lipson, M. Y., & Wixson, K. (1983). Becoming a strategic reader. *Contemporary Educational Psychology, 8,* 293-316.

Paris, S. G., & Mercer, M. (in press). Finding self in objects: Identity exploration in museums. In G. Leinhardt, K. Crowley, & K. Knutson (Eds.), *Learning conversations: Explanation and identity in museums.* Mahwah, NJ: Lawrence Erlbaum Associates.

Perkins, D. N. (1994). *The intelligent eye: Learning to think by looking at art.* Santa Monica, CA: Getty Center for Education in the Arts.

Roberts, L. (1997). *From knowledge to narrative.* Washington, DC: Smithsonian Institution.

Rogoff, B. (1993). Children's guided participation and participatory appropriation in sociocultural activity. In R.Wozniak & K. Fischer (Eds.), *Development in context: Acting and thinking in specific environments* (pp. 121–153). Hillsdale, NJ: Lawrence Erlbaum Associates.

Rosenzweig, R., & Thelen, D. (1998). *The presence of the past.* New York: Columbia University Press.

Silverstein, S. (1981). *A light in the attic.* New York: HarperCollins.

Smith, F. (1973). *Psycholinguistics and reading.* New York: Holt, Rinehart & Winston.

Snow, C. E., Burns, M., & Griffin, S. (Eds.). (1998). *Preventing reading difficulties in young children.* Washington, DC: National Research Council.

Stanovich, K. E. (2000). *Progress in understanding reading: Scientific foundations and new frontiers.* New York: Guilford.

Street, B. (1995). *Social literacies.* London: Longman.

The New London Group. (1996). A pedagogy of multiple literacies: Designing social futures. *Harvard Educational Review, 66*(1), 60–92.

van Allen, R. (1965). *Attitudes and art of teaching reading.* Washington, DC: National Education Association.

van Kraayenoord, C. E. (2000, July 11–14). *Features of communities of literacy practice.* Paper presented at the International Reading Association 18th World Reading Congress, Auckland, New Zealand.

van Kraayenoord, C. E., & Moni, K. B. (2000). At the beach . . . *Practically Primary, 4*(2), 35–37.

Vellutino, F. R., & Denckla, M. B. (1991). Cognitive and neuropsychological foundations of word identification in poor and normally developing readers. In R. Barr, M. L. Kamil, P. B. Mosenthal, & P. D. Pearson (Eds.), *Handbook of reading research* (Vol II, pp. 571–608). New York: Longman.

Wertsch, J. V. (1991). *Voices of the mind: A sociocultural approach to mediated action.* Cambridge, MA: Harvard University Press.

CHAPTER THIRTEEN

Cloaking Objects
in Epistemological Practices

Leona Schauble
University of Wisconsin, Madison

Although this book is about object-centered learning, objects are just the starting point for the authors of these chapters. The overarching theme of the section appears to be a consensus that it is time to dethrone objects from their traditional, privileged place as the center of attention in the museum. Instead, exhibit designers and visitors alike are being asked to shift their vision from the object qua object toward the practices that imbue these objects with meaning in disciplinary communities.

How can a museum help visitors effect this shift of vision? It is admittedly a challenging task, because the qualities that objects have — perceptible, static, enduring, and valuable — tend to make them more visible and salient than the practices involved in making science, art, or history. Forms of argument, inquiry, and expression are difficult to see and think about. For one thing, they are embedded in the functions, interactions, and goals of groups of individuals, so it is easy to mistake a small piece of behavior for the overarching pattern. As just one example, "activities" are not practices, but museums often aim at providing the former, and rarely at supporting the latter. Moreover, practices occur over time (sometimes long time scales), so they are difficult to "fix" and reflect on (for example, see Bazerman, 1988). Finally, the assumptions and motivations on which they rest often go unstated, so they are easy to misinterpret.

To make matters even more difficult for exhibit designers, many visitors tend to come to museums in an "entertainment" frame of mind, predisposed to shallow processing and browsing. The very plentitude and multiplicity of objects and experiences in a museum may well exacerbate this predisposition, especially in children, who are easily overwhelmed by too many things to see and do. Ironically, one of the reasons it may be difficult to get museumgoers to "try on" disciplinary perspectives is because they are already members of a different kind of community: a leisure-time, low-effort, entertainment experience community. A member of such a "community" may be neither prepared nor disposed to appreciate the kinds of practices in which historians, artists, and scientists participate.

Many museums explicitly acknowledge that they are competing for visitors with places like movie theatres and amusement parks. Perhaps for this reason, museums in general do a good job of "hooking" or interesting visitors, but a rather poor job of motivating extended follow-up. This is problematic because even the provisional adoption of unfamiliar epistemologies takes concentrated effort and some time. As Rennie and McClafferty (chapter 11) point out, helping people develop a sense of the relevant history, culture, or science requires at the very least supporting the kind of prolonged interaction that is most likely to result in learning.

And of course, prolonged interaction is a necessary, but not sufficient, condition for learning. Rennie and McClafferty's analyses show how deep involvement with objects and exhibits can nonetheless fail to accomplish what the designers intended. Visitors in general — and children in particular — can be quite inventive about the goals and uses to which they put objects and materials. Often, their inventiveness sidesteps the purposes that the museum staff had in mind, so that children sometimes spend considerable time pursuing activities that they find fascinating, but that fail to support the forms of learning that adults expected to emerge (for a good example see Gelman, Massey, & McManus, 1991). Somehow, Bain and Ellenbogen (chapter 9) explain, objects and built environments need to exemplify, or, if you will, participate in patterns of practice. In other words, museums need to find ways to incorporate their objects and collections in authentic epistemic frames. For example, how can we help a visitor appreciate how a historian "sees" a historical artifact? What contexts, narratives, disciplinary questions, and arguments does the artifact evoke for the historian? And how do these differ for a scientist contemplating a different object, say, a laboratory instrument? As Bain and Ellenbogen point out, history museums and science museums have somewhat different traditions with respect to their use of objects. In history museums, the effort is typically to place the object in context, so as to invoke the time and place from which it comes. Bain and Ellenbogen describe this as "being in the presence" of an historical object, or, they might well add, a historical place. The reverence that a visitor can feel during a visit to a Civil War battlefield or to the Civil Rights Museum in Birmingham, Alabama, comes from imagining oneself as a participant in that time, place, and situation. To support this kind of imaginative participation, the symbolism, function, and emotional resonance of objects are deliberately preserved, and sometimes enhanced by exhibit designers, because they are integral to "being there" via the object. Bain and Ellenbogen contrast this tradition of rich and layered contextualizations of objects in history museums with the typical use of objects in science museums. There, objects are often used to demonstrate a scientific phenomenon or principle. Because explanation and clarity are the goals, science exhibit designers often strip away context to maximize the probability that viewers will "see" the science in the exhibit. Usually, the desired focus is on neither the object nor its specific time and place, but on the process that it participates in or exemplifies.

But we know from studies of school learning and from contrasts of expert and novice reasoning that disciplinary epistemologies are by no means self-evident to laypersons. That should not be surprising because these forms of thinking are the distilled products of the history of a discipline. They often are communicated in genres (like scientific journals or historical accounts) that encapsulate a host of assumptions. These assumptions provide a rich background of meaning for bona fide members of the discipline, but not necessarily for outsiders. To provide just one example, interpretation is fundamental to both history and science, but most nonpractitioners do not know this. Instead, they tend to regard history as "the way things happened" and science as a "true" account of the way the world works.

To return to our original question, then, how can museums bring visitors into more nuanced relationships with objects and exhibits? The chapter authors in this section propose a variety of potential solutions. For example, Bain and Ellenbogen describe the Primary Source Network (PSN), a technologically based aid that poses a series of layered prompts for visitors. The purpose of the prompts is to expose the kinds of thinking and question-posing that a disciplinary expert might engage in spontaneously. It can also provide links to other resources (either collections in the museum or supplemental information from other relevant sources, like libraries or websites), so that deeper inquiry can be scaffolded and encouraged for those who choose to undertake it. An advantage of the PSN is that it can reside in the museum as part of the built environment. It is not possible to support disciplinary inquiry in the absence of others practicing the discipline, so the PSN simulates key parts of what the disciplinary community provides.

A different, but conceptually compatible solution is offered in chapter 10 by Palinscsar and Hapgood. Like Bain and Ellenbogen, these investigators emphasize the importance of immersing visitors into assuming what they call an "investigatory stance." Rather than portraying history or science as "method," they instead argue that it is this investigatory stance that is primary; method follows from the question being explored, the investigator's (and the field's) current state of knowledge about the question, and the resources at hand.

Palincsar and Hapgood suggest that museums are uniquely equipped to support a particular kind of investigation, one in which the objective is to learn from the investigations and interpretations of others. They call these "second-hand investigations." The idea is to display scientists thinking aloud about questions, artifacts, and evidence, via video replay, labels, narratives, or other means. These "texts" serve to mediate between the viewer and the museum object so that the text and the object together provide a perspective on the field of inquiry that might otherwise be hidden to an observer. The overall goal is to help visitors assume the perspective of the relevant disciplinary community — whether it is history, science, art, or some other discipline — where the object in question intellectually "resides."

Van Kraayenoord and Paris (chapter 12) take the idea of text even further, by playing out the conjecture that it may be fruitful to regard objects as a kind of text. At the most general level, reading texts and understanding objects are both processes of constructing meaning. In other words, they are suggesting that we think of "reading objects" as a form of literacy. Like other forms of reading, good "object-reading" needs to be sensitive to the epistemologies, strategies, and forms of talk (what van Kraayenoord and Paris call the *disciplinary seating*) that form the equivalent of "genres" of disciplinary culture. Like learning to read, becoming a skilled reader of objects may be an easier transition to effect with the right forms of assistance from more capable others, whether those are peers, exhibit designers, museum interpreters, teachers, or parents.

Of course, acquiring a repertoire of genres requires exposure to multiple examples of key types. This suggests that learning to "read objects" in a museum may be impeded if multiple exposure to key types is not provided. And unfortunately, designers often are not thinking about issues like these, which rely on consistency of message across the museum. Usually, the "grain size" for consideration of design is the exhibit, or at best, the gallery. As a result, museums are typically carved up into separate spaces, with little or no epistemological consistency communicated across galleries or even exhibits. It would be very difficult or impossible to grasp the major disciplinary genres of objects in a museum designed like this. Although an epistemological stance of a certain type might be elicited in one gallery or exhibit, a nearby exhibit might convey an entirely inconsistent or even incompatible view of the subject matter. What this suggests is that it may be desirable to take a broader view of design, one guided not by a goal for a particular exhibit or gallery, but by a coherent view of the museum as a whole. How can design be used to communicate what kind of place this is, what it is that we do here, and what community we are being initiated into? What broad repertoire of textual practices should the visitor encounter, and how are visitors best initiated into adopting these practices, even if provisionally?

In short, I think that van Kraayenoord and Paris have presented a serious design challenge, one that may come up hard against the way that museums usually do their business. Fortunately, Piscitelli and Weier provide an illustration in chapter 8 that shows that the challenge can be met. Their description of the exhibition "The Art of Eric Carle" is an impressive demonstration of how visitors — in this case, young children — can gently be initiated into forms of disciplinary practice — in this case, art. As children became artists, their encounters with art objects made by others were, in turn, revolutionized.

In the exhibit that Piscitelli and Weier describe, children's experiences with artwork were embedded in a context that provided multiple opportunities to create their own art in a variety of media and activity structures. Most impressive is the very careful and thoughtful programming that transformed this exhibit from a gallery into an artists' community. The programming included extensive preparation for the volunteer college student guides who sensitively assisted with children's initiation into the roles of artists and art interpreters.

One important object lesson from this chapter is the essential role of other people. Many museums have become resigned to the fact that they cannot afford human mediation, and consequently, exhibit designers often attempt to produce galleries that do not rely on it. In my view, this may be a big mistake. It is not possible to initiate visitors into a community that is not there. As the chapters in this section suggest, there are many tricks of the trade that can be used, including video, text, multimedia, and computer databases, to stand in for some of the aspects and functions of disciplinary community. Yet, the Piscitelli and Weier chapter reminds us that knowledgeable others are difficult to simulate, and we may lose much if we do not take every possible opportunity to encourage participation from the real thing. In this case, the university students were able to play their important role because thought and care were given to how this experience might also become an educational experience for them as well as for the young visitors whom they guided.

In general, museums might do more to situate active disciplinary communities within their walls, making the distinctions between museum and community center much more permeable. Of course, many museums do host the occasional working artist or scientist. This is no doubt valuable, but one expert does not make a community. In a disciplinary community, novices have the opportunity to observe a range of expertise, from beginners to old timers (Lave & Wenger, 1991). Novices (and those who have not yet joined the community) benefit especially from proximity to those who are just a bit more expert than the newcomers, because these individuals make visible the roles that the novice may next assume. For this reason, clubs and organizations, ranging from amateur astronomy groups to bird-watcher organizations to ham radio clubs, might profitably play a more central role in the museum, and special consideration should probably be given to those organizations that can put the collections of the museum to active and authentic use. Rather than meeting in a back room, these organizations would be most educative for visitors if their on-going intellectual work is made visible, and if their group standards for what counts as more expert bird-watching (or radio-building or badge-winning or vegetable-growing) can be public and shared. In other words, community organizations and clubs might well help make the practice and development of expertise — in a variety of fields — more open, public, and visible to outsiders.

The second message from the Piscitelli and Weier chapter is that museums need to become learning communities in at least two senses. First, as the authors in this section and I have been arguing, museums need to be places where disciplines are practiced, not simply exhibited. But second, they also need to be communities organized around empirical study — in this case, study of the most effective ways of initiating visitors into these disciplinary practices. In the Eric Carle exhibition, college students took as an explicit object of study the question of how to help young children appreciate both the processes and products of art. Perhaps because the visitors were children, it was understood that this would be a task worthy of sustained intellectual effort. Participants worked together to construct a shared base of common relevant knowledge and, when the exhibit opened, to retune and revise that knowledge in response to feedback — in this case, what appeared to work. Presumably, however, the community dissolved when the exhibition closed. It would be indeed exciting to pursue ways to make museum mediation a more enduring disciplinary practice, one organized around generating, sharing, and revising a common and growing base of knowledge about effective ways to help visitors make meaning with objects.

In sum, these chapters hold implications beyond those that they explicitly consider. One of these is the grain size and extent of the design space considered. It is not just objects and exhibits that communicate messages to visitors; it is the museum as a whole. Accordingly, it would be well worth attending to the coherence and breadth of messages conveyed by the museum as an intact place. A second issue is the multiple roles of people in the museum and ways of making those roles both more central and more visible. Finally, the chapters provoke some consideration about what it might mean to consider museum staff as members of a learning community, one organized around learning about effective ways of enhancing the educative experience of visitors. Ironically, each of these considerations suggests that designers, and not just visitors, need to look beyond "bare" objects, to focus instead on the messages and practices in which they are cloaked.

REFERENCES

Bazerman, C. (1988). *Shaping written knowledge: The genre and activity of the experimental article in science.* Madison: University of Wisconsin Press.

Gelman, R., Massey, C., & McManus, M. (1991). Characterizing supporting environments for cognitive development: Lessons from children in a museum. In L. B. Resnick, J. M. Levine, & S. D. Teasley (Eds.), *Perspectives on socially shared cognition* (pp. 226–256). Washington, DC: American Psychological Association.

Lave, J., & Wenger, E. (1991). *Situated learning: Legitimate peripheral participation.* Cambridge, UK: Cambridge University Press.

PART III

Conversations About Objects

CHAPTER FOURTEEN

Object-Based Learning and Family Groups

Minda Borun
The Franklin Institute Science Museum

HOW WE LEARN

We tend to think of learning in terms of the arrangements and procedures involved in school. This is how we in the United States and other industrialized nations master large, print-based bodies of information and achieve certification for adult status and occupations. However, it is not the only way we learn. Much of what we learn is part of the process of growing up as a member of a social group. We learn to walk, talk, eat, dress, cook, ride a bicycle, and acquire many other skills and associated knowledge without taking courses.

This less formal learning has been called *socially situated* (Lave & Wenger, 1991). We acquire knowledge through observation, imitation, and apprenticeship or through "guided participation" — interaction with more skilled members of our group (Rogoff, 1990). We also acquire this knowledge through interaction with objects. Object-based learning in museums has more in common with socially situated learning than with school-based knowledge acquisition. Museum exhibits are objects set in a context designed to promote understanding.

The learning unit in a museum is not the individual, as in a classroom setting, but the small group. In science and children's museums, it is a multigenerational group, most often a family or a school group of children and their adult chaperones. The "family" need not be a nuclear family and may consist of all kinds of related individuals or friends. In the following discussion of

245

family learning in museums, *family* means any small multigenerational visiting group.

Key to understanding museum-based learning is that there are children (usually of mixed ages) and adults who are *simultaneously* engaged in a novel learning experience. The museum exhibit is the occasion for the exchange of information and reactions among group members. The information may come directly from the objects on display or it may be an association to prior knowledge that is triggered by these objects. Family conversations at exhibits generally involve both sorts of information. "I try and relate exhibits to things in their own environment. They learn better if they know it's something that touches them every day. It's more interesting for them." [1]

The exhibit acts as a catalyst to conversation among family members. Objects, particularly interactives, stimulate conversation involving observations, recollections, associations, and connections to prior learning among members of the visiting group. The work of Crowley and Callanan (1998) looked at how exhibits evoke conversations between parents and children that facilitate the child's learning.

Although adults, most notably adult females, tend to assume the role of facilitator or "learning leader" (Borun, Chambers, Dritsas, & Johnson, 1997), children also bring information to the situation. Further, the object-based information is often new to the adults as well. Thus, in a museum, adults and children are *both* learners. "When everyone is involved in it, everyone's participating, the activity is successful."

THE LEARNING AGENDA

Families come to the museum with multiple goals. They are seeking a social experience for the group, they are interested in a valuable experience for the children, and they are definitely interested in learning. Although families differ in the extent to which they have mastered the skills involved in active family learning, it is clear that learning is on their agenda. "I want to make learning fun. I want them to enjoy learning about things. The museums make it an enjoyable experience rather than something that's forced."

In their study of family behavior at the National Museum of American History, Hilke and Balling (1985) found that 66% of family behavior functioned to acquire or transfer information and an additional 5% involved relating this information to past or future experiences of other family members. The family emerged as a flexible learning system that adapts well to museum environments.

Visitors come to the learning situation with all sorts of ideas about the topic being discussed in the exhibition. Many of these ideas would be seen as

---

[1] Quotations are from Philadelphia/Camden Informal Science Education Collaborative (PISEC) focus groups.

misconceptions by a subject-matter expert. In order to convey new information to visitors, it is necessary to address pre-existing conceptions (Borun, Massey, & Lutter, 1993).

Until recently, it was customary for museums to assume that they could present whatever information their curators deemed important without considering visitors' prior knowledge of the topic. However, cognitive science research has changed our picture of learning so that we no longer view the learner as a blank slate but realize that visitors bring their prior understandings with them and construct new syntheses based on the old. This research has important implications for communicating with museum visitors.

What people take away from a museum experience depends, in part, on what they come in with. If we think of learning as movement along a continuum from novice to expert, we can see that most of us are novices with respect to most learning domains. This does not mean that we are blank slates. Visitors bring their existing knowledge structures, including correct information and misconceptions, to the exhibit experience. They have lots of ideas on many subjects; however, these ideas may not correspond to those held by experts in the field. To help visitors move incrementally along the learning continuum in a given subject, it is important to find out their baseline conceptions.

NAÏVE NOTIONS AND OBJECT-BASED LEARNING

Objects and associated text can produce an "aha" or breakthrough perception that opens people to new understandings. Direct interaction with objects allows for visual and kinesthetic learning that can be far richer and more complex than text alone. "Someone can be doing it and other people can be watching and everybody likes it, everybody's fascinated."

A lecture on the four forces of flight may not convince people that moving air is holding up an airplane, but a demonstration of lift using airfoils in a wind tunnel (Fig. 14.1) can be quite powerful. "When he gets to do an actual experiment, it sparks his interest in learning more about that subject."

Explanatory text is necessary to provide the vocabulary and concepts through which to interpret the experience, but the memorable part of the experience comes from observing and manipulating objects. This is the power of the museum.

Unfortunately, too often, museum exhibits illustrate or "embody" concepts rather than "explaining" them. Principles are embedded in the workings of the constructed objects or are presented symbolically. For example, how many people have rolled a coin or a ball into a hollow, inverted cone and understood the connection between its path and planetary orbits? Or, using the same gravity cone (Fig. 14.2) device, how many people understand why the

FIG. 14.1.　Experience Lift — an airfoil in a wind tunnel

FIG. 14.2.　Gravity Cone — Why does the ball roll into the hole?

248

FIG. 14.3.   The Giant Lever — Can you lift 500 pounds by yourself?

coin or ball rotates faster as it approaches the opening at the bottom of the cone and what this has to do with gravity?

For expert viewers, who already understand the ideas involved, such devices are clever analogues for processes in nature, often delightful in their elegance. Unfortunately, the symbolism is lost on the novice visitor, who must base understanding on a label filled with technical terminology. The result is often hands-on without "minds-on"; objects are manipulated, but not understood.

On the other hand, if the device actually demonstrates the phenomenon, such as allowing you to lift 500 pounds with a giant lever, the concept can be seen in action (Fig. 14.3) and the connection is made.

Evaluation can play a crucial role in the development of experiences that allow visitors to conduct their own inquiries and arrive at new understandings. The process begins with front-end study to determine visitors' knowledge and possible misconceptions about a topic to be treated. Then prototype exhibits can be built, tested, and revised. The result will be experiences that create a conceptual bridge from the novice to the expert explanation.

Learning can be seen as an active process in which people select from, transform, and elaborate information to extend or revise existing cognitive structures. This view of learning sees it as a shift from naive or novice to expert structures in a particular field or domain — a shift toward increasingly powerful explanations that apply to a wider set of conditions (Carey, 1985; Gardner, 1991; Gentner & Stevens, 1983). Teaching then, is not simply a matter of conveying a correct understanding where there was no understanding before; rather, it must involve a process of conceptual change from a less sophisticated to a more sophisticated schema (Carey, 1986). Even a well-defined, clearly presented concept cannot be conveyed if the novice's conceptual structure is not prepared to accept it. The outcome will be either a failure to learn or a distortion of information to fit the novice's model. This constructivist view of learning has important implications for communication through objects in free-choice settings.

If careful front-end evaluation precedes exhibit development, widespread misconceptions can be addressed and altered by the exhibition. However, if the front-end analysis has not taken place, people will view the exhibition through a filter of existing preconceptions and their initial ideas will be unchanged or even reinforced (Borun, Massey, & Lutter, 1993).

NAÏVE KNOWLEDGE RESEARCH STUDY[2]

- "Without air pressure things would not fall."
- "It is summer when the earth is closer to the sun."
- "Moving air has more pressure than still air."
- "The rotation of the earth creates gravity."

These statements were made by visitors to The Franklin Institute Science Museum during the course of the Naive Knowledge Study — an investigation of visitor's ideas about gravity.[3] All of these statements represent widely shared beliefs with which scientists would disagree.

---

[2] Excerpted from *Curator, 36*(3), with permission of *Curator.*
[3] This project was supported by grant #MDR-8751396 from the National Science Foundation. Any opinions, findings, conclusions, or recommendations expressed herein are those of the authors and do not necessarily reflect the views of the National Science Foundation.

Long before receiving formal science instruction, people develop their own ideas about how the world works. These intuitive or "naive notions" are not indicators of developmental stages; they are held by adults as well as children. Studies of science students from elementary and middle school (Nussbaum, 1979; Pines & Novak, 1985) through high school and college (Clement, 1982; McCloskey, 1982; McDermott, 1984) indicated that students enter the classroom with preconceived notions about phenomena, notions that tend to persist despite instruction. Even students who give sophisticated answers to test questions often do not apply what they learn in school to experiences outside the classroom.

The Naive Knowledge Study at the Franklin Institute Science Museum took place over a 3½-year period ending in April, 1992. It was a research and application project to uncover alternative schema about the concept of gravity held by museum visitors and to test the efficacy of hands-on exhibits in altering these naive notions. Interviews revealed a recurrent and widespread set of misconceptions about the cause and effects of gravity (Borun, Massey, & Lutter, 1993). Inasmuch as gravity is a confusing topic and even experts disagree about its cause and nature, it is not surprising to find naive notions.

In connection with the Naïve Knowledge study, exhibits were designed to counter typical and persistent misconceptions and enable visitors to shift from the naive knowledge of the "novice" to the more sophisticated understanding of the science "expert." The study revealed that hands-on experiences with carefully worded labels can indeed alter naive notions and open the door to new understanding.

Respondents for the study were randomly selected from among visitors who came to the museum's astronomy exhibition and used the gravity cone device. Interviews were videotaped to provide a permanent record for review and evaluation. A wireless clip-on microphone was used to record the audio portion of the interviews. A video camera was mounted on a tripod nearby.

It was found that 50% of visitors, regardless of age (i.e., adults as well as children), believed that gravity needs air "in order to work." Thus, they reasoned, "there is no gravity on the moon, because there isn't any air." Existing museum devices that dealt with gravity did not address this misconception. It took a device (Fig. 14.4) specifically constructed to show that a ball will fall in an evacuated tube, to prove to visitors that the presence of air was unnecessary.

Using objects to demonstrate that the ball behaves in essentially the same way with or without air in the tube was a convincing way of altering the air misconception. This finding has important implications for science teaching. It indicates both the efficacy of uncovering and directly addressing naive notions and also demonstrates the instructional power of an object-based demonstration. Interestingly, in a related experiment in which people were shown the sentence "Gravity does not need air in order to work" without the

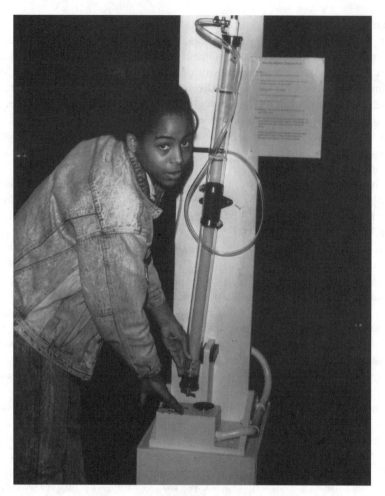

FIG. 14.4.   Gravity Tube — Gravity doesn't need air.

object-based experience to demonstrate this idea, the misconception was actually reinforced. People ignored the word "not" and more people thought that air was necessary after reading the statement than before reading it!

It is important to remember that naive notions are commonsense explanations held by people who are intelligent enough to have thought about the subject. They may be novices in physics, but they are certainly not naive people. What is interesting is the consistency and frequency of the misconceptions.

A common misconception about misconceptions is that they are held by children and replaced through formal instruction. Most previous research on naive notions is based on studies of children in classrooms. However, the

Franklin Institute findings indicate that naive notions are widespread among adults. There was no correlation between the incidence of misconceptions about gravity and age group. On the other hand, when we looked at the frequency of accurate responses, there was a significant trend toward an increase with age. Apparently, although the acquisition of expert science information increases with age, misconceptions are also maintained over time.

Through front-end evaluation, developers can gain a sense of how novice visitors "understand" phenomena. The novice view should then be compared to the expert view or desired final state. If there is no gap between the novice and expert views, a conventional teaching exhibit can be used. If there is a very large gap, it is probably advisable to rethink communication goals. If there is some correspondence, but also crucial areas of disagreement, it is important to address some of these problem areas in the exhibit and to build explicit connections between the novices' current approach and more sophisticated ways of looking at the topic.

Another complexity of object-based learning in museums is that the learning unit is generally a small, multiage group, most often a family. Conversations at objects are transactions in which information and emotions are exchanged among group members. The design of exhibits can enhance or hinder such exchanges.

Each family brings its unique culture — shared knowledge, values and experiences — to a museum visit. The museum in turn enriches the family culture through immediate and potential learning experiences. Family members can share the associations stimulated by objects immediately or long after the museum visit. This social definition of learning was a guiding premise for the Family Learning Project.

THE FAMILY LEARNING PROJECT

In order to explore how families learn in museums and what specific exhibit characteristics enhance the learning experience, four Philadelphia area museums (the Academy of Natural Sciences, the Franklin Institute, New Jersey State Aquarium, and the Philadelphia Zoo) formed PISEC — the Philadelphia/ Camden Informal Science Education Collaborative. Funded by a grant from the National Science Foundation,[4] with matching funds from the Pew Charitable Trusts, the group set out to define family learning, measure family learning at the four sites, develop exhibit enhancements to increase family learning, and measure the impact of these enhancements (Borun et al., 1998).

[4]This project was supported by grant #ESI-9355504 from the National Science Foundation. Any opinions, findings, conclusions, or recommendations expressed herein are those of the authors and do not necessarily reflect the views of the National Science Foundation.

Family groups were a natural unit for the study; family groups comprise approximately 60% of the visitors to museums in the United States (Dierking & Falk, 1994.) In a demographic survey conducted by the four PISEC institutions, families were found to make up 62% of the weekend audience (Korn, 1996). The more we know about the motivation, interests, and behavior of these families, the better we can plan exhibitions, programs, materials, and services.

The Family Learning Project had three phases, each a response to a research question.

Phase 1—What is Family Learning and How Can it be Measured?

Phase 1 was a research study to establish behavioral indicators for family learning. Visitors' behavior was studied at a test exhibit at each of the four museums. Behavior and conversation at the exhibits was recorded by narrating everything that family members did and said into a hand held minicassette tape recorder. Groups were interviewed on leaving the test exhibit. A definition of three progressively complex levels of learning (Fig. 14.5) was developed and used to score conversation and interview data. Note that the learning level schema includes connections to prior knowledge shared with other family members as well as the acquisition of information about the museum objects.

When families' learning levels were compared to the frequencies of thirteen coded behaviors, five behaviors were found to vary directly with learn-

ONE	
Identifying	One word statements or answers
	Few associations to exhibit content
	Connections to content miss the point of the exhibit
TWO	
Describing	Multiple-word answers
	Correct connections to visible exhibit characteristics
	Connections to personal experience based on visible exhibit characteristics, not concepts
THREE	
Interpreting and Applying	Multiple-word answers
	Correct statement of concepts behind exhibits
	Connection of exhibit concepts to life experiences

FIG. 14.5.   Learning levels

ing level: ask a question, answer a question, comment on or explain exhibit, read explanatory text aloud, and read silently. These behaviors were considered to be *performance indicators* of family learning and used as a measure of learning in phase 3 of the project.

It is important to note that hands-on activity was also significantly related to learning level. However, inasmuch as only two of the test exhibits were interactive, "hands-on" could not be used as a learning indicator in all four museums. The PISEC data do suggest that "hands-on activity" should be considered a performance indicator for participatory exhibits.

Time spent at the exhibit was also directly related to learning level; families with higher level scores spent significantly more time at the exhibit.

Phase 2—Do Specific Exhibit Characteristics Facilitate Family Learning?

Based on the museum literature, observations of family behavior, and discussions in focus groups with museum visitors, a list of seven characteristics of family-friendly exhibits was formulated. The characteristics are:

1. Multisided — family can cluster around the exhibit
2. Multiuser — interaction allows for several sets of hands (or bodies)
3. Accessible — comfortably used by children and adults
4. Multioutcome — observation and interaction are sufficiently complex to foster group discussion
5. Multimodal — appeals to different learning styles and levels of knowledge
6. Readable — text is arranged in easily understood segments
7. Relevant — provides cognitive links to visitors' existing knowledge and experience.

These seven characteristics were the basis for the development and evaluation of a "family learning component" (Fig. 14.6) associated with each of the four test exhibits. One component — an interactive explanatory graphic (zoo), an activity kit (Natural Science Museum), a carry-along kit (Aquarium), a multiuser experiment station (Science Museum) — was permanently installed at the test exhibit in each of the four museums.

Phase 3—Do Exhibits That Have the Seven Characteristics of Family-Friendly Exhibits Produce Measurable Increases in Family Learning?

The final part of the project was a research study comparing the frequency of performance indicators or "learning behaviors" for families that used the test

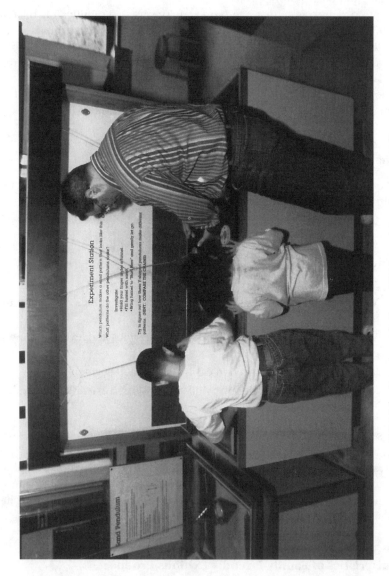

FIG. 14.6.   Experiment Station — Which pendulum draws a pretzel?

TABLE 14.1
Average Frequency of Performance Indicators/Family

	Control	Treatment
Science Museum	12.9	26.5*
Natural Science	12.3	24.3*
Aquarium	18.0	24.8*
Zoo	13.2	24.2*

*p < .05 (unpaired *t* tests)

exhibit plus family learning component (treatment group) to families that experienced only the original test exhibit (control group). Results (see Table 14.1) show highly significant increases in frequencies of learning behaviors for the treatment group.

Most of the demographic characteristics measured did not influence the frequency of performance indicators. For example, there were increases in performance indicators from control to treatment for all ethnic groups. However, gender and generation did have an effect. In both the control and treatment groups, adults had significantly more performance indicators than children, and adult females had significantly more performance indicators than adult males, girls, or boys. The latter suggests that adult females are "learning leaders" — they facilitate the family's learning experience.

OBJECT-BASED FAMILY LEARNING

The Family Learning Project demonstrates that exhibits designed to facilitate family learning can create a substantial and measurable increase in learning behaviors. Through collaborative research, the Family Learning Project found similarities in how families learn in a natural science museum, a science center, a zoo, and an aquarium. Despite differences in type of collection, test exhibit, and exhibit enhancement at the PISEC museums, all four enhanced exhibits produced significant increases in performance indicators and time spent at exhibits. The four exhibit enhancements or "family-learning components" were based on the seven characteristics of successful family-learning exhibits. Using the seven characteristics as a guide to exhibit development proved an effective strategy for increasing active family learning. The study indicates that the selection, construction, and arrangement of museum objects can influence the reading, learning, conversing and exploring that takes place at the exhibit.

Through in-depth study, the Family Learning Project found that families are learning in museums and that this learning can be enhanced and extended through thoughtful use of objects. By incorporating the seven characteristics of family-friendly exhibits, it is possible to create exhibits that are effective for a wide range of family groups.

GENERAL CONCLUSIONS

The research studies discussed in this chapter point to the importance of looking carefully at museum visitors, talking to them, and systematically studying the learning process in order to understand its dynamics in free-choice settings and to design exhibits with maximal learning potential. Exhibit developers need to test and modify exhibit prototypes so that the final product is accessible and relevant and so that it demonstrates, not simply embodies, ideas.

Visitors will enter the free-choice learning environment with prior knowledge and misconceptions that can interfere with their understanding of objects. It is up to the museum to conduct front-end research to uncover widespread misconceptions and treat them in exhibitions.

The Naïve Knowledge Study showed that it is crucial to begin the exhibition development process by conducting front-end evaluation studies to find out what visitors know, feel, and think about a planned exhibition topic. Widely shared misconceptions that could distort or block understanding can thus be uncovered and then treated explicitly. In this way exhibits can bridge the gap between novice and expert views. If exhibit developers do not take such misconceptions into account, visitors are likely to perceive objects through the lens of their pre-existing naive notions. Museums face a difficult challenge. They attempt to convey expert views to learners whose knowledge structures are widely varied. To succeed, exhibit developers must come to know their audience as well as they know their subject.

Finally, the learning unit in the museum is the small group. It is up to exhibit developers to design for groups, rather than individuals, so that visitors can have lively and meaningful conversations as they look at or interact with museum objects.

In order for museum objects to elicit the powerful associative responses that lead to family conversations, the exhibit must be physically and intellectually accessible to the members of the group. The seven characteristics of family-friendly exhibits summarize the requisites for this accessibility

Too often exhibits are designed for the individual learner. They are arranged along a wall or put in small glass cases or study carrels such that only one person at a time can view or interact with them. In order to optimize the learning potential of museum objects, they should be presented in a way that allows for group access and conversation.

We need to put aside classroom-based models of learning and look to the socially situated, object-centered interactions of the cultural group in order to understand and encourage museum-based learning:

You can't begin to understand the answers if you don't know what the questions are. Going there [to a museum], being exposed to things helps you to develop the questions. You see an interaction that you've never seen and you have an immediate question. As time progresses your mind is digesting it and you develop more questions.

REFERENCES

Borun, M., Massey, C., & Lutter, T. (1993). Naïve knowledge and the design of science museum exhibits, *Curator, 36*(3), 201–219.

Borun, M., Chambers, M. B., Dritsas, J., & Johnson, J. I. (1997). Enhancing family learning through exhibits. *Curator, 40*(4), 289.

Borun, M., Dritsas, J., Johnson, J., Peter, N., Wagner, K., Fadigan, K., Jangaard, A., Stroup, E., & Wenger, A. (1998). *Family learning in museums: The PISEC perspective.* Washington, DC: Association of Science-Technology Centers.

Carey, S. (1985). *Conceptual change in childhood.* Cambridge, MA: MIT Press.

Carey, S. (1986). Cognitive science and science education. *American Psychologist, 41*(10), 1123–1130.

Clement, J. (1982). Students' preconceptions in introductory mechanics. *American Journal of Physics, 50*(1), 66–71.

Crowley, K., & Callanan, M. A. (1998). Describing and supporting collaborative scientific thinking in parent–child interactions. *Journal of Museum Education, 17*(1), 12–17.

Dierking, L. D., & Falk, J. H. (1994). Family behavior and learning in informal science settings: A review of the research. *Science Education, 78*(1), 57–72.

Gardner, H. (1991). *The unschooled mind* (8, 143–166). New York: Basic Books.

Gentner, D., & Stevens, A. (Eds.). (1983). *Mental models.* Hillsdale, NJ: Lawrence Erlbaum Associates.

Hilke, D. D., & Balling, J. B. (1985). *The family as a learning system: An observational study of families in museums.* Washington, DC: Smithsonian Institution Press.

Korn, R. (1996). *PISEC baseline visitor study.* Unpublished manuscript.

Lave, J., & Wenger, E. (1991). *Situated learning: Legitimate peripheral participation.* New York: Cambridge University Press.

McCloskey, M. (1982, March). Naive conceptions of motion. Paper presented at the annual meeting of the American Educational Research Association, New York.

McDermott, L. C. (1984). Research on conceptual understanding in mechanics. *Physics Today, 37*, 24–32.

Nussbaum, J. (1979). Children's conceptions of the earth as a cosmic body: A cross-age study, *Science Education, 63*(1), 83–93.

Pines, L. A., & Novak, J. D. (1985). The interaction of audio–tutorial instruction with student prior knowledge: A proposed qualitative case-study methodology. *Science Education, 69*(2), 213–228.

Rogoff, B. (1990). *Apprenticeship in thinking: Cognitive development in social context.* New York: Oxford University Press.

APPENDIX: TEMPLATE FOR ASSESSING
THE FAMILY-FRIENDLINESS OF EXHIBITS

SEVEN CHARACTERISTICS OF FAMILY-FRIENDLY EXHIBITS	EXHIBIT NAME: FILL IN COMMENTS BELOW
MULTISIDED (Family can cluster around the exhibit)	
MULTIUSER (Interaction allows for several sets of hands or bodies)	
ACCESSIBLE (Comfortably used by children and adults)	
MULTIOUTCOME (Observation and interactions are sufficiently complex to foster group discussion)	
MULTIMODAL (Appeals to different learning styles and levels of knowledge)	
READABLE (Text is arranged in easily understood segments)	
RELEVANT (Provides cognitive links to visitors' existing knowledge and experience)	

CHAPTER FIFTEEN

Maps, Globes, and Videos: Parent–Child Conversations about Representational Objects

Maureen A. Callanan
Jennifer L. Jipson
Monika Stampf Soennichsen
University of California, Santa Cruz

Manipulation of three-dimensional objects affords children learning opportunities that are less available in situations that involve purely verbal or written communication (Rogoff, 1990). As discussed in other chapters in this volume, and in the education literature more broadly, the opportunity to touch and interact with objects is often very helpful for young children as they attempt to understand abstract concepts or processes. Inspired by Piaget's theory (cf. Piaget & Inhelder, 1969), psychologists and education researchers have posited various concrete-to-abstract shifts in children's thinking. For example, whereas preschool-aged children understand perceptually based analogies, older children understand analogies based on more abstract relational features (Kotovsky & Gentner, 1996). Educational methods have often been developed with such concrete–abstract shifts in mind. The manipulative materials used in early mathematics classrooms, for example, have long been considered essential aids in communicating abstract principles to young children. The usefulness of concrete objects as tools for abstract thought is not surprising, given young children's connection to the sensory reality of the here-and-now. In this chapter, however, we focus on a growing view that concrete objects do not always improve children's understanding of abstract ideas, and, in fact, that the sensory properties of certain objects, "representational objects," can even pose an obstacle to learning (Uttal, Liu, & DeLoache, 1999).

A *representational object* is an object in its own right, but it is also intended to be used as a symbol for some other entity (what we call the *referent object*). For adults, some representational objects, such as maps and scale models, are easy to think of in that way because they are clearly concrete objects, and their function as representations is also clearly understood by most people who use them. There are other representational objects, however, that may be less obviously thought of as both objects and representations. Photographs and videotapes, for example, are not usually thought of as objects in themselves. Instead, they are extremely transparent representations and immediately bring to mind the objects, people, and scenes that they depict. In this chapter we later consider three features of representational objects that may help to characterize the range of variation in this class of objects: representational objects can vary in their *salience* as objects, in their *similarity* to the referent object, and in their *familiarity* to the user.

Although some representational objects, such as maps and globes, are very commonly seen in children's homes and classrooms, several areas of research suggest that children may not understand that these objects are meant to be symbols. Without seeing them as symbols, children cannot possibly use these objects to improve their understanding of the objects that they represent. DeLoache and her colleagues (DeLoache, 1995; DeLoache & Marzolf, 1992) have shown, in a comprehensive program of research, that representational objects can often hinder young children's ability to solve problems concerning the objects that they represent. In her most famous work, DeLoache (1987, 1991) asked whether young children can use a scale model of a room (akin to a dollhouse) to reason about the hiding place of an object in a full-size (but otherwise identical) room. Children see a small Snoopy dog hidden in the scale model, and they are then asked to find the large Snoopy in the same place in the full-scale room. It is not until 3 years of age that children are consistently successful in using the information provided in the scale model to reason about the location of the referent object (DeLoache, 1991). Beyond the preschool years, Liben and her colleagues (e.g., Liben & Yekel, 1996) have shown that once children understand the symbolic nature of representational objects, such as maps, there is still a great deal of development needed before they fully understand the meaning of various components of the representations.

DeLoache's and Liben's findings raise questions about why young children find representational objects so challenging to understand. DeLoache (2000) suggests that children may have trouble achieving "dual representation," in other words, they may not initially be able to think of objects simultaneously as both objects in their own right and as representations for something else. Because the physical reality of these objects is so salient to young children, it may be difficult for them to get past that physical reality to reason about the thing that the object represents. Thus, DeLoache's work documents a striking developmental shift in children's understanding of representational objects; however, the source of that developmental change is less clear.

To investigate the mechanisms underlying the developmental transition that DeLoache has uncovered, it is important to consider the social contexts in which children experience representational objects. The importance of the social context is suggested by Tomasello (1999), who argues that because representational objects are a kind of cultural tool, observations of or interactions with other people may be needed for children to learn the functions intended for these objects.

The focus of this chapter is on exploring the role of children's everyday social interactions in their developing understanding of representational objects. In particular, the project focused on three types of representational objects often found in museums and other settings: maps, globes, and video. Representational objects are commonly used in museum exhibits, presumably because they allow visitors to explore objects that could not be literally brought into the museum. For example, a globe encourages one to think about the earth's properties and its place in the solar system. Various photographic and videographic media bring the visitor information about objects and events that would be difficult to view firsthand. Parent–child conversations around these objects were investigated as families interacted with them in the context of a hands-on children's museum. We were particularly interested in gaining information about the everyday contexts within which children may come to understand the links between these object-like representations and their referents.

The following review of the literature focuses first on the possible role of the social context in the development of dual representation, and then on aspects of representational objects that seem to affect the likelihood that they will be understandable to children. In the subsequent sections, we discuss previous research on three different types of representational objects relevant to the museum exhibits we observed: maps and aerial photographs, globes, and live video. Next we discuss our own research on three exhibits, each presenting children with one of these types of representational object. Finally, we consider implications and conclusions from this research.

SOCIAL CONTEXT OF CHILDREN'S EXPERIENCE WITH REPRESENTATIONAL OBJECTS

How might parents guide children in coming to understand the complex and abstract symbolic nature of representational objects? To answer this question it is important to investigate how parents and children talk about representational objects in museums as well as other informal settings. DeLoache (2000) points out that because of their limited experience with symbolic artifacts, children may need guidance from adults in order to even think of the possibility that something is meant as a symbolic object rather than an object in itself. As their experience with symbols increases, children are likely to develop more "symbolic sensitivity" and have a greater ability to recognize the symbolic nature of previously unencountered representational objects (DeLoache, 1995; DeLoache & Marzolf, 1992).

Because children's first reaction may be to deal with representational objects only as objects, parents may play an important role in helping children to see the representational nature of these objects. To date, however, most research on children's understanding of representational objects has focused on when children gain symbolic understandings, and not on how this understanding emerges. Two recent studies have begun to uncover evidence regarding the potential influence of social interaction on children's developing understanding. First, Troseth, Rozak, and Spry (1999) asked parents of 2-year-olds to encourage their children's understanding that video images can represent reality. They sent parents home with a camcorder for 2 weeks and suggested that they use real-time recordings of children's behavior to encourage children to see links from their own behavior to the video image. After the 2-week period, Troseth et al. found that children who had this experience were more successful than the control group on a task where they saw an object being hidden on video and then were asked to find the object. This finding suggests that familiarity with this particular use of video improved children's ability to use video as a symbolic medium. This research provides a first step toward understanding the role of social interaction in the development of representational insight. The next step is to ask more directly about the process by which these experiences may influence children's understanding. In another study, we have some preliminary evidence that adults' talk about representational objects may contribute to children's understanding of video as a representational medium (Soennichsen & Callanan, 2001). Two-year-olds who heard labels for the video images of objects and for their actual object referents were more successful later at using the video to find a hidden object than were those who saw the same video but did not hear object labels. From these two studies, we have some preliminary evidence that, at least with video, adult–child conversations may be helpful to children who are learning about dual representation. The research reported in this chapter extends this work by providing information about the dynamics of situations in which parents and children discuss a variety of representational objects.

This project is influenced by Tomasello's (1999) analysis of the reasons representational objects may be very difficult for children to understand. Tomasello points out that representational objects are cultural tools and that their intended symbolic nature may not be apparent to young children. In making this point, Tomasello extends DeLoache's dual representation argument, claiming that children may not only have difficulty decoupling the material and symbolic aspects of representational objects, but may also need guidance in understanding the intentionally communicative affordances of such objects. Our hypothesis is that parents are not likely to directly teach children about abstract concepts such as dual representation. Instead, parents may talk with children about the meaning of specific representational objects, treating the children *as if* they understand the bigger concept of symbolic representation. By helping children see that individual objects in specific situations are symbolic objects, parents could be teaching children an instance of the deeper notion of dual representation. We next consider three features of representational objects that have been elaborated in previous work: salience, similarity, and familiarity. With those features as a framework, we evaluate this approach using family conversations about maps, globes, and video.

THREE IMPORTANT FEATURES OF REPRESENTATIONAL OBJECTS: SALIENCE, SIMILARITY AND FAMILIARITY

As mentioned earlier, three aspects of the representation–referent relation seem especially influential in terms of children's appreciation of the symbolic nature of representational objects. They vary in their salience as objects, which can also be thought about as their "transparency" as representations. Photographs are transparent, that is, they bring to mind the referent object and are not salient as objects in and of themselves. Representational objects also vary in similarity to the referent object, which may have impact on their recognizability as symbols. They also vary in their typical familiarity to young children.

In a series of studies, DeLoache (1987, 1991) found that whereas 3-year-old children performed well in tasks requiring representational understanding, children only 6 months younger were not as successful. In subsequent studies, DeLoache and her colleagues turned their focus toward systematically identifying task variations that influence the age at which children demonstrate achievement of dual representation. Although DeLoache's findings show that scale models are generally understood as representations by the end of the preschool years, related work on globes (Vosniadou & Brewer, 1992) and maps (Liben, 1999) suggest that the developmental trajectory for understanding representational objects continues well into the elementary school years. Using DeLoache's research as a guide, Table 15.1 illustrates the impact of the three features of salience, similarity, and familiarity, in relation to children's understanding of different types of representational objects.

Salience of Representational Object

First, DeLoache argued that the salience of the model as an object itself can impede young children's ability to hold the dual mental images of object and

TABLE 15.1
Summary of DeLoache Findings as Relevant
to Salience, Similarity, and Familiarity

	Salient as an Object?	Similar to Referent?*	Familiar as a Representation?
Photographs	no	yes	yes
Video	no	yes	no (but familiar in other form)
Scale Models	yes	yes	no

Note. *Varies across studies.

symbol in mind. In one study, increasing a model's salience as a concrete object (rather than a representation) by allowing children to play with it in a nonsymbolic manner decreased the chances that 3-year-old children would reason with it as a symbolic object (DeLoache, 2000). Conversely, placing the model behind a glass window, and thus eliminating the possibility of playing with it as an object, led to improved performance in finding hidden toys (De-Loache, 2000).

In further support of the importance of object salience, DeLoache found that pictures are understood as representational objects at an earlier age than other symbols. Salience of a representational object can also be thought of in terms of how "transparent" the object is as a symbol. Pictures are quite transparent as representations; when parents point to a picture, for example, they are likely to talk with children about the object depicted rather than about the picture itself. As DeLoache's work with photographs suggests, to the degree that a representational object is transparent (and not salient as an object) it may be easier for children to "see through" the symbol to the referent (cf. Ittelson, 1996). Two-and-half-year-olds are able to use pictures as representations of objects, yet are unable to use scale models in the same manner (De-Loache, 1991, 2000).

Similarity Between Representational Object and Referent

Another important feature of representational objects is the degree to which they are similar to their referents. DeLoache varied the similarity of representation and referent and found important effects (DeLoache, Kolstad, & Anderson, 1991). For example, when physical similarity between a scale model of a room and the actual room was increased by making the rooms similar in size, even 2-year-old children were able to successfully understand the model–room relationship. Liben (1999) also discusses the idea that representations that closely resemble their referents come close to "re-presenting" the referent, therefore the connection may not be as difficult to comprehend as that between a referent and a representation that are less similar. Liben and Yekel (1996) found that children were better able to make map-room connections with maps in which the depicted objects more closely represent their referents (oblique maps), than with more abstract "plan" maps (with overhead or aerial perspective). Thus, children have an easier time understanding representational objects that have a high degree of similarity to their referents.

Similarity of a representational object to its referent is only helpful, however, if comparisons between the two can be made. Some representational objects that are commonly used by adults have referents that are not easily compared to the representation. Both maps and globes, for example, have referents that are not easily examined in their own right, namely specific geographical regions in the case of maps and the entire earth in the case of the globe. In these cases, children are likely to have a harder time considering the similarity between representation and referent. Extrapolating from De-Loache's work, when the referent is not available for comparison, it should be even more difficult for children to understand these representational objects.

Familiarity With Representational Objects and Symbolic Experience

The third feature of representational objects that may affect how likely children are to understand them is their familiarity to children. Research has demonstrated that children's ability to engage in spatial reasoning tasks is influenced by their familiarity and comfort with the testing space (Acredolo, 1982). Troseth, Rozak, and Spry (1999) have also reported evidence that preschoolers' experience with video predicts their understanding of video as a representation. Interestingly, however, just because representational objects are familiar to children does not ensure that they are understood. Globes are common in middle-income U.S. homes, yet Vosniadou and Brewer's (1992) research suggests that children well into their school years have difficulty with the notion that the earth is globe-shaped.

In addition to considering children's familiarity with particular representational objects, it is important to also consider their familiarity with those objects as symbols. Troseth and DeLoache (1998) discussed children's symbolic experience as part of the explanation for why pictures become easier to use as symbols between ages 2 and 2½ years. Children's typical experience with video may actually act against their understanding of video as symbolic. Because they see video mostly as a medium through which to view movies or previously recorded events, it may be difficult for children to interpret video as a representation of an actual ongoing event. As mentioned earlier, Troseth et al. (1999) found that parents were able to provide their 2-year-olds with experience that helped them understand video as a representation. Further, there is evidence from both DeLoache's (e.g., Marzolf & DeLoache, 1994) and

Liben's (e.g., Liben & Yekel, 1996) laboratories that children's experience with a simpler form of representation can transfer to more complex sorts of representations. This suggests that familiarity or experience seems to be an important factor in children's symbolic understanding.

In our research, we explored parent–child conversations about three museum exhibits that centered around representational objects varying in their salience, similarity, and familiarity. In the following sections, we consider research on children's understanding of each of the three types of representational objects explored in these exhibits: maps, globes, and video. We then present our findings on how parents talk with their children about each of these representational objects.

MAPS AND AERIAL PHOTOGRAPHS
AS REPRESENTATIONAL OBJECTS

DeLoache's work with scale models points to the difficulty that children have in conceptualizing something as an object (e.g., a dollhouse) and a symbol at the same time. Dual representation applies to maps and photographs as well. The first exhibit we examined was a set of aerial photographs and matching maps of several neighboring towns surrounding the museum. In this exhibit the representational objects are the photographs and maps, with the referent being the streets, buildings, and parks depicted. The maps and photographs were arranged along a wall with the maps mounted vertically on the wall and the matching aerial photographs mounted below them on an angled counter-like table. Each photograph was covered in plexiglas with a movable dome-shaped magnifying glass attached.

With regard to the three features of representational objects, the maps and aerial photographs were considered to be relatively low in salience. Table 15.2 presents an analysis of how the exhibits we studied compare to DeLoache's exhibits on these three dimensions. Although in other settings maps may be salient objects in their own right, the particular exhibit under investigation

TABLE 15.2
Summary of Observed Exhibits as Relevant
to Salience, Similarity, and Familiarity

	Salient as an Object?	Similar to Referent?	Familiar as a Representation?
Ideal (based on DeLoache)	no	yes	yes
Maps & Aerial Photos	no	difficult to assess	no
Globes	yes	difficult to assess	yes? (confusing?)
Video	no	yes	no

here was arranged such that paper maps were placed on a wall over a counter and were, therefore, inaccessible for children to physically manipulate. The aerial photographs were similarly unavailable as they were placed under Plexiglas. Thus, museum visitors were not likely to find these particular maps and aerial photographs to be salient as objects. The decreased salience of these representational objects should, according to DeLoache (2000), enhance their symbolic attributes.

Consideration of how similar maps are to the spaces that they represent suggests that despite surface similarities, the relationship is quite abstract. Although the aerial photographs in the exhibit directly represent actual geographical spaces, they are novel types of photographs and the perspective taken is one that tends to be unfamiliar to children. In a study of children's interpretations of aerial photographs, for example, children identified tennis courts as "doors," refused to accept a rectangle as an office building because buildings are bigger, and failed to find grass on the black-and-white image because "grass is green" (Liben & Downs, 1989). Thus, the buildings and streets that are represented in the aerial photographs are difficult to recognize from overhead views, making these photographs more like maps and less like photographs of canonical objects. In addition, the size differences between the representations and the spaces they depict is considerable, thus decreasing the similarity between the two and making it impossible for children to compare the map to its referent space except by using their memory for the space.

Finally, regarding the familiarity of maps and aerial photographs, different families were likely to have had varying experience with these kinds of representational objects. In general, it was anticipated that most parents would be very familiar with maps and relatively unfamiliar with the aerial photographs. In addition, because the museum in which this study was conducted attracts families visiting from other parts of the country and other parts of the world, families were expected to vary in the extent to which they found the depicted spaces to be familiar. Thus, the aerial photography exhibit, in particular, is unique in that parents may not be very familiar with either the medium of symbolic representation or the referents.

Children's understanding of representations of space (e.g., maps, aerial photographs, scale models) has received a great deal of research attention, particularly by Liben and her colleagues. In general, studies in this area suggest that by the time children enter preschool, they demonstrate an appreciation of the symbolic nature of maps. This understanding is remarkable in that preschoolers must come to think about a physical object (e.g., a map) as also having a symbolic function, what DeLoache (1995) referred to as attaining representational insight. Liben (1999), however, made the point that understanding maps as representing physical spaces is but the first step in gaining competence in map use. Many children who have made this step go on to reveal misunderstandings in map interpretation. For example, Liben & Downs

(1989) reported that several preschool children in their studies overextended the physical properties of maps to the referent (and vice versa), as in the case of one child who inferred that a road shown in red on a map meant that the actual road would be red.

Despite these misunderstandings, preschool children have been shown to successfully use maps in a variety of ways. In some situations, for example, they are able to use maps as sources of information as to the location of hidden objects (Uttal, Lio, & Taxy, 1995), and as tools to accelerate their learning of a route through a playhouse (Uttal & Wellman, 1989). Further, Liben and Yekel (1996) found that 4½- to 5½-year-olds were able to reverse their representational understanding and use their knowledge of a familiar room to interpret a map of the room. Interestingly, this last study revealed that all maps are not created equal. Children had an easier time making the room–map connection when presented with an oblique map (in which depicted objects resemble their referents) than when shown an overhead map. This finding reinforces DeLoache's argument that the use of symbolic information is facilitated when representation and referent are physically similar (DeLoache, Uttal, & Pierroutsakos, 1998).

GLOBES AS REPRESENTATIONAL OBJECTS FOR THE EARTH

Globes are another type of representational object for which children must use dual representation to understand the link from the globe to the earth. Because globes are very common cultural artifacts, one might think that children understand their function from an early age. Research on children's understanding of the shape of the earth, however, suggests that the dual representation problem is very difficult in this case as well (Vosniadou & Brewer, 1992). The second museum exhibit we investigated was called "Digging to China." The exhibit consists of a large globe (representing the earth) equipped with two small video cameras that display opposite sides of the earth. An accompanying video monitor presents the images from both cameras. Visitors use controls to find a spot on the globe, look at that image on the monitor, and then look at the other image to see what spot on the globe is at the exact opposite point. The idea is that you can find out where you would end up if you could dig through the earth (as in the phrase "digging to China.")

Compared with the scale models in DeLoache's research, globes are perhaps equally salient as objects and considerably more familiar as cultural artifacts. They are also regarded by adults as quite similar to their referents. This similarity may be lost on children, however, as suggested by a large body of research in developmental psychology and education that shows that even children as old as 7 years of age have difficulty truly understanding that the earth is a sphere (e.g., Nussbaum & Novak, 1976; Vosniadou & Brewer, 1992). This research suggests that, despite their exposure to globes as artifacts, children may not understand globes as symbols. Direct evidence on this point is not available, however.

In contrast to the research attention given to children's understanding of maps of physical space, children's understanding of globes per se has received little attention from researchers. One reason for this oversight may be that the symbolic relationship between a globe and the planet Earth is so obvious to researchers that the question of whether children appreciate the connection has been overlooked. Educators of young children may also overestimate their understanding of the globe as a symbol for the earth. In this section, we discuss prior research that suggests that an appreciation of the symbolic relationship between globes and the earth may be quite difficult to attain. We first present findings that suggest that young children may encounter difficulties in considering globes to be representational objects in addition to being interesting objects themselves. We then discuss research indicating that children's limited understanding of the earth itself may impede successful mapping of the globe-to-earth relationship. Thus, making the symbolic connection between globes and the earth may be challenging for any of three reasons: ability to achieve representational insight; ability to interpret the representational object (globe) as symbolic; and understanding of the referent (earth).

The work of DeLoache and her colleagues offers valuable information regarding the emergence of representational insight, as discussed earlier. In her work with scale models, photographs, and videos, DeLoache (1995) generally found that children's understanding of the symbolic link is available by 3 years of age. Children's confusion about the shape of the earth continues much later, however. Therefore, it is interesting to consider whether the globe as a symbolic object may be very challenging for children to use to gain information about the earth's shape. In everyday life, children may be likely to treat globes as objects in and of themselves and interact with them nonsymbolically. Unlike maps or photographs, which tend to be treated by parents and children primarily as representational objects (Liben, 1999), globes are particularly salient and interesting in their own right (e.g., they are colorful, fun to spin). Thus, depending on individual experiences, globes may first be considered to be amusing playthings and the insight that they are representational may be delayed.

Another possible obstacle to appreciating globes as models of the earth may lie in children's incomplete knowledge of the earth itself. Liben (1999) suggested that understanding the referent is essential to understanding representations. For example, she suggested that a child's difficulty interpreting a clover-leaf intersection on an aerial photograph is likely to be due to limited knowledge of clover-leaf intersections, rather than an inability to interpret the representation. We know that the degree of similarity between a symbolic object and its referent influences the success with which children are able to demonstrate representational insight (DeLoache et al., 1991). However, if children do not understand enough about the earth's shape to appreciate the physical similarities between a globe and the earth, it will be extremely difficult to make a representational link between the two.

Research examining children's mental models of the earth suggests that many children do not, in fact, initially consider the earth to be a sphere. Instead, studies in this area converge to show that children initially construct ideas about the earth based on information gained through perceptual experiences (e.g., the earth is flat). With time, however, children demonstrate attempts to merge their initial understandings with the scientific idea of a spherical earth and develop a variety of alternative models of the earth (e.g., flat disc, hollow earth, dual earth theory, flattened sphere; for a description of these alternative models see Vosniadou & Brewer, 1992). These "synthetic models" reflect children's attempts to resolve inconsistencies between their own perceptual experiences and information given to them by others (e.g., teachers, parents, other children). It is not until children are 10 or 11 years of age that they seem to have fully accepted the scientific model of a spherical earth (e.g., Nussbaum & Novak, 1976; Sneider & Pulos, 1983; Vosniadou & Brewer, 1992). This research is crucial in that children who do not understand the earth to be a sphere may find it more difficult to understand the relationship between a globe and the earth, regardless of their representational skills.

VIDEO AS A REPRESENTATIONAL OBJECT

The third exhibit we investigated as part of this project uses video as its symbolic medium. In this exhibit, while a model train goes around a track, a camera mounted on the train's engine sends a video image to a monitor. The video monitor is in a booth that looks like a stylized train engine. Children watch the monitor while controlling the movement of the small model train. Dual representation is embedded in this exhibit because children can respond to the video as an entity of its own or as a representation of the objects that the train "sees" as it goes around the track.

Real-time video is clearly not very salient as an object, hence it should be easier for children to achieve dual representation with video than with three-dimensional objects. In fact, Troseth and DeLoache's (1998) work has shown that 2-year-olds find it quite difficult to use information conveyed via video in their Snoopy hiding task, but that, similar to their performance with pictures, children begin to use video in a symbolic fashion between 24 and 30 months. Similarity between representation and referent is very high with video. In the case of the train exhibit, the similarity between the objects on the monitor and the three-dimensional objects that they represent is extremely high.

273

Further, the similarity is there for children to perceive firsthand. This contrasts with both the map and globe exhibits, where the referents are not available in the exhibits themselves.

The role of familiarity is also evident in children's developing understanding of the representational nature of video. It is likely that between the ages of 24 and 30 months children gain experience with video as a symbolic medium. Troseth and DeLoache (1998) pointed out that although many 2-year-olds have certainly been exposed to video, it is usually in the context of entertainment and make-believe. This may make it difficult for young children to consider video as something that can represent reality. As mentioned earlier, Troseth et al.'s (1999) study, as well as our own preliminary findings (Soennichsen & Callanan, 2001) suggest that children's conversations with parents may provide experience that contributes to children's ability to use video as a symbolic medium.

RESEARCH FINDINGS— MAPS, GLOBES, AND VIDEO

The main goal of this study was to explore parents' talk with children about representational objects to gain information on the process by which children might learn about symbolic relationships. In addition, we asked about whether children were jointly engaged with parents during these interactions. To do so, we examined 126 interactions between children and parents at the Children's Discovery Museum in San Jose, California, a hands-on children's museum (see Crowley & Callanan, 1998). Forty-two parent–child interactions were coded at each of the three exhibits. At each exhibit, half of the target children were aged 4 years or younger, and the other half were aged 5 and older. These age groups were selected due to our desire to compare the conversations parents have with children who are not yet in school to those of parents with school-aged children. These data were collected as part of a larger study of children's learning in museum settings (see Crowley, Callanan, Jipson, Galco, Topping, & Shrager, in press; Crowley, Callanan, Tenenbaum, & Allen, 2001). Families were approached as they entered the museum, informed about the research, and invited to participate. Families who agreed to participate were given age-coded stickers for their children to wear. When children with stickers approached targeted exhibits, video cameras were turned on. This project included only children who visited with one or both parents.

Coding of Interactions

In our analysis of these conversations, we first asked whether parents discussed representational objects in ways that might reveal the link between representation and referent. One strategy that parents might use to explain the representational nature of maps, globes, and video is to explicitly point out the representational link. We therefore identified cases where parents explained the *explicit link* between the representational object and its referent. For example, a parent at the train exhibit might say, "See the picture of the tree on the TV? And there's the real tree over there!" This strategy might be particularly helpful in those cases where the similarity between a representational object and its referent is not obvious or is not accessible, as in the case of the link between the globe and the earth. Furthermore, if familiar representational objects are used in unfamiliar ways, parents' discussions of explicit links could help to clarify the situation. Knowing that their child is familiar with video that is not "live," for example, a parent might make a point of indicating that this video is being shot at the present moment.

Even if parents do not explicitly explain the link between a representational object and its referent, there are more subtle ways that they might guide their children's understanding. In particular, parents might talk about a representational object as if it were its referent. This kind of talk is very common, for example, in conversations about photographs; parents often point to a photograph saying, "There's Daddy!" even though literally speaking they are pointing to a piece of paper rather than to the person depicted. We coded this sort of "transparent" talk about the referent, differentiating it into two subcategories. Parents might use *specific labels* for aspects of the referent with which children are familiar. For example a parent might point to an aerial photograph and say, "Look, there's your school!" Or they might use *generic labels*, naming aspects of the referent that are less familiar to the child, for example saying something like, "There's a river." Notice that if children do not understand the representational nature of the object, these sentences could seem nonsensical. Such a child might think, for example, "How could a piece of paper on the wall be my school?" Children who notice this contradiction, but who are trying to make sense of what their parents are saying, might begin to understand that the map, globe, or video is a representation for something else. We predicted that the specific label strategy might be more helpful than the generic label strategy in guiding the child to see that the object being discussed is a representational object. This is because children may be more motivated to figure out why their parent is labeling a familiar object while pointing to something else.

Finally, if none of these strategies were used, we coded the parents' speech as *not relevant* to the symbolic relation between representation and referent. This category also included interactions in which parents did not talk about the exhibit. In addition to coding parents' talk about the representational objects, we also asked about how children were engaging with their parents and the objects during these interactions. We were particularly interested in whether children seemed to be engaged in joint attention with their parents as the representational objects were being discussed.

TABLE 15.3
Percent of Parents at Each Exhibit Demonstrating Strategies

	Explicit link	Specific	Generic	Not relevant
Maps	17	52	9	22
Globe	5	67	5	23
Video	19	52	7	22

Frequencies of Categories of Talk

The frequencies with which parents used these different strategies are presented in Table 15.3. A chi-square goodness-of-fit test was conducted to explore whether parents used all strategies equally. This analysis revealed that parents did not demonstrate equal use of the four strategies ($\chi^2(3) = 75.21$, $p < .001$). Examination of these frequencies suggested that parents used more *specific-label* strategies than other strategies. Further, when reanalyzing parents' strategy use by exhibit, we found that a similar pattern was true across all three exhibits and that this pattern did not vary by children's age.

These results indicate that parents tended to talk about specific aspects of the referent while interacting with the representational objects. Further, parents rarely offered explicit explanations of the relationship between the representational object and its referent. This pattern of results is consistent with the prediction that although parents may not explain the abstract concepts of dual representation to their children, they may guide children in achieving particular instances of dual representation.

Although they were rare, the conversations in which parents explained the explicit link between representation and referent suggested that parents may sometimes provide children with explicit information about representational objects. For example, one parent pointed to the video image, saying, "You see that? That's the picture that the train takes." He then pointed to the real train and said, "And see, there's the real train right there." Another parent pointed to an aerial photograph saying, "This is what it looks like when you're in an airplane and you look down."

Salience, Similarity, and Familiarity

To further elaborate on patterns in parents' guidance, we return to the three important features of representational objects discussed earlier — salience, similarity, and familiarity — especially as they relate to these three museum exhibits (see Table 15.2). First, the maps and aerial photographs exhibit presents representational objects that are not particularly salient, so parent guidance is not likely to be needed on that dimension. As might be expected, then, parents rarely labeled the map or photo as an object itself. One exception was where a mother said, "This is a map of where Aunt Jenny lives." Much more common, however, was the kind of "transparent" talk where parents pointed to the image and labeled things as if the actual things were present, for example: "This is Hwy 101, the big road we drove down to get here," and "See, there's our house."

The depictions on maps and aerial photographs are somewhat similar to the objects they represent, but this similarity is difficult for children to assess, partly because the referent objects are not available for inspection. Further, the maps and aerial photographs are not likely to be familiar to children, or at least they present an unfamiliar perspective. Therefore, parents' guidance on the similarity and familiarity dimensions seem potentially informative, as in the following example:

> **Parent** (pointing to aerial photograph): "Can you find our house? We're on here. Right here."
> **Child:** "Where?"
> **Parent:** "This is where we are. Somewhere on here. Can you find our house? Where's your school? This is a picture from the air.... There's the middle school that you went to and right there is your house."
> **Child:** "Oh cool!"

The parent's explanation that a map is, in a sense, "a picture from the air" may help the child make the representation–referent connection by addressing the unfamiliarity of the perspective for the child.

A map is less similar to its referent than a picture or even a video image of an object, and this disparity was evident in another parent's directive to her child to see that "white dots" represent ponds at the map exhibit. The parent pointed to the aerial photograph and explained, "See, those are where our house is. See the pond? See our house is right there and see, those white dots, those are the ponds."

In contrast to the map exhibit, the salience of the representational object as an object is particularly a problem for the globe exhibit. The globe is a compelling object and parents could potentially guide children in seeing it instead as a representation for the earth. In our observations, however, we found that parents tended to treat the globe as an object, and rarely seemed to help children see that it could also be thought of as a symbol for the earth. By treating the globe not as a representation of the earth, but as an object in its own right, a parent's behavior reflects an assumption of the child's understanding of the earth–globe relationship, as in "See the globe that is showing where you are?" Examining the data in Table 15.3 reveals that explicit links were particularly rare in conversations about the globe exhibit. Parents may think that children already understand globes as representations for the earth and that they are not in need of further explanation. As discussed earlier, Vosniadou and Brewer's (1992) research suggests that this assumption on the part of parents may not be warranted. In a related study, Jipson (2000) explored parent–child conversations about the shape of the earth. Some of these conversations suggest that parents assume that children understand the globe as a model of the earth, and children's comments in those conversations also suggest that the assumption may be invalid. The following example from that study is from a 7-year-old's conversation with his parent during a part of the procedure where parent and child were asked to draw the earth:

Child: Can you draw what ever however you want?
Mother: Yeah, you can do whatever you want.
Child: What color is it?
Mother: What? The earth? What color is the water?
Child: Blue. Where should I leave the house? Should I do it on this side?
Mother: Remember when we saw the globe and then there are some parts that are green and some that are blue? And the green parts are land.
Child: Oh the globe doesn't live on the earth.
Mother: Who?
Child: The globe.
Mother: The globe?

Later, the conversation continued when they were asked to show where two children would live if one (John) lived in Australia and the other (Sally) lived in California:

Mother: OK you want to show me on there on the globe?
Child: (points at quilt on wall) That's a globe?
Mother: No sweetie, right on the globe right there (points to globe on table).
Child: That's a globe?
Mother: Yeah, so show me on that where Sally and John live.
Child: Right here, see right there. (pointing to drawing)
Mother: No, but on that one. Where's Australia?
Child: (looking at globe) Australia, Australia, Australia, Australia, Australia, Australia, Australia.
Mother: So where does John live?
Child: John lives in Australia.
Mother: OK so put him there and put Sally in California.
Child: Can I see where California is? California is that big.
Mother: Yeah, so show me on the globe.
Child: (looks on globe) This?
Mother: Mm hmm.
Child: This?

This conversation suggests that the mother is assuming some familiarity with the globe on the part of her child, but the child seems somewhat confused. If parents generally assume understanding that is not there, then familiar representational objects could elicit less explanation from parents and could take longer for children to begin to understand.

Finally, the video exhibit presents children with a representational object that is not at all salient (and arguably not even an object) and that is very similar to the referent. Consistent with our predictions, parents' talk about the objects in the video rarely mentioned the video image itself. Instead the same kind of transparent labeling seen in the map exhibit was apparent here. Parents often pointed to the video image saying things like, "Look at the coins," or "There's Daddy!"

Unlike the other two exhibits, the referent objects in the video exhibit are present and available for comparison to the representation. This allowed parents to point out the similarity between the referent and the representation. Parents talked about the video exhibit in ways that emphasized the link between the representation and the referent, as in the following example:

> **Parent:** "That's the train you're moving (pointing to the object). See that one right there?"
> **Child:** (standing on his tip-toes to look at the object) "uh huh."
> **Parent:** "And this is what it looks like if you were the train conductor (pointing to the object representation)."

Parents also often used the same term to refer to the object representation (video image) and the object itself, perhaps helping children to recognize the similarity between the two.

> **Mother:** (pointing to the video image) "See, the train?" (then lifting the child up so that she could look at the real train) "There, going around the track, right there. See the train? Look down there.... See the train? It's coming out the other side."

Children's Engagement

In addition to coding parental strategies, we also coded whether children were engaged in joint attention with their parents as the representational objects were being discussed. Each parent–child dyad was coded as either being jointly engaged or not at the time of each coded statement, and reliability was assessed. The data on joint attention are presented in Table 15.4. Chi-square analysis of the relationship between joint attention and parental strategy revealed that children's likelihood of being in joint attention with their parents varied as a function of the strategies parents used ($\chi^2(3) = 15.44, p < .001$). Of children whose parent discussed a specific aspect of the referent, 90% (65 out of 72) were in joint attention with the parent. There were fewer children whose parents talked about an explicit link, but they were also quite likely to be in joint attention (88%, 15 out of 17). In addition, all of the

TABLE 15.4
Number of Children in Joint Attention as a Function of Parental Strategies

	Explicit link	Specific	Generic	Not relevant
Joint attention	15	65	9	17
No Joint attention	2	7	0	11

children whose parents talked about a generic aspect of the referent were in joint attention (9 out of 9), but 60% of the children whose parents talked about nothing relevant were in joint attention (17 out of 28).

Joint attention is not an assessment of children's understanding, and future work on this topic is needed before we can understand the potential impact of parents' strategies on children's understanding. Further, it is not clear whether the strategies used by parents differentially encouraged joint attention or whether children's attentiveness motivated parents' use of certain strategies. This research does begin to suggest, however, that parents may be providing information that is potentially helpful as children begin to understand that these objects are not just objects in their own right, but also representations.

CONCLUSIONS AND IMPLICATIONS
FOR MUSEUM EXHIBIT DESIGN

The findings of this study are consistent with results from several related projects (Callanan & Jipson, 2001) where we observed parents conversing with their children about science in ways that focused on particular events rather than on deeper abstract principles. These findings are also in line with the work of Gelman, Coley, Rosengren, Hartman, and Pappas (1998) on parents' talk with children about category membership of various natural and human-made objects. Gelman et al. found that parents used subtle cues such as gestures to indicate shared category membership, but that they rarely gave explicit explanations about underlying category structure. In his commentary on that work, Keil (1998) argued that it would perhaps be unproductive for parents to give children too much detail about underlying scientific principles, and that it might be more appropriate to introduce children to the general domain and then let them explore the details on their own. We are beginning to formulate a model of how these fragmentary explanatory conversations may impact children's learning. We argue that by focusing on particular events of interest in the moment, and providing fragments of information, parents may be laying the groundwork for children to eventually build up coherent understanding of deeper principles.

In the conversations analyzed here, parents talked to young children as if the children understood representational objects for what they are. Although deep explanations did not abound, we argue that there was some guidance given that could help children to begin to attain dual representation. When parents name the referent while pointing at a representational object, for example, we argue that children are being presented with a puzzle to be solved. To make sense of what their parents are saying, they must come up with a nonliteral way to interpret the label. This conflict may lead children to begin to search for another way to think about the objects with which they are interacting. These sorts of conversations could perhaps be important motivation for the emergence of dual representation ability.

It seems possible that in some situations it could be unhelpful to children to have adults treat objects as if they are already understood. A speculative example is that the parents in our observations seemed to assume that their children understand that globes are models of the earth. Given parents' assumption that this must be obvious, they do little to clear up the confusion that results from the fact that the globe is a compelling object in its own right. It is possible, then, that children's confusion about the shape of the earth may not be helped by their exposure to globes, partly because globes may not be recognized as representations for the earth. Further research on this point should help to shed light on this issue.

Consistent with this point of view, and as mentioned at the beginning of the chapter, DeLoache's original work is sometimes taken as evidence that representational objects can hinder children's learning. Uttal, Liu, and DeLoache (1999) argued that the use of interesting manipulative materials in mathematics classrooms (e.g., Cheerios, marbles) may actually obscure the representational quality of those objects and make it more difficult for children to learn the abstract concept that is being represented. They cited Stevenson and Stigler's (1992) research reporting on the use of manipulative materials in Japanese math classrooms. Interestingly, a common practice in Japanese classrooms is to use the same manipulatives — simple tiles — throughout the early school years; this consistency may help children to develop an understanding of the representational nature of the objects. Uttal, Scudder, and DeLoache (1997) suggested that the most effective concrete object for encouraging learning is one that is interesting enough to hold a child's interest, but not so appealing that it ceases to have representational qualities for the child.

One contribution of the work presented here is to bring into focus not just the nature of various representational objects, but also the nature of the social interaction within which children experience these objects. The previous research reviewed here suggests that children are likely to appreciate the representational nature of photographs and videotapes by the time they reach the preschool years. Representational objects that are more salient as objects, such as globes and maps, are likely to take several more years to be fully understood. Our research suggests that parents and others may be able to help children understand the dual nature of these objects by talking about them both as objects and as symbols for other (more abstract) objects.

Children's museums often contain many representational objects. These exhibits may be designed without much background information regarding children's understanding of the dual nature of such objects. Also, the philosophy of museum design may not distinguish these objects from other sorts of objects. Constructivist theories in museum settings, for example, may lead exhibit designers to hide their intentions for exhibits, with the goal of encouraging open-ended exploration so that children can discover new affordances of objects. Tomasello (1999) argued that children (and adults) respond to human-made objects in terms of their "intentional affordances" as well as their physical affordances. The idea is that we have expectations that human-made objects have intended functions, and if they are not apparent to us, we may be confused about how to approach the object. Tomasello's approach raises intriguing questions regarding the interface of museum visitors' expectations and designers' intentions (hidden or otherwise). Further, our findings suggest that it may be beneficial to create opportunities for social interactions around museum exhibits containing representational objects.

Although our studies took place in the context of a hands-on children's museum, children's everyday lives are full of opportunities to explore and discuss representational objects with their parents. For example, when planning a trip, parents and children may look at road maps together to discuss their route. Or, when watching a video of a family gathering, parents and children may talk about the people seen on the tape. Of course, the most common instance of conversation around representational objects may be when parents and children together look at picture books, labeling the objects they see represented on the pages. Given the numerous representational materials of use in day-to-day living, our research easily extends to settings beyond children's museums. Children's conversations with parents serve as a setting for children to figure out the notion of an object that serves as both object and symbol.

REFERENCES

Acredolo, L. (1982). The familiarity factor in spatial research. In R. Cohen (Ed.), *New directions in child development: Vol. 15, Children's conceptions of spatial relationships* (pp. 19–30). San Francisco: Jossey-Bass.

Callanan, M. A., & Jipson, J. L. (2001). Explanatory conversations and young children's developing scientific literacy. In K. Crowley, C. Schunn, & T. Okada (Eds.), *Designing for science: Implications from everyday, classroom, and professional, settings* (pp. 21–49). Mahwah, NJ: Lawrence Erlbaum Associates.

Crowley, K., & Callanan, M. (1998). Describing and supporting collaborative scientific thinking in parent-child interactions. *Journal of Museum Education* (Special issue on Understanding the Museum Experience: Theory and Practice, S. Paris, Ed.), *23,* 12-17.

Crowley, K., Callanan, M., Jipson, J., Galco, J., Topping, K., & Shrager, J. (in press). Shared scientific thinking in everyday parent-child activity. *Science Education.*

Crowley, K., Callanan, M., Tenenbaum, H., & Allen, E. (2001). Parents explain more often to boys than to girls during shared scientific thinking. *Psychological Science, 12,* 258-261.

DeLoache, J. S. (1987). Rapid change in the symbolic functioning of very young children. *Science, 238,* 1556-1557.

DeLoache, J. S. (1991). Symbolic functioning in very young children: Understanding of pictures and models. *Child Development, 62,* 736-752.

DeLoache, J. S. (1995). Early symbol understanding and use. In D. Medin (Ed.), *The psychology of learning and motivation (Vol. 33),* pp. 65-114. New York: Academic Press.

DeLoache, J. S. (2000). Dual representation and young children's use of scale models. *Child Development, 71,* 329-338.

DeLoache, J. S., Kolstad, V., & Anderson, K. N. (1991). Physical similarity and young children's understanding of scale models. *Child Development, 62,* 111-126.

DeLoache, J. S., & Marzolf, D. P. (1992). When a picture is not worth a thousand words: Young children's understanding of pictures and models. *Cognitive Development, 7,* 317-329.

Deloache, J. S., Uttal, D. H., & Pierroutsakos, S. L. (1998). The development of early symbolization: Educational implications. *Learning & Instruction, 8,* 325-339.

Gelman, S., Coley, J., Rosengren, K., Hartman, E., & Pappas, A. (1998). Beyond labeling: The role of maternal input in the acquisition of richly structured categories. *Monographs of the Society for Research in Child Development.* Serial no. 253.

Ittelson, W. H. (1996). Visual perception of markings. *Psychonomic Bulletin and Review, 3,* 171-187.

Jipson, J. (2000). Parent-child conversation and children's understanding of the shape of the earth. Ph.D. dissertation, University of California, Santa Cruz.

Keil, F. C. (1998). Words, moms, and things: Language as a road map to reality. Commentary in Gelman, S., Coley, J., Rosengren, K., Hartman, E., & Pappas, A. (1998). Beyond labeling: The role of maternal input in the acquisition of richly structured categories. *Monographs of the Society for Research in Child Development.* Serial no. 253.

Kotovsky, L., & Gentner, D. (1996). Comparison and categorization in the development of relational similarity. *Child Development, 67,* 2797-2822.

Liben, L. S. (1999). Developing an understanding of external spatial representations. In I. Sigel (Ed.), *Development of representation: Theories and applications* (pp. 297-321). London: Lawrence Erlbaum Associates.

Liben, L. S., & Downs, R. M. (1989). Understanding maps as symbols: The development of map concepts in children. In H. W. Reese (Ed.), *Advances in child development and behavior* (Vol. 22, pp. 146-202). San Diego: Academic Press.

Liben, L. S., & Yekel, C. A. (1996). Preschoolers' understanding of plan and oblique maps: The role of geometric and representational correspondence. *Child Development, 67,* 2780-2796.

Marzolf, D. P., & DeLoache, J. S. (1994). Transfer in young children's understanding of spatial representations. *Child Development, 64,* 1-15.

Nussbaum, J., & Novak, J. D. (1976). An assessment of children's concepts of the Earth utilizing structured interviews. *Science Education, 60,* 535-550.

Piaget, J., & Inhelder, B. (1969). *The psychology of the child.* New York: Basic.

Rogoff, B. (1990). *Apprenticeship in thinking: Cognitive development in social context.* New York: Oxford University Press.

Sneider, C., & Pulos, S. (1983). Children's cosmographies: Understanding the Earth's shape and gravity. *Science Education, 67,* 205-221.

Soennichsen, M. S., & Callanan, M. A. (2001). *Parent-child conversations and children's under-standing of representational objects.* Manuscript in preparation.

Stevenson, H.W., & Stigler, J.W. (1992). *The learning gap: Why our schools are failing and what we can learn from Japanese and Chinese education.* New York: Summit Books.

Tomasello, M. (1999). The cultural ecology of young children's interactions with objects and arti-facts. In E.Winograd, R. Fivush, & W. Hirst (Eds.), *Ecological approaches to cognition: Essays in honor of Ulric Neisser. Emory symposia in cognition* (pp. 153-170). Mahwah, NJ: Lawrence Erlbaum Associates.

Troseth, G. L., & DeLoache, J. S. (1998). The medium can obscure the message:Young children's un-derstanding of video. *Child Development, 68,* 950-965.

Troseth, G., Rozak, K., & Spry, B. (1999). *This is your life: Understanding the relation between video and reality.* Poster presented at the meetings of the Society for Research in Child De-velopment, Albuquerque, NM.

Uttal, D. H., Liu, L. L., & DeLoache, J. S. (1999). Taking a hard look at concreteness: Do concrete objects help young children learn symbolic relations? In L. Balter & C. S. Tamis-LeMonda (Eds.), *Child Psychology: A Handbook of Contemporary Issues* (pp. 177-192). Philadelphia: Psychology Press.

Uttal, D. H., Lio, P.A., & Taxy, B. E. (1995). Seeing the big picture: Children's mental representations of maps. In J. Plumert (Chair), Developmental change in the coding of spatial location. Pre-sented at the biennial meeting of the Society for Research in Child Development, Indianapo-lis, IN.

Uttal, D. H., Scudder, K.V., & DeLoache, J. S. (1997). Manipulatives as symbols: A new perspective on the use of concrete objects to teach mathematics. *Journal of Applied Developmental Psy-chology, 18,* 37-54.

Uttal, D. H., & Wellman, H. M. (1989). Young children's representation of spatial information ac-quired from maps. *Developmental Psychology, 25,* 128-138.

Vosniadou, S., & Brewer, W. F. (1992). Mental models of the earth: A study of conceptual change in childhood. *Cognitive Psychology, 24,* 535-585.

CHAPTER SIXTEEN

Pathways Among Objects
and Museum Visitors

Kristine A. Morrissey
Michigan State University Museum

A father, his daughter, and his son crouch on the ground, examining the skulls of a beaver and a raccoon on a nature walk. "Look at those long teeth!" the daughter says, holding up the beaver skull. The father explains how the teeth will continue to grow if the beaver does not chew on wood, and his son talks about a related television show. They turn their attention to the other skull and continue looking, talking, and asking each other questions — sharing their knowledge, questions, and observations. Completely rooted in the immediacy of the moment, their attention is focused on the physical objects in front of them and on each other, each connecting this moment to other experiences and knowledge while fertilizing the soil of their knowledge base that will support future experiences.

Encounters with real things — be they from the natural or cultural environment — ignite curiosity, imagination, memories, and questions. Encounters with objects provide an opportunity for dialogue, inquiry, and conversation through which individuals find deeper connections not only to the world around them, but to each other as conversations twist around the object, the content, and the thoughts and experiences of each individual. Individuals learn *about* each other while they learn *through* each other. These conversations or interactions between individuals, in the presence of objects, are the foundation of learning and are core to the concept of museums as places where knowledge is created, discussed, reflected on, and passed on to future generations. By focusing on these interactions, and the ways objects influence these interactions, museums can better understand and facilitate the visitor experience.

OBJECTS TAKE US ON A JOURNEY

Christopher Vogler (1998), story consultant to such top grossing films as *The Lion King* and *Beauty and the Beast,* suggested that a plot is a journey from the ordinary "world of common day" in Joseph Campbell's language, through trials and challenges and ultimately, the return home, a different person. He wrote:

> At heart, despite its infinite variety, the hero's story is always a journey. A hero leaves her comfortable, ordinary surroundings to venture into a challenging, unfamiliar world. It may be an outward journey to an actual place; a labyrinth, forest or cave, a strange city or country, a new locale that becomes the arena for her conflict with antagonistic, challenging forces.
>
> But there are as many stories that take the hero on an inward journey, one of the mind, the heart, the spirit. In any good story the hero grows and changes, making a journey from one way of being to the next....(p. 13)

Encounters with objects are also journeys. They take us from the familiar and the known to secret or faraway places where ideas are challenged or supported and where various forms of interpretation serve as guides or mentors — sometimes leading us astray and other times providing the magic elixir to change us.

Like the mythic tales, encounters with an object can also take us on an inward journey, seeking that which is within, provoking a deeper level of awareness, a moment of intense connection to the immediate world and by extension, to each other. We can watch a butterfly in flight or touch the footprint of a dinosaur; we can read Francis Scott Key's handwritten draft of the national anthem, the scribbling of John Lennon, or ancient petroglyphs in a national park. Glazer (1999) wrote that these moments of openness, of intimacy with direct experience and intimacy with our perceptions, are sacred. Not grounded in religion, but rather in experience and awareness, he described *sacredness* as the ground of learning (p. 10).

> Sacredness is the practice of wholeness and awareness. It is approaching, greeting, and meeting the world with basic respect. What is sacredness as the ground of learning? It is rooting education in the practices of openness, attentiveness to experience, and sensitivity to the world. (pp. 11–12)

In an essay titled "The Grace of Great Things," Palmer (1999) offered a very simple definition of the sacred appropriate to this discussion of objects: "The sacred is that which is worthy of respect" (p. 20). He suggested that if we could recover our sense of the sacred, we would also recover our capacity for wonder and surprise, both of which are essential to life-giving learning. Life-giving learning is not about getting information, but about renewing the vitality of life and claiming our place in the world. In a society often distanced or distracted from direct experience — where we view war on a TV screen, order books online, and eat lunch as we work — museums, gardens, and zoos offer an opportunity to experience something real, to approach it with wonder and surprise. It may feel awkward to use the term *sacred* in this context; in reality we do not have the appropriate language to talk about these moments of connection, what we colloquially may refer to as the "wow" moments. These are not only the moments of being swept away by something magnificent, but also the quiet moments of awareness and affinity. When visitors share these times, when they openly and spontaneously respond to the objects and to each other, they are responding to the language of the object and using the lexicon of the objects to connect with each other.

THE LANGUAGE OF THE OBJECT

> Artifacts are alive. Each has a voice. They remind us what it means to be human — that it is our nature to survive, to create works of beauty, to be resourceful, to be attentive to the world we live in…. [they] court the mysteries of private lives, communal lives, lives rooted in ritual and ceremony. (Williams, 1991, p. 189)

In the 2000 campaign for president, Vice President Al Gore was plagued by the reputation of the president who preceded him and he wanted to change the way Americans viewed him; he wanted to connect his image to the ideal that is America. Could words alone do it? In a media moment, the 2000 Democratic Convention opened in Los Angeles, California, to a projected image of the Declaration of Independence and the announcement that one of the 26 original copies would now be housed and displayed in California. The Democrats used the powerful language of the object to place the history and the values of the American people side-by-side with Al Gore.

Artifacts, as well as specimens collected from the natural environment, represent and codify all that humans have experienced; they are a reminder or a record of beliefs, values, places, activities, and times. Because encounters with these objects can be and often are powerful, it is easy to imagine that there is something inherently powerful in the object itself. However, like all language, that of the object is subjective and dependent on the meaning others attribute to the object (Gurian, 1999). The bell from the *Edmund Fitzgerald* may be no more than a rusty shipwreck relic to one visitor. However, to the viewer who reaches out to trace the name of a childhood friend inscribed on the side of the bell, the object is a symbolic link to the lives of the sailors, the power of Lake Superior, and a moment in time when those men lost the battle against the sea. The value of an object comes not simply from its age or beauty, but from its ability to illuminate a part of the human experience, to provide a portal through which people can see their own experience in the context of a larger history and culture. The power of an object resides in the language it speaks and the language it provokes among viewers.

LANGUAGE AS KNOWING

How do I know what I think until I hear what I say? (Wells, 1999, p. 107)

Conversation is our account of ourselves. (Ralph Waldo Emerson, quoted by Wurman, 1989, p. 93)

The term *postmodernism* has been used to refer to a current school of thought where reality is viewed as subjective and the learner as an active participant in constructing knowledge. This view of reality is in contrast to the previous modernism view of reality as objective and the learner as a passive recipient of fixed knowledge (Reed & Johnson, 2000, p. 278). Museums have attempted to describe or understand the visitor experience in ways consistent with this postmodernism view using constructs such as meaning-making (Silverman, 1995), constructivism (Hein, 1998), and narrative (Roberts, 1997). These constructs share assumptions that: (a) the visitor is actively engaged in creating knowledge; (b) learning is a process, not a product; and (c) knowledge is not transmitted from one person to another, but constructed and continually negotiated and renegotiated. The role of the social group also has been recognized in current views of the ways visitors construct meaning, most notably in Falk and Dierking's (2000) contextual model of learning.

The view of knowledge as constructed or mediated relies heavily on the role of language and social interaction. A theoretical perspective, most commonly associated with Vygotsky but expanded on by others, suggests that social interaction not only promotes, but is a prerequisite for intellectual, social, personal, and cultural development (Moll, 1994). Language is fundamental to knowing and learning; it is not only the way learning is communicated, but it is the way learning happens — "the process by which experience becomes knowledge" (Wells, 1999, p. 106).

Jane Roland Martin's efforts to bring the female voice into the conversation of culture and education reminds us that to be educated is to engage in a conversation that stretches back in time (Reed & Johnson, 2000).

We are all inheritors neither of an inquiry about ourselves and the world nor of an accumulating body of information, but of a conversation begun in the primeval forest and extended and made more articulate in the course of centuries....And it is this conversation which in the end, gives place and character to every human activity and utterance. (p. 145)[1]

In museums, where most visitors are part of a social group involving mixed generations, the conversations of visitors are both inevitable and a remarkable resource to promote learning and enjoyment. The importance of language in the museum environment is supported by the Family Learning Project (Borun, Chambers, Dritsas, & Johnson, 1997; Borun & Dritsas, 1997). Their research identified five behaviors that correlated with learning in the museum setting: ask a question, answer a question, read text silently, read text aloud, comment on or explain the exhibit. Four of these behaviors involve spoken language, suggesting a conversation or interaction between family members. These interactions change not only how the individuals respond to the objects, but also how they relate and think about each other. "In any interaction we negotiate meanings about what we think is going on in the world, how we feel about it, and how we feel about the people we interact with" (Wells, 2000, p. 100). Language creates pathways between individuals and objects as it also creates paths that connect people.

PATHWAYS AMONG OBJECTS AND INDIVIDUALS

The interaction between the father and the children cited at the beginning of this chapter can be used as an example of how individuals create connections between themselves and objects. Central to this example and the subsequent discussion are four characteristics of the encounter. The encounter involved a group, language, an object, and different levels of maturity and experience. The interaction is illustrated in Fig. 16.1. The object (skulls) provided a stimuli, a focus of attention, and is represented in the diagram as O (object). The children and the father, each one unique in his or her response, also represent different sets of experiences and maturity and are represented in this diagram as A (adult) and C (child). The lines connecting the individuals and the object are the pathways that represent the encounters, the responses, and the interactions. Meaning is negotiated in unique ways on each pathway.

Five pathways are suggested in this model:

1. The child responds to the object (C–O)
2. The adult responds to the object (A–O)
3. The adult's response to the object is mediated by the child (A–C–O)
4. The child's response to the object is mediated by adult (C–A–O)
5. The adult and the child respond to each other (A–C)

[1]This quote is taken from Michael Oakeshott, *Rationalism in Politics and Other Essays* (London: Methuen, 1962, p. 199).

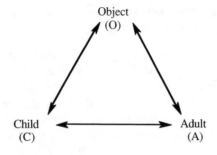

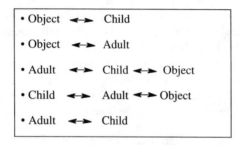

FIG. 16.1.   Pathways Model

PATHWAYS BETWEEN INDIVIDUALS
AND OBJECTS

In Pathways 1 and 2, the object speaks to the individual and the individual responds. The language of the object grows from its history, and its voice is that of each person involved in the creation, use, collection, care, disposal, acquisition, study, and display of the object. A paleontologist collected a particular fossil in Madagascar because it represented a particular time she was studying; a mother wove a basket in Ethiopia for her daughter's wedding to express her love and respect for tradition; a person donated a scrapbook documenting a time of war with the hope that it would teach future generations. Visitors begin a dialogue with an object only when they understand how the values, knowledge, and experiences of each of these individuals are encoded in the language of the respective object.

In the diagram of pathways (Fig. 16.1), the lines between the object and the individuals point in both directions, suggesting a continuous two-way dialogue. Many museums have developed ways to engage visitors in conversations and to bring these conversations into the narrative of the exhibit. Strategies include simple devices such as dropping a ball in a jar to indicate opinions, voting on environmental positions through a computer, and virtual conferences with individuals in other parts of the world. Perhaps the simplest and most common format is the comment card. At the Michigan State University Museum, we have been tabulating and reviewing comment cards since 1995 and find that responses typically include declarations of presence ("The Wilsons, Sept. 10"); responses to the experience itself ("Kids loved the guessing part," "I need more than an hour to look at all this mess — because I like it"); and critiques or compliments of specific messages as visitors articulate the fit between the museum's narrative and their own beliefs ("I liked it because it had real animals in it," "I am an American of Russian descent but an Arab at heart. Loved the exhibit," ". . . is this just more anti-fishing anti-hunting P.C. wrapped in the guise of science?").

In a recent exhibit, a Polish crested chicken displayed with a pair of sunglasses sparked a dialog between visitors via comment cards, including these:

> "What's up w/ the shaded Rooster? Very Glam!"

> "This is a place of learning. The sunglasses are completely and utterly unnecessary. It belittles the Polish crested chicken as a species. It is my fav. species and I don't like it."

> "I completely disagree concerning the sunglasses. This institution represents learning but certainly it should retain a sense of the comical; an imaginative addition. Looks glaringly like A. Einstein."

I witnessed a wonderful example of visitors' responses in Birmingham, Alabama. In a re-creation of the jail cell where Martin Luther King was held during the civil rights battles, visitors had thrown pennies through the rungs of the cell door to pile up on his cot. According to staff at the museum, the coin tossing apparently began spontaneously, presumably as a tribute to the memories of Martin Luther King's acts of civil disobedience, and the pile of coins continued to grow in both size and impact. Years later, I do not remember the labels or signage, but I do remember the coins left by other visitors as their part of the story and I remember my own sense of connection to other visitors and to Martin Luther King when I also tossed a coin into the re-created jail cell.

CHILDREN MEDIATE THE PATHWAYS OF ADULTS

The nature of the personal relationships, as well as the differences in perspectives between adults and children, mediates and often enhances the ways adults respond to objects (Pathway 3). For an adult, the presence and the unique perspective of a child create a path that integrates the experiences of self, child, and object. Although I have seen many examples of this in museum galleries, most compelling have been my personal experiences where the presence of my daughter changed how I responded to the object and to her. My experiences in art museums in particular changed completely when I began experiencing them with her. Her perceptions, reactions, and interactions with me created a path to the art that I had not found independently.

Not having any background in art history or any talents in artistic expression, for years I was a stranger to and at art museums. When museum friends tried to engage me, I was a compliant but unenthusiastic observer of art. During a visit to the Art Gallery of Ontario, my then 4-year-old daughter gazed at an 18th-century painting of a highly dressed young boy who, from the appearance of his clothing, lived a life very different from hers or mine. Looking into his face, she recognized his feelings and said, "That boy looks sad. I think his mommy is on a trip." Her emotions crossed the boundaries of time and place to connect with this boy, and recognizing his emotion as familiar, she attempted to understand the cause of his sadness in the context of her own experience. She learned the power of art to express emotion, and I learned more about how she felt when I traveled than the simple words "I missed you" could ever convey. As we both responded to the art, we also experienced each other in a way that was unique. I determined to follow the advice of a sign in the art gallery at that time and rather than taking the art too seriously, I let the art take me. Today I think of art museums as a wonderful place for family interaction where art stimulates ideas, thoughts, emotions, and reactions. I found my way to art through my interaction with my daughter.

ADULTS MEDIATE THE PATHWAYS OF CHILDREN

Adults mediate the ways children respond to objects and exhibits (Pathway 4). This may be through the sharing of personal connections that provides a way for children to see the object as it relates to the adult, or it may be through providing a view of the world that is based on a wider and larger set of experiences. A young boy, scooting by the skull of a mammoth, stops when his father says, "This was found in Kansas right by where grandma lives." A mother and daughter look at a piece of unfinished handmade lace with the bobbins still attached and try to project which bobbin would be used next, both developing a sense of appreciation and awe for the craft. A chaperone says to a group, "Hey, do you know why a dollar is called a buck?" and a small group of students gather to hear him explain that at one time a deer was worth one dollar in trade or sale and often deer carcasses ("bucks") were used to pay for a service or merchandise.

In these examples, the adults were not deliberately attempting to teach but were naturally responding to the objects, sharing their responses and joining the children in trying to understand what they saw. This collaborative approach to understanding and reacting to exhibits involves both the adult and the child as active participants in the learning process. Adopting a model of learning based on co-construction of knowledge puts adults in a natural role of co-learner. Adults can actively engage students in talking about what they see, reacting, asking questions, and displaying "a stance toward experiences and ideas — a willingness to wonder, to ask questions, and to seek to understand by collaborating with others in the attempt to make answers to them" (Glazer, 1999, p. 121). Museums encourage this type of collaboration when they use interpretive approaches that engage visitors in talking about the objects and encourage adults and children to express and share their natural responses and questions.

PATHWAYS BETWEEN VISITORS

> My vision of a brave new world is not the opportunity for me to create, but for us to create a maze which becomes the context for us to find our way to each other.... The task of a museum is to create an event that doesn't tell you how wonderful the designers are, but instead provides a context where you can feel better about and understand the people around you. (Schlossberg, interviewed by Wurman, 1989, p. 132)

Some years ago the Michigan State University Museum did an exhibit called "Fiestas de la Fe: Celebrations of Faith," illustrating the artistic and cultural traditions of the feast days of Posadas, Fiestas Guadalupanas, and Día de los Muertos as practiced by Mexicans in southwest Detroit — a study of continuity and change. I was stopped in this gallery one day by a man who wanted to know if he and his father could take pictures. The older man, his father, pointed around the gallery and with a broad, contagious smile said, "I wanted to show this to my son." He explained that his son was born in America and had never been to Mexico. The father proceeded to move around the gallery, positioning himself in front of several of the displays for his son to photograph. It was particularly telling that the man wanted the photograph of himself *and* the exhibit. The story captured, and indeed created, by those photos was not just the story of the exhibit or of this man's past, it was the integration of memory, objects, family, and emotion. It was the sharing and passing on of culture that happened in a particular way in the presence of these very real objects. Although the purpose of the exhibit was to share information about culture, the potentially abstract message became personal as the son learned the story of his own culture through the voices of both the museum and of his father. The objects in the exhibit provided an authentic and meaningful context where the older man could reveal and retell his story.

Museums have tremendous potential to help individuals connect not only to people in other places and times, but also to connect more closely to each other, to learn their own history (Silverman, 1995). The history and the authenticity of objects can draw out narratives within the individuals and create an atmosphere where it is only natural to share stories and narratives. In an exhibit about World War II, I learned more about my own father's experiences in the war than I had heard in the previous decade. In the following section, I share this story.

A Personal Story

Like most children of veterans, I grew up knowing little about the war or about my parents' experiences, and I probably showed very little interest. Some years ago, I went through an exhibit with my parents about the home-front activities during WWII. As we looked at newspaper headlines, uniforms, ration books, a Victory Garden cookbook, and other objects, I listened to stories and memories and gradually the abstract facts about the war were replaced or enhanced by very specific and personal images and words — Mrs. McGillicuddy down the street who traded ration cards with my mom; my dad's first train trip to Seattle when he enlisted; and December 7, the day that started with a trip out to Boeing to see the new B17 and ended when he heard the news of Pearl Harbor and volunteered to "ride shotgun" to a storage dump in the mountains to retrieve bombs and depth charges (wisely instructed by the driver to throw the charges out the window if the truck hit any bumps).

Walking through that history exhibit, my story, my own history, merged with the story of the exhibit, and I not only experienced the exhibit differently, but I experienced my father differently. Through our conversation, a new meaning of my history and of WWII evolved. My sisters and I recently encouraged him to record some of his memories. One of my favorites is next, about an incident in the early days of the war in the South Pacific that now embarrasses him for its sheer audacity but delights his family for the same reason.

A Gross of Eggs

One day I noticed several small crates of fresh eggs by the officer's mess tent. The idea of a fresh egg sandwich sounded very good. That night I worked out a plan. I got up early the next morning and went to the Marine that was guarding the food supply and held out a $20 bill and told him it was his if he would stay right where he was for ten minutes. I picked up a crate of eggs and walked into the jungle. I covered the crate with palm branches and went to the mess area, and selected the cook I would talk to. For $20, he agreed to put ten loaves of bread in the plane number I gave him.

I talked to another one of the electrical maintenance men to help fry and collect $1.00 per sandwich.(He wanted $40 to do it but settled for $30). Each plane carried a two-burner Coleman stove. It was common to be working on the planes in the evening and usually a pot of coffee was brewing in one of the Coleman burners outside the plane.

After supper, Bill (the $30 man) and I went down to the work area. Bill started the Coleman and I went for the eggs. The cook was next to the plane. I asked him to pass the word — egg sandwiches for $1.00. It wasn't long before there was a line waiting. I think it took about an hour to cook the 144 eggs and there were 144 satisfied sailors in the camp that night! (from personal notes of Jim Morrissey, Navy Aviation Radioman)

An encyclopedia can tell us that 70 million men and women fought on both sides in WWII and about 17 million of them lost their lives. These soldiers became people — young men and women — when I could imagine my father away from the farm and old enough to risk his life for his country, but still young enough to crave an egg sandwich and to stretch the rules to get it. I had gained both intellectual knowledge and the beginning of "emotional knowing." The story and the reality of the war had existed for decades, but it was the objects in the exhibit that, like a fish hook, snagged the memories and drew out the stories, and it was conversation that brought me into the story. The objects represented experiences, a time, and a set of values; they were the language of a set of experiences that I previously had no way to access. But my dad, in responding to the objects, in providing the stories that they represented to him, opened the pathway, taught me the language they spoke, and I became part of the conversation. Objects provide a way for us to connect to each other, to share our own stories and to continue the conversation of culture about the meaning of life and our own particular place in this world (Gurian, 1999).

IS ALL CONVERSATION LEARNING?

What makes a conversation meaningful to both visitors and museums? What facilitates the merging of the visitor's narrative and the museum's narrative where visitors are talking about objects and ideas and experiences that are related to the educational mission of a particular museum? Roberts (1997) discussed education as "fundamentally a meaning-making activity that involves a constant negotiation between the stories given by museums and those brought by visitors" (p. 14). Consider the scenario of a father and teenage daughter trying to identify a skull in an exhibit about animal weapons. In front of the skull is the label "Describe my teeth. How do I use them? What am I?" Because the skull is so large, they first suspect it is from an extinct animal. The teeth are large and flat — perhaps a grass-eating mammoth? But the daughter points out that the teeth are white. "Wouldn't they be dark if it was a fossil?" They wonder what contemporary animal it could be. "An elephant?" Then they lift the tab and read that it is the skull of a hippopotamus. "That's like an elephant. Aren't they both herbivores?" They then talk about the teeth of the elephant they saw in another exhibit.

This interaction involved observation, description, relying on prior knowledge, discussion, creating and testing hypotheses against evidence, imagination, asking questions, and even reading labels — processes that are part of knowing and part of learning to learn. It was also a social experience, and when the father and daughter discussed this interchange, it was apparent that it was also a moment of shared trust, each testing and showing the other how they thought. The vocalization of thought processes and sharing of an intellectual challenge provides an opportunity for both adult and child to understand how the other person thinks, how each approaches the world, and what they value — learning new ways of thinking about the world and about each other. This adult–child interchange met the goals of the father and daughter to share time together, and it also met the museum's agenda for visitors to learn about animal weapons (and ultimately about evolution, biology, and more importantly, the process and attitude of inquiry). It is interesting to note that this interaction included both conversation and thoughtful moments of reflection. A well-known pianist is said to have remarked that it was not the notes he played, but the pauses between them that made the difference. Although this chapter promotes language and social interaction, it is within the context of understanding that opportunities for reflection and introspection are equally important.

While designing the exhibit "Animal Weapons: Nature's Arm's Race," the development team at the Michigan State University Museum tried to follow an interpretive approach that balanced presentation of content with the creation of opportunities for the visitor to respond to objects and to experience science as they engaged in a dialogue of inquiry. The hippo skull described earlier was part of a module called "Your Turn ... What is it?" which challenged visitors to describe the teeth of three skulls and hypothesize the diet and identity of the animal. Through observations and conversations with visitors,[2] we found this simple form of interpretive engagement seemed to be extremely compelling. Children were able to participate on equal footing with their parents by using their skills of observation and description, and both adults and children were challenged to hypothesize and imagine within the safety zone of having an answer available. The opportunity to connect to each

---

[2] Visitor observations were conducted on 24 days, April through August, 2000, by Kelly McIntyre. Interviews were conducted on July 27, 2000, by Kris Morrissey and Kelly McIntyre. Comment cards were collected throughout the run of the exhibit (March–October, 2000).

other and to practice interpretation provided an opportunity for adults to better understand how their children think, to model ways they themselves face the unknown, and to collaborate in a dialogue of inquiry.

ENHANCING PATHWAYS

Exhibits and programs can be designed in ways that facilitate and support conversations where visitors seek out and create new pathways between themselves and objects. It requires museum personnel to think and talk about the kinds of conversations we want visitors to have during and after their experiences in our museums or programs and making meaningful conversation a goal through all stages of planning, development, and evaluation. For several years, Dr. Deborah Perry and I have conducted a workshop called "Designing for Conversation."[3] Built on the premise that conversation promotes learning and enjoyment, the workshop explores ways to facilitate conversation in and about exhibits. One of the activities that Dr. Perry developed is called "Enhancing and Inhibiting Conversation," where workshop participants wander through exhibits and identify characteristics of the design and the interpretation that enhance or inhibit conversations. Participants are quick to identify ways that conversations can be promoted once they use this goal as a lens to view the exhibit. (Many of the participants come to the workshop with wonderful experiences from their own institutions in designing exhibits that promote social interaction). Participant suggestions include space for groups to stand together, controlling background noises, labels that can be read aloud or at a glance and shared with children, interpretation that brings in voices or encourages visitors' voices, areas for docents or teachers to sit on the floor and ponder an object, objects that are familiar and connected to daily experience or likely to be more familiar with one generation to promote sharing, and providing opportunities to engage in dialogues of inquiry.

Designing for social interaction means expanding our planning conversations to include questions such as, "What do we want visitors to talk about in the exhibit?" "How can visitors' ideas become part of this story?" "What part of this story can visitors create or build?" "What do our objects say to visitors?" Visitor studies can promote this approach by focusing on what visitors talked about in the galleries, ways visitors shared personal memories, and how conversations in galleries encouraged visitors to look or think differently about the objects and their own connections to the objects and to the people with them.

---

[3] Many of the ideas expressed in this chapter have been influenced by discussions and activities associated with the planning and implementation of this workshop.

IN CONCLUSION: IS A MUSEUM
DIFFERENT FROM CABELA'S?

Cabela's® advertises itself as "the world's foremost outfitter of hunting, fishing and outdoor gear."[4] Their 225,000-square-foot store, which opened in Michigan in the fall of 2000, is expected to draw 6 million visitors a year, potentially making it Michigan's top tourist attraction. They have a library, a collection of specimens, a 65,000-gallon walk-through aquarium, a wildlife biologist on staff, a 35-foot-tall mountain replica with running waterfalls and a trout pond, and information kiosks with touch screens that identify animal species. The store also offers a cafeteria, meeting rooms, and a parking lot for RVs to spend the night.

During busy periods, customers are greeted in the parking lot by uniformed staff on horseback who direct them to open parking, where a van waits to whisk them to the front door. Inside, the displays and specimens are not merely a backdrop to commerce or simply a display of trophy mounts; they are engaging and conceptual. For example, one display shows eight musk oxen forming part of a defensive circle against three wolves. On the side is a musk ox on the ground, just taken by a gray wolf—illustrating concepts of predatory and defensive behaviors. Cabela's website states that they have "museum-like dioramas, sculptures and wild game trophies displayed in a showroom so extraordinary shoppers might forget they're in a retail store." Places like Cabela's and Disney World are probably successful at least in part because they know their audience, they know their product, and they make it easy and fun for their audience to experience their product. Is this education, entertainment, marketing, or a smart blend of all three?

Museums are not diminished by the success of institutions like Cabela's (and may even find opportunities for collaborations), but instead are challenged to consider and reflect on their mission and their guiding principles. It is the philosophy, the purpose, the context for collecting, studying, and displaying objects that defines an institution, be it a school, a museum, a national park, or a place of commerce. In an era where stores like Cabela's increase their appeal and revenue by mimicking museums, and where dinosaurs are auctioned by Sotheby's, institutions cannot afford to fool themselves that they are defined only by the objects they own, study, and present. Gurian (1999) suggested that although objects form the necessary foundation on which the definition of a museum might rest, they are not sufficient in themselves:

> The foundational definition of museums will, in the long run, I believe, arise not from objects, but from "place" and "storytelling in tangible sensory form," where citizenry can congregate in a spirit of cross–generational inclusivity and inquiry

---

[4]See for example, their website at http://www.cabelas.com.

into the memory of our past, a forum for our present, and aspirations for our future. (p. 181)

As a special place of gathering and sharing, and as a repository of objects that signify what we know about the world, museums provide a forum for the exchange of views, beliefs, joys, and fears, a place where individuals come together to learn, to teach, to create meaning, to find their connections to the world and the people around them. Museums today are challenged to use objects to help us all more clearly see not only the special qualities of objects, but the special qualities of ourselves and our relationships to others — to use objects to increase and strengthen the pathways between ourselves and others and between ourselves and our communities and our landscapes.

REFERENCES

Borun, M., Chambers, M. B., Dritsas, J., & Johnson, J. I. (1997). Enhancing family learning through exhibits. *Curator, 40*(4), 279–295.

Borun, M., & Dritsas, J. (1997). Developing family-friendly exhibits. *Curator, 40*(3), 178–192.

Falk, J. H., & Dierking, L. D. (2000). *Learning from museums: Visitor experiences and the making of meaning.* New York: AltaMira Press.

Glazer, S. (Ed.). (1999). *The heart of learning: Spirituality in education.* New York: Jeremy P. Tarcher/Putnam.

Gurian, E. H. (1999). What is the object of this exercise? A meandering exploration of the many meanings of objects in museums. In *Daedalus: Journal of the American Academy of Arts and Sciences, 128*(3), 163–183.

Hein, G. (1998). *Learning in the museum.* New York: Routledge.

Moll, L. C. (1994). *Vygotsky and education.* New York: Cambridge University Press.

Palmer, P. J. (1999). The grace of great things: Reclaiming the sacred in knowing, teaching, and learning. In S. Glazer (Ed.), *The heart of learning: Spirituality in education* (pp. 15–32). New York: Jeremy P. Tarcher/Putnam.

Reed, R., & Johnson, T. (2000). *Philosophical documents in education.* New York: Longman.

Roberts, L. C. (1997). *From knowledge to narrative: Educators and the changing museum.* Washington, DC: Smithsonian Institution Press.

Silverman, L. H. (1995). Visitor meaning-making in museums for a new age. *Curator, 38*(3), 161–170.

Vogler, C. (1998). *The writer's journey* (2nd ed.). Studio City, CA: Michael Wiese Productions.

Wells, G. (1999). *The dialogic inquiry: Toward a sociocultural practice and theory of education.* Cambridge, UK: Cambridge University Press.

Williams, T. T. (1991). *Refuge: An unnatural history of family and place.* New York: Vintage Books.

Wurman, R. S. (1989). *Information anxiety.* New York: Bantam Books.

CHAPTER SEVENTEEN

Objects of Learning, Objects of Talk: Changing Minds in Museums

Gaea Leinhardt
Kevin Crowley
University of Pittsburgh

In the increasingly fierce competition for leisure time and educational spending, museums are seriously challenged by edutainment, the Internet, CD-ROMs, and 500-channel satellite TV. For example, if a child is interested in dinosaurs, 20 years ago a parent would have been likely to take him or her to the museum to see some fossils. Today, many parents would probably begin by taking the child to the computer to search the World Wide Web, where a quick search reveals thousands of dinosaur web pages.[1] If the family did not find a site among these thousands that satisfied the child's curiosity — or if the family found a great site that whetted the child's appetite for more dinosaur knowledge — the parent might decide to take the child to Barnes and Noble to browse through several shelves of books about dinosaurs and one or two bins of CD-ROMs such as Microsoft "Dinosaurs." On the way home, the family could stop at Blockbuster to pick up one of the National Geographic videos or perhaps even a copy of "Jurassic Park." There is no reason to wait until the weekend to visit a museum to find out about dinosaurs. It is easy to tap instantly into a flood of pictures, video, and text about almost any topic in art, science, or history.

---

[1] In early 1999, a Yahoo.com search on the word "dinosaur" revealed 32,727 web pages; two years later, in early 2001, the same search uncovered more than 224,000. Narrowing down these sites to just those that deal with "fossils" reveals a set of about 31,000 sites; narrowing those down to those that are for "kids" reveals a set of 2,830 sites. By the time this book is published, the number of sites, and probably the usefulness of the best sites, will have increased again.

Why should anyone bother to visit a museum to see the actual artifact when virtual copies are so easy to come by? The current museum research literature does not provide a coherent answer to this question. Many of the recent studies focusing on learning in museums have been conducted in the context of interactive exhibits, mostly in the domain of science and technology (e.g., Allen, 1997; Borun, Chambers, & Cleghorn, 1996; Crowley & Galco, 2001). These studies have correctly focused on the role of interactive hands-on activity, with either an implicit or explicit comparison to the passive learning of didactic instruction. Although this is appropriate for hands-on science centers, it is less useful for artifact- and collections-based institutions, which, after all, exist to collect, to conduct research on, and to display pieces of art, history, and natural history that are far too valuable to put into interactive settings.

Studies conducted in art and natural history museums have often been directed at understanding the effects of signage or other mediation devices on visitor content learning (McManus, 1989). These are valuable studies, but they are not directly related to the question of how artifact-based museums can provide unique educational experiences. For example, one conclusion of such studies is that layered text can be effective at providing appropriate educational context for an artifact (e.g., Blais, 1995). This may be important to maximizing the learning once a visitor is in the museum, but it directs attention away from what is the unique part of the experience: the artifact itself. CD-ROMs or web sites are far more efficient vehicles for layered text or other structures that allow a presentation to adapt to varying levels of domain expertise. If layered text is the important educational element, museums are an inefficient way to present that information, and they do so to a much more limited audience than does a good web site.

So why *should* people bother to visit museums when virtual copies of most objects in museums are so readily available? In the first part of this chapter, we consider four unique characteristics of learning from objects in museums and then trace these characteristics through two examples of visitor learning. The four characteristics are *resolution and density of information, scale, authenticity,* and *value.* The two examples, drawn from our recent museum learning research, are teachers learning to plan field trips to a history center and groups of children interacting with autonomous robots in a children's museum. In the second part of the chapter, we explore the conversations of a pair of visitors engaging with objects in an African art exhibition in order to see how conversation develops around objects.

EVERYDAY LEARNING, MUSEUMS, AND THE ROLE OF OBJECTS

What is it about museums that makes them unique learning environments? Museums are places where the objects and messages have been selected as ones of high cultural value — whether one is referring to a specific art collection, historically salient artifacts, or a collection of bones or scientific findings. Sometimes objects are included in museums because they are unique examples of a category — the oldest, largest, rarest, or most complex of their kind. Sometimes objects are presented for the exact opposite reason — to be common evocations of an interesting or important group, time, or place. Objects are displayed in systems designed to encourage visitors to consider a particular take on a discipline and to encourage reactions such as amazement, mystification, realization, and personal connection.

In his role as a discussant at our Museum Learning symposium at the 2000 American Educational Research Association, Howard Gardner challenged the field of museum learning in general, and those of us in the Museum Learning Collaborative in particular, to document the "genius of the museum" as a unique learning environment. First, consider what is *not* likely to qualify. In contrast to the systematic and extensive presentation of disciplinary argument and evidence in a textbook, museum exhibits are opportunistic and incomplete. The aspects of a topic that are addressed in an exhibit depend on the objects that can be conveniently assembled; in fact, curators often identify objects in the earlier stages of design and then work backwards to connect them to aspects of disciplinary knowledge in the final exhibition (Knutson, 2001). In contrast to the linear arguments that can be built up in textbooks or essays, museum exhibits cannot be based on strong assumptions about what visitors have seen or understood in an exhibition prior to viewing any particular element within it. Visitors choose their own path through exhibitions and, even when they follow what may be the desired flow, they rarely view every element (Serrell, 1997). Similarly, diverse paths through exhibitions make museums much weaker vehicles for narrative than are novels, movies, or television shows. Narrative is sometimes presented in museums (Roberts, 1997), but typically it is narrative in the broader, sociocultural sense, meant to engage visitors in conversation and debate rather than story-telling in the strict dramatic or historical sense (DeBlasio & DeBlasio, 1983). Finally, in contrast to web pages or other media, museums are very slow to update their content in response to innovation and advance. Furthermore, the web and the media can be accessed spontaneously at little or no cost when a learner questions, whereas museum visits are special, premeditated, and relatively expensive events (in terms of time, organization, and money).

From the standpoint of how they best support learning, one might think of objects in museums as collections of examples. Learning, when it is carefully orchestrated in classrooms or when it emerges from spontaneous activity, requires examples. Examples are the evidence that needs to be explained by any acceptable concept or theory. As learners study examples, the examples are unpacked and connected to existing declarative, conceptual, and procedural knowledge (Atkinson, Derry, Renkl, & Wortham, 2001; Leinhardt & Ohlsson, 1990). The essential features of good examples are that they characterize the core structure of an issue or domain and, through their specifics, make the organization and application of domain-specific knowledge more veridical and flexible (Leinhardt, 2001; Young, 2001). Thus, when they are unpacked and connected, they carry the specifics that are most important to the pedagogical or practical goals of the learning situation.

We think of objects in museums as a special case of example-based learning. There are four features of objects that make them unique nodes for ideas and their elaboration.

1. *Resolution and density of information.* Real objects, as opposed to two-dimensional representations of those objects, maintain veridical resolution and density of information. Photographs and drawings can embody many important visual features of an object, but are abstractions for which the photographer and artist decided which characteristics to preserve and which to ignore. A photograph of a complete painting may allow viewers to appreciate composition, but subtle gradation of color and brush-stroke technique are lost. Similarly, the ragged edges of decomposing clothing or fine twists of rope from an unearthed mummy combine in especially vivid ways. Other features available only from objects are those that cannot be photographed — the smell and sound of standing next to an elephant at the zoo, the texture of a leaf at the botanical garden, or the heft of a cast iron colonial stew pot at a history center. Although many of these features could be described completely and perhaps even represented in close approximations of reality, the holistic collection of features for an object cannot be efficiently represented in the absence of the object. For example, a series of pictures from different zoom levels might be able to address issues of both brush stroke and composition in the same painting, but the viewer sees these as separate abstract presentations rather than a smooth perceptual zoom as he or she moves from standing yards away to standing inches away from a painting.

2. *Scale.* In contrast to pictures, drawings, and photographs in which scale either is absent (it is the size of the book page) or requires a mathematical transformation (for example, a person standing next to a dinosaur bone), objects in a museum are in their actual scale. In many cases the smallness or largeness of the object is precisely the characteristic most worth noting. Clearly, being dwarfed by the hulking skeleton of a diplodocus is a powerful moment in the life of many children. Likewise, for adults, examining a recovered space capsule may often lead to stark realizations of how small and seemingly unprotected the cockpit is. In a culture awash with sport utility vehicles and minivans, most of us would feel vulnerable and naked driving to the store in a vehicle of that size, let alone orbiting the earth, re-entering the atmosphere, and splashing down into the Pacific Ocean in it.

3. *Authenticity.* Our third construct, authenticity, exists only in the interaction between specific objects and our history and culture. Thus, Napoleon's

campaign bed is authentic because we believe it is actually the bed that he slept in, and we know that to be the case because someone who we call an expert said it is. The response to this authenticity is that the visitor stands right next to, and in some sense shares, the object with Napoleon. In the Henry Ford museum, this concept expands out to the underlying belief system of Henry Ford himself, which was that objects have auras that are tangibly communicable. Although fewer people today share Ford's faith in psychic mechanism, we think many would acknowledge that there is a moment of awe and a sense of historical connection when we stand next to objects connected to venerated or loathed individuals and events. We think many might also acknowledge the same sense of a personal connection with everyday objects of extreme age in museums — perhaps while looking at the scores and indentations on an arrowhead and imagining vividly the moment when an ancient hunter carefully chipped it out of flint, or looking at the worn, uneven threads of homespun garments, or perhaps thinking about how many dinosaurs were ripped up and wolfed down through the jaws of a fossilized T-Rex.

4. *Value.* It is often the case that authentic objects of cultural import are also valuable, but it is not always the case that valuable objects are authentic as we have defined it. By value, we refer to an object's uniqueness and, in many cases, its monetary value. Because generally we do not have in our possession objects that have value in terms of the larger culture, being in the actual room with the crown jewels invites us to imagine being the owner or possessor. Similarly, a recent exhibit on aluminum at the Carnegie Museum of Art included an aluminum car — the Plymouth Prowler. Although the car is somewhat expensive and exotic, it is certainly not culturally or historically valuable. Yet it was one of the more popular elements of the exhibit, perhaps in part because most visitors would like to drive around in it but will never get the chance.

We now consider how these dimensions play out in two examples of learning from objects in museums. Each of these examples is drawn from the ongoing work of the Museum Learning Collaborative. Funded by a consortium of federal agencies, the Museum Learning Collaborative (MLC) is exploring the role of conversation as a process and outcome of museum learning. Elsewhere, we elaborate on aspects of conversation that serve to parse, connect, and explain aspects of the museum visit (Leinhardt, Crowley, & Knutson, in press). Like many other museum learning researchers who have explored connections between museums and everyday or classroom learning (Borun, Chambers, & Cleghorn, 1996; Falk & Dierking, 2000; Gelman, Massey, & McManus, 1991; Gleason & Schauble, 1999; Paris, Troop, Henderlong, & Sulfaro, 1994), our approach sometimes led us to focus on what makes museums similar to other learning environments. One of us (Crowley) has even gone so far as to term museum learning "mundane," arguing that, although some real insights and breakthroughs may occur in museums, the most common kind of family learning and the one that museums should design for is more related to families practicing habits of scientific literacy such as explanation and hypothesis generation (Crowley & Galco, 2001). Although comparing museum learning to everyday or classroom learning may help us understand some aspects of the learning that occurs in museums — especially in interactive science and children's museums — such comparisons do not account for all the learning experiences in museums, nor do they allow us to characterize the specific genius of museums as sites for learning. We suspect the genius of the museum exists somewhere in an analysis of how unique and powerful objects support learning. In the Museum Learning Collaborative we think that that support is in the form of conversations (Leinhardt & Crowley, 1998; Schauble, Leinhardt, & Martin, 1998), conversations that get elaborated as small clusters of individuals engage with objects.

Burning Bus

We start with an example of a powerful object located in a history museum, the Birmingham Civil Rights Institute (BCRI) in Birmingham, Alabama. According to the museum's web site (http://bcri.bham.al.us), the purpose of the Institute is to document the events and display objects from the Civil Rights Struggle:

> The Institute's historic galleries trace the footsteps of those brave men and women. The journey moves from the era of segregation to the birth of the Civil Rights Movement and the worldwide struggle for civil and human rights. Along the way, exciting multimedia exhibitions depict dramatic events that took place in Birmingham and other cities, events that stirred the conscience of a nation and influenced the course of an international human rights struggle.

The museum is located across the street from the 16th Street Baptist Church, which was bombed during the struggle resulting in the deaths of four young girls. Inside, the museum sets the stage for the visitor who moves through a fairly prescribed set of displays, from early Jim Crow laws exemplified by a shop with various signs through Martin Luther King's jail cell and the march on Washington. There are several major sections that the visitor moves through after an introductory film: Barriers, Confrontation, the Movement, Procession, Milestones, Human Rights. Photographs, sound, and lighting all contribute to a sense of the visitor being there as opposed to just looking at objects and images. One of the most prominent features in the Movement Gallery is a burned-out bus. The bus is a very precise replica of the Greyhound bus that had been bombed and burned.

Consider the bus in relationship to our object features. The most prominent of the features is scale. The bus is life-sized; one walks around it, feels small next to it, and feels enormously vulnerable when realizing that, even with its enormous size, it was not big or strong enough to protect the riders. The density and detail of information, from the charred sides and interior to the shiny chrome of the areas not touched by flame, are both realistic and evocative: Here is where the fire spread; these seats, like those I might have been sitting in, were completely burned . . . those less so. These are personal evocations prompted by the scale of the bus and the density of information; that is, the association is dependent primarily on the relationship between the individual's historical experiences and the object. Both the constructs of value and authenticity, because they are social constructs, are more complex to determine. The bus is an actual Greyhound bus, so it is authentic in that sense, but it is not THE bus that carried the freedom riders and was bombed and torched. The value is in part that the museum got a real bus, but the value resides more in that visitors are prompted to consider their own experiences with buses and the assumptions of safety and protection we usually make while in a bus.

Our example of the burned-out bus is drawn from a study in which 50 pre-service teachers went to the BCRI as part of a social studies unit in their normal training program (Gregg & Leinhardt, 2001; Leinhardt & Gregg, in press). The student teachers had conversations in small groups before the visit and again after the visit. They drew semantic nets of their personal concepts about the Civil Rights Era before and after the visit, and they designed activities centered on the BRCI for their students. These young people had an average age of 22 and none of them was alive during the civil rights struggle or the Vietnam war. As local residents of Alabama, they had heard about the period but tended to view it as a part of the past or as an intensely personal struggle. Regardless of their own ethnic background, they tended to believe that the conflicts and struggles associated with the time were between African Americans and European Americans.

Before the visit to the BCRI, not one single student, when talking in their small groups, mentioned the Freedom Riders, the attack on the bus, or the biracial nature of the group of Freedom Riders. Nor did they talk about them when discussing what they might see at the BCRI or what might be emphasized. Only two student teachers included Freedom Riders or the bus in their webs of ideas before the visit. *After* the visit, all but one of the groups mentioned the bus, and for the majority of the groups, it was the first thing they talked about and they returned to it often. At the individual web level, the message is the same: Two of the 50 students mentioned either the bus or the Freedom Riders in their previsit webs whereas afterwards all but eight did. Furthermore, many of the preservice teachers frequently mentioned in their postvisit webs the fact that the Freedom Riders were both Black and White.

The object of the bus, with its vivid destruction and all that that implied, served to anchor the other historical information about the civil rights workers, their ethnic make-up, their physical route from Washington to New Orleans, and their abrupt ending in Birmingham. The small-group discussions do not have elaborate examinations of the bus and its meaning, but the conversations reflect our basic assertions of why objects are memorable and significant locations for mediating the "important part" of the story.

Here is the voice of authenticity:

> — *I was surprised at the actual bus.*
> — *Yeah*
> — *Was that the ACTUAL bus? I mean, I don't know.*
> — *Yes, it was!*
> — *It was? OK. Well it didn't say that it was, but it looked, like, like what I was reading,*
> — *I'm only ... it was*
> — *OK. And that glass (from the broken windows)*
> — *Yes. Yeah I was surprised to see that ...*

According the BCRI web site, this was not the actual bus but a Greyhound bus similar to it. Even though this group had a misconception about the authenticity, it is noteworthy that they had a bit of questioning and followed that up with a check from text. The main point here is that the vividness and strength of the impression was extended because they believed that to have been the real bus.

Here is the voice of detail or resolution from two other groups also discussing the bus:

> — *The bus, that bus. It was symbolic to see that stuff on the bus ...*
> — *The Freedom Riders*
> — *Yeah, where they busted the windows and all that. And you hear stories about that kind of stuff but when you see it, it makes it more real.*

[Later in the discussion]

> — *I don't think I knew anything about the Freedom Riders. I don't think I did. I'd heard about the March to Montgomery and the speeches and the segregated water fountains and ... but I didn't know anything about the Freedom Riders.*
> — *Most of it, I had a feeling that I kind of heard about almost all of it but it was like a real surface knowledge about it. So, I guess the new stuff for me was the in depth ...*

A second group has a slightly different take on the issue of resolution or detail:

> — *The bus. The bus*
> — *Freedom ...*

— *Yeah the Freedom Rider's bus. That scared the crud out of me.*

— *I felt like someone was going to jump out and attack me!*

— *Everything was realistic. It looked just like I would have thought it. I was surprised but it's like, I would have thought it to be like that—*

— *UmHum*

— *Something like a burnt out bus.*

In this last section, the detail and authenticity merge with the very first idea in the previous quotation; the bus is iconic and symbolic, "something like a burnt out bus." This third group of preservice teachers went on to mention four more times that they did not really know about the Freedom Riders, they did not know that there were White people involved, and they did not know that White people had been hurt or arrested. As they said later on, "I did not know how many White people stuck up for the Black people ..." The bus was the transport for that idea. The idea that both groups participated is very powerful. For this set of young prospective teachers, the comfortable cover that "it was how they were raised" (therefore they could not be expected to have behaved differently in the face of injustice) had been lifted by the presence of a few remembered White people on a bombed-out bus. If those people had worked to help right a wrong, why not others? The authenticity and explicitness of the bus carries that concept home:

— *The bus was ... I mean, I knew a little about what that was but to actually see that and to read more about it. And didn't realize that there was so much violence that went on, you know the ride. When they were traveling.*

— *I learned how brave people really were and now, I thought about, if this was happening today, would I be as brave as those people were to do the sit-ins, to do the um, you know the bus boycotts, do all those things where they were in risk of their lives every day. I mean, there was just ... Hard to see how I would do it now.*

Why is the burned bus such a powerful object in the BCRI? We think there are several reasons. Buses are iconic. We can all conjure a mental picture of a bus in our mind, and most of us even today can imagine a silvery, sleek Greyhound bus. "Busness" is a construct, it is totally ordinary, we almost all see many every day. We can imagine ourselves climbing the steep steps, walking back toward an empty seat, settling in for a long or short ride. What we cannot imagine is our bus being blown apart by a bomb. Seeing the results of that shatters the safe, solid image, and it is that precise conflict that makes the bus so valuable.

We can consider what changed for the student teachers with respect to the bus. From a cognitive point of view, we can assume that all of the preservice teachers had a mental construct of bus, even a construct of a Greyhound bus (as distinct from city buses). We know that they had a concept of the Civil

Rights Era. However, the Civil Rights Era concept was less vivid, less real, and less specific than what we believe the concept of the original bus was. What happened was that a new concept with a vivid image developed — the concept of a bombed and burned bus. The bus concept became connected in a very powerful way to the original bus construct and to the concept of the Civil Rights Era. The object and its icon became a bridge between two abstractions. We believe that for some time into the future, thoughts about the Civil Rights Era will evoke a particular image of a particular bus and everyday thoughts about buses will be haunted by a particular bus in the BCRI and its evoked history.

That is our cognitive tale of the bus. Socioculturally, what do we think took place? This is more complex. A group of European American and African American preservice teachers connected in quite different ways to their own historical past. The museum offered an affordance for its visitors to connect to the everydayness and the uniqueness of a bus. The impersonal historical record that had vacuous labels — such as struggle, injustice, prejudice — was enlivened by the appropriation of the meaning of an object. As a group, the preservice teachers had seen, shared, and thought of ways to make active use of a particular object in the activities and practices of teaching that they were all trying to develop. For many of us, the Civil Rights Era is in our personal historical memory; for these students, it is not. We think that, for these students, the bus and what it symbolized altered their sense of identity. The bus provided a shared evocation of details that could be discussed in concrete terms, and it connected the group members to the question: If I were there, then what would I have done? European American students had, prior to this experience, excused themselves as being the products of their families — but the riders of the bus were also products of their families, yet they stepped out of their historical contexts; for African American students, the assumption that they would have been in the struggle, too, may have been shaken because the realism of the violence and the loss of life and injury became more palpable.

When the Object is "Alive": Autonomous Robot Playmates in a Children's Museum

Our second example is drawn from observations and interviews with groups of children and adults interacting with two prototype autonomous robots at the Pittsburgh Children's Museum. The idea for the prototypes was to program the robots to act like ducklings who attempt to engage children in a game of "follow-the-leader." The robots used sonar to detect objects in front of them and were programmed to back away from targets coming close to them and to follow targets that were moving away from them. When the robots detected no targets in front of them, they were programmed to move forward rapidly until they found another object. Only the front three sonar units were active on the prototypes, which meant that the visitor needed to be directly in front of the robot in order to be noticed. Because of the robots' relatively narrow "visual field," visitors had to move slowly to get the robots to track them. Mounted to the top of the robots were two speakers that produced quacks — specific kinds of quacks were associated with specific actions on the part of the robot.

From the moment they came rolling and quacking onto the museum floor, children and adults were fascinated by the robots. At one point, a large school group had moved upstairs, leaving the first floor mostly empty except for the robots and the adults involved in prototyping them. It took us a little while to notice that, although the kids had all moved up to the second floor, they remained fixated on the robots, pressing their faces against the windows in the second floor railing. It is unusual, especially in a place that is as interesting as a children's museum, to see such sustained focus on a particular object.

We think a great deal of this interest in the robots relates to the dimension of authenticity and value. It might at first seem strange to the reader to think of robots pretending to be ducks as authentic. However, although robots have long been a part of popular culture, it is likely that these were the first real autonomous robots that the children had ever met. Thus, although children may think they are very well acquainted with robots and their abilities, they are at the same time almost completely without relevant authentic experience when they approach real robots for the first time.

The role of this extensive yet impoverished knowledge was made clear in an age-related difference we noted in how children related to the robots. Toddlers and preschoolers were more likely than elementary school children to spontaneously touch the robot. One boy, who appeared to have just mastered walking, toddled straight up to one of the robots and, without hesitation, grabbed onto it. The robot, programmed to avoid obstacles, tried to back away, but found its path blocked by an exhibit. Trapped between the exhibit and the child, the robot tried a series of small turns and forward lunges, looking for an opening to resume its wandering and get back to playing follow-the-leader. But the child, oblivious to the robot's predicament, began playfully pushing against it and touching a lot of the hardware. At one point he almost switched it off, prompting an adult nearby to tell him not to press that button or the robot would go to sleep. This boy, like other young children we observed, was applying the standard children's museum script to the robots: Run up to an exhibit, press and pull whatever is there, and wait to see what happens. The younger children appeared to encode the robot as just another machine — a vacuum cleaner or a remote control toy.

This reaction of the young children was in stark contrast to the way the school-aged children reacted to the robots. The older children acted much more like children do when they approach strange dogs on the street or when they approach sheep or goats at petting zoos. Older children approached the robot warily, moved their arms and legs slowly, and constantly looked up at the nearby adults for confirmation that they were doing OK. Even after they began playing follow-the-leader, most of the older children appeared to hold their bodies and faces more rigidly than normal. These older children appeared to us to be a little nervous and unsure, but intensely excited. The older children knew enough about robots to recognize that they were looking at one and that it really did appear, at least in some sense, to be alive.

Once the feature of authenticity is established, the features of scale and resolution and density of information become important to the kinds of learning that could be supported by the object. Sometimes this learning was accurate. As a fictional technology, robots are often portrayed as having quasihumanoid form and often are human-sized or larger. The prototype robots were cylinders about two feet high with a lap-top computer and speakers on top. One girl at first was not sure she was really looking at robots, telling us: "Robots usually have hands and arms. I didn't think they would be this small."

Other times, the interaction of familiarity with resolution and density of information had unintended consequences. In an interview with us, a boy repeatedly talked about how the robot had an eye and could see him. Despite our assurances that the robot does not have eyes and navigates through use of sonar, the boy insisted he was right. He finally got fed up with us and marched over to the robot, pointing at a red LED that was the power indicator on one of the speakers: "See? Here's his eye." Another pair of children told us that the robot had been talking to them, telling them to "Wait, wait, wait." In fact, all the robots could say was "quack, quack, quack," but these children had interpreted "quack" as "wait," perhaps because they assumed the robot spoke English and perhaps because the robots kept falling behind the leader. In both cases, children might be portrayed as looking to the object to find evidence to support assumptions based on their familiarity with fictional as opposed to actual robots.

The way in which resolution of information was most important was in children learning that robots can be much less competent that humans at seemingly simple tasks. Fictional robots are often depicted as having abilities that equal or surpass humans. However, experience with the real robots quickly dispelled at least part of this notion. The natural way to play follow-the-leader would be for the child to walk forward facing away from the robot. However, because the prototypes could only track a visitor who moved slowly and stayed within the relatively narrow area covered by sonar, the main activity that emerged for children was to learn how to shape their behavior so that the robot could track them.

The most successful children either kept looking over their shoulder or learned that it worked better if they walked backwards, facing the robot. In addition to letting the child monitor the robot's progress, walking backwards had the added advantage of naturally slowing the child's movement and thus making it easier for the robot to track him or her. Other children discovered that it was much easier to control the robot if they walked toward it and had it back away from them. Pushing the robots was easier because the robots seemed to have a slower back-up speed, because it was easier for the child to monitor them, and because children naturally slowed down their walking so that they would not bump into the robots. Even so, the robots often got confused in the small, busy spaces of the museum. The fragile abilities of the robots to do something as simple as follow-the-leader led some children to tell us that they did not think these robots were very smart. One boy said, "It's like a little kid! It doesn't know how to play [the game]."

Reflections on Burning Buses and Quacking Robots

How did interaction with the robots change children's understanding? Probably, the most important change was in calling the certainty of their understanding into question. As most of their prior knowledge about robots was probably derived from fiction, the modest appearance and severe behavioral limitations of real robots may have led to restricting certain aspects of the category that may have once been widely applied. For example, many children learned quickly that robot behavior was rigid and fragile, and that somewhat unnatural and exaggerated human behavior was needed for the robots to succeed in playing follow-the-leader. Any prior assumption about human-like abilities in children's understanding of the category "robots" was most likely challenged and pruned by these interactions with authentic robots. Children also learned that robots could be two feet tall and could act like ducks — we subsequently interviewed children who have not seen the robot about this idea and most find it initially to be preposterous. Thus, for the first time, many of the children had some hard specifics that they then needed to account for in their broader knowledge of robots.

How did the object of the burned bus change the student teachers' understanding? In contrast to the case of the robots, the learners were very familiar with authentic examples of buses. They were also familiar with many elements of the history of civil rights in America. The encounter with the bus at the BCRI served to drastically alter the original concept of "bus" and to reify the "struggle" portion of the civil rights struggle. The vividness of the bus lay in features of scale and detail. Its power to change understanding rested with the ways in which clusters of student teachers used it to mediate their own concepts of the civil rights era and everyday bus travel. Thus, in this case, the object served to elaborate and instantiate familiar ideas as well as to connect two fairly distant and previously unassociated ideas.

In the first part of the chapter we characterized museums as places where systems of objects exist that support learning conversations, and identified four features — resolution and density of information, scale, authenticity, and value — that make objects unique. These features draw visitors to the object and press the object into the experiential repertoire of the group. Thus, talk can refer to a simple label for the object, but it can also contain a considerable amount of descriptive detail, which in turn can lead to speculative explanations. This allows different members of a group to respond to different specific features of the object. We argued that objects are best thought of as examples that create nodes around which existing knowledge can be restructured and into which new knowledge can be integrated.

Although we referred to these four properties as belonging to objects in museums, it is important to note that none of these exists independently of the visitors. This is most clearly true of the last two properties, authenticity and value. Each of these exists only in the interaction between the object and the culturally specific identity and knowledge of the visitor. The first two of these dimensions — resolution and density of information and scale — might at first appear to be "objective" properties of objects. After all, regardless of who is looking at a dinosaur skeleton, the bones will look big and will have certain kinds of textures and colors. Yet it is important to note that not all visitors experience even objective properties in the same way, and, even if experiences were roughly equivalent, the learning will not necessarily be the same.

In other words, objects do not speak for themselves. Particularly in the case of children, parents and teachers are the ones who need to speak for the objects. It is precisely the features that make objects most powerful that children have the most trouble with, because in many cases they do not have the requisite prior knowledge to make sense of the example. Thus, parents and educators in informal learning environments are challenged by the problem of mediation. It is interesting to note that, for the student teachers visiting the BCRI, the need to mediate for children was a driving force in their learning. Their task was to use the visit to plan activities for students, and a challenge that drove much of the learning and conversation was around issues of how to highlight, intensify, and, in some cases, defuse the power of museum objects.

In our examples of learning from objects, all of our visitors knew about the objects that they saw. The teachers knew about buses and about civil rights and the children knew about robots. What happened in the mediated encounter with the objects was that the objects grew into nodes of social value and salience with specific detailed features. The examples became enriched, attached, meaningful, and focused. This kind of learning is not unique to museums; as we mentioned at the beginning of this chapter, television, web pages, and books can also support the transformation of a vague concept into an anchor point for learning. However, we believe that the museum is unique in its capacity to provide situations in which those nodes (powerful object-based examples) that can and will be usefully extended will be found.

LEARNING CONVERSATIONS OVER TIME

So far in this chapter, we have not acknowledged the tension that exists between the Museum Learning Collaborative's vision of learning as the accumulation and enrichment of the mundane and the implied assumption of Gardner's remarks in searching for the genius of the museum — that learning is an act of sparkling insight. The deep consideration of objects — the topic of this volume — has forced us to try to resolve these differences. We take as our analog *punctuated equilibrium* from evolutionary biology. Punctuated equilibrium is the resolution in evolutionary theory between the pure, slow, natural selection explanation of evolution, and the cataclysmic, sudden, environmental shift view that imagines steady states with moments of rapid change. Punctuated equilibrium accommodates both the gradualist, cumulative, elaborative view and the sudden, insightful, unique view. We believe that museums are places where the unique object — bus or robot, for example — can have a powerful impact; but we also believe that the thousands of other objects present in the BCRI or the Pittsburgh Children's Museum, which were perhaps less noticed but helped to set the total stage for learning, were also significant.

We consider learning, in the MLC context, as *conversational elaboration* (Leinhardt & Crowley, 1998; Leinhardt, Crowley, & Knutson, in press). By conversational elaboration we mean that visiting groups to a particular museum exhibit may have a set of experiences that enable them to discuss the thematic and object-based content of the exhibit in more complete, analytic, synthetic, and explanatory ways than they were able to do before or without the visit. This means that the conversations are elaborated in two ways: First, the structural form of the conversation can move from list-like identification or labeling to analytically engaged or explanatory; second, the conversations move from almost aimless exclamations to thematically connected ideas. The idea here is that one of the benefits of going to a museum is that one can share that visit experience with friends in real time and in a later recounting and that it is the details of those conversations that are both the processes of learning and one outcome of it.

Is conversational elaboration the only outcome of museum visits? No. But it is one. And we would argue that it is a valued and valuable one. We use our capacity for discourse in many ways: to manage our time and plan, to give directives and orders, to gain simple information, and to have conversations whose goal is social cohesion and appreciative sharing. White (1995) suggested that this latter conversational aspect of our lives is of considerable interest and relatively rare. In the context of the MLC, we focused on this particular type of discourse as an area where visiting a museum might have a positive discernable impact.

If conversational elaboration is something that occurs as a result of a visit to a museum, then when exactly does that take place? Does it occur as a kind of summation? Or does it accrue gradually throughout the course of a visit and continue to grow even after the visit has ended? If conversational elaboration does develop, then how does it develop? The purpose of the second part of this chapter is to examine one group's visit to a museum exhibition in a manner that helps us to actually see the growth of conversational detail and specificity over a short period of time and to help trace the moment-to-moment alterations in the conversations in a manner that permits us to speculate how conversation develops.

The pair of adults we focus on represents part of what we refer to as a coherent group — they are familiar with each other and have a pattern of interaction that stems from prior experiences together. They also have a particular task, to make sense of and to share in the experience of the visit to this particular exhibition. For each visit, they must renegotiate the terrain. Because the purpose and layout of each exhibit is unique, a vocabulary for referring to objects, describing them, and evaluating them and their display must be developed. The visitors need to establish a pacing of their tour as well as a path through it. They need to orient themselves with respect to each other and the content: What is familiar, what is foreign? Do they "like it?" Do they "get it?"

As the visit progresses, the work of orientation and stance is established and the visitors find themselves freer to discuss the particulars of the material and to perhaps engage with the subtleties of the curatorial premises: Why is this object here and not there? Why do the labels give this information and not that? What exactly is the "message?" Occasionally they may take a moment to renegotiate the path or anticipated duration of the visit, but mostly they engage with each other and with the objects in the museum. As the visit ends, they return to the management of the visit itself — where they will go next, establishing the time, general way-finding behaviors through time and place.

The Setting and the Methodology

Our particular example of a visit takes place at the Carnegie Museum of Art (CMA) in Pittsburgh, Pennsylvania. The CMA is located in a cluster of buildings all donated by one of the patrons of the city, Andrew Carnegie — the Carnegie Library, the Carnegie Music Hall, the Carnegie Museum of Natural History. All of these buildings are interconnected and are in sight of Carnegie Mellon University. The CMA is the most recent addition to the cluster, fashioned in the modernist tradition of wide low stairs, abstract fountains, and slabs of glass; it fits and contrasts well with the neoclassical style of the adjoining buildings.

Inside the building there is a flight of deep, low, flat stairs. It is said that the stairs were deliberately designed to make fluid automatic movement up them impossible; the visitor cannot stride up on alternating legs but must pause either every step or every other to insert an extra step. This feature is designed to force the visitor to slow down and look around. At the top of the stairs, a small landing area divides the permanent collection (to the left) from the temporary and visiting exhibits (to the right).

The *Soul of Africa* exhibition was showing at the CMA during the summer of 1999. The exhibit represents 10% of the 2,000-piece Swiss collection of Han Coray. Coray did not himself visit Africa. He developed his collection between 1916 and 1928 because of his interest in and devotion to the particular artistic features of African art. In particular, he admired the abstract and primitive feel of the material, which stood in contrast to the prevailing European artistic milieu. The exhibition consisted of 200 pieces of 19th- and 20th-century art: masks, sculpture, ritual furniture, jewelry, textiles, and musical instruments. The exhibition was organized around the curatorial themes of Art and Leadership, Rank and Prestige, Life Transitions, Supernatural World, Remembering the Dead, and Music. The objects themselves were placed in a decidedly artistic stance with wall colors and mountings designed to emphasize the aesthetic aspects of the pieces (Stainton, in press).

The exhibition was not "easy." Those formally trained in art could quickly see the similarities of line, form, and distillation that connect with modern art sensibilities and that pervade the collection, whereas the less trained might tend to see an anthropological exhibition displaced into an art venue (see Stainton, in press, for an elaboration of this idea). Aesthetics were less easily captured than was a sense of craft and accomplishment, and throughout there was the tension between modern and primitive — the former encompassing simplicity by choice, the latter encompassing simplicity by circumstance. The visitors could, if they chose, float through the exhibition with their own preconceived notions intact or they could engage and be challenged by what they saw. What we address here is how the engagement evolved and was reflected (or not) in the conversations.

The data are taken from a larger series of studies designed to validate the instrumentation and theory of the MLC (Leinhardt & Crowley, 1998). The specific data come from a sample of 12 groups of visitors to the *Soul of Africa* art exhibit. Camilla and Harold (pseudonyms) from Las Vegas, the group we focus on here, had come to the museum as a part of seeing the sights of Pittsburgh, not particularly to see the African art exhibition. Their interactive style was extremely pleasant and cordial. Camilla visited museums quite frequently and evidently saw it as what one did when visiting a new place. Harold did not go to museums often and had what might be described as a bemused tolerance for the activity.

Before touring the exhibition, Camilla and Harold were wired with light-weight portable microphones. They were instructed to visit the exhibit as they naturally might and informed that the researchers would be noting where they were in the exhibit hall. As they toured, the researcher marked their stops on a map and noted phrases from the current conversation to help us later synchronize the stop with the on-going audio recording.

The tape was partitioned based on a combination of location and talk. A segment consisted of a coherent set of talk about a particular object or grouping at a particular place. The total number of segments for the visit was grouped into five equally sized (in terms of number of segments) chunks. The five chunks were viewed as five phases of the visit. The chunks varied with respect to the amount of time and the actual amount of talk that took place within them; only the number of segmented "stops" stayed relatively constant. There was nothing magical about the division into fifths beyond the fact that it allowed us to view the first chunk as settling down and orienting, the second through fourth chunks as the main substance of the visit, and the last chunk as the process of disengagement and exiting. Thus, by contrasting the *second* and *fourth* chunks, we can see a bit of how the conversation evolved over the course of the visit.

Each segment was coded in terms of the structural and thematic features of the talk. The structural features of the segment included listing or identifying, synthesizing in a personal manner, synthesizing in an object manner, analyzing, and explaining. The thematic features of the talk, reflecting themes of the exhibit, were function, craft, beauty, and social meaning. We viewed analyzing and explaining as more complex than listing or synthesizing, and we considered discussions of beauty and social meaning as more challenging than discussions of function and craft. Each segment was coded for one and only one structural feature and for as many thematic features, if any, as were mentioned. Examples of the coding follow.

List:
   — *Hmm, used for hunting*
   — *huh?*
   — *It's a hunting whistle*
   — *Ok*   *(function)*

Synthesis:
   — *Storage boxes*
   — *Cosmetic boxes, like what they use today 'cept they're different shapes, they have something like what you guys use now*
   — *Elaborate*   *(function)*

Analysis:
   — *gosh, look! I love the way these figures have their hands positioned under their chins*
   — *Look at that one, it looks like, let's see if there is a reason they're called bow figures*
   — *Those have their hands right here on their stomach*   *(beauty)*

Explanation:
- *— Anthropomorphic cups*
- *— Drinking cups*
- *— For Palm wine*
- *— Because it, well the more elaborate your cup is the higher you were in the ranking in the tribe, the more important you were*
- *— Oh there is a double cup there. I guess you get this when you get married and drink stuff*
- *— Or where they had a ceremony, maybe they were going to share*
- *— Share drinks?*
- *— You had to share with someone*   *(social meaning)*

Analysis and Results

In order to give the overall feeling for how Camilla and Harold's visit evolved, we give a brief numerical description. Second, to get a sense of the developing and social nature of the visit, we describe the overall visit in terms of the gradual evolution of explanations.

Harold and Camilla had 42 segments overall and 9 segments in their second chunk, which comprised 77 lines of dialogue, as shown in Table 17.1. Three of the segments in the second chunk were list-like, comprising 13% of the lines of talk; one segment included synthesis between objects, comprising 6% of the lines of talk; three segments were analytic, comprising 43% of the lines of talk; and two of the segments were explanatory, representing 35% of the talk. Thus we see in the early part of the visit that this couple devoted almost 80% of their talk to analyzing and explaining a few objects. Over the nine segments, Harold and Camilla discussed functional features on six occasions, craft aspects twice, and issues of beauty and social meaning once each.

In the fourth chunk of the data, Camilla and Harold had 102 lines of dialogue and 8 segments. None of the segments were lists. One segment was an object-based synthesis comprising 8% of the dialogue lines. Four segments were analytic and comprised 33% of the dialogue lines. Three of the segments were explanatory and comprised 61% of the dialogue lines. Thus, explanatory

TABLE 17.1
Harold and Camilla, Analysis of Conversational Structure

	Chunk 2		Chunk 4	
	Segments (9)	% Lines (77)	Segments (8)	% Lines (102)
List	3	13	0	0
Synthesis	1	6	1	8
Analysis	3	43	4	33
Explanation	2	35	3	61

discourse went from 33% to 61% of the discussion space while list-like behavior dropped out completely. With respect to the thematic aspects of the
talk, two segments dealt with craft, two with function, and three with social
meaning. When we consider the combination of structural and thematic features together, we can see that not only did the structure move from list to
explanation, but also thematic discourse moved from functional descriptions
to explanations of social meaning concerning the objects.

Another way of tracing how the visit evolved is to examine one kind of discourse, explanation, over the entire visit. Explanations can be offered about
the content of a display, the meaning of the display, or the intention of the dis-
player or curator. But to explain something requires both asking and answering a query (Leinhardt, 2001).

Harold and Camilla engaged in nine explanations. Their first explanatory
segment occurred in the first chunk. It dealt with a functional theme and emphasized the composition and purpose of the "neck collars." Interestingly,
Harold saw the collars as both old-fashioned "back then" and as unique to the
African contexts. In contrast, Camilla immediately connected the collars to
men's necklaces, which are still in use in the United States. The second explanation occurred just two segments later when Harold tried to figure out "How
does this tie in?" to the other objects they were looking at. He and Camilla
were confused and puzzled by the relationship of groups to the dead — they
wondered, do the living take care of the dead by doing the necessary cere-
monies and gifts or do the dead take care of the living by watching over them?
They understood the idea that the dead in some sense were to be appeased,
but they were confused by the statuary for baptism of the dead. Again it was
Camilla who clarified the two positions although she did not resolve them:

> But they expect the living to be in a position to take care of the dead or if they
> have not [they have] made that decision. But they have, there is also a belief
> that they are allowing the ancestors to control what's going on in present day
> life among the living. Cause the ancestors would, could be [ruffled]. They con-
> sidered them spirits which could punish, if something were going wrong.…
> Whereas the religious practice you're talking about is baptism of the dead.
> The other is more to insure their salvation. Not a control of…

In the next explanation, a part of Chunk 2, Camilla introduced the ambigu-
ity once more. They were examining a variety of cups and noticed one was
double — two distinct cups in the shape of back-to-back heads, joined at the
neck. They discussed the social rank implied by the carving on the cups and
then discussed why it would be a double cup. The explanation focused on
both function and social meaning. Harold suggested it was a marriage cup —
similar to our own customs — while Camilla noticed that it might just be for
sharing in a ceremony of social significance not necessarily marriage.

But it was two explanations later where Camilla and Harold engaged most
deeply. They had come to "Nailman," a wooden figure of a man studded all

over with large iron nails — it was a show-stopper of an object for most visitors. In their discussion, it was Camilla who jumped to the conclusion that the figure was a voodoo doll, used to harm or curse others. Harold questioned whether that was really the case. They both then read the label copy. They discovered that "it's not voodoo dolls, it's different . . . because the reason for it was different. Like if you take some type of secret oath. I guess for contracts, legal decisions. I think it used . . ." Camilla concurred but noticed that there is implied power in the nails and the act of nailing. Thus the nails could heal or exact revenge if the contract were broken. Therefore the nailman might be, in Camilla's logic, a forerunner of the concept of voodoo dolls. She continued her reflection of forerunner by saying, "[S]ome practices were brought down from generation to generation. And they just changed, their *use* has changed."

Harold and Camilla have found a device to support engagement. The device originally was "them versus us" (as with the neck collar), but with the Nailman exploration, they shift and discuss "then versus now." Although the exhibition is in fact quite modern (20th century) and the objects themselves not particularly old, this couple focused on time rather than cultural differences to act as a lens for interpretation. The advantage of their approach was that they could constantly construct a problem space of finding where a concept or artifact played itself out in present societies. Harold and Camilla made four further explanations of objects in the exhibition. All but one dealt with the thematic idea of social meanings.

Harold took the lead in one of these explanations, where he was trying to understand initiations for young men. He started by saying, "Secret societies. Good old forerunners of the Elks! . . . I'm not going there, but once again what you are seeing, you had all these different tribes that had a certain procedure they used for guiding the young boys to manhood. . . . All of them had a way of teaching boys how to become men." From there, Camilla connected these rituals to those of the American Indian and then circled back to comment on the lack of such guidance and training in the modern context of America. Both Camilla and Harold pressed to interpret the particular cultural constants that link the alien objects to their own American experiences. What they avoided, however, was any deep engagement in the aesthetics of the exhibit. They noted when things were pretty or skillfully carved or delicate or glittery, but they never commented on the artistry or form of objects — the lines, scale distortions, and mixed media that so captivated the artists of the early 20th century remained invisible to or unnoted by this couple.

CONCLUSIONS

We began this chapter by wondering why people should continue to come to museums and with a concern about the relative emphasis on the unique or the mundane as the best lens for research on museum learning. We have presented two conceptual frames to help us consider these issues. The first proposed four features of objects that make them unique and powerful kinds of examples. The second proposed a particular way of examining conversation as a mediating process for learning. Visitors come to expand on what they already know and to experience what they have only imagined, and to see beyond the mundane to the unique. Just as they can come for multiple reasons, visitors can learn in multiple ways. As we saw with the preservice teachers at the BCRI, the encounter with the bus challenged them to reconsider their understanding of the Civil Rights Era by attaching to a mundane concept (a bus) a vivid distortion (burned). As we saw in the case of children at the Pittsburgh Children's Museum, encountering a real robot prompted a revision of a fairly extensive but romantized knowledge base. In the case of Harold and Camilla at the Carnegie Museum of Art, we saw a couple finding a way to evolve a system for exploring, over a series of African artifacts, connections between the familiar and the alien.

In some ways these findings lead us to consider the very identity of museums themselves. When museum researchers document the rapt engagement of young children in science museums, one might conclude that museum learning must have a hands-on feature or no powerful learning can take place. This assumption is clearly false because museums are also places of quiet contemplation. Similarly, when we at the Museum Learning Collaborative focus on the social features of conversational elaboration as the mechanism of learning in museums, we do not mean to suggest that visitors must talk all the time in deep and meaningful ways. This assumption is clearly false because museums are also places of solitary exploration and of trivial chatter. So, too, when a volume is devoted to objects in museums as the agents of impact, we must be cautious because the layered accumulation of multiple experiences, of multiple moments of contemplation, of multiple objects is essential to the thing that is a museum and the learning that takes place there.

ACKNOWLEDGMENTS

We thank our collaborators in these studies: Madeleine Gregg and her student teachers from the University of Alabama, the Pittsburgh Children's Museum, Mobot, Illah Nourbaksh, Rose Russo, Catherine Stainton, and the Carnegie Museum of Art. We also thank Joyce Fienberg for her assistance with the manuscript. Preparation of this chapter was supported by the Museum Learning Collaborative, funded by the Institute for Museum and Library Services, the National Science Foundation, the National Endowment for the Arts, and the National Endowment for the Humanities. The opinions expressed are solely those of the authors and no official endorsement from the funders should be presumed.

REFERENCES

Allen, S. (1997). Using scientific inquiry activities in exhibit explanations. *Science Education* (Informal Science Education — Special Issue), *81*(6), 715-734.

Atkinson, R. K., Derry, S. J., Renkl, A., & Wortham, D. (2001). Learning from examples: Instructional principles from the worked examples research. *Review of Educational Research, 70*(2), 181-214.

Blais, A. (Ed.). (1995). *Text in the exhibition medium.* Québec City: Société des musées québécois.

Borun, M., Chambers, M., & Cleghorn, A. (1996). Families are learning in science museums. *Curator, 39*(2), 123-138.

Crowley, K., & Galco, J. (2001). Everyday activity and the development of scientific thinking. In K. Crowley, C. D. Schunn, & T. Okada (Eds.), *Designing for science: Implications from everyday, classroom, and professional science* (pp. 393-413). Mahwah, NJ: Lawrence Erlbaum Associates.

DeBlasio, M., & DeBlasio, R. (1983). Constructing a cultural context through museum storytelling. *The Journal of Museum Education: Roundtable Reports, 8*(3), 7-10.

Falk, J. H., & Dierking, L. D. (2000). *Learning from museums: Visitor experiences and the making of meaning.* Walnut Creek, CA: Alta Mira Press.

Gelman, R., Massey, C. M., & McManus, M. (1991). Characterizing supporting environments for cognitive development: Lessons from a children's museum. In L. B. Resnick, J. M. Levine, & S. D. Teasley (Eds.), *Perspectives on socially shared cognition* (pp. 226-256). Washington, DC: American Psychological Association.

Gleason, M. E., & Schauble, L. (1999). Parents' assistance of their children's scientific reasoning. *Cognition and Instruction, 17*(4), 343-378.

Gregg, M., & Leinhardt, G. (2001). *Learning from the Birmingham Civil Rights Institute: Documenting teacher development.* Manuscript under editorial review.

Knutson, K. (2001, April). *Creating a space for learning: Curators, educators, and the implied audience.* Paper presented at the annual meeting of the American Educational Research Association, New Orleans.

Leinhardt, G. (2001). Instructional explanations: A commonplace for teaching and location for contrast. In V. Richardson (Ed.), *Handbook for research on teaching* (4th ed., pp. 333-357). Washington, DC: American Educational Research Association.

Leinhardt, G., & Crowley, K. (1998). *Conversational elaboration as a process and an outcome of museum learning.* Museum Learning Collaborative Technical Report (MLC-01). Pittsburgh, PA: Learning Research & Development Center, University of Pittsburgh [Available at http://mlc.lrdc.pitt.edu/mlc].

Leinhardt, G., Crowley, K., & Knutson, K. (Eds.). (in press). *Learning conversations in museums.* Mahwah, NJ: Lawrence Erlbaum Associates.

Leinhardt, G., & Gregg, M. (in press). Burning bus, burning cross: Pre-service teachers see Civil Rights. In G. Leinhardt, K. Crowley, & K. Knutson (Eds.), *Learning conversations in museums.* Mahwah, NJ: Lawrence Erlbaum Associates.

Leinhardt, G., & Ohlsson, S. (1990). Tutorials on the structure of tutoring from teachers. *Journal of Artificial Intelligence in Education, 2*(1), 21-46.

McManus, P. M. (1989). Oh, yes, they do: How museum visitors read labels and interact with exhibit texts. *Curator, 32*(3), 174-189.

Paris, S. G., Troop, W. P., Henderlong, J., & Sulfaro, M. M. (1994). Children's explorations in a hands-on science museum. *The Kamehameha Journal of Education, 5,* 83-92.

Roberts, L. (1997). *From knowledge to narrative.* Washington, DC: Smithsonian Institution.

Schauble, L., Leinhardt, G., & Martin, L. (1998). A framework for organizing a cumulative research agenda in informal learning contexts. *Journal of Museum Education, 22*(2&3), 3-8.

Serrell, B. (1997). Paying attention: The duration and allocation of visitors' time in museum exhibitions. *Curator, 40*(2), 108–125.

Stainton, C. (in press). *Voices and images: Making connections between identity and art.* In G. Leinhardt, K. Crowley, & K. Knutson (Eds.), *Learning conversations in museums.* Mahwah, NJ: Lawrence Erlbaum Associates.

White, H.C. (1995). *Where do languages come from? — Switching talk.* Unpublished manuscript, Columbia University, New York.

Young, K. M. (2001). *Learning to write from examples: The effects of number of examples and presence of scaffolding on student understanding and writing.* Unpublished doctoral dissertation, University of Pittsburgh, Pennsylvania.

CHAPTER EIGHTEEN

Leveling the Playing Field through Object-Based Service Learning

DeAnna Banks Beane
Association of Science-Technology Centers,
Washington, DC

Myla Shanae Pope
John A. Johnson Achievement Plus Elementary School,
Saint Paul

I was in eighth grade at Ramsey Junior High and the Science Museum of Minnesota was opening up a new exhibit hall called the Experiment Gallery and was hiring youth explainers for it. Regardless of my personal drive, competitive spirit, and strong parental support, somehow I had gotten the impression from my environment — especially my teachers — that boys were more "math and science-minded" and that there were no people of color doing anything related to these subject areas. Nevertheless, I applied to become a youth explainer.

Four years later in my preparation to attend college, I took the ACT (American College Testing) exam during my senior year in high school. The last part of the exam was on science reasoning, the section that I had not expected to do well on; but my reading and other scores would make up for the anticipated lower scores in science. However, to my surprise, the science reasoning section had several questions related to pendulums. I really do not remember the questions being really easy or hard, I just remember doing them.

Eventually I received my exam scores. What amazed me most about my breakout scores is that I did not do best in reading, a subject I felt I was definitely good in. Nor did I receive my best scores in writing. My highest score was on the science reasoning section! I was both puzzled and excited. I had never studied pendulums is school! I reflected on how I, who was not really connected to or fond of science in my elementary years and had just made the grade, was able to make a high grade in science on a standardized test. Thinking back, I remembered that "Pendulums" was the major lab I was trained in as one of the first twelve youth explainers at the Science Museum of Minnesota.

— Myla Pope, St. Paul Public Schools[1]

The basic premise of this chapter is that sustained interactions between adolescents, people, the environment, and objects of a science museum, over time, can have transforming effects on adolescents. Both authors have been involved with YouthALIVE! (Youth Achievement through Learning, Involvement, Volunteering, and Employment), a national museum-based initiative of the Association of Science–Technology Centers (ASTC).[2] YouthALIVE! programs make these sustained relationships with museums accessible to adolescents from underserved communities. DeAnna Beane serves as project director for the national initiative. Myla Pope, during her 9-year involvement with youth programs at the Science Museum of Minnesota, was first a participant and later, a staff member. Our observations of these programs strongly suggest that their impact can be particularly significant for girls, minorities, and adolescents who, because of low-income status, have had limited opportunities to explore science in supportive, enriched environments. We maintain that to develop the confidence and competence required for future career options that include science, adolescents need regular access to science-rich environments. For some, this may begin in the primary or middle grades with well-equipped classrooms and teachers who not only have mastered basic science concepts and inquiry-based pedagogy, but also communicate the expectation that all students will be successful in science. For others, positive introductions to scientific activity comes from family, friends, neighborhood afterschool programs, or science centers and museums. However, many adolescents lack access to the kinds of on-going activities, school experiences, family resources, and lifestyles that enable them to become confident science learners. While acknowledging the existence of other of interventions designed to address some of these inequities, we offer the science center or science museum as a highly appropriate intervention resource for developing science competence in underserved adolescents.

Our experiences have led us to view the science museum as much more than a collection of objects. Like Schlereth (1992, p. 102) we embrace the idea of the museum-as-object. While defining the museum as a site where people primarily use objects to learn about themselves and other people, he encouraged us to think of the museum as an "intriguing assemblage of material cultural evidence" and challenged us to look at the museum-as-object. Even for

---

[1] This opening extract by Myla Pope is one of nine presented here as reflections on her experience as a participant in a museum-based youth program.

[2] The Association of Science–Technology Centers Incorporated, is an international nonprofit organization of over 400 science centers and museums in the United States and 42 other countries.

the most casual visitor, science centers and science museums present intriguing assemblages of evidence of what people have learned about the natural world and the wide range of technological applications of that knowledge. Modern science museums also encourage visitors to explore science concepts for themselves, often using the same kinds of objects and methodologies that scientists use in their investigations. Visitors are immersed in a culture of objects, staff, exhibits, and programs that have been shaped by the work of scientists. There is much to learn about this fascinating object, the museum. How is this place organized? What is its mission? What purposes do the exhibits serve? Who comes here and why? For adolescents who initially may be intimidated by the vastness of science, the science museum can indeed be an object, an entity to be explored, understood, and utilized for learning about science, self, and others. Our multiyear involvement with museum-based youth programs that intentionally recruit adolescents from underserved populations has led us to conclude that programs that provide authentic work experiences have direct cognitive and emotional benefits for adolescents. Although all youths can benefit from these programs, the probability of positive impact on the observable affective and cognitive development is even higher for adolescents who, because of their cultural or economic backgrounds, have previously lacked regular access to the science museum, its objects, exhibits, programs, and people. In this chapter we describe the common elements of the YouthALIVE! programs, and provide a more detailed exploration of one program, Lab Partners, which was developed at the Science Museum of Minnesota.[3]

The opening quotation, and others by coauthor Myla Pope, are drawn from her reflections as an alumna of the first cohort of Lab Partners at the Science Museum of Minnesota. Myla's long-term involvement in the museum's array of youth programs provides valuable insight into aspects of her cognitive and affective development during adolescence. With Myla, we explore the role of the science museum in an African American adolescent's transformation from a "science avoider" to a "science doer." We note the ways in which her early employment opportunities and ongoing involvement with a museum, its staff, and objects supported her developmentally. We describe how, in a collaborative, object-centered environment, she (a) began to learn science in order to help museum visitors more effectively, and (b) developed a much deeper understanding of other young people and their lives. Finally, we suggest that because these programs offer user-friendly access to science

---

[3]Developed in 1991, Lab Partners provides paid employment to eighth and ninth graders; 12 individuals during the school year, and 15 in the summer. They assist visitors in using the experiment gallery and the physics exhibits. The program, modeled after programs working with teens in California and Ohio, was started at the Science Museum of Minnesota by Mary Ann Steiner, current director of (the Museum's) Youth Science Center (Madzey-Akale, Donohue, & Cady, 1999).

and technology — within an environment that intentionally addresses the developmental needs of adolescents — the programs could, with some refinement, become a resource for encouraging and nurturing future teachers and scientific or technical workers. We contend that Myla's experiences are a powerful demonstration of how objects and social interactions inherent to science centers and museums can provide the context for significant cognitive, social, and emotional development in underserved adolescents.

THE NEED FOR INTERVENTION

To gain a perspective on the significance of the science museum experience as a cognitive intervention, we have only to look at science and mathematics participation patterns in the larger picture. Over 25 years ago educators and researchers began identifying factors that were thought to contribute to the underrepresentation of females and minorities — particularly African Americans, Hispanic/Latinos, and Native Americans (Beane, 1985). According to the National Science Foundation, in 1995, these three groups comprised 23% of the U.S. population but only 6% of the nation's science and engineering labor force. Although women, who constitute 51% of the population and 46% of the labor force, have made progress in the past 20 years, they still comprise only 22% of the practicing scientists and engineers. Academic preparation for science-related careers requires competency in higher level courses in mathematics as well as science. In general, on standardized measures of achievement in science and mathematics, non-Asian minority elementary and secondary school students (comprising over 30% of America's total school enrollment) do not perform as well as their European American and Asian American peers (Campbell, 2000). This disparity in performance on national assessments in science and mathematics strongly suggests that the underrepresentation of African Americans, Hispanics/Latinos, and Native Americans in science and technology career fields has its origins, primarily, in their precollege experience, beginning with the elementary and middle school education or earlier. By the time they enter high school, girls often have learned to avoid science, particularly the physical sciences. As Myla's story suggests, they do not see themselves of succeeding in a "boy's" subject. Race and ethnicity, gender, and socioeconomic status too often become determinants of the quality of schooling and out-of-school enrichment opportunities available to these young people (Clewell & Braddock, 2000; National Center for Education Statistics, 1998). Generally, experiences with science in and out of school are neither appropriately challenging nor positive for females, minorities, and students of low socioeconomic status. By eighth grade, female students are less prone to like physical science than males (Beaton et al., 1996). Myla's attitudes toward and participation in science were similar to those of most children from the underrepresented populations — until a caring middle school teacher and a museum intervened.

> As a child I never came here (to the Science Museum). In elementary school, science had an aura of mystery — something that only those "special students" could understand. We did not have science class every day. You could choose the "Rocks and Ripples" course or other science classes as enrichment courses, but otherwise you did not have science. The science classrooms seemed kind of eerie. You could look at stuff and some of it was quite strange. There were plants, but there were also a lot of different containers with dead animals, fish tanks, microscopes and small, round dishes with tiny things in them. There were eggs that they were going to turn into baby chicks. On the walls were all kinds of posters; the planets I knew, but there was a huge chart with letters, numbers and weird phrases.
>
> The students in these classes were all White! Although the boys seemed to be enjoying themselves, the few girls seemed to be grossed out and uncomfortable. Clearly, science was "out of my league."
>
> My world of science changed completely in the eighth grade. Mrs Hoskins, the science teacher and my first African American teacher, approached the class with the Science Museum of Minnesota opportunity. Mary Ann Steiner from the Museum interviewed me and I was hired.

YouthALIVE! MAKING SCIENCE ACCESSIBLE

It is assumed that museums are for everyone, but seldom does a museum visitor stop to ask who is not here and, more importantly, why not? Some science centers and museums have for many years explored creative solutions to these equity issues; however, the focus has traditionally been on outreach to elementary-aged children or families. Aside from the possibility of a brief school field trip, adolescents, particularly teenagers of color or from low-income communities, were largely overlooked. Myla's story, like that of other young people in YouthALIVE!, suggests that access to the objects, exhibits, and people in science centers provides adolescents with hands-on experience with scientific topics. Additionally, science centers can play a significant role in helping young people realize their potential — as learners, as teachers, and as contributors.

In 1991, with support from the Wallace–Reader's Digest Funds and considerable planning, ASTC launched YouthALIVE!. Through the program, ASTC staff has worked directly with 72 science centers, children's museums, zoos, aquariums, and botanical gardens that have made a commitment to implementing and sustaining structured opportunities for adolescents to develop the competencies needed to make a healthy transition into adulthood (Association of Science-Technology Centers, 1999). Acknowledging the need for broader opportunities for adolescents from minority and low-income communities, participating science centers have developed partnerships with schools and community organizations that serve these communities. Although YouthALIVE! programs are open to all adolescents, museums work with their community partners to identify young people who seem to be most in need of this type of experience. In 1999, over 60% of the 2,000-plus YouthALIVE! participants were African American and Hispanic/Latino — populations mentioned as being severely underrepresented in science and technology career fields. In addition, well over half of the YouthALIVE! participants were residents of low-income communities (Association of Science-Technology Centers, 2001). In general, participants of these programs live in neighborhoods that are not always able to offer adolescents much in terms of assets that research has found to be essential for healthy adolescent development. Examples of those important community assets include a challenging academic environment, educational enrichment, mentoring by a network of adults, career exploration, high tech access, and meaningful employment.

The ultimate goal of YouthALIVE! is to establish a sustainable network of science centers and museums with the capacity to support positive youth development through service learning, particularly for underserved youth. Although a few of the programs have been intentional about nurturing future scientists or information technology workers, most do not consider this to be the primary goal. Despite differences in program objectives, all programs adhere to a common set of basic principles, and the adolescents report a more positive attitude toward science as a result of their participation in the program. These principles of best practice (see Fig. 18.1) emerged from lessons learned during the first 4 years of the initiative, as science centers and museums began to apply the research on adolescent development to the design of youth programs.

Dinosaur skeletons in a natural history museum, sharks in an aquarium, computers with digital cameras in a technology center, giant lenses and prisms in a science center — the objects, like the programs, are as varied as their host institutions. All the YouthALIVE! programs have been designed to bring objects and adolescents together in highly productive ways that are beneficial to both the institution and the adolescent. Whether interpreting exhibits, performing demonstrations, assisting with fabrication, leading outreach activities, caring for small animals, or assisting with a day camp, the young people use object-based activities to help the museum meet its mission. The training and nurturing they receive in executing these responsibilities support their cognitive, social, and emotional development in these unique environments. These science centers and museums have become community institutions that contribute valuable assets to the lives of adolescents.

A Search Institute report (Scales & Leffert, 1999), for example, compiled 40 research-based assets that comprise the building blocks of healthy adolescent development. These developmental assets have been clustered into two

These principles form the cornerstone of Youth ALIVE! programs

- Both the needs of the institution and the needs of the youth are met through the program
- The entire museum's environment is committed to integrating participants into the fabric of the institution.
- The programs operate year-round and participants have at least 120 contact hours each year.
- The rules and the expectations for the participants in the program are appropriately flexible.
- Participants work in small groups with sensitive staff members and/or mentors who challenge the young people intellectually.
- A positive peer culture is nurtured as participants from diverse backgrounds work together on common tasks.
- Participants are given responsibilities commensurate with their developmental needs.
- Participants are engaged in tasks that are of interest to them and enhance their perceptions of their own capabilities and future.
- Participants are provided stimulating opportunities to make connections between their museum experiences, career possibilities, and educational paths.
- Program staff recognize the importance of family support and seek to involve the families of the targeted youth.

FIG. 18.1.   YouthALIVE! Programs

categories — internal and external. *External assets* are related to what the community and family must provide and *internal assets* are personality characteristics that enable a young person to flourish. External assets are environmental structures and practices that provide support, empowerment, boundaries, expectations, and opportunities for constructive use of time. Internal assets involve an adolescent's commitment to learning, positive values, social competencies, and positive identity. Family and school are integral parts of the average adolescent's life, but for many young people, these two institutions alone cannot provide sufficient opportunities for constructive use of out-of-school time. Equally as challenging for families and schools is the creation of effective vehicles that enable adolescents to make meaningful contributions to a larger world and motivate them to pursue new knowledge and skills beyond minimum classroom requirements. Through YouthALIVE! programs, science centers and museums are providing underserved young people with many of the essential developmental assets taken for granted by their more affluent peers, while making science learning and teaching a part of their daily lives. The degree to which family and community (including the museum) offer sufficient external assets can determine the degree to which an adolescent may grow and emerge as a healthy, productive young adult with a sense of purpose and positive identity.

It is common for adults to think of adolescence only as a time of confusion, raging hormones, and emotional turbulence; it is easy to forget that this is the time when they must begin to define who they are, what they have to offer, and what their role is in the world around them — the search for identity (Erikson, 1968). Effective youth programs honor that search for identity. Like YouthALIVE!, they provide knowledgeable, caring adults as mentors and a safe environment in which adolescents can explore ways of being useful or needed. They offer multiple opportunities for experimenting with new behaviors and attitudes and making decisions. Adolescents are stimulated intellectually, they experience competence and achievement, plus, they enjoy and benefit from the social interaction with peers.

LAB PARTNERS

Of the youth programs affiliated with YouthALIVE!, we selected the Lab Partners program as the context for much of this discussion for several reasons. First, the relationship between adolescent and exhibit (and objects) was "symbiotic" from the start. The development of the exhibit could not proceed without the input of the adolescents who would first learn from the exhibit's objects, then later facilitate the visitors' experiences. To do this job well, the adolescents needed the objects. Conversely, the exhibit "needed" the adolescents who would maximize visitor engagement with its objects. Second, the program did not necessarily recruit young people who were avid science students. Third, the program addressed the developmental needs of young adolescents by providing committed adults, meaningful work, opportunities for intellectual stimulation and competence, and a positive peer group. Fourth, Lab Partners and the fabrication of its related exhibit areas were designed as learning experiences for adult museum staff as well as the newly recruited adolescent. The fifth reason for us to discuss Lab Partners as an exemplary program is because Myla Pope's continuing involvement with the Science Museum of Minnesota began with Lab Partners.

Concurrent with the launch of YouthALIVE! nationally, the Science Museum of Minnesota began front-end work on the development of an exhibit gallery for middle school students. With support from the National Science Foundation (NSF), the museum began creating the Experiment Gallery, a set of 10 physical science exhibits designed to encourage adolescent visitors to experiment with selected phenomena in their own way. Exhibit topics included light, sound, electricity, gravity, and pendulums. The NSF grant also supported the development of Lab Partners, a program for eighth graders. This program was designed to meet two important needs of the museum: (a) the need for "in-house experts" who could help staff learn more about designing exhibits and a gallery space that would appeal to young adolescents; and (b) the need for a diverse staff of peer explainers or interpretive facilitators for this gallery. Thus, the partnership between museum staff and the eighth grade Lab Partners was mutually beneficial. The staff had a ready audience to try out new ideas and could gain honest and immediate feedback from the adolescents. These young people had ongoing support and coaching from two key staff members. Mary Ann Steiner, the youth programs manager, visited schools and community-based organizations to recruit Lab Partner applicants. After they were hired, she helped these new young workers adjust to the museum environment, introduced them to the requisite job skills, and encouraged them to reflect on their experiences. Science content workshops, which Myla describes later, were lead by J. Shipley Newlin (Jay), the Museum's Director of Physical Science. Newlin and Steiner prepared the Lab Partners for the important services that they were expected to perform for the museum and its visitors.

Although the Lab Partners' principle interactions were with Jay and MaryAnn, Myla reminds us of the larger context with which the youth program was introduced. Lab Partners did not operate in a vacuum and its participants were cognizant of that. Surely, in the case for these newcomers, the Museum's entire staff comprised a significant element of the "museum-as-object."

> It was a big adjustment for the Museum to have a group of youths as workers. Among some of the people in the Museum, a lot of feelings surfaced, and I knew they were probably related to the idea of "change." It's amazing to think back to that time and to see all of the positive things that are happening now.

MUSEUMS AS VEHICLES FOR SERVICE LEARNING

Advancing the public's understanding of science is central to the mission of a science center or science museum. To understand how a youth program can successfully address both the developmental needs of adolescents and the mission of the institution, we look at the service learning and the science learning that occur when adolescents participate in the public service work of a science museum.

> I didn't expect to be at the museum for nine years. I just thought it was going to be an eighth grade thing; I'd be here for eight months and that would be it.

Every time I thought it was over, the Museum found another opportunity for me. The summer after 11th grade I was a camp counselor for the Museum's River Girls program. It hurt me to see the range of issues facing some of these girls of color. I began to understand the learning-related roadblocks that they placed in front of themselves. It was a mental roadblock. You could see it when they would laugh and clown at the wrong times. They were in an environment where they didn't know something. So, they had to make it seem like they didn't care. I care deeply about girls and people of color. I had to deal with this roadblock. To be able to reach people, you have to learn to meet them where they are, allow them to be comfortable enough to come out of their shell, to knock down that road block, and to realize that it's OK not to know something. We needed to figure out a way to do this together. I learned so much; it allowed me to see some things that I hadn't seen in life. And that was good. (Myla, February 1999 interview)

Developmentally appropriate youth programming requires museums to be flexible enough to create new opportunities as adolescents mature. Young people who may have begun their science center or museum involvement as fifth or sixth graders in an after-school enrichment club usually require an expanded set of experiences by the seventh or eighth grade. Middle school is the ideal time to introduce young people to service learning, but the benefits of such experiences can be equally significant as adolescents mature. Although Myla's *service* learning experiences in the museum environment could not begin until she had participated as a Lab Partner, her observations about what she learned as a rising high school senior working in a summer science camp points to the potential impact of service learning in adolescent development. As a museum camp counselor, she developed a deeper understanding of teenage girls who shared her racial heritage but whose life experiences had been quite different from hers. That interaction helped her learn more about herself. Personal growth has been mentioned by other young people who are assisting younger children with educational enrichment experiences in similar programs.

Unlike schools where service learning is often finite, extracurricular, or focused on short-term projects, YouthALIVE! programs represent a unique type of service learning because these youth development experiences match some of the major tasks of adolescence with the service needs and resources of one institution — the science center or museum. YouthALIVE! programs are, however, similar to school-based service learning programs in that these museum-based volunteer and paid experiences are intentional in promoting adolescents' learning. They require the learner to be engaged directly with other people — those providing services and those being served. These engagements constitute a significant learning process because they bring a distinct set of new experiences. The adolescents are: (a) working together in a group to plan and carry out service activities; (b) adjusting these activities to fit the tastes and needs of people who are often very different from the learner; (c) encouraged to reflect on the meaning of these activities in their own lives and in the lives of those they serve; and (d) provided with incentives to develop effective habits of performance in joint endeavors and to assume growing responsibilities in such relationships (Schine, 1997).

The four elements identified by Schine — teamwork, responsive "customer service," individual and group reflection, and high performance expectations — are generic to most work-based YouthALIVE! programs. Clearly, any one of these elements alone would elevate the experience of providing a service. It is this combination of elements that contributed to the evolution of the Principles of Best Practice for YouthALIVE! listed in Fig. 18.1. These elements provided the springboard for discussions and activities related to education plans, college, careers, as well as community issues around which young people could develop service projects. For example, the young people in one Midwestern science center applied for and received a grant to take hands-on science activities to youths in the local juvenile detention center and to organize a museum experience for families from a nearby homeless shelter. The museum's objects were central in the young people's planning and interaction with the new audiences that they had selected. Their science museum's objects and exhibits had become so familiar that the adolescents felt quite capable of sharing them in new ways with new learners.

One way of describing the outcomes when the museum environment is the vehicle for service learning experiences would be to consider the attributes inherent in helping others: a sense of caring, of responsibility, of self-worth, and of connectedness. Assisting museum visitors and staff can contribute positively to an adolescent's quest for identity. Although little rigorous research is available on the impact of service learning, the work of Scales and Blyth (1997) supports our observations about the effects of participation in YouthALIVE! programs: adolescents' sense of social and personal responsibility increases. In addition, many adolescents in these museum-based programs viewed the experience as an opportunity to develop the personal skills, attitudes, and behaviors for success in the workplace. Of equal interest to us is the frequency with which participants report their surprise at how much they enjoy teaching younger children, and the number of alumni who mention a desire to "work with kids" or "give something back." Moore and Allen (1996) found that the frequency and duration of involvement in service activities can have a positive effect on adolescents. YouthALIVE!'s museum-based programs are expected to engage adolescents for a minimum of 120 hours over the course of a year. This duration of involvement in rendering service under the ongoing guidance of caring adults offers time to develop a heightened value of importance for helping or supporting growth in others. This may help account for the common "giving back" attitude of youth-organized outreach projects described earlier.

Moreover, in YouthALIVE! programs, service learning is complemented by a workskills component, particularly as young people mature into paid, part-time positions. Although the element of service remains at the core, attention is given to the basic skills needed to enter the workforce successfully, such as interpersonal skills, allocating resources, acquiring and managing information, understanding systems, and using technology appropriately. These skills have been identified by the U.S. Department of Labor[4] as essential for successful workforce entry. Most of the skills are addressed within the context of the adolescents' roles as exhibit explainers, demonstrators, teaching assistants etc. Staff and peer feedback — provided by reflection, coaching, and evaluation — is critical to a young person's development as a competent worker and is built into these kinds of programs.

EMPLOYMENT AS MOTIVATOR

Many YouthALIVE! participants report that prior to joining the program, they had little interest in science and little, if any, interaction with the museum. For most, the motivation was a part-time job and the opportunity to earn money, as this statement by another Lab Partner indicates.

> Back in 1991, I was in eighth grade and frequently attended the Boys and Girls club on the West side of Saint Paul. One day, Mary Ann Steiner was there to recruit kids for some jobs at the Science Museum. I do not come from a wealthy family, so the idea of a job and income caught my ear fast. That's how I got into the Science Museum with my first job as a Lab Partner interpreting the exhibits, pendulums, colors, and gravity. Many of those exhibits weren't self-explanatory. I don't know where I would be right now if I hadn't gotten in that early and learned the skills and discipline of keeping a job at that point. (February 1999 taped interview with Eric [Caucasian male], currently a 3rd-year computer technology student, Brown University)

Many others like Eric, who want or need money, are attracted by the nature of the work — assisting the public in a safe and "cool place." Their sustained involvement in science is directly related to their desire be successful in providing services to museum visitors. The experience affords them opportunities to both learn science from the staff and objects of the museum, and develop the skills and positive attitudes required to effectively facilitate the science learning of others.

---

[4]In 1990, the U.S. Department of Labor's Secretary's Commission on Achieving Necessary Skills released its report (SCANS), establishing a common core of skills that constitutes job readiness.

MUSEUMS AS VEHICLES FOR SCIENCE LITERACY

Museum-based service learning usually requires the adolescent to facilitate the visitor's engagement with the objects and exhibits. There is the expectation that the adolescent will develop sufficient understanding of the relevant concepts to provide a successful experience for the museum visitor. With adequate training and support from adult staff, adolescents can fill an important need on the museum floor; their presence and their willingness to talk with visitors bring a unique energy to the exhibit galleries. Moreover, in this rich informal science environment, the adolescents develop new competencies in science while doing their jobs. Sometimes the learning opportunities here compensate for those lacking elsewhere, including schools, as Myla's account at the beginning of the chapter reveals.

NOVICES, EXPERTS, AND OBJECTS

In the opening of this chapter, as Myla connects her performance on the standardized test to her experiences, she is prompted to reflect on the nature of her initiation into "doing science." What she describes is not only her first encounter with pendulums; it is also an account of one aspect of her own cognitive development, nurtured by a community of learners — experts and novices — engaged in a collaborative process. Two intertwined elements contributed significantly to Myla's progression from "science avoider" to "science doer." One was the social context — a "community of learners" formed by the museum staff, Lab Partners, River Girl campers, and eventually museum visitors. The other involves this community's use of objects in science learning.

Consider Myla's reflections in light of the work of researchers engaged in studies of cognition and development. Rogoff (1998) is part of a growing group of developmental psychologists who advocate for a more inclusive view of human development, one that goes beyond the traditional focus on middle-class European American families. Rogoff's (1994) studies of how children growing up in different cultures learn to operate in their home environments and various community institutions might be particularly appropriate in exploring the sociocultural influence in Myla's case. The museum, as a community, offered Myla and her fellow Lab Partners a new culture with its own values, norms, language, history, practices, and traditions. Although objects were obviously important in their lives prior to joining the museum community, the role of objects here was quite unlike that of home, school, church, the library, the playground, or the grocery store. In the museum culture, the development of exhibitions and presentation of objects are central to the mission.

The opportunity to manipulate objects in and of itself would not be likely to result in the kinds of learning we can infer from Myla's reflections. We must factor in the sociocultural activities of Myla's museum community for a better sense of the importance of the interaction between Myla, other learners, objects, and the staff. Rogoff's (1994) community of learners concept was based on the premise that learning and development occur through participation in collaborative activities that are explicitly related to the community's history and practices. The collaborators are a combination of mature members (the *experts,* Jay and Mary Ann, both of whom were experienced museum professionals) and less mature members (the *novices,* Myla and her adolescent peers, who were new to the museum). The Lab Partners joined this new community expecting to develop learning relationships not only with museum staff, but also with museum visitors. Perhaps it is this interchangeability of roles or the awareness that all members of the community are learners that contributes to the sense that learning is occurring in a natural or unconscious manner, a characteristic of effective informal learning environments.

All members in a community of learners share responsibility for the tasks at hand, with the mature members contributing overall orientation and direction. Lab Partners is a community model that demonstrates Rogoff's contention that the roles of novice and expert are indeed shared or interchangeable, with all members feeling safe and valued. Jay and Mary Ann, the experienced museum professionals, relied on the Lab Partners to teach them effective ways of engaging young adolescents in the learning of physical science concepts. The experts and novices shared responsibility for authentic tasks in their quest for an "adolescent-friendly" physical science gallery.

Myla's Introduction to Lab Partners and Pendulums

When I began training, the structure was nothing like I had imagined. First, the other Lab Partners, did not appear to be science geniuses. Everyone was down to earth and our group of twelve represented many cultures. I felt comfortable with my peers of Lab Partners.

We were there before the exhibits were installed and our training took place behind the construction walls. Jay Newlin, a program leader and exhibit developer, worked with the Lab Partners. We played with materials, discussed what we saw happening, and compared it to something we had seen before. We were not lectured to, nor did we have to write down and memorize facts. As a group we would play with things that taught a specific concept and come up with our own ideas of what to do, our own experiments. Later, we would have a round-table discussion on the principles that were at work.

I had never heard the word pendulum before, but was able to make sense of it when looking at a clock with a swinging pendulum. Before that I did not know that the swinging thing was actually a pendulum that measured something. As a group we talked about what they were and did. After making pendulums, we discussed what we saw and compared our observations with our partners and the group. When we noticed something, Jay or Mary Ann might say, "Well what you are noticing is the frequency of the pendulum. So how can you make a pendulum have a slower or faster frequency?"[5] We would talk about how we would achieve this goal and try out our ideas. I also remember using the swinging pendulums to trace waves on butcher paper and in sand. We were able to see how a pendulum makes waves and how, with frequency changes, the size of the waves changed. During this process we learned factual information.

Learning to Play; Playing to Learn

Before the exhibits were up, the lab partners did activities with balls, weights, and string. I remember measuring out different lengths of string, and using weights. One of the hardest parts of this type of training was learning how to play. I had never been taught a subject through play and manipulation. Up to that time I would always follow directions to make something happen, but if told to try something with objects that were unfamiliar to me I would just sit there. I am very task and goal oriented. It was hard for me just to play with objects but I was okay with observing what was happening, discussing what I saw, and working toward a goal. At first, I saw balls, strings, and weights. Later I saw pendulums, waves, and pieces of science. I did not even think I was doing science because I was playing with things related to the exhibits in the experiment gallery. We would make hypotheses and carry out a set of experiments to test our questions. Jay or Mary Ann, our mentors, would take it further by discussing the principles. At no time did I feel like I did not fit in or that I could not understand the information; I was part of the learning. All of our individual experiences and/or knowledge were always acceptable. Our comments were never degraded! Everyone was learning something. The learning may have been about a principle, a cultural group, or ways to communicate with others. The things I was learning, the people I was being exposed to, the overall experience and the opportunity intrigued me.

"Learning to Play . . ." offers a perfect example of Myla's growing understanding about the value of "playing" with objects for her own learning and teaching. In learning to play, she was actually learning to select, change, and experiment with variables in her own way. Hakkarainen (1999), in discussing Leont'ev's work on the social needs of play, observed that "Play as an activity type aims at the mastery of mastering. . . . It produces general flexibility and disposition to change one's approach when facing the concrete demands of the situation" (p. 234). This suggests a relationship between play and the development of some of the problem-solving skills that schools value. The ability to delight in play, which comes so naturally to young children, is all too

---

[5]Pendulums swing back and forth at a regular rate because of gravity. The longer the string, the longer it takes for the pendulum to make one complete swing forward and back. The frequency is the number of complete cycles or back and forth swings that occur in a specific unit of time (i.e., swings per minute). Without an outside force, friction generated by the weight moving through air will cause the pendulum's swing to get progressively smaller.

frequently lost as students grow older and become acclimated to the mores of the classroom. Yet, metastudies of even the earliest hands-on science curriculum programs found that students in activity-based programs demonstrated substantial improvement in science content, perception, logic, language development, and mathematics. They also expressed a more positive attitude toward science. (Shymansky, Kyle, & Alport, 1982). What the Lab Partners and these activity-based science programs had in common was the manipulation of materials/objects as a key component of the learning process.

Myla's ACT scores indicate that in those informal, but purposeful, sessions in the museum she was indeed learning. She describes her initiation into an environment that encouraged play, collaborative investigations, and discussions with peers. She appears to be making a mental comparison between the way her learning experiences were structured in school and these new experiences in the museum. She found that to learn from objects — to direct her own learning — she first had to learn to play. She had to manipulate the string, weights, and balls without any preconceived results in mind, testing her observations, and developing her own explanations

Service — Motivation for Science Learning

A key part of my motivation was that I knew I had to learn this information in order to explain it to visitors. It was a part of my job. I did not want to sound foolish or uninformed when working with the staff, training my peers, or assisting the visitors. One thing that I will carry with me through life is that it is okay not to know something and tell somebody that you do not know. I was not expected to know everything about everything in order to work in the Experiment Gallery. This really changed some negative feelings I had about science. I thought that in order to learn and teach so a profound subject, you had to know everything about it! But you don't. Mature people can admit not knowing and understand that they are constantly learning themselves.

Another aspect of our training focused on how to approach and engage visitors during their time in the Experiment Gallery. As a group, we came up with a list of ways to approach visitors. We talked about questions to use with the visitors so that they felt challenged and yet comfortable in experimenting with the exhibits. After our initial training, we had follow up meetings and journals in which our concerns, issues, and suggestions were aired. The journals were a way to talk about how our day went in the exhibit gallery and problems we had working with visitors. There was an issue with many of the Lab Partners feeling like older visitors tended to move away from us because we were young. Mary Ann scheduled bi-weekly staff meetings to discuss these kinds of issues.

Lab Partners — Emerging Experts

As the exhibits were placed on the floor, the lab partners in small groups were trained on the three different activity stations. My specialty was the Pendulum Lab. Much of the training we had done prior to the station being put up was helpful in understanding the Pendulum Lab. Now we were able to play with the experiments in the actual lab. The Pendulum Lab was next to the big exhibit where you changed the frequency of the two pendulums to make a design on a postcard. There were sign up forms for visitors to sign up for a 15 minutes in the lab. Visitors could work with a large pendulum, changing its length and weights on a time clock and use a computer to start and record the pendulums' movements. A stopwatch could be used to determine the number of swings the pendulum made in a specific period of time. There were flip cards with suggested directions, if the visitor needed them.

Once the fabrication was completed, our training in the lab consisted of reviewing the materials and the experiments that were suggested on the cards to be completed by the visitors. The three of us being trained would look at the cards, read them, and work on the challenge. Once we completed the challenges, we thought about the questions that may be asked of us during the visitors' experience. Sometimes we explored the answers to these questions in the same way we played with materials before the exhibits were up. We identified things that we didn't like about the lab. For example, on some of the cue cards, the wording was too complex or too much. We actually suggested some ways to make the wording clearer and more interesting. The pendulum in the lab was too difficult to manipulate, to change its length on its weight. Changes would make it easier for visitors to experiment with the pendulum. All of our suggestions were encouraged and acted on by Jay, Mary Ann and the exhibit developers. They really wanted our input.

My attitude about science was changed by my role as a Lab Partner, the adult and youth staff that I worked with, and the activities that I became involved with. Working with other students my age created a whole new peer group for me: I developed relationships with the other Lab Partners. We were so different, yet we all were initiated into something totally new and, if we were not supportive of one another, everything could have fallen apart. We were connected and shared new skills and techniques with one another. I talked to my family daily about my interactions with my coworkers, my supervisors, and the visitors. My parents talked to me about the different dynamics of the work world: how to deal with non-supportive staff; how to address conflict in a positive way, and how not to be intimidated by the White visitors who seemed uncomfortable with my teaching them and their children.

I would practice working with visitors by using my family as guinea pigs and getting suggestions from them. I guess talking to my brother, Marcus was exciting to him because he became a Lab Partner when he was in the eighth grade! In a short period of time at my job, I had developed a totally different perspective of science

Constructing Deeper Meaning

Focussing on just the Pendulum Lab made me sort of isolated. As a Lab Partner, I had no idea of how activity stations as well as all the other exhibits in the hall related. I understood the principles of each lab and exhibit but at the same time I isolated the information to each specific lab or station. It had to be years later,

I am not exactly sure when, but it HIT ME! All of the labs and activity stations had a connection to one another! Frequencies are explored in all the labs and in every station; the wave is created by the rate of movement. This is true for a pendulum, an instrument's sound, or a siphon bringing up water. That was why it was important for visitors to manipulate how fast or slow an object moved. When I was a Lab Partner, I did not see this dynamic.

Perhaps the 14-year-old lab partners were not yet developmentally ready to master the overarching principles of physics that unified the physical science labs and exhibits. However, the nature of their experiences, as they prepared for and assisted visitors, enabled them to construct basic knowledge from which richer understanding could develop. The learner may make more sophisticated connections long after the original learning experience. This was certainly true in Myla's case.

WHAT MYLA'S STORY CAN TEACH US

Adolescence has been characterized as a time of great transitions — often with dramatic physiological, anatomical, emotional, social, and cognitive changes. Programs designed to support and enhance young people's development during these years must attend to multiple and often complex needs. Obviously there are many variables to be considered when looking for the lessons here, but it is certainly worth the effort, if only to raise awareness of the need for formal studies of the elements and outcomes of these kinds of museum-based experiences (Schauble, Beane, Coates, Martin, & Sterling, 1996).

It is possible that, because the learning experiences were embedded in the place or situation in which the new knowledge and skills were to be utilized, we can view the Lab Partner model as a form of apprenticeship. In doing so, we can relate it to the model of cognitive apprenticeship proposed by Brown, Collins, and Duguid (1989). According to them, cognitive apprenticeships involve the development of the concepts and cognitive tools necessary for the authentic activities of the situation. Jay's expert role in the Lab Partners' community was to facilitate the development of scientific reasoning through exploration of physical science activities. These cognitive skills would be essential to the adolescents' future success as employee/explainers in the exhibit gallery. Wherever adolescents serve as exhibit explainers or interpreters in science centers and museums, their work centers on objects and information. They must spend a period of time as "apprentices" to museum staff who are either explicit with the requisite knowledge or who, like Jay, model and coach them through to a level of mastery. In most YouthALIVE! programs, the adolescents are in active partnership with experts — adults or experienced older youth who model and support the adolescents in mastering the visitor service behaviors appropriate to the museum setting. Over time, these novices begin to emerge as experts who confidently engage the less experienced — the visitors. Even after coaching them through the transition to part-time museum employees, the original museum experts try to keep in place the qualities of successful communities of learning — collegial bonds, mutual respect, reflection, performance assessment, and collaborative problem solving. Myla and other "graduates" of these kinds of communities not only seem to know how to manage their own learning but can also support and lead others.

Myla's science education prior to eighth grade appears to have been sporadic and textbook driven. Why did the science museum learning experiences make such an impression on her? Dewey and Piaget, giants in the early work on how children learn, may contribute generally to our understanding here, particularly Dewey's emphasis on giving as much attention to the methodology of science as he would give to the knowledge acquired, the learning by doing (Archambault, 1964). More recent research findings in cognitive science lend powerful insight into the cognitive development involved in Myla's journey. Myla engaged in an inquiry process and progressed from a "novice" who had never heard the word pendulum, to an "expert" as symbolized by the moment when she recognized the relationship between all of the labs and exhibits in the physical science gallery. Moreover, she was able to describe that relationship accurately. Central to the inquiry process is the posing of questions about phenomena. To what extent was her learning dependent on changes in the brain stimulated by in the inquiry process? Lowery (1998), in writing to help educators become more aware of the impact of recent advances in brain research on science education, summarized relevant findings about how learners move from novice to expert. In reminding us that the brain absorbs data only through the senses, Lowery helped science educators in both formal and informal learning settings refocus on the role of objects and opportunities to manipulate them. Engagement with multisensory, laboratory-oriented science activities allows the brain to absorb new data. Science centers and museums, through their interactive exhibits, capitalize on this relationship between sensory input and learning. For Myla and her peers, this began with learning to "play" with objects that would eventually be used to construct pendulums.

The learner must be allowed to explore, manipulate, and experiment with the object, relating it to his or her prior knowledge. The Lab Partners worked individually, in pairs, and as a group constructing pendulums, identifying and testing variables, and comparing results. Each activity with the objects built on what was gained from prior, related activities. Their brains stored the new knowledge in clusters that were organized into systems. These exploratory and experimental activities may strengthen the connections between storage systems in the brain, making transferability more likely. By manipulating the objects, the learner begins to explore relationships and discover patterns. It is the emerging expert's ability to utilize accrued knowledge to recognize and interpret patterns that distinguishes him or her from the novice. Myla acknowledges that only after several years did she see the relationship between the activities of the various physical science exhibits. It is important to realize that she was able to make those connections because her manipulation of those objects as an eighth grader had enabled her to store sufficient knowledge. For most learners, the absence of opportunities to "mess with" the objects makes it more likely that the knowledge will fade over time.

In the current science education reform movement, schools and teachers are being challenged to utilize hands-on (object-based) curricula and instructional methods like inquiry because they are consistent with findings from modern cognitive science. Neuroscience is beginning to clarify the efficacy of Dewey's early call to recognize that children "learn by doing." Piaget's work, even as it is disputed, helped us to realize that there is a relationship between learning and development (Wadsworth, 1988). Anyone working with adolescents would do well to remember these relationships. Although content remains important, today's science classrooms are expected to give more attention to inquiry as a process for developing the mind characteristics of science-literate citizens. Myla's recognition of sophisticated patterns, and later her performance on the science reasoning section of the ACT, were indicative of the effectiveness of her collaborative, multisensory laboratory experiences at the museum. Her performance also indicated that she had transitioned into the stage that Piaget would have considered formal cognitive operations. It is also interesting to note that Piaget used pendulums to set up problem-solving challenges in some of his studies of cognitive development in children and adolescents (Wadsworth, 1988).

Myla, an African American female, who as an elementary school child had accepted the stereotypes about science and those who can engage in it, has vividly described only a portion of her adolescent journey to science literacy. We selected these segments from her many experiences in the museum because her reflections offer a glimpse into the kind of long-term learning and interest that can occur from well-planned, developmentally appropriate, informal science education. Myla was surprised at her high performance on the science reasoning section of a standardized examination 4 years after she was a Lab Partner. This suggests that, despite her ladder of successful experiences in the museum, she had yet to fully internalize a new sense of herself as one who successfully engages in science. Her description of her experiences in the museum indicates a growing but still ambivalent confidence in her ability to understand science concepts. Her supportive family found ways to encourage her, even though her journey into science and the Science Museum was a new experience for them all. In Lab Partners, she found new friends — peers interested in doing science activities and knowledgeable, caring adults who played the roles of both teacher and learner. For the first time in her life, she enjoyed the on-going support for doing science. Her "science-support system" included significant others like family, new friends, mentors, and a science teacher who looked like her and encouraged her involvement.

She began to understand that in a "hands-on" environment, she could actually enjoy learning science. She was given the time and encouragement to persist in "playing" with the string, weights, and balls until she understood how a pendulum works and the role of variables in its operation. She was able to connect what she was doing to what she had seen in grandfather clocks and help visitors to her Pendulum Lab do the same, using the big clock stationed beside the entrance to the Lab. She was able to compare the patterns of movement in her lab with patterns of movement in other exhibits in the Experiment Gallery.

Myla Today

I truly believe that my greatest works can be accomplished through teaching. I love working with inner city populations. I went into my undergraduate studies with the idea of working on the prevention of delinquency. I wanted to intervene in young people's lives in a positive way. Now I plan to teach! In the graduate program, it seems so strange — yet so divinely orchestrated — that everyone in the program, my instructors, other students, and even I have concluded that I would be a wonderful science teacher. The museum has served as my playground for science learning since the eighth grade. I no longer see science as a foreign subject! I see it as an area of study where one can play, explore, devise theories, test ideas, and recreate. It really does not matter if I am right or wrong. What matters is that I know how to find the answer! I really like the idea of teaching science to primary students, and bringing inquiry and a hands-on approach to the classroom.

As Myla progressed through college, we often discussed her growing determination to find ways to intervene in the lives of underserved children and youth. For the year following her graduation from college, she worked full time as an education program coordinator at the museum. Currently, she has completed her final semester in the Collaborative Urban Educator Program at the University of St. Thomas in Minneapolis. Equipped with a Master of Arts in Teaching, she has accepted a position in Saint Paul, Minnesota, as a fourth-grade teacher in an elementary school with a student population that is 45% African American.

CONCLUSIONS

Stepping back from Myla's story, we raise broader but related issues. Are the formal and informal educational institutions of the United States adequately preparing *all* of our children for their future roles as knowledgeable, caring, responsible citizens, capable of and interested in assuming vital roles in a rapidly changing world? Judging by today's workforce, the answer is "no." We are experiencing critical shortages of computer engineers, computer scientists, systems analysts, and teachers — especially minority teachers of mathematics and science. In 1996 there were approximately 346,000 vacant information technology positions in the United States (Reinert, 1998). By an Act of Congress in 1998, the cap on immigrants entering the United States on temporary visas to work as information technology professionals was increased from 65,000 in 1999 to 115,000 in 2000 (Smith, 1999). Despite economic fluctuations, the U.S. demand for highly skilled information technology workers is expected to continue, reaching 3.5 million by 2008 (Cooke, 2000).

Many school districts began the 2000 school year with increased enrollments and teacher shortages. The U.S. Department of Education predicts that more than two million new teachers will be needed by 2009 (Hussar, 1999). Creative but insufficient temporary measures are being tried to address immediate needs. In 1998, according to the Council of Chief State School Officers (1999), 36% of the students in the U.S. public schools were from minority populations. Only 8% of chemistry teachers and 12% of biology teachers, however, were minorities. Oakes (as cited by the Council of Chief State School Officers, 1999), found that the participation of minority and female students in mathematics and science is influenced by the characteristics of their teachers. Having a teacher who looks like these students can help counter long-held stereotypes about who can do science. School districts have been aggressively recruiting teachers from other fields and other countries — especially professionals with mathematics and science expertise. Despite these efforts, one of the largest urban districts opened the 2000 school year with over 9,000 teachers on emergency credentials. To help staff New York City classrooms for the 2001–2002 school year, approximately 700 teachers from overseas were hired. Likewise, several other large urban public school districts — Chicago, Atlanta, and Los Angeles — also now recruit abroad to help meet their teacher shortages (Sheridan, 2001). Myla's counterparts in Boston, Miami, Philadelphia, St. Louis, San Francisco, Durham, and other cities across the nation reflect untapped potential that could be developed to help meet these serious needs.

The authors recognize that the ultimate solution to these kinds of workforce shortages rests in the country's capacity to adequately educate our children and retrain its workforce. There is a growing body of research on how learning occurs. Certainly, there are ways in which some of the new science curricula can be utilized to develop competent science learners. While encouraging all schools to move quickly to bring these tools to all teachers and students, we must once again acknowledge the "uneven playing field" existing in school districts. We suggest that the experiences with YouthALIVE! and programs like Lab Partners at the Science Museum of Minnesota make a strong case for extending an infrastructure of out-of-school programs to complement the in-school experiences of underserved children and adolescents. Such programs, building on what is now known about youth development and the importance of sensory-motor activities in cognitive development, would bring together the objects, people, and environment of museums to create communities of learning that would stretch beyond the obvious intersection of museum needs and adolescent needs. These museum-based communities would provide adolescents with support, safety, empowerment, and expectations, while continuing to employ a service-learning model that nurtures cognitive and social competencies, positive values, and a positive sense of identity. Importantly, while supporting the affective development of adolescents, they would also be intentional in building connections between the service learning that helps the museum fulfill its mission and the many related careers that are accessible through additional education and training.

Who am I? Where do I fit in this world? Who needs me? What can I learn to do well? Finding answers to these universal questions is the real work of adolescence; but adolescents cannot find these answers in a vacuum! As a novice, Myla needed a cognitively stimulating community in which to play with objects, explore new ideas, and develop new competencies. She needed situations in which to practice and perfect those competencies. She needed supportive mentors and peers. She needed to know that she was a contributor and that her knowledge, skills, and energy were valued. She needed to experience the gratification of knowing that she had successfully introduced science concepts to others. Along the way, she developed the confidence and competence to begin preparing for a career as a teacher. Because her learning community was a science museum with its object-based culture, she is now able to speak of teaching science in an elementary school classroom.

In closing, we suggest that the kinds of long-term experiences discussed in this chapter can help thousands of underserved adolescents have safe places in which to begin answering those universal questions. The very nature of their service in science museums, and the strategies they practice for utilizing objects to make learning exciting, make them prime potential candidates for careers in teaching. Like Myla, they will know that not only does their museum need them, but that — with skills — they can fill an important role in the larger society. Let us cultivate that potential!

REFERENCES

Archambault, R. (1964). John Dewey on education: Selected writings. Chicago: University of Chicago Press.

Association of Science-Technology Centers, Incorporated. (1999). *Program profiles YouthALIVE!: Directory of programs 1995-1999.* Washington, DC: Author.

Association of Science-Technology Centers, Incorporated. (2001). *From enrichment to employment: The YouthALIVE! experience.* Washington, DC: Author.

Beane, D. B. (1985). *Mathematics and Science: Critical filters for the future of minority students.* Washington, DC: American University.

Beaton, A. E., Martin, M. O., Mullis, I. V. S., Gonzalez, E. J., Smith, T. A., & Kelly, D. L. (1996). *Science Achievement in the Middle School Years: IEA's Third International Mathematics and Science Study.* Boston: Boston College.

Brown, J. S., Collins, A., & Duguid, P. (1989, January–February). Situated cognition and the culture of learning. *Educational Researcher, 18*(1), 32–42.

Campbell, G. (2000). United States demographics. In G. Campbell, R. Denes, & C. Morrison (Eds.), *Access denied: Race, ethnicity, and the scientific enterprise* (pp. 7–42). New York: Oxford University Press.

Clewell, B. C., & Braddock, J. H. (2000). Influences on minority participation in mathematics, science, and engineering. In G. Campbell, R. Denes, & C. Morrison (Eds.), *Access denied: Race, ethnicity, and the scientific enterprise* (pp. 89–137). New York: Oxford University Press.

Cooke, S. D. (2000, April). The information technology workforce. *Information Impacts Magazine.* Retrieved September 11, 2001, from the World Wide Web: http://www.cisp.org/imp/apri/2000/cooke/04_00coke.htm

Council of Chief State School Officers (1999). *State indicators of science and mathematics education: 1999.* Washington, DC: Author.

Erikson, E. H. (1968). *Identity: Youth and crisis.* New York: Norton.

Hakkarainen, P. (1999). Play and motivation. In Y. Engestrom, R. Hiettinen, & R. Punamaki (Eds.), *Perspectives on activity theory* (pp. 231–249). Cambridge: Cambridge University Press.

Hussar, W. J. (1999, August). *Predicting the need for newly hired teachers in the United States to 2008–09.* U.S. Department of Education (NCES). NCES 99-026. Washington, DC: U.S. Government Printing Office.

Lowery, L. (1998). How new science curriculums reflect brain research. *Educational Leadership, 56*(3), 326–330.

Madzey-Akale, J., Donohue, T., & Cady, J. (1999, November). *Youth Science Center Program Evaluation Report* (p. 21).

Moore, C. W., & Allen, J. P. (1996). The effects of volunteering on the young volunteer. *Journal of Primary Prevention, 17,* 231–258.

National Center for Educational Statistics. (1998). *Condition of education 1997.* Washington, DC: U.S. Government Printing Office.

National Science Foundation. (1999). *Women, minorities, and persons with disabilities in science and engineering: 1998.* Arlington, VA: NSF 99-338.

Reinert, J. R. (1998, March 24). Testimony on educating our workforce with technology skills to compete in the 21st century. Joint hearings before the Technology Subcommittee of the Committee on Science and the Early Childhood, Youth, and Families Subcommittee of the Committee on Education and the Workforce, United States House of Representatives. Retrieved September 11, 2001, from the World Wide Web: http://www.ieeeusa.net/forum.POLICY/1998/98mar24.html

Rogoff, B. (1994, Fall). Developing understanding of the idea of communities of learners. *Mind, Culture, and Activity 1*(4), 209–229.

Rogoff, B. (1998). Cognition as a collaborative process. In D. Kuhn & R. S. Siegler (Eds.), *Cognition, perception and language, Vol. 2, Handbook of child psychology* (5th ed., pp. 679–744). New York: Wiley.

Scales, P. C., & Blyth, D. A. (1997). Effects of service-learning on youth: What we know and what we need to know. *The Generator: Journal of Service Leadership, 17,* 6–9.

Scales, P. C., & Leffert, N. (1999). *Developmental assets: A synthesis of the scientific research on adolescent development.* Minneapolis: Search Institute.

Schauble, L., Beane, D., Coates, G., Martin, L., & Sterling, P. (1996). Outside the classroom walls: Learning in informal environments. In L. Schauble & R. Glasser (Eds.), *Innovations in learning: New environments for learning* (pp. 5-24). Mahwah, NJ: Lawrence Erlbaum Associates.

Schine, J. (1997). Editor's Preface in J. Schine (Ed.), *Service Learning. Ninety-sixth Yearbook of the National Society for the Study of Education* (pp. vii-viii). Chicago, IL: University of Chicago Press.

Schlereth, T. (1992). Object Knowledge: Every museum visitor an interpreter. In Museum Education Roundtable, *Patterns in Practice. Selections from the Journal of Museum Education* (pp. 102-112). Washington, DC: Museum Education Roundtable.

Sheridan, M. B. (2001, September 11). Employers Look Beyond Borders for Prospects. *Washington Post,* A1, A9.

Shymansky, J., Kyle, W., & Alport, J. (1982, November/December). How effective were the hands-on science programs of yesterday? *Science and Children,* 14-15.

Smith, L. (1999, August 5). House subcommitte on immigrations and claims. *Tech Law Journal.* Retrieved December 21, 2000, from the World Wide Web: http://www.techlawjournal.com/cog106//hlb/19990805smi.htm

Wadsworth, B. (1988). *Piaget's theory of cognitive and affective development* (4th ed.). New York & London: Longman.

CHAPTER NINETEEN

The Object of Experience

Sally Duensing
University of Bristol and the Exploratorium

> We are surrounded by objects. Our lives are spent identifying, classifying,
> using and judging objects . . . they are things precious, beautiful, boring
> frightening, lovable. We are so used to objects . . . but objects have their ex-
> istence largely unknown to the senses.
>
> — Richard Gregory (1970, p. 11)

Gregory's phrase "existence largely unknown to the senses" refers to experience. Much of Gregory's visual and auditory perception research work has explored relations of experience and the perception of objects. Reflecting this
perspective, the chapters in this section explore the important relationship of
experience in determining the kinds of interactions and conversations that
people have with objects.[1]

In multiple ways authors looked at the types of experiences, prior experience, and experiences with the object itself, that shape conversations through
enabling people to build up new functional, representational and symbolic
meanings and understandings of objects. Although the authors explored
these relationships from different disciplines or perspectives, I found it interesting that there was a large degree of overlap in the areas that they each
explored. Also, throughout this section there was a strong shared value of

---

[1] Note: As with the other chapters in this book, throughout this commentary I use the terms
exhibit and *object* interchangeably.

promoting people's ability to understand and communicate to others some of the representational and symbolic aspects of objects.

Additionally, the authors explored ways in which experiences are not equal. Most of the chapters examined how different kinds of interactions with objects could enhance or diminish people's communication and understanding as a result of those interactions.

In this commentary I discuss some of these prevalent and shared ideas raised by the authors regarding relationships of experience, objects, conversation. I first look at some of the ideas regarding prior experience and then look at some of the ideas regarding the results of experiences and conversations with the object itself.

I also explore two areas regarding conversations and objects that I felt were underemphasized or missing in the chapters in this section. One area concerns the context of the object — how the object is displayed in relation to other objects, in relation to the museum, and in relation to the broader cultural context of the object and of the museum. Although context is the focus in Part I of this book, it also plays a major role in determining the kinds of conversations that can and do occur with objects in museums. The second area that I felt needed further mention is regarding the inclusion of visitor voice in the museum. I briefly describe some ways in which museums have begun to make use of visitor's perspectives, as part of the object or as the object itself on the museum floor.

PRIOR EXPERIENCE

What I found of particular interest was the way in which all of the authors addressed ideas of prior experience from their very different perspectives. For example, Morrissey (chapter 16) explored ways in which an object can encourage visitors to share prior experiences in sharing with others personal stories and experiences with objects. Pope and Banks Beane (chapter 18) regarded the whole museum as an object and addressed ideas of access to this object being determined by prior experiences. Crowley and Leinhardt (chapter 17) discussed the important influence of the perceived value and authenticity of objects, two perceptions that are created by past experiences.

Borun (chapter 14) and Callanan, Jipson, and Soennichesen (chapter 15) emphasized an object's paradoxical capacity to be both an object in itself and a symbol of something else. Prior experience was discussed in both chapters as a major influence in determining how people are able to see the dual meanings or representations of the larger or more abstract ideas that the object can communicate. The authors all spoke toward ways in which representations are learned and are not inherent in the objects.

Borun framed her discussion of prior experience from the idea of the novice and the expert. She looked at how those different levels of experience impacted the visitor's conceptual meaning making of objects, discussing how the symbolism or more abstract ideas of the object might be lost on the novice museum visitor. Callanan et al. explored prior experience with objects from a child development perspective. They looked at ways in which specific kinds of prior experience can help to facilitate a child's perception of more abstract aspects of objects.

OBJECTS OF EXPERIENCE

In addition to prior experience, many of the chapters discussed how experiences with the objects themselves in the museums can enhance representational and conceptual understandings. Borun gave an example of an object's ability to enable people to confront and alter a common misunderstanding, and also found that this misunderstanding was actually reinforced by text if the object was not present. In her research she found that a common misunderstanding by all ages was that if there is no air, there is no gravity. She described an interesting account of how this misunderstanding could be decreased through an exhibit that allowed museum visitors to see that a ball behaved in essentially the same way with or without air in a tube. In her research Borun found that this was "a convincing way of altering the air misconception." Conversely, in displaying a piece of text that said, "Gravity does not need air in order to work," without the related exhibit, Borun found that the misconception was actually reinforced.

Crowley and Leinhardt also described a study that showed how assumptions could be altered through interactions with the object. Observing children interacting with an exhibit on robots at a children's museum, they noticed that the children's prior and often erroneous assumptions about robots were challenged. They said that although the children that they observed often seemed to have expectations about what a robot could do, that did not match what happened when they interacted with the actual robots. Many of the children were able to adapt and adjust their behavior with the robots to begin to change their own understandings about what robots can and cannot do. Crowley and Leinhardt said, "Thus for the first time many of the children had some direct evidence to be accounted for by their broader knowledge of robots."

This is similar in some ways to research work that Feher and Rice (1988) conducted at the Reuben Fleet Science Center. At specific exhibits, visitors were encouraged to make predictions of what might happen. At an exhibit on light and shadows, for example, visitors were asked to predict the shapes of a shadow that would be created by a small bead as it was illuminated by light sources of different shapes. Visitors would then be encouraged to see if the outcome matched their prediction. In addition to providing an avenue for people to make more conscious their expectations, this also often encouraged further questioning of the phenomena of the exhibit. It also provided a way for the museum staff to more clearly see a visitor's expectations and in some cases modify the exhibit to enable people to refute or confirm their expectations and assumptions.

OBJECTS OF DESIGN

Most of the authors also addressed ways in which experiences with objects are not equally effective in enabling people to perceive the object's representation in their interactions with it. Borun, Crowley and Leinhardt, and Callanan et al. explored different ways in which the features and design of the objects could impair or enhance representational and symbolic understandings through interaction.

Crowley and Leinhardt discussed ways in which an object's scale, resolution and density of information can greatly enhance the interest and access to ideas of the object. For example, they said that the "color and brush stroke of paintings, sound and smell of an elephants . . . life size cockpit, ragged edges of cloth from a mummy, all can add layers of experience not possible through descriptions."

Callanan et al. and Borun both spoke to the importance of the object's representational side being salient for museum visitors. Both chapters gave useful examples in which people more easily perceived representations when the interaction with the object reflected the more symbolic or conceptual component of the object. Callanan et al. described research that shows how certain experiences with objects could even negatively influence a child's ability to perceive its representation elements. They said that "allowing children to play with objects in a nonsymbolic manner decreased the chances that 3-year-old children would reason with it as a symbolic object."

Borun described two classifications for interactive exhibits that address the salience of its representational communication. She referred to exhibits that provide direct experience of an object's representational elements or concept as "demonstrative." The interactive exhibits in which the concept is less apparent she called "embodied." Borun contrasted the kind of direct experience a museum visitor can have with the idea of leverage through using an exhibit on levers that enable one to lift 500 pounds, with the common "gravity cone" coin-rolling exhibit in which one can see that the coin increases its rotational speed as it gets closer to the center. She felt that a less direct, more embodied interaction occurs in the gravity cone exhibit because the change of speed of the coins does not directly demonstrate gravity, which is the stated conceptual intention of the exhibit in most museums. However, with levers, she argued, the phenomenon is demonstrated, not just embodied.

A close parallel is evident in the idea by Callanan et al. that the salience of a representational object can be judged in terms of how "transparent" the symbol is as a symbol. For example, they described ways in which the symbolic or representational role of photographs might be relatively easy for children to see immediately inasmuch as the object, a paper with patterns, is not the salient feature, but what these patterns represent is salient and more closely resembles the thing it is intended to represent. Photographs, they said, tend to be almost exclusively used as the representations of the things that they represent rather than as objects themselves. Callanan et al. contrasted this with a globe in which the spherical nature of the globe seems to be more dominant for children than its more abstract role as a representation of the earth.

The degree of salience or directness of representation is not always apparent to people familiar with the more symbolic elements of the object. Callanan et al. and Borun both said that research studies point to the importance of looking carefully at museum visitors, talking to them, and systematically studying the learning process in order to understand its dynamics in free choice settings and to design exhibits with maximal learning potential. Both chapters stressed the need for exhibit developers to test and modify exhibit prototypes so that the final product is accessible and relevant. Borun said, "Museum staff often seem to think that the symbolic aspects of the object are apparent and miss the fact that people come in with a range of different kinds of experience that shapes the interactions and meanings that they make with the objects."

OBJECTS OF CONVERSATION

In addition to elements of the objects that influence people's ability to see its more representational aspects, most of the authors looked at elements that influence an object's capacity to elicit conversation. For example, Borun said, "Objects, particularly interactives, stimulate conversation involving observations, recollections, associations, and connections to prior learning among members of the visiting group."

Fortunately, this was not seen as simple or automatic. Most of the chapters also went on to discuss that this was not just a cause and effect process. Authors discussed different ways in which design could greatly influence, both positively or negatively, the quantity and quality of conversation generated by interactions with objects.

Crowley and Leinhardt discussed the significance of scale and authenticity of objects through descriptions from their study of visitors' conversations after interacting with an actual Greyhound bus in the Birmingham Civil Rights

Institute. Crowley and Leinhardt said that the authenticity and explicitness of having a real bus that appeared to be burned out like one that actually was bombed in Montgomery, Alabama, during the Civil Rights Movement had the power to provoke conversation and new insights. For example, they said, "We can imagine ourselves climbing the steep steps, walking back toward a free seat ... what we cannot imagine is our bus being blown apart by a bomb. Seeing the results of that shatters the safe solid image, and it is that precise conflict that makes the bus so valuable."

Both Borun and Morrissey described methods they have used in museums to encourage staff to consciously attend to design elements that can encourage conversation and saliency of the conceptual and symbolic ideas of the objects. Borun described her in-depth study, the Family Learning Project, findings concerning family learning that can be enhanced and extended through thoughtful use of objects. This work led to her creating seven characteristics of family-friendly exhibits for a wide range of family groups.

Morrissey's example was a workshop called "Enhancing and Inhibiting Conversation," where participants wander through exhibits and identify characteristics of the design and the interpretation that enhance or inhibit conversations. She said that museums staff are quick to identify ways conversations can be promoted once they begin to use this goal as a lens to view the exhibit.

In addition to physical design features that can encourage or discourage conversation, ways in which the conversations themselves could be a positive or negative influence were discussed. Callanan et al. described ways in which parents could aid this understanding in children through their conversations, saying that parents conversations could help children see that individual objects are also symbolic objects. Callanan et al. speculated on the possible usefulness for children when their parents spoke with them about objects "as if" they understood the symbolic nature of an object. "When parents name the referent while pointing at a representational object, for example, we argue that children are being presented with a puzzle to be solved. To make sense of what their parents are saying, they must come up with a nonliteral way to interpret the label. This conflict may lead children to begin to search for another way to think about the objects with which they are interacting. These sorts of conversations could perhaps be important motivation for the emergence of dual representation ability."

OBJECTS OF QUESTIONS

These puzzle-like situations that Callanan et al. described are similar in intent to an overall goal for the exhibits at the Exploratorium in San Francisco and for many other science centers in which intrigue and personal interest is thought to be promoted through generating surprising interactions with objects. The director of the Exploratorium, Goéry Delacôte (1997) thought of exhibits as question-generating tools that can create a learner-driven environment. Delacôte felt that a destabilizing experience can encourage visitors to raise their own questions through creating a situation in which one is confronted with an unexpected event or result.

Encouraging an awareness of incomplete understanding can be motivating through creating a need to know more. A desire to solve a problem can be evoked because one is not satisfied with a current state of knowledge. To know the boundaries of knowledge does not have to seen as limiting but instead can invite learners to think further about how to find out the answers.

But knowing that you do not know something does not automatically generate curiosity to find out. Related to these discussions on prior experience and people's ability to see the representational aspects of objects, prior experience also can influence the levels of curiosity and amount of questioning between people and objects. For example, in a lecture given in February 2000 to a science society in Bristol, Gillian Thomas, former chief executive officer of the Bristol Millennium Science Center development project in the United Kingdom, told the story of teaching science to Iranian immigrant women in France. When asking them to predict, speculate, or question what might happen when different things were added to each end of a simple balance, she found that the women had no questions or rather no curiosity, nor any prediction about what would happen. They had no experience with it, and because they had no experience, she felt they had no motivation to explore the situation.

The difference in response by people to puzzling, destablizing situations also relates to the potential engagement, excitement, and energy of inquiry described by St. John (1999). To be motivating and not limiting, he said that you know that you do not know something that you feel you should know. And he also said that the questioning or inquiry process itself is a skill that can become more effective, more generative through learning. "You have to find just the right point of ignorance. But it has to be proximal. If it too far away, it is not useful. Hubert (Dyasi) and I described that as our 'proximal zone of ignorance'" (St. John, 1999, pp. 12–13).

Although a playful variation on Vygotsky's (1978) Zone of Proximal Development, the idea of a Zone of Proximal Ignorance, ZPI, offers an interesting way to think about some of the issues regarding questioning, conversations, and objects. Thomas's balance was outside the zone for the Iranian women. Globes as a representation of the shape of the earth are outside the ZPI for many children in the article by Callanan et al.

Conversely, the puzzling "as if" situations with objects such as aerial maps and photographs, in which children seemed to be able to see more easily the nonliteral, were within the ZPI. With those objects, the children felt encouraged to puzzle over an adult's reference to find another way to think about objects with which they are interacting.

The museum environment as a whole can also be considered in this regard. In the Pope and Banks Beane chapter, for example, the museum was able to not be a foreign, overwhelming, or impenetrable place, but instead was within a ZPI for adolescents through in-depth work experience in these rich environments.

As with designing more salient ways for objects to communicate their representational facet, a ZPI perspective points out that in the design of exhibits, programs, and museums, the developer needs to consider these zone differences and look for ways that visitors can gain a glimmer of intrigue and not a deluge of unknowing.

OBJECTS IN CONTEXT

> There are as many contexts for an object as there are interpretive strategies.... Those who construct the display also constitute the subject, even when they seem to do nothing more than relocate an entire house and its contents, brick by brick, board by board, chair by chair.
> — Barbara Kirshenblatt-Gimblett (1991, pp. 389–390)

In addition to the exhibit design factors already mentioned, there is the context of the object itself. Exhibits and objects are not experienced in isolation but exist in environments that need to be considered as well (Rogoff et al., 1993). It was surprising to me that the immediate setting in which an object is presented, as well as the cultural contexts of the institution, if mentioned at all, was only cursorily addressed by the authors in this section.

Borun briefly mentioned, without elaboration, that her research work indicated that the selection, construction, and arrangement of museum objects can influence the reading, learning, conversing, and exploring that takes place at the exhibit. Early in their chapter, Crowley and Leinhardt also briefly mentioned that a museum best supports learning through having a collection of objects that are a collection of examples. But neither they nor the other authors discussed to any degree some of the ways in which context could influence the conversation and interactions of people with objects. All of the authors looked at the object's influence on the interaction in a museum context, but they did not look at the museum context's influence on the interaction with the object.

For example, Morrissey gave a striking example of the symbolic power elicited by the presence of an original Declaration of Independence at the Democratic Convention. She talked about the strong role of the object in this setting, but not the role of the setting on the object. In a different context —

the next election in the United Kingdom of a prime minister, for example — the symbolism, conversations, and meanings elicited might be quite different.

Another example is Crowley and Leinhardt's extremely powerful account of the impact of a replica of the burned out Greyhound bus at the Birmingham Civil Rights Institute in Birmingham, Alabama. They said that the association is dependent primarily on the relationship between the individual's historical experiences and the object. However, as with the Morrissey example of the Declaration of Independence, Crowley and Leinhardt did not mention that the context of the bus is also equally important in the kinds of experiences it generates. The stories and exhibits surrounding the bus in the museum, as well as the context of the museum itself being in a building that is across the street from the 16th Street Baptist Church, all potentially contribute to the visitor's experience, conversations, and learning. To Crowley and Lienhardt's statement that the museum's "impersonal historical record and labels on struggle, injustice, prejudice, was enlivened by the appropriation of the meaning of an object," I would add the converse and say that the appropriation of meaning of the object itself is enlivened by the labels and historical records.

In addition, any discussion of the importance of the *cultural* context of an object was only implicitly addressed in this section's chapters. Morrissey mentioned that objects have no value independent of the viewer and stated that the "meaning comes from how viewers use the object to reconnect to the memories, the values, and the ideas that the object represents." And implicitly, Pope and Banks Beane talked about including different cultural perspectives in museums through their examples and discussion on important outcomes by involving adolescents from backgrounds that are underrepresented in the cultural context of museums.

There is a growing body of literature on relationships of culture, context, and interaction with museum objects (Bradburne & Janousek, 1993; Brah & Coombes, 2000; Clifford, 1991; Coombes, 1994; Corrin, 1994; Duensing, 2000; Karp & Lavine, 1991), primarily in art and natural history museum fields. Much of this work concerns the display of objects with the assertion that the display itself is a cultural object.

Also there have been a number of fascinating exhibitions on the power of context in determining the kinds of meanings and conversations that are derived from interactions with objects (Vercoe, 1996; Weschler, 1996). Looking at displays of objects in ethnographic collections, Coombes (1994), in *Reinventing Africa,* described how the context of the object is a reflection of multiple current cultural practices in her case study that explored the presentation of African objects in British Museum environments. She said ethnographic collections of a museum represent "the material intersection and negotiation of state, institutional and professional politics" over a specific period of time.

Even in the seemingly politically neutral arenas of science centers, I have seen ways in which that cultural context can influence various forms of interactions and conversations of an exhibit (Duensing, 2000). For example, with a mirror exhibit and activity table with Lego-blocks activities at a science center in Trinidad and Tobago, there was a tone of competition-like interactions and conversations. This form of interaction reflects the strong emphasis of competition in many aspects of Trinidad life. I had never considered these two exhibits as competitive prior to seeing these interactions in Trinidad.

In the mirror exhibit called *Star Tracer,* one tries to trace the outline of a star while looking in a mirror at one's hand. It is a difficult task to do because the movements seen in the mirror are opposite from what one is actually doing. We have a similar exhibit at the Exploratorium, and what I focus on and have often described to others about this exhibit is the striking sensory conflict experience you have between what you feel your hand doing and what your eye sees. I had never thought about it from a competition perspective. However, when this exhibit was described by two different staff members, competition was what was highlighted. One staff member said that he liked *Star Tracer* because you could set up a mini competition with a friend. It was "kind of a competitive thing. Because you can go (do) a little competition with your friend to see who can do it, and maybe (see) who can do it faster." Another staff member said that *Star Tracer* was a popular exhibit because you could compete against yourself and that people liked it because they like competition.

At the Lego building blocks activity table, mini competitions would form. When talking with the science center's director of education about the popularity of this activity table, I thought she was going to say something about the appeal of the open-ended quality of building things with Legos. Instead, her perception was that competition was the reason for its popularity: "They do that as competition, 'Let's see who can build, whatever, first.' "

Although it was not on the physical or cultural context of the object itself, the ideas in the Callanan et al. chapter most directly emphasized relationships of conversations, objects, and cultural context. They discussed the importance of the social context in the development of children's perception of the dual representation of objects. Through a sociocultural focus, they looked at the social contexts in which children experience representational objects. The implication is that the context of the object can be created by the different perspectives of the visitors themselves. That implication brings me to the concluding part of this commentary that looks at ways interpretation, conversation, and object can combine to become an object in itself.

MY OBJECT OF OBJECTS

The painting ... can be anything depending on who's looking at it. (Esner, 2001)

I conclude this commentary by looking at how the visitor perspective itself can be used as an object on the museum floor. This intent is different from taking the visitors to a specific place or level, novice to expert for example. This other intent is not to take people to any one place but is instead to create a forum of perspectives, opinions, voices for people to see and begin to understand the range of experiences, symbolism, and representations that objects can and do have.

Focusing on the variations of visitor's interpretations is, for me, one of the most significant object of objects in museums. The importance of inclusion of diverse voice was implied by Pope and Banks Beane when they said, "It is assumed that museums are for everyone, but seldom does a museum visitor stop to ask who is not here and more importantly, why not?"

In looking at the special ways in which museums support learning, Crowley and Leinhardt mentioned that rather than the more singular and/or linear narratives of movies, novels, or television, the specialness of museums is that they are not linear and are usually not singular narratives. The authors say that instead of a singular narrative "in the broader, sociocultural sense," museums are "meant to engage visitors in conversation and debate."

Including some of these conversations and debates on the museum floor has the potential to be a powerful reflective tool for people to gain a deeper understanding and appreciation of themselves and of each other. For example, Morrisey wrote about a visit to the museum with her father in which she was able to gain new insight about her father through hearing his personal stories about the object that they both were encountering. Other visitors might have also appreciated hearing her father's stories.

Morrissey mentioned but did not elaborate on a growing direction in many museums — the use of visitor voice or visitor perspectives with objects and exhibits. She mentioned some of the methods museums have developed to bring visitor voices into the narrative of the exhibit from simple devices such as dropping a ball in a jar to indicate cultural background, voting on environmental positions through a computer, and virtual conferences with individuals in other parts of the world. Increasingly, there are a variety of ways in which a museum's exhibits and programs are being used as forums in which diverse communities can learn from each other in various exchanges of perspectives and points of view.

In a recent exhibition on human memory at the Exploratorium, the visitor's stories became some of the exhibits. For example, in an exhibit on childhood memories, visitors were asked to write their earliest memories in books that other visitors could read. The visitor experience or perspective was the object.

Presentations of controversial issues in certain exhibitions are also increasingly making use of visitors' perspectives. Exhibitions on genetics in several different museums have included visitor opinion-posting forums on ethical dilemmas in genetic research. Some forums were simple paper-posting areas; others were on computer. In almost any format, I have been impressed with the large amount of time visitors spend writing as well as reading other's responses.

Additionally, these "perspectives as objects" exhibits can provide places to generate communication and learning among communities that might not normally interact. For example, as part of a public science awareness week, United Kingdom university engineering students created a display in a shopping mall about a range of risk situations. They asked the public to write their responses to the level of risk for each situation. What became apparent was that the public paid attention to aspects of risk that the engineering students had not considered. The students said that they were intrigued and surprised by some of the differences of perspectives on the risk issues that were presented; some of the responses were not what they would have predicted. In addition to learning that their assumptions about what the public thought were incorrect, the engineering students learned other ways to think about some of the risk issues. They said that they saw the need to modify some of their own perspectives and ways of communicating.

Many of the ideas mentioned in the chapters of this section could possibly be extended in some intriguing ways by including different perspectives as part of the exhibit. For example, in the exhibits on globes, photos, and maps described by Callanan et al., the different meanings given to the object by the children could be posted. A brief commentary label could be added on things for parents to notice about the children's perceptions and how this relates to developmental research questions and understandings about objects and meaning-making. Also, it could be interesting to see if the children's own perceptions expand through this metacognitive process of describing or drawing their interpretations of objects and looking at other children's ideas.

My main point in bringing in visitor voice in this commentary is that it could be valuable to think about ways in which the visitor's perspectives might be made more accessible to different groups of people to further enrich the experiences, interactions, and conversations of people with the objects. Most importantly, providing forums in which people contribute and reflect on their own and others' ways of experiencing and thinking about objects, and perhaps in doing so create a new hybridity of perspectives, is conceivably one of the most important and unique functions of museums.

This section as a whole highlights the value of understanding multiple perspectives and experiences with objects in a museum environment. Morrissey illustrated this value, saying, "Encounters with objects provide an opportunity through which individuals find deeper connections not only to the world around them, but to each other as conversations twist around the object, the content, and the thoughts and experiences of each individual. Individuals learn about each other just as they learn through each other. Knowledge is created, discussed, reflected upon and passed on to future generations."

REFERENCES

Bradburne, J., & Janousek, I. (Eds.). (1993). *Planning science museums for the new Europe.* Paris: UNESCO.

Brah, A., & Coomes, A. E. (Eds.). (2000). *Hybridity and its discontents.* London: Routledge Press.

Clifford, J. (1991). Four Northwest coast museums: Travel reflections. In I. Karp & S. Lavine, (Eds.), *Exhibiting Cultures, The Poetics and Politics of Museum Display.* Washington DC: Smithsonian Institution Press.

Coombes, A. E., (1994). *Reinventing Africa: Museums, material culture and popular imagination.* New Haven, CT: Yale University Press.

Corrin, L. (1994). *Mining the museum: An installation by Fred Wilson.* Baltimore, MD: The Contemporary; New York: The New Press.

Delacote, G., (1997). *Science venters and inquiry.* Presentation to the International Education Research Academy Conference, San Francisco.

Duensing, S. (2000). *Cultural influences on science museum practices.* UMI Dissertation Services, Ann Arbor, Michigan.

Esner, R. (2001). In the eye of the beholder. On cultural contexts and art interpretation. *Journal of Museum Education, 26*(2), 14–16.

Feher, E., & Rice, K. (1988). Shadows and anti-images: Children's conceptions of light and vision, 2. *Science Education, 72*(5), 505–520.

Gregory, R. L. (1970). *The intelligent eye.* London: Weidenfeld & Nicholson.

Karp, I., & Lavine, S. (1991). *Exhibiting cultures: The poetics and politics of museum display.* Washington, DC: Smithsonian Institution Press.

Kirshenblatt-Gimblett, B. (1991). Objects of ethnography. In I. Karp & S. Lavine (Eds.), *Exhibiting cultures: The poetics and politics of museum display* (pp. 389–390). Washington, DC: Smithsonian Institution Press.

Rogoff, B., Chavajay, P., Mistry, J., Göncü, A., & Mosier, C. (1993). Guided participation in cultural activity by toddlers and caregivers. *Monographs of the Society for Research in Child Development,* Serial No. 236, Vol. 58, No. 8.

Rogoff, B. (in press). *The cultural nature of human development.* London: Oxford University Press.

St. John, M. (1999). *"Wait, Wait! Don't Tell Me!" The anatomy and politics of inquiry.* The 1998 Catherine Molony Memorial Lecture (pp. 12 & 13). New York: City College Workshop Center.

Vercoe, C. (1996). Postcards/Signature of Place. *Art Asia Pacific Journal,* Vol. 3, no. 1.

Vygotsky, L. S., (1978). *Mind in society.* Cambridge, MA: Harvard University Press.

Weschler, L. (1996). *Mr. Wilson's cabinet of wonder.* Vintage Books.

Author Index

Subject Index